SHOUTING OUT LOUD

ALSO BY AUDREY GOLDEN

I Thought I Heard You Speak: Women at Factory Records

Audrey Golden is the author of *I Thought I Heard You Speak: Women at Factory Records* (White Rabbit, 2023), which recenters the story of Factory Records—the famed Manchester label and cultural phenomenon—from the perspectives of more than seventy-five women who were central to nearly every aspect of Factory, but whose voices have largely been excluded from written and visual depictions of the label to date. Her writing has also appeared in *Maggot Brain*, The Quietus, the *Guardian*, *DIVA*, *American Book Review*, and other venues. She is station manager of Louder Than War Radio, where she presents the show *Breaking Glass*, which illuminates women in music. She earned a BA in film studies from Wesleyan University, a JD from Wake Forest University School of Law, and a PhD in literary studies from the University of Virginia. She lives in New York with her husband and their two cats.

SHOUTING OUT LOUD

LIVES OF THE RAINCOATS

AUDREY GOLDEN

DA CAPO

New York Boston

Copyright © 2025 by Audrey Golden

Jacket design by Tyler Comrie

Jacket photograph © 1978 by Shirley O'Loughlin

Jacket copyright © 2025 by Hachette Book Group, Inc.

Hachette Book Group supports the right to free expression and the value of copyright. The purpose of copyright is to encourage writers and artists to produce the creative works that enrich our culture.

The scanning, uploading, and distribution of this book without permission is a theft of the author's intellectual property. If you would like permission to use material from the book (other than for review purposes), please contact permissions@hbgusa.com. Thank you for your support of the author's rights.

Da Capo
Hachette Book Group
1290 Avenue of the Americas
New York, NY 10104
grandcentralpublishing.com
@grandcentralpub

Originally published in hardcover in July 2025 by White Rabbit Books in the United Kingdom.

First US Edition: July 2025

Da Capo is an imprint of Grand Central Publishing. The Da Capo name and logo are registered trademarks of Hachette Book Group, Inc.

The publisher is not responsible for websites (or their content) that are not owned by the publisher.

Da Capo books may be purchased in bulk for business, educational, or promotional use. For information, please contact your local bookseller or the Hachette Book Group Special Markets Department at special.markets@hbgusa.com.

Library of Congress Cataloging-in-Publication Data has been applied for.

ISBNs: 978-0-306-83590-2 (hardcover), 978-0-306-83592-6 (ebook)

Printed in the United States of America

LSC-C

Printing 1, 2025

For my Matin

CONTENTS

Foreword by Greil Marcus   ix

Author's Note: On Methodology   xv

Introduction   1

LIFE NUMBER 1   9

LIFE NUMBER 2   145

LIFE NUMBER 3   287

Notes   365

List of Images   372

List of Interviewees   374

Acknowledgments   376

FOREWORD
AN OLD RAINCOAT WON'T EVER LET YOU DOWN
BY GREIL MARCUS

Have you had some good friends on the road with ya?
Who'd stand by you through thick and thin
Here's to Ana and Gina, Vicky and Anne, Palmolive and Shirley

—after Rod Stewart, "An Old Raincoat
Won't Ever Let You Down," 1969

In late 1975, two young art students in London find themselves at what turns out to be the first public performance of a band called the Sex Pistols. The four people on stage plainly have no idea what they're doing, but seem to be having a wonderful time doing it—and with a queer kind of vehemence, as if something is actually riding on whether the performance comes across or not. A light that over the next years will go on for countless people goes on for the two women in the crowd: We could do that. We could get up in front of other people and say what the world looks like to us, and see if they have anything to say back.

One woman plays guitar, the other bass. They have no background in music; a violinist they bring in has. A drummer, late of the Slits, the first all-female punk band, comes on board. They call themselves The Raincoats, a name so perfect for a London band it's hard to believe no one has used it before, but there they are.

They begin to play shows, whatever they can get. Working with a resolutely independent, not to say anarchist, little London record outfit, in 1979 they make an album. They're a punk band, but even in the punk milieu, where chaotic noise is the currency, they sound like no one else, as if they're still learning to play, or unlearning what they played the night before. Even the Mekons' songs are predictable, or rememberable, compared to theirs. They make another album, and then a third. They never escape the small-time; it's not clear they mean to. In 1983 they call it a day and go on to other callings.

But if the band is soon forgotten, the music press chronicling the next small things as if they'd never been, the records, as few copies as there may have been still traveling, find their way into the world. In the early 1990s, in the town of Olympia, Washington, around the try-anything-anytime Evergreen College, people begin to pass cassettes among one another, to gather around their Raincoats records with the obsessiveness and awe, the shock of hearing themselves captured in the music of people so far away and unknown to them, people not quite real, as blues collectors in the 1950s and 1960s gathered around their rare 1930s 78s of such Mississippi blues artists as Charlie Patton, Son House, Skip James, Robert Johnson, all whom carried such a faraway strangeness that they seemed to be calling out from the dead, even though some of them were living, and would soon be performing again, to audiences they could not have imagined existed. The same thing happened in Olympia, as people heard what the first two Raincoats once heard in the Sex Pistols. They form their own bands, their own little groups of public speakers: Kathleen Hanna, the singer for the most notorious, Bikini Kill, unfurls what she has learned from The Raincoats like a flag, like one of her songs: "punk wasn't a genre— it's an *idea!*" One of the most celebrated and dedicated musicians in the world, once part of that Olympia milieu, Kurt Cobain, the leader of Nirvana, becomes the Raincoats' most determined fan. He has his record company put out the old albums again, and like Skip James appearing at the Newport Folk Festival generations after his last record sold its few hundred copies, The Raincoats ("Seeking them out," Golden quotes the Bikini Kill manager Liz Naylor of their Olympia followers, "talking about them as if they were some ancient oracle! You'd have thought they were ninety, one hundred years old, but they must have been what, *maybe forty* at the time?... It makes them part of some kind of fairytale, doesn't

FOREWORD

it? You have to find them, if they're really there at all,") re-form, with a different violinist, a different drummer, and with Nirvana's Los Angeles record company make their own new album. They are about to tour the world with Nirvana when their champion kills himself and everything goes away.

But the story, somehow, doesn't end—can't, won't, it isn't clear, but as that lightbulb grows dim, the urge, the instinct to climb the ladder and screw it tight again will not go away. In the first decade of the next century, the band begins to play again, as always with new drummers, now in galleries and museums, not ratty clubs or even decent theaters—"It's one extreme or the other with The Raincoats," says the second violinist. "CBGB or MoMA, nothing in between!"—but that old raincoat, that old idea that you talk the talk of freedom by never letting a piece of music find a final shape—"where someone would say, 'I'm the bassist and I'll play the song this way each time,' we never had that in The Raincoats," says the first violinist. "Every time we played, we'd be starting fresh, playing in a slightly or wholly different way"—still kept them from the drizzling rain of stale culture, the same old jokes and complaints anyone has heard a thousand times before. In their last performance merely of this moment, at the sleek White Cube gallery in London, they played their song "In Love," and, as always, it seemed impossible—impossible that it ever achieved any shape, that after nearly half a century it had held its shape just to the degree that you could recognize what it was, with the certainty that you had never really heard it before. Today the Sex Pistols are about to embark on a new tour, with a tattooist in place of the singer who once stared down the world and made it flinch, promising to play the songs from their one, forty-eight-year-old album as close to how they're supposed to sound as they can manage. The Raincoats are biding their time, the cloth somehow never wearing thin.

This is the story Audrey Golden tells in *Shouting Out Loud: The Lives of the Raincoats*, a book that in a way that evades the cliches generated by countless previous books about groups of musicians is as much about the band's audience, and its own role in the creative life of the band, as the band itself—and as it goes on,

– xi –

through decade after unlikely decade, as loss leads to persistence, as failure means most of all that an ending remains unwritten, the story generates undying drama and pathos.

But along with the story of the band, running through the book, taking on more resonance, more melody and rhythm, is the story of the oddness of the Raincoats' music, how and why it is not like that of anyone or anything else—how and why its quality of abstraction, of just-out-of-reach of any listener or any member of the band herself, is not jazz, is not dub, is not punk in any comparable sense (Golden quotes John Lydon, quotes Johnny Rotten of the Sex Pistols, saying in 2009 that the first Raincoats' album is "the sole record he'd choose to represent 'the punk years'"—because, you can think, compared to The Raincoats the Sex Pistols sound like a conventional band), but an act on its own terms, a clearing of the ground and the thrill such an act makes that leads others to take their place on their own ground. As with the extraordinary tale Golden tells of a 1978 show the nascent Raincoats played in pre-Solidarity Warsaw: "By the second night, members of the audience were singing along—they'd taped the first show, gone home, obsessively listened, and learned the words phonemically; most couldn't speak."

Again and again, over Golden's three hundred and some pages, that story itself finds new forms. From Jean-Marc Butty, an off-and-on Raincoats drummer since 1996: "With The Raincoats, it is never about putting on 'good' shows—now, they want to put on a good show, but more, they want to share something that's completely remote from the preoccupations of other bands. And that's something that's refreshing, that is freedom... Sometimes you learn more by watching someone who doesn't know how to play technically... They didn't have formal technique and didn't want it, because they found a way to be challenged by something else that's very strong, that almost cannot be named." A musical aesthetic that to Kathi Wilcox of Bikini Kill translated into an argument about selfhood, about identity, about community, about politics in the fullest sense of the word: "The Raincoats stepped out of this orbit, neither male or female—another kind of being! They taught so many women that there are other ways to play music

FOREWORD

or be in a band without having to perform any version of gender. They weren't trying to be feminine or not feminine, and it didn't feel like they were trying to occupy any kind of particular gendered identity—they were being themselves and showing you that you were also free to be yourself."

It comes down, finally, to what the Raincoats' first violinist, the classically trained Vicky Aspinall, saw in their guitarist Ana da Silva, bassist Gina Birch, and drummer Palmolive, what their second violinist, Anne Wood, would see as well: their "limitations were also the groundwork for the flowering of their creativity." And that is the heart of the Raincoats' life in punk, as they found it and, by now, as much as anyone, define it. Enormous feeling is released by very limited technique. It's the moment, somehow recaptured permanently, when an anonymous person dares to demand that someone listen to her, and only then discovers that she has something to say, that she likes saying it, that one thought and feeling leads to another, that she likes being talked back to—whether it's peope in Warsaw living under Soviet rule who she will never meet, students and hangers-on in a college town in the Pacific Northwest, the musician next to her trying to follow her lead but also lead her to follow her, or the echo of her own sound, her own speech, in her own head.

AUTHOR'S NOTE
ON METHODOLOGY

The many lives of The Raincoats have been propelled by the band's commitment to experimentation and evolving forms of collaboration. The research for this book is an extension of that spirit. In writing it, I sought to use new forms of narrative writing to bring together overlapping stories of and about the band into a single chronicle that reflects the many facets of those experiences. From the start, The Raincoats supported this experiment with a radical openness. They facilitated connections with many people in the story regardless of their varied experiences. And they invited me into their sonic and material worlds, sharing with unfailing generosity their memories, artifacts, and insights. These years of work gave me a taste of what it is like to collaborate with The Raincoats. I could not have written this book as I did without such an approach.

Much of this book has been constructed through almost two hundred hours of oral history interviews I conducted with nearly a hundred storytellers, including The Raincoats themselves, and in-depth research into the band's own object-based material archive.

During an early discussion of my intended process for the book, Shirley O'Loughlin, longtime Raincoats manager and collaborator, said, "The idea of this oral history thing is really important, because everybody remembers things in such a different way. They've got their own feelings, their own experience, and it's all relevant." And she's right: One of the notable aspects of narratives based on oral history work is that experiential knowledge gets elevated, which allows individual memories and truths to overlap, diverge, and sometimes even contradict one another.

I chatted with Tobi Vail of Bikini Kill right around the time she was reading a pre-publication draft of Kathleen Hanna's memoir (*Rebel Girl: My Life as a Feminist Punk*, 2024), and Tobi said she was grappling with these vagaries of memory herself. "We definitely remember things very differently," she told me, referring to Kathleen's writing. "And that's what happens—she talks about how she remembers things, and I remember them differently. Sometimes, I'll think I know exactly what I'm talking about, like, *that did not happen in 1986. There's no way.* And then I'll look back at something and realize, *oh, it did. Totally.*"

Memory is ambiguous, and the interviewer's role is extremely important in drawing out an interviewee's memories and specific moments of experiential knowledge they've locked away. It's not just about what interviewees remember on their own when they're presented with a certain subject like The Raincoats, but the specific questions raised and the way those questions are asked. One interviewer might bring out entirely different responses than another in the same storyteller; the interviewer's background and framework shape the material that emerges in the dialogue.

I've written extensively about oral history practices elsewhere, so I won't belabor these points here. All this is to say, you'll see details in this book that may or may not appear in other chronicles of The Raincoats, and that might confirm or contradict what you think you know.

Various portions of this book also draw on materials contained in the extensive Raincoats archive that Ana da Silva has collected for more than forty years. "I'm not obsessively an archivist," Ana initially told me when she mentioned the archive, noting, "It's all in a cupboard." When I asked what she'd kept, mentally running through my own training in special collections archives, Ana replied, "I have two scrapbooks, but the rest got shoved into boxes." *OK, definitely manageable,* I thought. When I eventually saw the collection, my jaw dropped: nearly an entire flat's worth of physical objects, not to mention additional born-digital materials.

I spent months processing the archive, which involved photographing more than 4,000 physical objects for recordkeeping and compiling their data into methodical categories: artwork and proofs, correspondence, diaries and diary pages, handbills and posters, film

AUTHOR'S NOTE: ON METHODOLOGY

and video footage, legal documents, lyrics drafts, magazine and news clippings, merch, music and instruments, photographs, press and promotional materials, setlists, zines. Each time I thought I was getting close to nearing completion, I'd hear from Ana or Shirley that they'd found another folder or box of materials.

For several decades now, feminist scholars have pointed to the importance of women archiving their own stories, given that official repositories housing biographical archives have traditionally retained only those items related to the lives of men. For women, archiving their own lives and work becomes an act of resistance. Historian Honor Sachs points out how such materials offer opportunities for large-scale reshapings of historical memory and the figures central to it. Indeed, for people traditionally marginalized in historical accounts, including women and people of color, archiving becomes an intervention "against larger tendencies to erase the past," archivist Eira Tansey observes. According to Tansey, archiving is thus a political "act against forgetting, by informing larger communities that traces of the past still exist." And as Sachs clarifies, "Approaching documents [in archives] as living artifacts whose history as material objects continues long after the events they record took place can, ultimately, provide new perspective on the ways that we remember, shape, and understand the past."

This isn't to suggest that archives are in any way objective representations of any particular point in a given past. They're constructed, like all histories—shaped by those who assemble and arrange them. As historian Elizabeth Yale highlights, "No archive is innocent."

Yet the very fact that a Raincoats archive exists also speaks back to the anarchic time signature created by The Raincoats in their music. I'm drawn to the words of cultural historian Andreas Huyssen here, who suggests it may be possible "to resist the dissolution of time in the synchronicity of the archive."[1]

"I suppose I *am* the keeper," Ana confesses.

There is an essential connection between oral history and archive-based work that helps to shape a book like this one: Both underscore that there's never just one way to tell a story. In the same way that oral history interviews reveal how multiple perspectives can coexist in the realm of experiential knowledge at the same time, material object-based archives reveal, as Jacques Derrida suggests in *Archive Fever*, that relying solely on a single archive to present a "History" with a capital H suppresses the alternate lower-case histories around which the archive has been collated. Any material archive, historian Francis X. Blouin observes, offers one window—among many—into a past.[2]

I consider this book—constructed from a Raincoats material archive built by Ana, as well as an archive of oral history interviews and additional research materials collected by me—to be a layered feminist archive unto itself. The way I've curated this composite archive intentionally echoes many of the forms contained within it: fragmentary moments recorded in private journals, epistolary notes on leftover papers, clipped and recorded images and stories assembled alongside one another. It is both a granular account of a band written out of punk histories by the journalists and authors who've been the gatekeepers, and a broad-reaching chronicle that weaves in and out of the private and public, the local and the global. In many ways, it's a record of my own exploration of The Raincoats at this point in time with the materials I collated and in which I researched.

It's thus my hope that the archive that is *Shouting Out Loud: Lives of The Raincoats*, and the myriad interwoven archival materials central to producing it, will one day help readers, scholars, and other thinkers to shape a new kind of thinking: about the role women's archives play in radically remaking historical knowledge. But rather than tell you precisely how I want you to read the text that follows, or how to interpret my use of objects from the Raincoats material archive that Ana constructed or words from the oral history archive I built, I hope you'll take ownership yourself of what's contained within. I'll end with the words of scholar Maryanne Dever here, who says, "If we want to know what a feminist archive is, what feminist archiving looks like or what archival tools and theoretical dispositions feminist researchers might require, then we will only know in times to come."[3] That future, like the continued existence of The Raincoats, is yours to help create.

INTRODUCTION

You can't tell the story of UK punk without The Raincoats.

You can't tell the story of Rough Trade and the rise of independent record labels without The Raincoats.

You can't tell the story of rock revolution behind the Iron Curtain without The Raincoats.

You can't tell the story of New York City's downtown scene and its legendary venues without The Raincoats.

You can't tell the story of Riot Grrrl without The Raincoats.

You can't tell the story of American indie pop without The Raincoats.

You can't tell the story of noise rock without The Raincoats.

You can't tell the story of queercore without The Raincoats.

You can't tell the story of grunge and the Seattle sound without The Raincoats.

You can't tell the story of experimental music and rhythmic innovation without The Raincoats.

You can't tell the story of sonic weapons against political oppression without The Raincoats.

You can't tell the story of music-based performance art without The Raincoats.

You can't tell the story of the modern art museum in the twenty-first century without The Raincoats.

You can't tell the story of feminist footholds in the music industry without The Raincoats.

You can't tell the story of Sonic Youth, Bikini Kill, Big Joanie, or trailblazing bands yet to form without The Raincoats.

And you can't tell the story of The Raincoats without these encircling tales and the myriad voices within them.

The Raincoats are integral to nearly every independent and revolutionary music history that has emerged over the last fifty years. Founded by two pioneering women—Gina Birch and Ana da Silva, young art students in 1977—The Raincoats' approach to sonic experimentation, art, and politics distinguished them in punk-era London and produced fierce, inimitable sounds that reverberated throughout the counterculture of the 1980s and beyond. They are, and have always been, a singular phenomenon.

And yet, almost fifty years later, the band's story remains curiously underground, largely absent from broader cultural narratives of who and what shaped alternative music. It is clandestine knowledge. References to The Raincoats carry more currency at indie record store counters and among subversive musicians and their fans than they do in the ever-narrowing idol worship that passes for music "History" in our time. Listeners and devotees quietly pass fragments of The Raincoats' story between them like co-conspirators. But obscurity need not entail forgetting. The story of The Raincoats is as urgent and captivating as the music they make. And their direct influence on artists like Sonic Youth, Nirvana, and Bikini Kill—not to mention the broader movements of Riot Grrrl and queercore—leaves no question as to their importance. In many ways, Raincoats aficionados revel in the nature of their shared esoteric knowledge of the band. Yet at a certain point in sonic history annals, the absence of The Raincoats' story signals more than just inadvertent omission.

This lacuna is even more striking because as a band The Raincoats have lived not just one life but three: the first taking place largely in London, from 1977 to 1984; the second starting unbeknownst to The Raincoats in the late 1970s in the city of Olympia, Washington and thriving until 1996; and the third beginning in the early 1990s but fully taking shape after the turn of the new millennium. The first life was born of their own conscious efforts to bring into being this band, this sonic force. Their second and third lives materialized through manifold voices and experiences of artists whose own projects were conceived, to greater and lesser degrees, in reference to The Raincoats. Those artists, in turn, have propelled public knowledge of The Raincoats across geographic

INTRODUCTION

time and space, sustaining their life force well into our own time, up to—and assuredly beyond—the publication of this book.

Since their formation in 1977, The Raincoats have been many things to many people. To Gina Birch and Ana da Silva, the two original cofounders of the band, The Raincoats have been a collective that catalyzed a new definition of punk forged through experimentation and play. For other members of the band during its first life—such as Palmolive, Ingrid Weiss, Richard Dudanski, Charles Hayward, and Vicky Aspinall, a critical and equal comrade throughout—The Raincoats offered much the same. It was the band's second life that both inspired and ultimately led Kurt Cobain to become part of the story himself. He tracked down Ana at her cousin's antique shop in Notting Hill in 1992—an oft-told tale that has now taken on the status of myth—and sparked a resurrection of The Raincoats that included CD reissues and a new record on the American major label Geffen's "indie major" DGC (which released Nirvana, Sonic Youth, and Hole). The third life has been shaped by overt intersections of art and music, as well as ongoing questions about performance as a personal and political tool for cultural change. It's a life that has moved outside the band members' own experiences to take on an existence all its own.

In America, from the late 1970s and well into the 1990s, The Raincoats became an emblem of feminism, exploration, and courage. Artists who identified as gay or queer saw themselves in the band's bold spirit and found power within themselves to create indomitably, shedding the constrictions placed on them by a homophobic society mired in discriminatory politics. Those in Olympia, Washington who sought to use music as a weapon against misogyny, capitalism, and the stifling boundaries of mediocrity pointed to The Raincoats as the bedrock of their own revolutionary lineage. As for the artists who'd catapult the two words "Riot Grrrl" into international nomenclature, their odysseys wouldn't have been possible without The Raincoats providing a foundation to a history of feminist resistance.

And as the new millennium crept forward, the entire art world finally heard the message of the Guerrilla Girls and began evaluating the culpability of galleries and museums in perpetuating patriarchal narratives of cultural history. Naturally, The Raincoats played a role in reshaping those stories, too.

All the while, across time and space, the irreducible element of The Raincoats' music has been its focus on experimentation, particularly with timekeeping. Throughout the book that follows, speakers across generations and genres refer to the atypical nature of Raincoats' time signatures, so exceptional that no listener can pinpoint a meter; the rhythms and durations shift in the midst of songs, across album tracks, and as the band performs live. The consistency of the timing—a product of the emotional registers of the artists at any given moment—is in its inconsistency. In its ameliorative rhythmic volatility, The Raincoats' music reveals that we all have the capacity to reshape and keep our own sense of time, and in so doing, the power to grant our work perpetual life.

The form of this book takes a cue from that distinctive Raincoats time signature. Each of the sections and individual chapters do not aspire to a single literary consistency; rather, they're the product of my own experimentation. While researching and writing, I listened only to The Raincoats; sometimes I let the music flow through me in the background, almost subconsciously while I wrote, and at other times I'd stop writing and sing along at my desk. This book is the product of a particular magic that happens when you immerse yourself in another's creative work and allow it to become you, to shift your own emotional and intellectual production in such a way that it becomes the framing device and, in some ways, the whole.

Through this experiment of my own, I found myself breaking the bounds of narrative time. Seemingly tangential events could punctuate a particular moment I was crafting in print, or a memory from the past or future could startle me, demanding to be let into the present temporality of the story. The Raincoats' music, in the language of Russian theorist Mikhail Bakhtin, develops its own chronotope, its own time-space configuration constantly reshaped by the erratic beating of the human heart. Hearing The Raincoats so thoroughly that one's own output is shaped by its ever-changing and always-emerging mortal time signature is to realize both the psychological and cognitive power of music. Therefore, it makes sense to use the concept of overlapping and

INTRODUCTION

ongoing lives as the overarching structure for a book like this; lives within a life, never entirely demarcated by the parameters of time as we assume they exist.

To break outside the constraints of time, the boundedness of duration, can transform the way we perceive the world. In The Raincoats' music, there is no available metronome through which to "keep time" aside from the internal and psychic rhythms that guide our hearts into unknown worlds of experimentation—a process the band has sparked across decades and will continue to catalyze even as ordinary time, marked by changing calendars and backward-forward chronologies, marches onward. In those seemingly fixed notions of temporality, The Raincoats will remain timeless, forever precipitating an eternal return.

In that timelessness, it becomes clear that their story is not just their own—it belongs to all of us who keep the band's spirit existent. The question of afterlives becomes irrelevant because the time signature created by The Raincoats offers them to us in perpetuity.

POSSIBILITIES
varied ways.　　　　　ends longer
　　　　　　　　　　　ends loose

　　　　　　　　Eva Hesse, diaries, 1965[1]

Thus I am concealed in things as fiery energy. They are ablaze through me, like the breath that ceaselessly enlivens the human being, or like the wind-tossed flame in a fire. All these things live in their essence, and there is no death in them, for I am life.

　　　　　　　　　　　Hildegard of Bingen, from
　　　　　　　"A Vision of Love," *c.* 1163–1174[2]

Gina and Ana performing in Warsaw, 1978

LIFE NUMBER 1

They took individual breaths before the first life of The Raincoats could begin.

ROADS TO THE RAINCOATS

Ana da Silva was born first. She grew up in Madeira, an autonomous island region of Portugal on the African tectonic plate, about 320 miles west of Morocco. Ana was brought into a world bounded by the Estado Novo dictatorship, which lasted from 1933 to 1974. Her family was Catholic (as mandated by the state), but they forged opportunities to absorb outside cultural influences. Ana's mother, a language teacher, urged Ana and her sister, Maria Helena, to study English in Bournemouth. It was the mid-1960s. "The Rolling Stones had one album out, and *A Hard Day's Night* had just come out," Ana remembers. She didn't have a lot of money, but she bought a few records and saw the Rolling Stones live. Her first encounter with visual art occurred on a surreptitious family trip to Paris, where her uncle was working. She was especially enthralled with the Impressionists, whose paintings she understood as "not copying nature, but interpreting it in your own way," she says. "That's how my mind thinks, too, and how it sympathizes."

She first played a guitar in Germany, another place she traveled for language study. An American girl taught Ana "just a few chords" before she returned to Madeira, where Maria Helena bought Ana a guitar of her own. Together, they'd play Joan Baez and Bob Dylan songs, and Ana's world was forever changed.

Years later, amid student protests against the dictatorship, Ana wrote her university thesis on Bob Dylan. "Everybody was doing literature and poets, but for me, Bob Dylan was *it* at the time," she says. Choosing that topic was about bucking the rules and reorienting herself in cultural time. "In Portugal, we never learned anything from the twentieth century. Everything was before—even at university. I always felt that I wanted to learn what's happening *now*, and not just what's past. The past is interesting of course and informs the present, but I wanted to learn about the now, so I wrote about Bob Dylan." She took her thesis with her when she moved to London in 1974 with eventual plans to attend art school. She ultimately decided on Hornsey College of Art.

Seven years on from Ana's emergence into the world, Gina Birch was born in Cambridge and grew up in Nottingham, "in a family who really wanted life to be safe for their children," she says. "My brother was a bit older than me, and he was the boy, so everyone was really careful he got the good education whereas with me ... I realized that this very safe place was kind of throttling me. So I went right off the rails in every way I could. I needed adventure."

Gina knew she belonged in art school. She'd stay in the UK but set her sights further afield, making the island her oyster. She and her friend Alex Michon (who went on to make clothes for The Clash, direct an art gallery in London, and write future press releases for Gina's art exhibitions) decided to hitchhike across the country in 1975 to check out art schools. ("It was safe to hitchhike then," Gina smiles). On their odyssey, they made a stop with a friend at Saint Martin's School of Art in London. It was early November. There just happened to be a music gig planned in the school's common room, and Gina and Alex figured they might as well go. Listed on the poster: Bazooka Joe, an unnamed support band, and a bar. By all accounts, an ideal introduction to art school, even though neither Gina nor Alex would ultimately enroll at Saint Martin's.

On that fateful November 6 on Charing Cross Road, they stood in the Saint Martin's common room while the Sex Pistols—in their first-ever appearance—opened for Bazooka Joe (John Ellis, Danny Kleinman, and Stuart Goddard aka Adam Ant) to a small audience of art students and local Londoners. "We didn't know anything about punk or what was going on, but we just really loved these people, the Sex Pistols, playing this music and were really startled by it because they were so different, and so fresh. And *like us* in this way. We felt we could relate to them. There was none of the typical posturing ... well, if there *was* posturing, it was the kind of posturing we would have done! No distance, no 'star thing,' and it was so powerful." Gina refers to the connection the Sex Pistols made with the crowd and the unexpected sense of inclusivity in that performance space—something she'd never experienced at a music venue before. She'd have the same feeling again, and even more powerfully, when she saw The Slits a couple years later. Gina recognized a new kind of performance art.

She decided on Hornsey College of Art for herself and moved into a West London squat in 1976. It was on the second floor of a house at the end of Monmouth Road, a dead-end street near the famous Portobello Road. In the twenty-first century, townhouses lend an undeniable elegance to the street. But in the 1970s, anyone could get a room for free. The artist Neal Brown had already taken up residence on Monmouth Road when he helped Gina get her room, and they became close friends. They were the same year at Hornsey, and when they started classes that fall, they met a fellow art student who was also new: Ana. "I'd just arrived in London, and I really fell into something," Gina says.

HORNSEY COLLEGE OF ART

Hornsey College of Art, originally named Hornsey School of Art, was established in 1882 on Crouch End Hill in North London. By 1968, Hornsey had become known as a center of leftist protest. That year, a group of students occupied the main college building for six weeks, seeking a radical reconceptualization of art and education in the UK. The *New Left Review* described the sit-in as the "Hornsey coup," calling it "the most successful student power movement ... in Britain."[1] Tate Britain would later depict that moment as "a revolution—the overthrow of the established government by those who were previously subjected to it."[2] The occupation ended with the administration fleeing the building. Students and staff proceeded to run the college according to their own terms.

The student protesters drafted manifestoes outlining their goals: control of student union funds, overhaul of non-egalitarian assessment methods, and eradication of the capitalist structures inherent in the school's education model. Art is not a vocation learned through narrow means, they argued, but an expansion of cultural understanding and mode of participation in political change. Woodcut student-made posters for the sit-in carried slogans like "Smash the System" and urged community involvement.[3]

Hornsey was never the same again. The college took up temporary residence in Alexandra Palace (a grandiose venue in North London and longtime home of the BBC) until a new site was completed in 1979. The school sustained that sociocultural memory of revolution. It drew Gina, Ana, Neal, and others, and it brought radical artists from across Europe and the Americas to work with students. The "uprising," as the Tate would deem it, was so influential in the history of London arts culture that the museum put on a special *Journeys into the Past* exhibition in 2010, drawing on its archives to remind contemporary audiences of the continued significance of that 1968 moment at Hornsey.

The Tate's reference to Hornsey sparked something. By 2016, history exhibitions went up around London to memorialize the city's revolutionary past, largely centered on visual art and music. Hornsey appeared on a large exhibition map, but not because of the 1968 student sit-in. At the *PUNK: LONDON* show that year, celebrating "forty years of subversive culture," Hornsey was identified as a key part of London's radical cartography thanks to The Raincoats. An icon on the map depicted Hornsey with the notation that it was where Gina and Ana met, and where The Raincoats got their start.

SQUAT LIFE IN LONDON

Squatting and the ethos it grew out of in the 1970s were central to shaping an atmosphere in which experimentation, play, freedom, and sonic revolution were possible. So much of the punk music that ultimately emerged from West London revolved around that kind of communal life, and for The Raincoats, Gina's squat on Monmouth Road in particular.

Unplanned spaces are the ones where creative processes are most likely to occur—where artists can shape and be shaped by the lack of structure around them. At the same time, that idea hasn't always held true for urban locales evincing decay and maligned as

"Lend Us Your Ears," 1981

so-called eyesores and safety hazards. Yet for a brief period of time, empty Victorian terraces (rowhouses) and warehouses made the rise of punk, and the DIY art scene enveloped within it, possible. "In 1976, West London had been abandoned by wealth and money," Gina says, "and I was an art student squatter in Westbourne Grove for years. We really felt like the streets were our own."

Squatting—taking up residence in otherwise uninhabited structures—is a historical feature of mid-twentieth-century Britain, a product of wartime housing shortages brought on by Axis bombings. Homes in London,

Birmingham, Glasgow, and other major cities were rendered uninhabitable. A UK housing equity researcher dug up figures suggesting more than thirteen million British households had been displaced by 1945.[4] The area of West London around where the upstart record label and shop Rough Trade would pop up a few decades later—where Gina would also squat and The Raincoats would rehearse—was virtually untouched by the bombing campaigns that had devastated large swaths of London.[5] Living spaces were intact, but few people wanted, or could afford, to reside there.

By December 1948, the Universal Declaration of Human Rights was created. Although it has never had the force of law, it permeated the general Western consciousness, shaping ideas for standards of living. The document named legal entitlements to a residence and to housing as human rights.

That general sensibility combined with the work of housing activists led to postwar squatting movements. A grassroots anti-fascist activist group known as the "Vigilantes" promoted squatting, and the movement took hold across gender lines. Starting in the 1960s, squatting became part and parcel of counterculturalism in cities across Western Europe. By the 1970s, squatting became a particularly common practice for artists in London. Upon being threatened with eviction, one community of squatters near Monmouth Road even declared independence from the UK in late 1977. The residents described their secession as "part publicity stunt, part theatrical protest," with no actual intention to create a new nation state. As those squatters recall, there was no actual need to secede; they were already living in a place with an entirely different set of rules.[6]

For many art school squatters like Gina and Neal, their occupation served as resistance against the highbrow art gallery system. Squatting offered "physical space for the display of art and as a system of power relations."[7] They made and showed work that came to "embod[y] the radical new artistic practices of the counterculture movement, closely intertwined with a growing appreciation of vacant urban space."[8]

On Monmouth Road, a creative revolution was happening at the end of the cul-de-sac. Neal moved into his squat in 1976, right around the time the Sex Pistols supported the 101ers—Joe Strummer's pre-Clash band—at the nearby Nashville Rooms. He ended up in Monmouth Road thanks to the French Situationist Michel Prigent and Simon Cassell of the 101ers. Neal even used Simon's vintage funeral hearse (frequently deployed at 101ers' gigs) to move his limited belongings out of his parents' home and into the vacant space. In September of that same year, Gina arrived and needed somewhere to live. Neal had claimed a room on the top floor of the building, waiting for the right person to join the collective of artists occupying the space. "I chose well, in inviting Gina," he says. Gina moved in almost immediately and became part of the squatting community. Neal helped her to acclimate quickly. "As a friend of Joe Strummer's original band, the 101ers, with Richard Dudanski, who was right next door," Gina says, "he was quite enmeshed in everything that was happening."

Their building had been abandoned by the landlord and was in a state of decay. "Spectacularly scenic in its ruination," Neal laughs. Like other once-grand residences in Notting Hill, their 1864-constructed home was "a once very pretty building on a pretty little street, allowed to decline into phenomenal decay," Neal describes it. Primarily Victorian architecture, these were stately homes adorned in white stucco, like multitiered traditional wedding cakes. By the 1960s, the stucco and paint were falling off, revealing the construction techniques underneath. The decay had its own sense of disintegrating beauty and caught the eye of film directors and production crews, including for the 1983 movie *Runners*, starring James Fox, who was then best known for his role in Nicolas Roeg's *Performance* (1970). The film crews shot exterior and interior shots at the squat, and Neal and Gina even did some "set decorating" in their respective rooms.

For Gina, squat life on Monmouth Road brought punk energy into everyday life: "That kind of energy where there were people who enjoyed nonsense poetry, conceptual art, and all the things I fell in love with that had been written about in books," she says. "Like Dada, but better!" Gina laughs. "And that newness was about in the energy where I was living, and at Hornsey. And I think with punk, we were trying to draw those parallels to the art we were making and the way we were living."

Simon Bramley, a fellow artist and friend from Nottingham, moved straight into Gina's spare room in 1977. "It was a quite close community," Simon says, quickly explaining the music and art "crossover" contingent on Monmouth Road: Gina, Richard Dudanski, and Esperanza Romero (sister of Paloma Romero, better known as Slits and Raincoats drummer Palmolive).

Gina became extremely close with Richard and Esperanza (who'd later be married). "They were like family," she says. "When I first moved into Monmouth Road, Neal had taken me to the squat tearooms and there I had first set eyes on Richard and his brother Patrick, both wearing cool trilby-style hats. I knew they would be fun to get to know." Richard and Espe, as she was known to her close friends, lived next door to Gina. "They were much more experienced at squat living than I was," she explains. "I had left home and moved into a space with only cold running water and two gas rings on the floor, bare floorboards, no window coverings. I was used to a few more home comforts and being surrounded by friends. Here, I was very alone a lot of the time and not sure how to make life better. Sure, it had its brilliant freedoms and life was often exciting, but I was also lonely and uncertain." Amid those feelings, Richard and Espe became Gina's adopted family, and she "practically lived in their flat." They made Gina feel like Monmouth Road was truly home. And thus, she eventually brought other friends in, too, including Petra P from Nottingham and New York musician Amy Rigby.

For some, Monmouth Road was a transient space, which ultimately proved beneficial to The Raincoats in the long run. As squatters abandoned their posts, Neal, Gina, and others could expand their own spaces. Neal got a second adjacent room and part of the basement, which became a rehearsal area for the 101ers and others on the scene. "Gina and Ana used to play down there," Neal recalls, adding, "It was wonderful to be able to play music loudly." It wasn't always all fun, of course. "On one occasion the rehearsal area was both flooded and set on fire at the same time," he laughs. Pre-Raincoats, but after her firing from The Slits, Neal also remembers Palmolive hiding out in that basement, trying to avoid Ari Up's mother, Norah. "Norah chased Palmolive around London, wanting her drum kit back," Neal explains. Palmolive took refuge in the Monmouth Road rehearsal area, along with the drum kit. "Much as I liked Norah and loved The Slits," Neal says, "Palmolive was a higher cause."

LIFE NUMBER 1

Eventually, when The Raincoats became an official entity, that basement space became a regular rehearsal venue. One of Neal's lasting atmospheric memories of the squat is the sound of The Raincoats' second album, *Odyshape*. He heard the material so many times, in so many different incarnations—"To such a degree, more than any other listener, it has its own special circuit in my brain," Neal says. Since he was imbibing those *Odyshape* rehearsals during a period of time when he was "really depressed and holed up, listening to The Raincoats underneath me," he'll always describe those songs as "fractured, vulnerable"; his own experience and memories indelibly permeate the music for him.

Ana didn't live in a squat, but in a council flat nearby off Golborne Road market, a spot that was and remains an eclectic community. "It was in this flat that we first rehearsed when Nick, Jeremie, and Kate played with us," Ana says, referring to future Raincoats members, "and where we composed a few of the songs on the first album." There, she overlooked the rail lines, and those train tracks would become a trope in Ana's art and life; she'd occasionally draw them on her face, two stark lines, before performing, and they appeared across the poetic lyrics she wrote. Those tracks were so prominent in the physical space where she lived and made music that a writer for the music magazine *ZigZag* described the living space as "cluttered up with drums and guitars and . . . the continual noise of trains passing by."[9]

Ana's living space might not have been in the same state of physical dilapidation as Gina's, but it was imbued with its own sense of fragility, marked by the loneliness and confusion Ana felt on moving to London. From that flat, she wrote lyrics to various Raincoats songs including "The Void." Ana recalls, "I felt confused and baffled about life, trying to figure it out, and trying to figure myself out." The industrial image and sound of the rail lines became integral to her sonic vision. "The railway line became like a friend to me."

The culture of the neighborhood was shaped by its residents. "It was all a big community thing," journalist Vivien Goldman says, referring to the general area around Westbourne Grove. Vivien shared a flat with Geoff Travis of Rough Trade, a friend from university. "For a while, he used the space as a sort of B&B for Rough Trade artists," she laughs. "*Everyone* stayed at that house." It had the spirit of a squat, and Vivien suggests it might as well have been. She lists scores of artists who came through, temporarily making the living space their own. It was there that Vivien learned about The Raincoats. "If anybody was in the Rough Trade orbit, they were like extended family," she says.

That same squatting culture of sustaining and sharing with fellow travelers would play an unexpected and important role in bringing the music of The Raincoats over to the crucial geographic nodal point of Olympia, Washington. As Jean Smith of punk duo Mecca Normal explains, she first heard The Raincoats thanks to her bandmate, David Lester. "David became aware of them because he lived in a squat in London around the time The Raincoats were active," Jean says, adding, "David had an excellent grasp of feminism." Thanks in part to his squatting experience, he introduced Jean to a number of female-fronted bands like Crass, Au Pairs, Poison Girls, X-Ray Spex, and The Slits, in addition to The Raincoats. Vicky Aspinall, who'd soon join The Raincoats on violin, was also in a squat in Brixton. "It was terrible," she laughs.

Squatting had its advantageous aspects, but "there was also a darker side," Neal explains. "Although no one owned a squat, people were territorial." Neal and Gina became politically active in their community to ensure they could keep the building. "It was a fight," he says, "but housing is so important." Although needing a place to live and seeking a creative community were their initial reasons for squatting, in the later years on Monmouth Road, Gina and Neal's purpose became more aligned with the political aims of early postwar squatting movements. They became founding members of a housing cooperative to formalize their living situation. "There was a whole statutory process," Neal recalls, "and we were very unusual in that, in our negotiations, we were actually on record at the British Houses of Parliament where they discussed us in the House of Commons. Not at great length, but they discussed us." After "endless committee meetings," Neal says, they eventually earned the right to retain their ownership interests in Monmouth Road.

LIFE NUMBER 1

BAND BEGINNINGS

From the deteriorating squats of London and the community they incubated, new things grew, and those "unoccupied" spaces helped to produce a diverse range of artists. Since the very beginning, Ana and Gina wanted their band to be seen and appreciated as art. They were never just musicians; they were making a new kind of sonic artistry. Kim Gordon of Sonic Youth captured that ethos decades later, saying, "I've never seen myself as a musician. I see myself as an artist that makes music and writes, and I feel the same way about Gina and Ana."

Gina and Ana met at Hornsey, but neither started art school with plans to form a band. They were two artists, from different parts of the world, honing their respective crafts. Gina wanted to create larger-than-life paintings while Ana was interested in working on a smaller scale. Yet they both trusted their instincts and sensibilities; they shared a sense of their own potential and power. In the very early Raincoats days, Gina remembers, "Ana and I were almost more like colleagues than really close friends." She continues, "When I met Ana, she was twenty-eight, and I was twenty, soon to turn twenty-one. It makes a big difference at that age ... life experience is huge. I hadn't lived away from home before. I was mischievous, shy, and adventurous, but I was also a girl from the provinces who had only left the UK shores for a few days once before." Despite their different backgrounds, their working relationship grew, and the distinctions in their approaches to art began to form a dynamic that would become the heart of The Raincoats. Stark differences, punctuated by synergies.

Gina says, "It was quite scary because I felt completely inadequate. Ana only knew a few chords, too, but because she'd studied languages and written poetry, she could imagine lyrics in a way I couldn't." But, Gina continues, "I had a lot of energy, and a real passion for art and creativity. We had very different perspectives, so we made for a very interesting marriage."

Two very different perspectives, two very different people. "You need that weird juxtaposition, almost opposites" to create meaningful art, Gina suggests. As soon-to-be Raincoats manager and collaborator Shirley O'Loughlin describes it, "There's always been a mutual respect between Ana and Gina, but the dynamic of their relationship and that tension is the fire in the belly. They have ultimate respect for each other, but sometimes the tension stretches things so much that it seems it's going to break, and sometimes it's just magnificent. When they're together on stage, there's magic."

The Raincoats—or the very idea of a punk band that might grow into The Raincoats—got started thanks in part to a roadie named Kevin from The Clash ("known as 'Roadent,'" Gina notes). He was talking to Gina and Ana about punk, and they were keen to get involved themselves. "I'd seen the Sex Pistols, but I didn't really know what was going on," Gina says. "My life was changing at that point because the world was opening up in a brilliant way, revealing all sorts of creative energies, and punk was another level of that. Before, the things I fell in love with were written about in books—conceptual art, Dada, nonsense poetry, and the energy to it. So we didn't really know what punk was, but we knew it had this same kind of tremendous energy."

Kevin knew Ana had been cutting her friends' hair and her own. "He asked me if I'd cut his hair, but really badly . . . it was all that kind of spirit," Ana says. Through Hornsey, Ana and Gina began hanging around with other art school punks and squatters with connections to The Clash, The Slits, and everything in between. Along with friends in tow, they began attending gigs together, often tagging along with Ana's cousin Manuel (he had a car and could drive them). They were enlivened by the scene and got to talking one day in the pub underneath Hornsey. Ana and Gina were thinking it at the same time: *We should start a band.* "We didn't really know if we could do it. At that point it was just percolating as an idea, a fantasy, a fantastical idea. But we *took a photograph*, the band, so that's what makes it real!" Gina laughs. "We took these baby steps towards the possibility of having the group."

Right around that time, Ana and Gina bought the first Raincoats instruments. Ana picked up an electric guitar in a market, along with a small amp she could carry. "It was a really terrible guitar," she laughs, "but I didn't know the difference between that and a Gibson or a Rickenbacker. I just knew it made noise." Gina nervously stepped into Macari's Musical Exchange, a West End instrument shop that was already known as one of the most popular and well respected in London. That location on Charing Cross Road, where Gina bought her first bass, was established in 1958 by two brothers whose descendants kept its doors open for sixty years. It's actually the very same spot where Gina took her own daughter, Honey, instrument shopping decades later.

It's pretty to think there was something innate in the atmosphere at Hornsey that made an experimental punk band seem like a possibility, a new way of making art that spoke back to the "Hornsey coup." But in fact, the opposite is mostly the truth. At the time, Ana lamented that Hornsey tutors simply weren't interested in music as art, and it was Gina's art school boredom that became the kick she needed to buy a bass. One day in 1976, Gina was sitting in an art and politics lecture. "I always hoped that art and politics lectures could lift my spirits, inspire me, but sadly this was not the case," she says. She got a lunch break, went for a couple of drinks and then headed to Macari's. "With great trepidation, I entered Macari's," Gina recalls. "I had never been in a music shop before, and I was about to buy an instrument I had no idea how to play. 'What's the cheapest bass guitar you have?'" she'd asked. A store clerk handed her a bass that cost £30. "When asked if I wanted to try it out, I shook my head and left with it, wondering what would happen next." She just wanted to get it home even though she didn't have an amp. "I think I plugged it through my little record player, playing along to Toots and the Maytals records."

But once they had those instruments, it was official: They were starting a band.

There were no gigs lined up, but they did decide on a name: The Raincoats. "The most important thing is the name of the group, not the music, my cousin told us," Ana smiles. "So we started saying the names of objects, pieces of clothing. Manuel suggested, 'What about raincoats?' I really liked that idea. Maybe coming from sunny Portugal, the idea of London and all that rain, it seemed appropriate. Maybe the idea of an object. So we decided on 'The Raincoats' for the time being."

Everyone's got their own idea about the origins of the band name. "Before I joined, I remember asking Ana, 'Where'd the name come from?'" *says Jeremie Frank, who'd briefly become a Raincoat for a short period on guitar.* "And she said because she spoke Portuguese, she liked how the English word 'raincoat' sounded." *Thurston Moore of Sonic Youth says he thought the name referred to a condom, a feminist joke. For Rob Sheffield, eventual* Rolling Stone *writer and longtime fan,* "the name just seemed really cool." *Lois Maffeo, punk musician and writer from Olympia, remembers being drawn to the band name immediately when she first bought a copy of the Rough Trade compilation* Wanna Buy a Bridge? *(filled with various artists on the label) in 1982.* "It wasn't provocative or aggressive, but somewhat prosaic. Just the name of an article of clothing," *Lois says.*

"But *that* Raincoats, *that* wasn't even a band, really. It didn't happen," Ana says. They never played a gig and barely considered rehearsing together. It was just a name, a concept. Nonetheless, other things started to fall into place. A guy named John Herlihy asked Ana to join a new band he played guitar in. She agreed to go to a rehearsal, but she found it "too stiff, too organized." She called it quits after attending just one rehearsal, but not before she got the phone number of John's drummer, Nick. She thought he might be someone she could work with musically in the future.

But most importantly, perhaps, Ana and Gina went to see The Slits.

SEEING THE SLITS

"The Slits gave us permission that night!" Gina exclaims. "The idea that we could be on that stage. And I *really* wanted to be on that stage."

Ana and Gina went together to see the very first Slits show on March 11, 1977 at the Coliseum "cinema" in Harlesden. The Slits were on a bill with The Clash, Buzzcocks, Subway Sect, and a late-night showing of kung fu films. It cost £1.50 entry. (Unbeknownst to either of them, Shirley O'Loughlin, who'd soon become an essential component of The Raincoats, was also in the crowd that night.) Seeing The Slits awakened something in the two art students, who stood together shouting along with the band. This show felt different from any they'd seen before it. There were powerful women on stage. Ari Up was unlike anyone they'd ever witnessed, and they were drawn to Kate Korus (later to be replaced by Viv Albertine) on guitar. "When I saw Palmolive on stage, I didn't even know what she was doing exactly, but I just loved seeing it. There was so much joy coming out of her," Ana says.

Part of processing the gig, for Gina, meant bringing The Slits to play at Hornsey. "The only show I ever promoted," Gina says. It was scheduled to take place in the art studios in Alexandra Palace. "They were bringing a PA that Don Letts had sourced, but for ages, the studio stood empty—they were so late, and I was worried they just weren't going to show at all." They did, eventually, "and it was great," Gina says. "But by the time they arrived I had cut most of my hair quite short ... What is it about cutting your hair off when you are in a state?"

Seeing The Slits was ultimately what both Gina and Ana needed to give The Raincoats another go.

LET'S DO IT

In the summer of 1977, Ana traveled to Madeira to spend time with family, and Gina decided to commit to a renewed focus on the bass.

A friend of Gina's taught her E-A-D-G bass tuning, and she began learning the notes to everything on *Funky Kingston* by Toots and the Maytals. As she got comfortable with the instrument, she realized an exciting but unorthodox way to play the bass: to approach it visually, looking for root notes in patterns. "Once you find a root note, you realize there are all these other notes you can dance around a root note with," Gina remembers. "I didn't know how music was constructed, but I was beginning to see visual patterns while I was listening, so I started trying out different things to

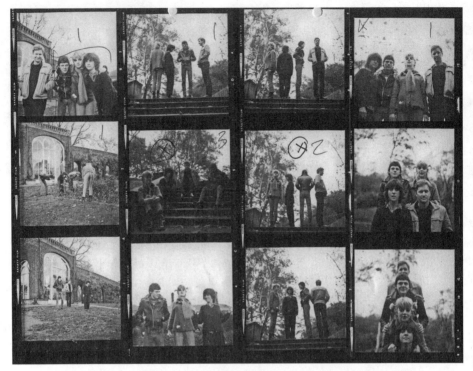

Contact sheet from the very first Raincoats photo shoot with Ana, Gina, Nick, and Ross, captured by Shirley in 1977

see what would happen." Her art school training was shaping her understanding of sonic representation. By the time Ana returned to London from her summer in Portugal, she and Gina got together for another go at The Raincoats—a jam session, essentially.

Meanwhile, more pieces were falling into place. Geoff Travis from Rough Trade asked Ana (she worked behind the counter at the record store) if a friend and newcomer to London, Ross Crighton, could stay in her spare room since he had nowhere to live. "It was a small flat," Ana laughs, "but I'd come from Portugal, so I didn't own anything, so he fitted in there perfectly." He played the guitar and also wanted to start a band. Although Ana played guitar, she and Gina thought they could use another guitarist. Ross was in.

The Raincoats only needed to find a drummer.

LIFE NUMBER 1

THE RAINCOATS NEED A DRUMMER

For the first but certainly not last time, The Raincoats found themselves in need of a drummer. That realization—"we need a drummer"—would become a refrain in the lives of The Raincoats, and one that would ultimately link Ana and Gina to artists including The Slits, the 101ers, This Heat, Robert Wyatt, Bikini Kill, Sonic Youth, PJ Harvey, the Velvet Underground, Stereolab, Tiger Trap, Lois Maffeo, and more. But back in 1977, for the first time, The Raincoats just needed someone capable of putting sticks to skins.

"We were never looking for a steady beat," Gina says. "For The Raincoats, it has always been the school of heartbeat playing. Something that can gain momentum unexpectedly, slow down, and surprise."

There wasn't much discussion when Ana remembered she had Nick Turner's number—good thing she'd gone to that lone rehearsal of John's band. Ana got in touch, and Nick was excited to be invited to join. The Raincoats had their first drummer.

"He was very enthusiastic," Gina recalls. "But I never got the sense he was into the politics of the whole thing." Nick was the youngest of the group. He'd just finished his A-levels and had been studying during the year of punk. "So I hadn't done spectacularly well, let's just say that," he laughs. He got started in a band with Toyah, and he'd fallen in love with the first Patti Smith record. Just right—Ana's kind of person.

What would this band be called? While Ana and Gina had never formalized the band name, the earlier idea, The Raincoats, stuck. In an interview with *ZigZag*, Gina suggested it was a practical choice. "We just kept the original name—The Raincoats," Gina said matter-of-factly.[10]

THE TABERNACLE: NOVEMBER 9, 1977

With the addition of Nick on drums, The Raincoats could play their first gig.

Thanks to the squatting community in West London, everyone was mostly in the know about who was in a band. Richard

Dudanski—Gina's squat neighbor and friend—asked if The Raincoats wanted to open for his new band, Tymon Dogg and the Fools (Tymon Dogg, aka Stephen Murray, was another squatter on nearby Westbourne Park Road). Joe Strummer had just laid the 101ers to rest, and Richard was frustrated, but he and Tymon Dogg started playing together. By early November 1977, they were getting ready for a gig at The Tabernacle.

Gina and Ana were apprehensive—"Downright scared!" Gina laughs—but agreed to be on the bill. "We just turned up," Ana says. Up to this point, they'd only been playing with portable amps and a single microphone.

Prior to the gig, Nick invited the art teacher from his school, Shirley O'Loughlin, to a rehearsal in Ana's living room. It was a fateful invitation. Shirley had met Ana before, casually, around the Rough Trade shop when Ana was on the clock, but The Tabernacle gig would soon bring Shirley into The Raincoats.

The performance also produced The Raincoats' first gig poster. As an early supporter of the band, Neal Brown was all over the marketing effort. He scrawled out with pencil, in all caps, on brown newspaper roll:

THE RAINCOATS
(GINA BIRCH & ANA DA SILVA)
PLUS TONGUES OF FIRE
PLUS DOLL BY DOLL
7.30 WED 9 NOV. AT THE
TABERNACLE POWIS
SQ W.11. NO BAR BRING
A BOTTLE. PARTY
AFTERWARDS AT GINAS

50p

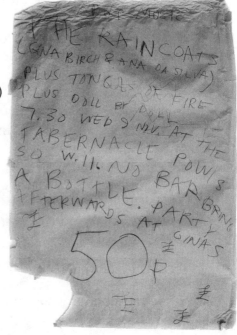

LIFE NUMBER 1

The Tabernacle was established in 1887, built as an "iron church" so named for the use of cast iron in its construction. The word "tabernacle" was much older, dating to biblical times and denoting an immovable structure. By the mid-nineteenth century, the architectural design had become popular for places of religious worship. Churches known as "tin tabernacles" were popping up across the UK, constructed with cheaper materials such as corrugated iron.[11] The Tabernacle that would ultimately be repurposed as a punk venue had a garden in front, and the structure itself was built as a rotunda with two turrets on either side and a red-brick facade.

The Tabernacle was just around the corner from Gina's squat and Ana's flat, and the venue was also in its early days of punk fame. "All these punk shows happened at The Tabernacle around that time," Nick explains. "Joe Strummer played there all the time, and he played the encore that night," he says and smiles, still giddy to think of it. Shirley arrived with her friend Glenn Marks and Toyah Willcox (who famously starred as the pyromaniac in Derek Jarman's film *Jubilee* that same year, whose audition photographs were taken by Shirley, and with whom Shirley was briefly in a band herself). "We played just one show as 'The Streets' and I borrowed Nick's drum kit with Nick next to me, keeping me in time!" Shirley laughs.

The gig would be Ross's first and only as a Raincoat. The pressure of playing live was too much. He left the band without a second guitarist. Ana and Gina weren't certain they had something worth continuing. Nick was eager to keep going, but like he says, "What'd I know? I was just a baby." As Ross exclaimed at the time, "I never want to do that again!" He hid behind the amp the whole time because of his stage fright, in which he wasn't alone. Gina adds, "I was quite terrified and didn't feel like we were ready for it, but Richard convinced us we could do it. But we hadn't become ourselves yet. We were very undercooked, like the cake mixture before you put the sugar in."

"We were all terrified!" Ana laughs. "I went on stage and thought, *Oh my God, what am I doing? Who am I to be up here, doing this?*" Gina continues, "I went back to college and my tutor said, 'Don't give up the day job,' and I felt that was the feeling—that we hadn't cracked anything, that we were a long way from the starting point." So much for Hornsey supporting experimental art!

Yet it was the start they ultimately needed, and important voices around the early Raincoats convinced Gina and Ana they had a real spark. "There was a real exuberance to it," Jude Crighton, Ross's partner and fellow Rough Trade employee, remembers. Shirley adds, "I thought they were brilliant!"

They played all the songs they'd written by that point, maybe five in total, although versions of the songs at The Tabernacle were years away from those that would ultimately appear on records. Years later, they recall playing "Hey Hey We're The Raincoats," "Only Loved at Night," and "Black and White," along with "Life on the Line" and "No One's Little Girl." Ana and Ross had written "Life on the Line" together and Gina had been working on "No One's Little Girl" lyrics in the time leading up to the gig. The latter would go on to become a quintessential song in the lives of The Raincoats, the first for which Gina ever wrote lyrics, and one that artists in decades to come would cite as evidence of an unrivaled Raincoats sound.

"Life on the Line" was a song Ross began alone, from a dark place. He'd witnessed a suicide on the London train tracks and put his emotions into print. He and Ana later crafted the song together in their shared flat. When it came time to record the first Raincoats LP, some of the lyrics to that song got altered in the studio at Berry Street—at the suggestion of a producer. The full weight of Ross's emotional lyrics was lost. He never took offense and doesn't have a clear memory of what the original words were supposed to be. Ana says it's one of the regrets she carries when looking back on early Raincoats work. "We should have kept all of Ross's lyrics."

At The Tabernacle after-party at Gina's squat—advertised rough and ready on Neal's poster that Ana happily grabbed from the venue and kept for safekeeping—Ana and Shirley got to chatting and Shirley quickly realized how much they shared. They'd catalyze one another's creative impulses all the way to the present.

LIFE NUMBER 1

WE NEED A GUITARIST

With Ross afraid to take the stage again, The Raincoats needed a new guitarist. For a brief moment it was Kate Korris (née Korus), an original cofounder of The Slits who'd later form the Mo-dettes. Kate played one gig as a Raincoat at Hornsey in December 1977 before she, too, parted ways with the band. "I do remember she had a song called something like 'Selling It, Selling It, Nine to Five,' and I thought it was about prostitution," Gina says. "And it *was* about prostitution, but not in a way I understood at the time. It was about prostitution—only in the sense that we're all prostitutes, selling ourselves for capitalist work and money. But I remember thinking, *I can't possibly sing 'No One's Little Girl' if Kate's in the band!*" Compared with Kate's fiery feminism, Gina saw her own lyrics as docile.

Nobody remembers exactly how Kate became a Raincoat for a night. Neal had a girlfriend who lived in a nearby squat with Kate's then-boyfriend, John "Boogie" Tiberi, so it's possible he made the connection. (And Kate wouldn't be the last member of The Slits to join The Raincoats, another union made possible through London squat living.) But in the meantime, The Raincoats needed a new guitarist. Again.

Ana was working at a restaurant in London while making Raincoats plans. A guy from Hornsey showed up for dinner with an American woman named Jeremie Frank. He mentioned Jeremie's guitar skills, so Ana invited her to come round and meet the band. "She turned up with a huge hat with big feathers and a black cape," Ana laughs, "and we thought, *Oh my God, what is this?* But she could really play." Gina laughs, too. "All I remember about Jeremie, other than that she could really play guitar, is she had a song about giving her body to science when she died."

From her initial entry into The Raincoats, Jeremie's fashion suggested she might not share the same ideology as the others. "We were just punks going to the charity shop for our clothes and imagination. It was a way of expressing ourselves," Ana says. Jeremie came from a different school of rock and thought she'd need to look glam on stage, modeling her style on T. Rex and

Bowie. That said, the cape she wore to the first Raincoats rehearsal was less of a fashion statement and more of a reflection of the sociocultural pressures women face. "I never wore clothes that fit, tried to cover myself up a lot of the time, and had a lot of body issues I was only able to deal with years later," Jeremie remembers. She learned from The Raincoats that fashion is always part politics. "Back then," Jeremie says, "I wasn't thinking about women's rights, gay rights, civil rights in general, but I look back on my time in The Raincoats and realize that's when my sense of those rights started to develop. I didn't know you could even choose clothes and makeup to *avoid* looking pretty, anti-feminine, as a statement. Now I do, and I have The Raincoats to thank."

BEHIND THE IRON CURTAIN: WARSAW, APRIL 1978

In early spring 1978, The Raincoats became the first punk band to play behind the Iron Curtain. The soundtrack to democratic revolution.

"Somebody told us the last band that had been in Warsaw was the Rolling Stones a few years before. So although I'm not comparing us to the Rolling Stones," Ana says, "it was us and the Rolling Stones."

It all started at a gig at The Chippenham pub in Maida Vale in January or February of that year. Simon Bramley, the performance artist and old friend of Gina's who'd moved into her spare room in Monmouth Road, was putting on a show with the duo Thom Pucky and Dirk Larsen, who performed together as Reindeer Werk from 1973 to 1981. They collaborated with Fluxus artists, such as Joseph Beuys and other conceptual artists, basing their own work on the idea of "Behaviouralism," designed to, as Pucky explains it, "make people aware of their 'conditioned behavior.' This anti-conformity also translated itself on the wider platform of the punk revolution."[12]

That night, Simon invited Reindeer Werk to create one of their Behaviouralism "workshops" in conjunction with his own performance titled *The Cost of Living*. Simon's capitalist critique drew extracts from a government budget speech, set them to a drum beat, and featured more than a dozen "citizens" on stage with paper bags over their heads, responding to the numerical figures read aloud by Simon. "A fantastic spectacle," Simon calls it forty-five years later. Reindeer Werk's performance was "basically lying on the floor and squirming around, some kind of Behaviourist contortions on the floor," Simon says. Meanwhile, he'd been in touch with some artists in Warsaw about the idea of taking *The Cost of Living* beyond the Iron Curtain. Initially, Reindeer Werk was meant to join him, but some logistical complications ensued. The Raincoats—the other group on the bill that night at The Chippenham—got the gig instead. Given the politics in Warsaw at the time, "We never expected it to actually happen," Simon reflects. But within a couple of months, the friends and bandmates were en route to Poland.

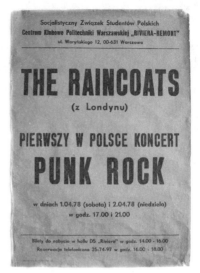

Poster advertisement for The Raincoats in Warsaw, Poland, 1978

To stage a punk gig in Warsaw was itself an act of resistance, something to which protestors in Poland had become warmly receptive. By the late 1970s, former student activists who'd been part of the Prague Spring uprising a decade prior had broadened their intellectual community to include younger student activists coming of age. The Student Solidarity Committee formed in Krakow in 1977, and by 1978 a young and substantial democratic opposition began to demand reform.

On March 25, 1978, just a week before Simon and The Raincoats departed London for their long train journey eastward, *Europa-Archiv*, the long-running publication of the German Society for Foreign Affairs in Bonn, ran a headline story: "'*Dissidenten' und Wirklichkeit*" ["'The Dissidents' and Reality"]. Circulated in the West, it illuminated for Western readers a rising dissent behind the Iron Curtain, centered in Warsaw. Two days later, London's *Evening Standard* ran a quarter-page photograph of The Raincoats above a title story, "These Punks Have Polish." The headline used a homonym to play on assumptions about punk style at the time and the region to where The Raincoats were headed. The piece slyly read, "Poland gave us Chopin and Rubinstein. Now we are returning the compliment by giving them this lot. They are a Portobello Road-based new wave band called The Raincoats, and they leave today to play at least three dates in Warsaw as guests of the Polish Government."[13]

As Ana, Gina, Nick, Jeremie, Simon, and Ana's sister Maria Helena traveled by rail through France and into West Germany, *World Today* drew on the March 25 article in *Europa-Archiva*, but this time for a broad English-speaking readership. Across newsstands, the paper announced the power of Polish dissent in an article titled "Poland at the Crossroads." It would prove to be a crucial political junction that The Raincoats would help to cultivate.

On March 27, 1978, The Raincoats boarded the night train from London and headed east, with plans to appear on stage at the polytechnic in Warsaw, a component of the "flying university" system, for a series of events known as the International Artists' Meeting ("I AM").

Polish resistance had become somewhat synonymous with the "flying university" — private spaces where lectures and performances were held and samizdat publications[14]* were produced.[15] The locations were fundamental gathering spots for young Poles eager to create revolution through art. Acknowledging the rising political dissent in his country, especially among university students, artist and cultural activist Henryk Gajewski opened the Post Remont gallery, an underground experimental arts and education center without a designated base. The location's home, as it were, existed

---

* Samizdat was "a clandestine practice... of circulating manuscripts that were banned, had no chance of being published in normal channels or were politically suspect." Nickolas Lupinin, "Samizdat," in *Encyclopedia of Russian History*, ed. James R. Millar, 1347 (Thomson Gale 2004).

wherever the democratic opposition was present. Gajewski organized the "I AM" in 1978 and became one of the key figures to introduce punk—and with it, a new wave of dissenters—in Warsaw.

For would-be Polish punks, Gajewski was a phenomenon. The club spaces he established offered a kind of freedom to students and political outcasts that couldn't be found anywhere else.

To bring punk to Warsaw was to introduce color to the gray monotony of living under Moscow's thumb in the satellite state. There was incentive, especially for students and activists working against the oppressive communist government, to avoid

Ana, fierce, in Warsaw

being seen; grey was a necessary political reality. Even those Poles who were punks at heart avoided style statements, despite being enamored with images of Vivienne Westwood style coming out of London. While The Raincoats eschewed the esthetic that typified punk at that time, they nonetheless stood out from the Eastern crowds. People stared at their clothes, their hairstyles, their shoes. The Raincoats were visual symbols of freedom punctuating the monotonous landscape. Tomek Lipinski, who served as the band's guide in Warsaw, still remembers them as being "like space aliens" who'd descended upon those surveilled streets. Until The Raincoats clocked in, the Warsaw opposition didn't know with certainty that punk was real. And neither did the communist officials who sought to prevent the punk ethos from taking hold.

Before they even reached Warsaw, the passage between worlds was palpable. "It was sort of spy novel-ish," Nick Turner amusedly recalls, recounting a full search of the band's belongings at Checkpoint

Charlie, complete with East German guards, machine guns, and Alsatian dogs. He suspects they were looking for Western books and records. For Ana, it was the sheer length of time the train had to stop that presses on her memory: "We were at the border for ages, sitting there amid East German guards with guns. The railway was a bit high, and you could look down, where below there were old-fashioned cars. And it was almost like a black-and-white spy film. The lights were all dim. But of course maybe your imagination starts to run away when you're in East Berlin." Jeremie remembers the experience similarly, like entering a fictional world: "We were followed on the streets, and our hotel rooms were searched. It was still very much a satellite state of Russia, represented by the Palace of Culture in the center of Warsaw that replicates the one in Moscow."

"It was quite heavy at times," Ana reflects. "Where we played, there were only certain people who could come. Gina wanted to invite a person working in the hotel restaurant, but it was all very strange, and we didn't understand everything that was happening." For Jeremie, the dangerous politics of the place became obvious after she returned to the band's hotel one afternoon. The day prior, she'd been walking through the city, documenting the constructivist architecture with her camera (Jeremie was an architecture student eager to capture the alien buildings of Warsaw from her own perspective). She stored her camera and the used film safely, ready to develop it upon her return to London. But those images would never be developed—Jeremie opened the hotel room door to find it ransacked, all the film stolen. Even the partially used roll in her camera had been snatched. Of course, the camera itself was safely intact; this was no monetary-based burglary.

Naturally, then, in gray Warsaw where uniformity was key to survival, there was a sense of paranoia in the air—for The Raincoats, as well as for the Polish punk-rockers-to-be. "There were a couple of people who went around with us," Ana says, remembering Tomek Lipinski and Iza X, "and we thought they were OK, but I didn't know to what extent they were supposed to spy on us when we got there." In actuality, Tomek and Iza weren't spying on The Raincoats; they'd volunteered to be their guides given their involvement in Gajewski's salon-style happenings. Tomek describes

LIFE NUMBER 1

The Raincoats' arrival in Poland as the most important moment in his life, showing him the revolutionary possibilities of sonic outsiderness. The band invited Tomek to their hotel to listen to cassettes they'd brought. "They played us all the best music, and they also brought things from London punk boutiques. They said, 'We have hair dye here. Why don't we dye your hair?'" He couldn't say no. He remembers going into their hotel "more or less normal," as far as Warsaw goes, and finding his way back out into the street with "radiant pink cyclamen hair, suddenly a completely different person ... In this grey reality, I suddenly had cyclamen hair, and that made me a space alien, too. I'd always *felt* like an alien here," he says, as he discusses the political reality of Warsaw at the time, "but I was officially alienized." Standing out from the crowd could be dangerous, but the inspiring presence of The Raincoats made Tomek eager to shed his furtive esthetic.

The Raincoats played two nights in Warsaw in the same venue: the Riviera Remont at the polytechnic. The "Remont Club," Maciej Magura, another student activist who played an MC-style role over the two nights, calls it. The four-walled nondescript enclosure was where "we punks, a very small group of outcasts, used to hang out," Maciej explains. So they all knew The Raincoats were coming and were anticipating the gigs.

The Remont was located just south of where a ten-foot wall had been constructed to imprison the city's Jewish population during the Nazi occupation. It was established as a performance and gallery venue in the 1970s, an intentionally unremarkable old space that could comfortably fit a few hundred people inside, and up to six hundred if you crammed everyone in. The Riviera Remont, as it's now called, continues operating and is known fondly as the "artistic mecca" of Poland's capital city.

The Londoners entered early to set up. When the doors opened to the eager crowd outside, "It was like a storming of the amphitheater in my memory," Jeremie recalls. Simon went on first with his spoken-word performance, *The Cost of Living*. Only this time it was "cobbled together with the youth in Warsaw who were slightly bemused about it," Simon remembers. "We had fifteen or twenty Polish youths with paper bags over their heads [the 'citizens'] on stage with The Raincoats, and a 'prime minister' with a stocking over his head, shouting extracts of the Chancellor's budget speech (five pence on a packet of cigarettes, eight pence, ten pence on a bottle of wine, etc.), and this was relayed to the 'citizens,' who'd have to clap their hands and stomp their feet to the instructions. We formed lifelong relationships with the Polish contingent, who were about to get conscripted into the army and sent to Afghanistan, as I remember it."

The audience roared with reverence when The Raincoats took the stage, as if transported to Hyde Park for the famously packed Rolling Stones or Queen gigs. Fans lifted Jeremie off the stage, the green snakeskin boots she'd had made especially for the shows flying into the air at the ends of her legs. "We were like heroes in Warsaw," she exclaims, lifting her arms as if to emulate all those fledgling Polish punks helping her to crowd surf back in 1978.

Behind Nick's drum kit, a small piece of paper hung on the wall with a one-word hand-scrawled message: SOLIDARITY. It's difficult to see in the photos, a small act of resistance within the larger sonic one taking place. "They were already trying to get the message across for Solidarity," Jeremie says.

As a result of intense political activism, Polish workers won the right to strike in August 1980, and they formed an independent union called, simply, Solidarity.[16] While Solidarity had a specific referent, the word also conjured a sense of political revolution, freedom, and independence made possible by the brave students and workers who came together to challenge Soviet oversight and power.

By the second night, members of the audience were singing along—they'd taped the first show and gone home, obsessively listened, and learned the words phonemically; most couldn't speak English. "It sort of felt like we were pop stars or something, which felt weird," Ana recalls. The Raincoats had only been together for a few months, played only a handful of gigs, and hadn't recorded anything. Yet they showed up ready to open eyes, ears, and minds to a new way of being. The Raincoats were punk rebels in Warsaw for two nights, long before fans back across the wall to the West would hear their song "Fairytale in the Supermarket." The Warsaw underground was starving for something revolutionary, and The Raincoats offered it to them in droves.

The trip became an inspirational nodal point for The Raincoats, too. On the train trip home, Jeremie wrote a song called "Warsaw" about the pervasiveness of the color gray. And in the early hours of the morning, as the band passed through East Berlin and ultimately back into the West, Ana wrote "You're a Million," a song that would become a centerpiece of the band's self-titled record a year later. The lyrics reflected the immediacy of Ana's experience in Warsaw, in which she recognized traces of her upbringing inside Portugal's Estado Novo dictatorship: "My feelings were killed by laws / The walls that surrounded my city / Stop here."

A few weeks later, The Raincoats received a package of large-format photographs at the Rough Trade shop, sent from behind the Iron Curtain. While Ana's sister Maria Helena had taken some prominent shots of the band onstage and had filmed the performances on Super 8, a young Polish photographer called Jerzy Kośnik had captured The Raincoats within the broader space of the venue, depicting the first moment that Warsaw art students and other burgeoning punks saw a band that would change their lives. He included a note with the images:

> I send you pictures (66 units) by registered letter. All of them are made in big format. That's my present for you.

THE RAINCOATS NEED A DRUMMER (AND GUITARIST TOO)

After returning to London and playing together a few more times, The Raincoats fired Nick. "I was really shocked," Jeremie remembers, not realizing Nick was about to be let go. "I guess we thought he wasn't right for the band," Gina recalls. The Raincoats were going to need a new drummer.

Nick was significantly younger than the rest of the band, and he'd been moving down a musical road that didn't feel quite suited to The Raincoats' direction. They all met at a pub, and Ana and Gina suggested it was time to part ways. "I was disappointed to leave the band initially," Nick says, "but Ana and Gina were absolutely right, in retrospect—I wasn't right for The Raincoats." He moved on to a more aggressive style of drumming with surf rock band The Barracudas and later the supergroup Lords of the New Church—alongside Stiv Bators of the Dead Boys, Brian James of The Damned, and Dave Tregunna of Sham 69. Still, Nick marvels, "All anyone cares about still is that I was in The Raincoats." He found success with The Barracudas, and "real fame with the Lords, but the coolest thing is still that I'm a footnote in The Raincoats' history, so it's a good thing."

Soon, Jeremie would depart, too. Her style always seemed like a stark contrast to Ana and Gina, and she was running up against student visa problems. If she didn't resume full-time studies in architecture in London, she'd have to return to America.

Richard Dudanski stepped in on drums—easy enough, he was a close friend living in the squat next door to Gina, and it was only temporary. Yet finding someone on guitar would be slightly more complicated. Luckily, the early connections The Raincoats were cementing within the worlds of music, performance art, and visual art started to come to fruition. At Hornsey, Gina had befriended Julian Maynard Smith, who'd later become a prominent London-based artist working across theatre and other visual mediums. Some years before he enrolled at Hornsey, Julian had been at architecture school with Patrick Keiller, who'd himself go on to become an acclaimed filmmaker. "As students of architecture, we were thrown out," Patrick says, referring to himself and Julian. "We were told to take a year off. It was 1968, 1969, and we got wrapped up in the climate of the times. I went back, but Julian only went back for a week before later going to Hornsey." Julian and Patrick remained friends.

"This may be a false memory now," Patrick continues, "but I think Julian was at the Panorama [Room] bar at Alexandra Palace and saw me play guitar." Patrick laughs, explaining his electric guitar "debut" in that space. His experience was limited to acoustic guitar in a casual folk band. "I'd never played a solid body," he says, "and when I showed up to join The Raincoats, I had a Höfner," referring to a German hollow-body electric. "It wasn't completely out of whatever you call it, because Joe Strummer had one, too," Patrick muses. "But it was quite difficult to play. I used it during my six weeks or less in The Raincoats."

Julian had known Gina's band was seeking a guitarist, so he recommended Patrick. From the beginning of his time as a Raincoat, Patrick recognized the impermanence of the privilege. "I knew it would be temporary, and it was very brief. I assumed they wanted a band with all women." (It wasn't actually the case, but Patrick wasn't the only one who came to the same conclusion once the future lineup with Palmolive and Vicky was solidified.) "It was also a rather disorganized period in my life," Patrick continues, "when I was migrating between being a frustrated architect and a filmmaker."

A DEMO

Patrick played just one live gig with The Raincoats and then recorded on the band's first demo.

On November 10, 1978, for one night only, Patrick was one of The Raincoats at the Cryptic One Club. "I remember how it looks, and I see myself now on the stage, as if I were in the audience, but of course, I wasn't," he reflects. Palmolive of The Slits was there too, off to the side, playing tabla. It would be the last Raincoats show of 1978. Afterward, they recorded a two-song demo at Spaceward Studios in Cambridge.

As would be the case for The Raincoats' eventual *Fairytale* EP, they made the demo tape at Spaceward because Rough Trade had paid for recording time for the Stiff Little Fingers, but the notorious band from Belfast didn't end up using all of it; they were quick in the studio. The demo was an opportunity for Geoff to hear what The Raincoats' songs were sounding like, with help from sound engineer and studio owner Mike Kemp. It was just two tracks: "Fairytale in the Supermarket" and "In Love."

"When we first started the band, Miles Copeland, who had the label I.R.S., invited us to join the label. We just didn't like the vibe," Ana remembers. "So when Geoff asked us to do a demo, I felt really honored because I liked Geoff a lot and respected him."

Ana, Gina, Patrick, and Richard played on the demo. Ana and Geoff thought Patrick's guitar sounded too much like "Here Comes the Night," the track by Them. Decades later, Patrick says, Geoff is still bringing that up. The Raincoats were already rethinking the lineup.

HELLO, PALMOLIVE

After the demo, Gina and Ana realized they were all the guitar the band needed. But drumming was another issue. In early 1979, The Raincoats needed a permanent drummer if they were going to make a record.

Richard filled in at a handful of shows but wanted to start his own band. As luck would have it, the squatting social network came to the rescue. Palmolive had just been booted from The Slits, so Richard—partner of Palmolive's sister Espe—suggested The Raincoats invite her to join them. "We almost couldn't believe it," Gina remembers, and Ana confirms, "That was one of the happiest days of my life, I must say, because I just idolized Palmolive." While Gina and Ana already had most of the songs written that would become the *Fairytale* EP and *The Raincoats* self-titled LP, Palmolive "had her own style of playing and brought that to everything we'd written," Ana says. "Ana and I *loved* The Slits, and we loved her drumming," adds Gina. "We knew she'd bring rhythms we couldn't have written, and she did."

For many Raincoats fans, the lineup with Palmolive is canon. What few realize is that the former Slits drummer was planning to leave the music business by the time she agreed to join the band. While others were drawing energy from London's upstart punk scene, Palmolive was fed up with the whole experience. But, she really liked The Raincoats. She and Gina were casual friends, and Palmolive knew she'd be able to work well with Ana, too, so

LIFE NUMBER 1

Palmolive on the drums, Acklam Hall, 1979

Flyer for The Raincoats gig with Gang of Four at The Nashville

"Rather than throwing everything out the window *right now*," she decided, "I'll do one record with them. I'll do this one, final thing." Palmolive was in The Raincoats for less than a year—she started and left in 1979—but it was kismet.

Like Ana and Gina, Palmolive had her own sense of rhythm, a keen sense of the politics of play, and a desire to experiment. She also brought an entirely idiosyncratic style to her drumming. The heartbeat of Palmolive's drums was derived from her love of dancing and a desire "to bring something unexpected." Before The Slits, she'd had no plans to become a musician and always thought of herself as "fake performing" when she'd give music a try. But when punk exploded in 1976, it was a "no-brainer" for Palmolive to become a drummer. She always felt like she was a little reserved, so sitting in the back of the stage behind the drum kit seemed natural. There was a comfort in that spot on the stage. And although she'd never seen another female drummer, she remembers, "I didn't feel I needed to see another woman drum to just do it—I became a drummer!"

Even though she knew she'd be leaving, Palmolive was 100 percent *in* as a Raincoat, and she never had second thoughts about it. "The amazing and great thing," she says, "is that they were very excited that I wanted to work with them, even though they were very sad it would be brief. But it wasn't *them*—it was *the system*, and I always wanted to convey that to them." Ana and Gina understood, and Shirley, who was becoming the de facto manager, did too. Shirley asked Palmolive if she'd be willing to stay to do an EP, an album, and a tour—a limited timespan that could be counted in months. That seemed fair to Palmolive, and she agreed. She became a Raincoat. Charles Hayward of This Heat remembers seeing The Raincoats play an early gig with Palmolive on drums and immediately became a fan. For the first time, he says, he understood the drums as "a fourth melody instrument."

But Palmolive's plans to leave were always present. She wanted out before she lost herself to what she called the "treadmill" of the music industry: an endless cycle of recording records, journalists writing nasty pieces, and touring. "I wasn't sure I could ultimately go to the places I needed to be if I stayed in The Raincoats, in the music business," she says. The Raincoats kept themselves distant from the corporate hand of the industry, but they couldn't eradicate the system that plagued Palmolive. She recorded the *Fairytale* EP and *The Raincoats* LP, and played a total of twenty-nine shows with The Raincoats in 1979 before taking her leave.

THE RAINCOATS MEET THE SLITS

With Palmolive joining The Raincoats, a historic connection between them and The Slits was cemented. In 1979 and for decades to come, the music press would link the bands any time references to female-fronted or feminist punk bands arose. Neither would use those descriptors themselves, but they became commonplace nonetheless. Palmolive's tenure linked The Slits and The Raincoats, and the bands released debut LPs the same year. Beyond those similarities, The Slits and The Raincoats only had gender in common. However, in a sonic world where there were very few women, writers couldn't help but draw the comparison. Although, to state the obvious, nobody draws connections among male-dominated bands on the basis of sex.

"It was like two totally different boyfriends," Palmolive laughs loudly as she recalls playing with The Slits versus The Raincoats. "Very different personalities!" There was a shared set of internalized values, perhaps, which neither band discussed but knew were present. "We knew we were going to listen to each other, going to value each other," she says.

Palmolive was and remains in a distinct position to reflect on the similarities and differences between the bands. "On stage, both The Slits and The Raincoats had a really committed following," Palmolive says. "But the mayhem of Ari Up!" she laughs. "Nobody could equal that. Nobody in The Raincoats wanted that, anyway."

The Slits and The Raincoats actually shared a song, Palmolive's "Adventures Close to Home." When she wrote it for The Slits, Palmolive remembers her bandmates asking what the song meant; they didn't get it. But Palmolive wasn't taking a traditional approach to songwriting. She was going into herself, trying to process her own experiences through writing. So, when she brought the song to The Raincoats, she felt it fitted into the band's shared knowledge that music can be emotional and experimental. Palmolive knew The Raincoats would never ask what the song meant; they got it. She felt "there was a kind of poetry" in how The Raincoats allowed her to explore her interiority. The commercialism of The Slits fell away, and the song grew out of her in a way that it only could have with The Raincoats.

The Raincoats shared bills with The Slits in the short years of their first life, and music journalists would forever link them.

"Even for me, it's hard to think of The Raincoats without thinking of The Slits," journalist Vivien Goldman says. "But it's not just because they're women, it's because they're both part of this shifting sense, like the sea and the tides moving toward a new and organic approach. They made it possible to become part of a flow." She continues, "To talk about The Slits and The Raincoats together, the comparison is like talking about the Pistols and The Clash." Part of a historic movement. Writers like Vivien would ultimately ensure that female artists of subsequent generations couldn't learn about The Slits without The Raincoats, and vice versa. "But the bands couldn't have sounded more different," Dick O'Dell, former manager of The Slits, emphasizes. "It's impossible to compare the sound."

Twenty-five years later, while being filmed by Lucy Thane for a documentary in 1993,[17] Ana told Kathi Wilcox of Bikini Kill: "We weren't any more like The Slits than we were like anyone else, except the fact that we were women ... you just have to forget about that shit."

From the very first Raincoats review and into the twenty-first century, the bands remain connected in varied print comparisons and analogs. "There's a spatial sense, a spatial memory, too," Vivien says. "We were in all those clubs together, part of a new organic, intuitive way of making music." And that connection, even if you read it as a dubious one, has led female and marginalized artists in the decades following the first life of The Raincoats (and the only life of The Slits) to see that there's more than one way to be a woman who makes music. "Two different kinds of radical approaches to space," Vivien nods knowingly.

WE NEED A VIOLINIST

It's difficult to think of The Raincoats' sound without that radical, scratchy violin. Ana and Gina loved the Velvet Underground and the timbre John Cale's viola brought, but they never considered adding a violinist until Palmolive suggested it. It became a key element of their experimental sound, one which took root shortly before they recorded their first record.

"Palmolive was obsessed with Tymon Dogg at the time, and he was a violin player. She was also getting very interested in this Indian guru, and Tymon was into that, too," Gina says. "So Palmolive said she'd like a violin player. But she had this idea of a kind of classical violin sound. We went for the kind of scratchy, John Cale viola sound."

Enter Vicky Aspinall.

Vicky was a classically trained musician from a young age. With a mother who was an opera singer and music teacher, it might have been inevitable. She started playing piano at six years old and picked up the violin around ten. She practiced a lot, joined youth orchestras, and enjoyed a sense of musical community before studying at the University of York with English musicologist and composer Wilfrid Mellers. At York, "there was an electronic studio, which I was itching to get into," Vicky recalls, "but it was very much a male domain." She did end up joining an electric string quartet, founded by a viola player "who played that viola like Jimi Hendrix," she says. The violist wrote the arrangements, but it was Vicky's first experience of playing in a way that bucked against the classical norm. The other violinist in that quartet later joined the Mekons, while Vicky wrote a thesis on Black music and rebellion, listening to artists like Al Green, Marvin Gaye, and Stevie Wonder, and moved through scat vocals, jazz-funk, Herbie Hancock, Miles Davis, and Nina Simone. "Nina Simone was a big love," she says, "and then punk happened." She went to see The Clash in Leeds,

Vicky playing her violin in Porchester Hall, 1979

"which was a revelation, the energy was mind-blowing, but it wasn't really my scene at the time." Instead, she joined the feminist music collective Jam Today.

Jam Today existed in London from 1976 to 1979. From the first gig on, the collective displayed a banner that read, "JAM TODAY FOR WOMEN." The group was integral in the Women's Liberation Movement (WLM) and advocated for women's rights by sonic means. The collective formed the feminist record label Stroppy Cow, reclaiming a derogatory term a man once yelled at the group. In an effort to eradicate male violence from venue spaces, Jam Today also pioneered women-only gigs and wrote music with overt lyrics demanding economic, social, and legal freedoms for women – language that arose from constant, in-depth discussions about contemporary politics.[18] Jam Today was one of several self-declared WLM feminist bands, including Northern Women's Liberation Rock Band, Ova, the Stepney Sisters, Sisterhood of Spit, and Henry Cow. Vicky calls it "all quite niche."

LIFE NUMBER 1

Vicky wasn't so comfortable with the female-only aspect of the Jam Today gigs. "I didn't feel that was the way to go," she says, suggesting venue spaces should be safe and welcoming to women without being separatist. But her involvement with the Jam Today community brought new knowledge. Vicky remembers being amazed by the music of Lindsay Cooper and Georgie Born of the experimental collective Henry Cow, a group formed in Cambridge in the late 1960s and featuring male and female multi-instrumentalists with an anti-commercial, feminist ideology. (Georgie Born would later play cello as a session musician for The Raincoats on the *Odyshape* track "Dancing in My Head," and Vicky later worked with Cooper and Born in her post-Raincoats days.)

The "women in music" community was "sort of bubbling up at the same time as punk, but completely unrelated to it," Vicky explains. "You'd think, looking back at punk, there were no other women musicians—or not many—but there were *loads* of them. They just weren't in rock or punk groups necessarily." And from that community of female artists, musicians experimenting with transdisciplinary genres and sounds, Vicky answered an ad to join The Raincoats.

"I don't know exactly what I was looking for at the time," she laughs, "but I went into the Compendium bookshop in Camden and saw the advert, and I was intrigued by it. Everyone says I took it off the wall so nobody else could respond," she notes, alluding to the mythmaking that has gone into the story of The Raincoats, "and to be honest I don't know if I took the advert with me. But I do remember ringing Gina and speaking to her in her squat. Neal Brown answered the phone, and I could hear all this music going off in the background while I was waiting for Gina to pick up. It sounded like reggae, and I thought, *Yes, this is going to be interesting.*"

Vicky went to see The Raincoats play shortly thereafter in the Cryptic One Club, the unlikely yet fashionable venue in the basement of a church. That Friday night in November 1978 was the one gig with Patrick Keiller on guitar, Richard Dudanski on drums, and Palmolive on tabla. It was also the only show where Palmolive played but *didn't* sit behind the drum kit.

"I could only see part of the band through an old archway," Vicky remembers, "so it was intriguing." She recalls Palmolive looking "so passionate and alive." While The Raincoats seemed "rough and ready" to Vicky, they also struck her as unlike anyone else she'd ever seen. She asked her friend Annie, who she'd brought with her to the gig: Could Annie imagine Vicky playing with The Raincoats, knowing her background in classical and experimental music? Her friend said simply, "Yeah, why not? They seem cool!" So Vicky went to a rehearsal in the basement of the Monmouth Road squat. "The one that's always talked about," Vicky laughs, describing "a mattress against the wall, a toilet on the floor, and we're all squeezed in. I could hardly move my bow, but they played me 'Fairytale,' and that was it. It was so exciting, so different and new in all sorts of ways. I left Jam Today and started rehearsing with The Raincoats, and that was that."

ROUGH TRADE

You can't tell the story of The Raincoats without Rough Trade, and you can't tell the story of Rough Trade without The Raincoats (even though some have tried to do the latter).

Almost from the opening of the shop and label, Ana worked behind the counter. Shirley started working for the record label too officially in October 1978, in production. Gina didn't become a Rough Trade employee until 1984, but The Raincoats have been part of the Rough Trade family from the beginning.

"There were eight of us at Rough Trade, and it was a brilliant learning curve for everyone, because none of us knew what we were doing and didn't have the knowledge to run a label or a shop. But because no one was interested in having Rough Trades all over the world, we learned from each other and it became empowering," Shirley says. "And it gave us a way to empower other artists and shops in the UK once we knew how to make a record, knew how to book bands, so we said, 'Let's share that.'" But the most important thing, Shirley emphasizes, is that "Geoff was a feminist and a socialist, and he encouraged that kind of empowerment, and thought it was really important to have women involved."

"The way the shop worked is that people would come and talk to us, and if we really liked them, we'd ask them to do some shifts behind the counter," Geoff explains. As for the record label, "we had the idea that everything would be a fifty-fifty profit share right from the beginning to make it fair for the musicians." He laughs, emphasizing there was "never any ambition to become a great record label, the Motown of West London." Rather, the label arose from a desire to support local musicians. Geoff ascribes the bold output of Rough Trade as part and parcel of "the fearlessness of youth, the fearlessness of not worrying about any limitations."

"It was always a sort of socialist model," Shirley explains, "where everybody got paid the same. I think it was something like forty quid a week at that point. And we had meetings where everyone had their say, and that was really important—having women's voices represented was so important to Geoff, and so important to us."

Geoff centered gender inclusivity at Rough Trade with a "real mix of male and female musicians." To everyone there, that equality of representation "just seemed normal," Geoff says, but now seems "revolutionary from the outside looking in and looking back." There was no shared sound, but rather a shared ideology. "There was a spirit among them, the threads of originality and innovation, and politics and feminism, that linked them all," Geoff explains of the Rough Trade artists. None of them "conformed to any one model of a band," except they all shared the same politics. "Nobody at Rough Trade would have been willing to work with anyone who *wasn't* a feminist," Geoff underscores. Ana points out that Geoff never went around identifying himself as a feminist, but was indeed one in practice, "and that's the most important thing," she says. Shirley calls Geoff "a most perfect ally."

Women populated Rough Trade in all its aspects, from the label to the shop to the booking agency. Sue Johnson was a director of Rough Trade Music, Sue Donne ran mail order, Caroline Scott handled accounts, Sue Scott and Gill Sheehan were in distribution, and Jude Crighton was shop manager. Shirley created a Rough

Trade booking agency that booked bands onto stages across Europe and America. "So when you see these stories and books about Rough Trade where the writers don't interview the women or don't name them, it's not because they weren't equally important to Geoff," Shirley says. "Writers who exclude the women involved erase a deeply significant part of the history and get me wound up like something else." Ana remembers Geoff asking her to come work at the shop and saying "he wanted women in there so guys who came in to buy records would learn how to speak to women and understand women were part of the record business. Just the fact he wanted a positive female presence there, a visible one, was why I started working there. And that was a very good beginning."

At the end of 1982, the Rough Trade record shop split off from the distribution and label. Jude, Pete Donne, and Nigel House "carried it on from that point, always with the same feeling of being open to new thoughts, new ideas, and equality," Jude continues, explaining how they'd occasionally stock used records as time went on, but running Rough Trade remained rooted in its principles. "If people came in and wanted to sell things that were racist, sexist ... *No*," she says firmly.

When it came to record contracts, Rough Trade was all about equality. The terms of the contracts were for a finite period so bands retained ownership of their work. "The contracts for the EP, the self-titled, *Odyshape*, and *Moving* were all for five years," Shirley explains of The Raincoats' records, "and the deal was always a fifty-fifty split. How it worked was Rough Trade would front the studio costs, all the production, manufacturing, and distribution costs, and after all costs were recouped there was a fifty-fifty profit share, or seventy-thirty in the band's favor for licensed albums. It was great for us because the first album did really well, and throughout the relationship we were partners," she says. "That kind of a relationship with a label—a partnership that involved deciding everything together—it was really a perfect thing."

"It might seem like a small thing," Ana adds, "but it just explains Geoff and who he was then, and who he is." At the end of the day at Rough Trade, she remembers, "Geoff would come into the shop and sweep it. On hindsight, he could have very well asked me, or

LIFE NUMBER 1

someone else working there, to do it, but that was Geoff. He didn't delegate these kinds of jobs to other people."

Even when Rough Trade became a known entity, it remained a vibrant work environment. Gina started in the mid-eighties as a record company assistant. Around the same time, Mike Holdsworth was hired in Rough Trade distribution, and Gina invited him to a party at her place. "I didn't go because I was too embarrassed to ask anybody where the address was," Mike laughs. "Gina and all those people were so cool, and I was a green, naive kid from New Zealand." He knew about The Raincoats because he'd bought the Rough Trade compilation *Wanna Buy a Bridge?* before immigrating, and he used to scour the music presses. "So I was very aware of The Raincoats, and I couldn't possibly ask someone for Gina's address!" Gina spotted him at a gig a few weeks later. "One of those rare London winter nights when it snowed," he says. Rough Trade brought them together, and they'd end up getting married thirteen years later (after living together for all that time).

Meanwhile, despite the love connection the label and its distribution arm made, Rough Trade went into receivership in 1991. In Shirley's estimate, Rough Trade likely owed a lot to Mute and Factory Records (which was about to go bust itself a year later). By 1993, Geoff reacquired Rough Trade Records thanks to an infusion of funds from Derek Birkett at the English indie label then known as One Little Indian (now One Little Independent). Allison Schnackenberg essentially became Rough Trade's head of A&R, and One Little Indian ran the label. In the meantime, Geoff was managing bands with Jeannette Lee of Public Image Limited (PiL), including Pulp and The Cranberries, while inviting Gina to collaborate creatively with his bands. "He often asked me to join discussion groups and design album covers," Gina remembers, but she was "always too shy." Yet Geoff's requests for Gina to be music video director on a range of projects did come to fruition—work that Gina started as early as 1991 with her much-loved video for Daisy Chainsaw's "Love Your Money." By 2000, Geoff and Jeannette officially formed a new Rough Trade partnership that gave them back the label with financial backing from Martin Mills of the Beggars Group.

Today, when Geoff pictures Rough Trade in his mind, he sees an early image of The Raincoats standing outside the shop with David Thomas of Pere Ubu. "Those are *some women!*" David says, smiles, and pounds his fists when he's asked about his friendship with The Raincoats. "*Some damn women!*"

Ultimately, Rough Trade would not have been what it was, or maintained its legacy in the present, without The Raincoats. They've always been "simply part of the fabric of Rough Trade," says Geoff.

RECORDING A FAIRYTALE

What's the price of making a fairytale? A total of £3,611.83, it turns out. Those were the handwritten costings The Raincoats received on a piece of lined paper from Rough Trade.

February 1979 was The Raincoats' first official time in the studio. Rough Trade had again booked Spaceward in Cambridge for Stiff Little Fingers, which meant The Raincoats could record after hours. "Geoff told me Stiff Little Fingers had finished recording super quick, and Rough Trade had about five days left—so did we want to go and record first thing?" Shirley explains. They all loaded into the Rough Trade van and headed up to Cambridge. Jude closed the Rough Trade shop early that night so she could get up to Spaceward in time to witness The Raincoats making their first record. It wasn't uncommon for bands to use studio space for a lower cost in the middle of the night when another band had booked during the day or finished early; it was economical and made recording possible for up-and-coming artists. Ultimately, recording *Fairytale* during the graveyard shift hearkened back to the very founding of the studio's origins.

Mike Kemp opened Spaceward in 1976 at 19 Victoria Street in Cambridge after working late into many early morning hours, on a student salary, to build a 16-track studio. Founder of UK punk label Raw Records, Lee Wood

The Raincoats with Geoff and Mayo in Spaceward Studios
during the *Fairytale* EP Session, 1979

was the first major studio customer, and Raw bands like The Psychos, The Users, The Hammersmith Gorillas, The Killjoys, and The Soft Boys were among the first bands to record there. Spaceward was "a couple of converted basements," Kemp remembers, *"more like a student place than a showbiz thing."* He recalls Robyn Hitchcock describing the studio *"like a space capsule with beer."*[19] Kemp ultimately reflects on Spaceward as a *"small link in the chain of punk history."*

Ana confirms that Spaceward was "very small, with a 16-track desk." Jude likes to think about Spaceward's "open-minded approach," referring to its interest in "recording sounds that weren't clean."

The Raincoats didn't care about tools of production—they aimed to keep the unpolished, visceral sounds of the band playing together, as if live. No overdubs. In part for practical reasons, that's how the first studio recording went. Geoff Travis says he and Mayo Thompson—the two "producers" credited on *Fairytale*—"had a lot of nerve calling ourselves producers because we'd never really done it before." He laughs and explains: "Mayo was in Red Krayola so he had some technical knowledge, and I guess I thought, *Well, that would be a good thing for a producer, right? So my main function as a 'producer' was to see if it was sounding good."* Yet even if Geoff and Mayo had more producer cred, they wouldn't have changed that first Raincoats EP in any fashion. As everyone at Spaceward that night remembers, The Raincoats just played live, their raw sound captured perfectly. "There was no trickery. The idea was to capture them as they were, because even then they had that particular swing that was quite unusual, and we wanted to capture the maximum amount of feeling and emotion they brought," says Geoff.

The pair of producers was an unlikely one on the surface. Geoff speaks softly with a London accent, and although he founded Rough Trade, describes himself as "musically illiterate, can't sing, pretty tone deaf." Mayo has a booming voice with a thick Houston accent that betrays his ties to Texas. He must have seemed an unexpected entity in the middle of Cambridge, yet as a founder of the Red Krayola—and its multidisciplinary, experimental focus—he became an immediate friend to The Raincoats.

As Gina tells it, "Even during our first single recording, I bonded with Mayo, jamming in the live room together, quietly, finding a sympathetic player who made me feel like I was going somewhere interesting on a six-string guitar. He later invited me to join Red Krayola and I have been included on many different projects with Red Krayola over the years."

When The Raincoats broke up in 1983, Gina joined the Red Krayola and toured with Mayo and the band. She spent nearly a year in Düsseldorf, Cologne, and New York with Mayo's collective, which included Lora Logic of X-Ray Spex and Essential Logic, who'd played on The Raincoats' debut LP. Around that same time, the Red Krayola signed to Carmen Knoebel's Düsseldorf label Pure Freude ("Pure Joy"), an intimate Raincoats connection that would become critically important just a year after the band's studio time at Spaceward.

At first, it was difficult for Vicky's violin to find its sync with The Raincoats. She was keen to try "something bluesy, quite fancy," as she describes it, yet "there was a shared sense I needed to be playing the polar opposite." She remembers Mayo "having a word

LIFE NUMBER 1

in her ear" to *play less, play less*, "take it down, just play one note and pedal over the intro." For Vicky, that night was her real starting point as a Raincoat, a new way of visualizing the music. "It had to go minimal, so that's what I learned how to do," she explains, defining the "aggressive but sparse" style she developed.

"When I first heard The Raincoats rehearse," Mayo recalls, "my only question to them when they finished was had they heard the Velvet Underground because of the violin. I wasn't advocating that they necessarily take it as a directive, but should bear it in mind in terms of generating something new and completely unique." Mayo and the other Raincoats urged Vicky to listen to John Cale, to the abstract sounds his viola emitted with the Velvet Underground, suggesting she "take a cue." They wanted Vicky "screechier," Geoff laughs. "We probably hurt her classical music sensibilities, but she seemed to accept it in the end."

"It was a bit of a struggle to get the violin sound right," Jude remembers, "and we were all saying to Vicky about the violin, *it sounds too NICE! It needs to sound ROUGHER!*"

As the only classically trained member of the band, Vicky had to do a kind of unlearning because, for the other Raincoats, their "limitations were also the groundwork for the flowering of their creativity," as Vicky describes it. She was eager to create something new and never wanted to replicate what others, including John Cale, had already done. "They brought something out in me," she reflects. She learned a mode of experimentation she hadn't considered before, "using tremolo, pizzicato, sliding up and down and creating white noise."

"And," she continues and laughs, "I lost *a lot* of bow hair. I used to get my bow re-haired once a month, because I was attacking the strings and the bow hairs would be just flying off. I learned how to make the violin a percussive instrument ... whacking it, attacking it, an intensely physical relationship."

For Mayo, "it was just ace stuff they were working on, so refreshing, completely different from the men's bands and the women's bands that were around." And to this day, he says, "I prefer The Raincoats right across the board." Unlike their Rough Trade contemporaries at the time of *Fairytale*, they were "more interesting musically and played with a charm and conviction that was absolutely convincing."

The Spaceward recording session was actually filmed for London Weekend Television, as the broadcaster Melvyn Bragg was working on a program about Rough Trade. "They take their anti-commercial recording principles into the studio," the voiceover narrates, "so it's not just lack of resources that make them choose to record in the basement of a terraced house. They make do-it-yourself records and homemade studios a matter of policy." The camera reveals a markedly tight space, barely enough room for all four musicians to play, let alone the handheld camera sweeping above and below their instruments. "We measure the success of a rock record by how happy the band are with the recording," Geoff tells the interviewer, not by the number of sales or any perceptions from the press. "If we're all convinced it was good," he says, referring to the artists and employees of Rough Trade, "and the rest of the world was convinced it was lousy, we'd be quite happy to stay in our insane asylum alone."

The Rough Trade family immediately approved of *Fairytale*, and Geoff reveled in the unique joy of working with The Raincoats, a band built around "individual characters with their own individual strengths." It was in Spaceward that he first saw what everyone would come to know as "that classic contrast between Gina and Ana, what made The Raincoats really work." Geoff explains, "A tension between two front people is what makes a truly great band, and the tension between Ana and Gina brought a kind of emotion to their music in that studio," and continues, "That tension makes the band, and it has always made their music." Mayo adds, "But it was a good tension, part of the basis of human nature, not just some disagreement about how the band should be packaged and sold."

Rough Trade's no-frills approach to capturing The Raincoats' essence on *Fairytale* helps explain the record's magnetic impact far beyond Spaceward. For Kathi Wilcox of Bikini Kill, who discovered the *Fairytale* EP the following decade, the title track will always have the greatest resonance of any Raincoats song. Everyone of her generation fell in love with "The Void," which Ana would dedicate to Kurt Cobain after his untimely death, but in Kathi's eyes, "Fairytale" is the standout. "It starts revving up like a motorcycle and then it just takes off. And in the first few seconds, the lyrics, 'no one teaches you how to live.' That's pretty intense for a fourteen-year-old, and that resonates and feels true." Kathi first heard the song on one of the original 7-inch EPs—a hand-me-down from her stepbrother in the mid-eighties, after The Raincoats had disappeared from the public. "Even now," she says, "I was listening to 'Fairytale in the Supermarket,' and I immediately started to cry because it took me right back to a time period where I hadn't been in a long time."

When The Raincoats recorded the song "Fairytale," they had no way of knowing the long and immortal life it would have, or the role it would play in influencing new generations of women to pick up instruments and experiment with sound and vision in a way they'd never have otherwise thought possible.

DIY SLEEVE DESIGN

In the Rough Trade contracts for each of The Raincoats' recordings, Shirley crossed out some boilerplate language: "The artwork and promotional material including packaging shall be mutually agreed by the Licensor and the Licensee." This bit of negotiation reflected something core to the band's ethos, which began with the *Fairytale* EP. The Raincoats have always wanted, and largely received, creative control. They made the term "do it yourself," or DIY, their own. For The Raincoats, DIY meant using the means of production available to them to make record sleeves and promotional materials, by hand, that reflected each of their training as artists. While complications with creative control would arise in the nineties when they signed with Geffen, in the band's first life, sleeve design became an extension of The Raincoats' experimental creative process.

Artwork for the back of RT 003, The Raincoats' self-titled album, 1979

Jude Crighton has vivid memories, still, of Ana's interest in windows. "The cover of *Fairytale in the Supermarket*, that was the window view out of Ana's flat," she recalls. "I was doing windows all the time then," Ana chimes in, "and I still do windows." Jude nods, "Ana was *always* drawing windows."

The cover of the *Fairytale* 7-inch EP was a cream color, alluding to the readily available newsprint on which Ana often did window sketches. The back was bright blue. "Palmolive wanted something more colorful, so the compromise was the front got made like I wanted—I mean, I'd done the drawing—and the back was colorful, like she wanted," Ana explains.

Artwork for Raincoats sleeves, posters, handbills, and advertisements quickly became a central point of collaboration among Ana, Gina, and Shirley, with Ana directing the artwork design conceptually and preparing for print.

For the front cover of *The Raincoats* album, Vicky found the book *Pictures by Chinese Children* in Compendium (the same shop where she'd seen the advertisement for a Raincoats violinist), and everyone fell in love with a painting in it by Pang Hsiao-Li. Vicky thought the image "seemed to capture some of the collective vocals" on songs like "No Side to Fall In," as well as "the collective nature of the band." Gina created the lettering—"The Raincoats"—and Ana adapted the image into a record sleeve by removing the Chinese script at the top and turning the background that celebrated shade of pink. It was a saturated stand-out color that could hardly escape the notice of record shoppers flipping through record bins. For the vinyl labels, Ana drew borders in dark black ink for the A-side and B-side and wrote out the track names with the same pen. Then she smeared them with water.

The same design process took shape for *Odyshape*. The band saw a Kazimir Malevich painting in a German art museum while on tour, and that image became the inspiration and image for the LP sleeve. Ana purchased the Malevich poster and brought it home, reworking it into an album cover with hand-drawn letters spelling out "THE RAINCOATS" on the left side and "ODYSHAPE" on the right by Gina. Initially, the artwork archives reveal, the band was thinking about titling the record "ODYSHAPES," with a plural "S" at the end. For the back of the sleeve, Ana completed the repetitive, abstract sketch, with song titles and copyright info in her own hand. She experimented with wetting the crayon to get intentionally smudgy lines.

When it came to their third album, *Moving*, Ana initially attempted a slightly more polished look. Rather than handwriting, she began testing out a range of existing fonts. Yet ultimately, The Raincoats were too enamored with the process of creating by hand. Ana developed a font with her own handwriting for the front of the record, the text that would read *Moving*. The band selected Pantone 574 for the background army green shade and 485 for the crimson red.

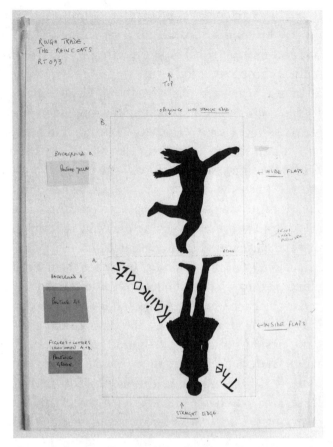

Artwork for the sleeve of The Raincoats' 7-inch single "No One's Little Girl" b/w "Running Away"

The 7-inch single from *Moving*, "No One's Little Girl" b/w (short for "backed with") "Running Away," gave Shirley a chance to get especially creative. In Picasso style, she sketched and cut out various paper dolls of a figure "running away" for the B-side. She experimented with the form, sometimes ripping its edges, sometimes creating the shape as relief. She took a similar approach for the cover, a Degas-inspired silhouette of a figure in a skirt standing between the words "The Raincoats." Gina designed the 12-inch *Animal Rhapsody* vinyl. She did the font by hand in pink and gray, adding a sketch that depicted her own idea of a "Honey Mad Woman," one of the B-side tracks.

LIFE NUMBER 1

THE FIRST AND LAST GROUP BUS TOUR (SPIZZ, KLEENEX)

May 11 to June 5, 1979

Ana's 1979 tour diary—the first in a series of diaries that would become a rich archive of personalities, reflections, memories from the band's life on the road—opens with signatures of all the touring artists, some with their invented and playful nicknames:

Gina Brains
Vicky Biscuit
Shirley-Whirley

In the photobooth during the 1979 bus tour

At the top of the first page, Ana's name appears in full, along with her flat address at the time—the one on St Ervans Road that sat just behind the rail lines. The diary captures photographs of the bands on stage and behind the scenes. Sketches by Ana, Gina, Marlene Marder (from the band Kleenex), and Klaudia Schiff (also in Kleenex) explore the banalities of tour life: Ana's drawings of a carton of orange juice, robes hung on the back of a door. Gina writes the first page:

> Kleenex, The Raincoats and the Swell Maps entertain under the flyover.
>
> Acklam Hall filled up with people who we'd never seen before. And I hardly saw anyone who usually comes to see us. Only Geoff [Travis] and about two others danced to the Swell Maps. You could see Geoff's head bobbing up and down in a sea of static heads. "No one understands them," it's true, but it was a nice evening. Wish they'd come with us on tour. Wendy [Glaze] said it was the perfect gig. She never enjoyed a gig so much. People were generally very complimentary but several people seemed quite concerned that once we got out of London the audiences would either react badly or not react at all to us. We shall see! 450 (more or less) people went to the gig.

Marlene also kept a personal diary during the tour.[*] After Acklam Hall, she was starstruck as she wrote, "Siouxsie was there . . .!!!" and reflected, "I feel totally at ease with The Raincoats. Most of all around Ana, Shirley, and Vicky. I also really like Palmolive. I haven't really spent a lot of time with Gina yet."[20]

Ana wrote the entry for the second gig at Whitcombe Lodge in Brockworth, at which point Spizz Energi had replaced Cabaret Voltaire as the third touring group in the van (rumor has it Cabaret Voltaire's girlfriends didn't want them with so many women). Ana notes:

---

[*] Marlene Marder's diary was translated by Jen Calleja in 2023. All subsequent references to Marlene's diary are taken from this translation.

LIFE NUMBER 1

We went for a walk and we went on stage with muddy shoes. A man liked us at Acklam Hall and came all the way from Bath to see us. We had no cheese sandwiches—only rotted meat. Somebody threw a glass which smashed by Gina. The "fans" didn't have a word to say to us, except to ask for autographs, badges and drumsticks. Couldn't find a face in the audience. 346 tickets were sold.

Caroline Scott joined the party for the gig in Hampstead, and Marlene jots that they were given "apples with a worm" on May 17. Along the tour, Ana and Shirley bought copies of *Melody Maker*, *Sounds*, and the *Record Mirror* to track reactions to the gigs and their recently released *Fairytale* EP. When they got to Lowestoft, Ana described a "funny gig—people seemed to want to dance." Shirley wrote: "The fans were really into contact, particularly tits and bums! Also kissed on the face." By this point, Ana's getting fed up with the so-called "fans" who were in attendance. She writes, imitating the questions she'd been getting:

> Can I have a badge, please? Can I have your wallet? Can I have your T-shirt? Can I have a souvenir? Can I have your jacket?

They make it to Leeds, where Ana makes note of "three good gigs at the Fan Club (F Club). Atmosphere—sweaty, smoky, packed (at least in the front!). The walls kept dripping."

Dave McCullough, now notorious for the sexist reviews he wrote of The Raincoats and Kleenex (and possibly others) in the pages of *Sounds*, dismisses the bands as "boring," and can't help himself as he focuses on the physical attributes of the female artists on stage. Of Kleenex, he writes, "the bassist . . . looks uncannily like a dead aunt of mine" and he describes Klaudia's vocals as "squeaky." He calls The Raincoats "difficult." Ana clips the full review, marks the particularly frustrating portions of McCullough's writing, and writes herself:

> GOD SAVE DAVE McCULLOUGH
> GOD SAVE DAVE McCULLOUGH AND HIS BRAINS
> GOD SAVE DAVE SOUR GRAPES

When they approach Manchester, it's Vicky's birthday. In orange ink, Gina writes out the happy birthday song to her. On the same page, in yellow marker, a note reads, "I lost ½ my front tooth. (Palmolive is mean. She won't allow me any artistic lisence [sic].)" Following a late May show in Liverpool, Vicky writes, "Palmolive grumpy cos snare drum broke halfway through, and both bows fucked." The Kleenex drummer Regula, like Palmolive, was also making plans to leave her band. Marlene reflected, "The Raincoats have the same problem with Palmolive that we have with Regula. Only Paloma isn't (yet?) as messed up as Regula. She ordered herself a taxi and left after the gig, by the way. I'll be glad when it's June."

The Raincoats lament the continued days of rain, and by the time they play Sheffield, they're ready to call it quits. The punters got violent, and it wasn't enjoyable for any of the bands that night. Shirley explains, "It was a gig that we should never have done. Rough Trade hadn't checked it out properly beforehand." They play a couple more shows before arriving in Nottingham, which Ana describes in the diary as "Gina's hometown, if there is such a thing." The last gig is back in London at the Albany Empire. Everyone writes their own farewell in the diary. Ana's entry ends simply, "I don't regret it."

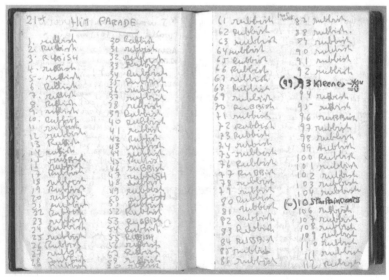

Two-page spread from Ana's 1979 tour diary

LIFE NUMBER 1

"We went on tour for twenty-eight days," Gina says, looking back, "and it was quite traumatic, to be perfectly honest. We were in a van with two other bands, we were all tired, and all probably a bit fed up with one another. I was just really uncomfortable. I think I knitted and listened to music the whole time."

The hours in the van were long, and they'd often involve extended distances. Ana and Gina sometimes felt they were traveling from one end of the UK to the other—"from Glasgow to Brighton," Ana says. They each passed the time with Sony TC-525 portable cassette recorders (recommended by Mute Records founder Daniel Miller), finding solitude amid a sense of chaos. Vicky remembers Gina constantly listening to the German experimental band Can on her Sony. Gina confirms it. "So much Can in the van," Vicky laughs. It was perhaps the only thing that saved Gina from the irritation of Spizz Energi. Both Shirley and Ana agree—Gina didn't have a good time on the tour, and it nearly felt like The Raincoats would end.

"Regula was leaving," Ana remembers, referring to the lead singer of Kleenex, "so she was hardly talking to the others, and Palmolive had decided she was leaving . . . there was this tension." Both Gina and Vicky remember Palmolive sitting silent in the van with headphones on, her pre-imagined music industry escape growing closer by the day. "She was already phasing herself out," Vicky says. "I can see her, sitting with headphones and not speaking to anyone. It already felt as if she was exiting." That sense of dispersion permeated the tour atmosphere. As the end neared, Marlene reflected on the parallel problems in Kleenex and The Raincoats. "The Raincoats have split problems too," she wrote in her diary. "Paloma wants to leave. Vicky and Ana don't really get along. Gina wants to go back to school."

"There was always an understanding: I will do the tour, and then I will leave," Palmolive explains. "That led to some conversations that were hard, and I wanted to say it's not a personal thing. I do think Ana and Gina knew me more, so they understood, but Vicky couldn't understand because she didn't know me as much . . . it wasn't selfishness, but I needed to breathe a different air. I have to choose my life."

"But a really good thing happened after the tour," Gina bounces back, "which is that we went into the studio and essentially recorded *The Raincoats* live. So that's the good thing I'll try to remember."

Suffice to say the tour wasn't the glamorous experience anyone was hoping for. Yet the gigs themselves were exciting, and The Raincoats found audiences across the UK to be largely receptive. By this point, Shirley was on her way to becoming the official Raincoats manager, and much more. "I never wanted to be seen as just the manager," Shirley explains. "I'm quite good at that, and really good at organization, and all the rest of it. But from the early days, it's been so much more than that. I've done photographs and artwork, esthetics, decision-making ..." She smiles and continues, "So I always describe myself more as a collaborator. I've always felt like a part of the band." Thurston Moore of Sonic Youth concurs: "Shirley is so important to the whole story. She was really the conduit." Without her, The Raincoats might not have made it back into the studio with Palmolive to record *The Raincoats*.

AN EPONYMOUS LP

Shirley had to convince Palmolive to record the self-titled LP. "She wanted to leave after the tour," Shirley says, "and I was the one who kind of persuaded her to stay just a little longer. I said something like, 'Look, please come and record this record. It's really fresh, and it would be terrible not to record it!' She'd never recorded anything except a Peel session with The Slits—which for me was the best Slits record—and I didn't want to lose that magic for our record."* Palmolive agreed to it.

The Raincoats was recorded at Berry Street Studio in a basement in Clerkenwell. The studio opened in 1970 as a relatively sparse yet professional recording space frequented by dub and reggae producers, and it also held sessions with prominent artists—ranging from Elton

---

* "The Peel Sessions" were a feature on BBC Radio 1 from 1967 until 2004, curated by presenter John Peel. Each session featured three or four live songs from a single artist, "rough and ready mixes of some of the world's most weird, wonderful and wired bands."[21]

LIFE NUMBER 1

Rough Trade poster for The Raincoats' self-titled album

John to The Slits and Radiohead. Geoff and Mayo were back as producers, and Adam Kidron was brought on as an engineer.

"Engineering is about finding out what sound somebody has in their head and replicating it somehow—either through trial and error, or through experience. And on the first Raincoats album, it was really about experimentation," Adam explains.

"He was so young!" Shirley remembers, and Ana chimes in, "I think he might have been a teenager, but he had a lot of confidence in himself." That confidence arose from Adam's upbringing, Ana suspects. "His parents were successful, and politically active as socialists. They were respected writers, and his sister became a respected filmmaker, so when you've got parents with that kind of confidence, they make you feel that you can do anything." Gina confirms that Adam's background shaped him: "His mother and father were closely associated with Pluto Press [a London-based revolutionary political press established in 1969] and they were very much part of the Hampstead intelligentsia." She remembers The Raincoats being invited to "play some of the parties at various venues," and to attend dinners at their home. They played one such Pluto Press party in November 1981 at Dingwalls, Camden at the invitation of

Adam's sister Beeban Kidron. And at one of those dinner parties, Gina recalls "once showing up to discover James 'Blood' Ulmer over there!" She adds gleefully, "I think I sat next to him ... and he talked to me about Mayo." For Gina, all of this meant Adam has a political sensibility that made him "the best person in a way" to work with The Raincoats. At the same time, Adam's appreciation for pop was always "driving him in another direction," Gina says.

In addition to inviting the band to play Pluto Press fetes, Beeban played a key role in Gina's later work. She bought Gina her first Super 8 camera, bringing it back from Hong Kong and setting in motion another stream of The Raincoats' creative output.

"I remember Geoff saying that our emotions were quite on the surface, and I think it must be that we were bickering during the mixing," Gina says. "A hallmark," Geoff laughs, remembering the disagreements. "When we all agreed on things, it was *beautiful*," Gina continues, "but sometimes we had to really fight for what we wanted, argue with each other about what we wanted, and sometimes I'd change my mind." She describes herself as "a bit more flighty, and a bit more of a comedic person," while Ana "was always slower to change her mind, to be convinced of anything, because she was always more considered in the first place."

Gina laughs. "It really *was* a democracy, though, because that's how democracy works, right?"

"We had just been on tour, so the songs were quite well rehearsed actually," Ana explains. "So basically, we went into the studio and recorded a live album. There are hardly any overdubs, and all the instruments were recorded at the same time. The only thing we ended up changing after was the drums on 'No Side to Fall In,' but you can still hear them a little bit coming through on one of the other microphones." Ana's solo on "The Void" was also something studio-created. When the first day of recording was over, she decided to do it differently after having the studio experience. It wasn't something she'd considered while The Raincoats had been playing the song on tour, and that album version would become historic in the subsequent lives of the band. Kismet.

LIFE NUMBER 1

Suggestions to "add some production" at Berry Street were met with resistance from The Raincoats. Ana remembers Adam suggesting, "Add some reverb," which was promptly shut down. "No, no! I'm still quite a purist," she laughs.

They brought in friend Lora Logic, from feminist punk bands X-Ray Spex and Essential Logic, for the fourth track, "Black And White." As Lora remembers it, "Geoff organized this studio outing for me, like he organized others." She turned up at Berry Street as a session player with a soprano sax (she usually played alto or tenor), and recalls, "It was my first time recording that I played the soprano, so that was a challenge for me." Lora explains how the instrument is "not very comfortable to play," but it was the right one for the song. And it gave Lora a chance to "be spontaneous." She heard the song just a couple times before improvising her own part, and The Raincoats were happy for her to bring her own sonic voice to their music. "They wanted me to be me, and that was refreshing," Lora says.

"We did the whole thing in three weeks," Ana continues. "Two weeks to record, one week to mix." They'd often stay until sunrise the next morning, arriving back to their respective flats or squats around 5 a.m. "And when we came home, we'd always smell of studio—the smell of equipment (the materials get this sort of smell from having all the electricity go through it, I think) and cigarette smoke, and maybe some beer spilled on the floor," she laughs. "It wasn't posh, but it was what Rough Trade could afford."

When *The Raincoats* was released on vinyl, the same year as the *Fairytale* EP, The Raincoats were elated to hold their records in their hands. "It had all become real!" Gina exclaims. For Ana, "It meant that we were really doing something, and nobody could take that away from us . . . It was just the existence of the objects that really made me so happy."

Sales were never the goal, but for what it's worth *The Raincoats* sold quite well.

PALOMA LEAVES

Following Palmolive's departure, Rough Trade would forever refer to the lineup with her as "The Original Raincoats." It wasn't exactly accurate given the band's earlier incarnations, but "The Original Raincoats" were the first to record anything. The music press would often use the line "Old Raincoats."

In 1979, Palmolive spoke to Vivien Goldman for *Melody Maker* about her decision to leave. She reflected on repressive boundaries in the British music industry, speaking more harshly about that form of tyranny than what she experienced previously under the final years of the Franco dictatorship in Spain. "I'm not happy with the surroundings. To me it feels restrictive, compromising too much, this rock business," she told Vivien. "It's the same old shit—with education and everything you end up building a wall around you by the time you're nineteen."[22] She officially left The Raincoats behind and headed for the Indian subcontinent.

Steve Shelley of Sonic Youth, and later of The Raincoats himself, says, "There's no better story for a drummer than if you leave, because you become a complete mystery, and that's why I just love the Palmolive story. That story was so fun as a fan ... Tell Palmolive I'm her number one fan."

But for the band, it was less about mystery and more a logistical problem. "So *The Raincoats* came out and we didn't have a drummer," Ana reflects. "I thought Gina believed touring was the worst time in her life, and we didn't have any new songs. It seemed like it should be the end, and the whole thing made me quite anxious. I found it quite difficult emotionally ... I just take things to heart."

THE RAINCOATS NEED A DRUMMER (AGAIN)

With Palmolive's departure, The Raincoats needed a drummer ... again. And it wouldn't come close to being the last time.

A new drummer happened along by word of mouth—most likely, she'd seen the ads The Raincoats had run in *New Musical Express* and

LIFE NUMBER 1

Melody Maker that read simply: "The Raincoats are looking for a female drummer."[23]

"This young woman just approached me on Portobello Road!" Gina marvels, remembering her first encounter with Ingrid Weiss. "I remember being in Ladbroke Grove, somewhere up near the long stretch of Portobello Market," Ingrid says, "and I saw Gina in the street. I got up the courage, walked up to her and said, 'I know you're looking for a drummer, could I come along and try out?' I don't even remember how I learned they were looking for a drummer, maybe just because I'd seen in *NME* that Palmolive left, so I knew they'd want to find someone else." Ingrid was only eighteen years old.

She started drumming in the garage of a friend's house, using "a stack of *NME*s and a biscuit tin" as instruments, because her parents weren't supportive of her music. "Palmolive was my hero, and it was because of her I became a drummer," Ingrid says. Though she initially cut her teeth on makeshift instruments, Ingrid eventually became friends with a slightly more established group of artists who rehearsed in what she describes as a "dirt church on Archway," which is now the Jacksons Lane Arts Centre. "There was a drum kit there!" she exclaims. She started honing her craft and eventually bought her own silver Pearl drum kit for her upstairs bedroom in her parents' house. "I remembered Palmolive had one, so that's what I needed to get. And our next-door neighbor was a drummer, so I wasn't the only one making noise!" She practiced, and practiced, and practiced.

To audition for The Raincoats, Ingrid showed up at the rehearsal space they were borrowing from This Heat: "Cold Storage, in Brixton," she recalls. "Well, it was technically called something else," Ingrid laughs, "but it was *freezing* in there." Charles Hayward, drummer with This Heat and a later addition to The Raincoats himself, explains that it was quite literally a "meat fridge that This Heat turned into a studio." Since The Raincoats needed a place to rehearse, This Heat offered up Cold Storage when they weren't using it. "And that's how I got to know The Raincoats," he says.

"I remember cutting my fingers on the drum kit, so there was blood spurting—as happens with drummers!" Ingrid notes. Charles vividly remembers Ingrid auditioning on his "quite rare and beautiful" drum set. He should have known it was going to get quite bloody, he says now, because he could see immediately that Ingrid was "a very raw drummer, very visceral." Charles laughs out loud as he remembers, "She bled *all over* this drum kit, and Gina, Ana, and Vicky were very worried that I was going to be very worried, but of course, no actual damage—just covered in blood. I could live with that!"

"I think it went fairly well because they said I could join," Ingrid remembers, all blood aside.

"Ingrid was great," Ana says. "She had so much spirit. But I just couldn't connect with her." Ingrid was the youngest in the band now, and Ana the oldest. "Ingrid had just turned eighteen, and I think Ana was thirty then," Gina explains, "so they really just didn't see eye to eye with one another in any way. That kind of age difference later on doesn't seem like anything at all, but when you have someone who's a teenager and someone who's thirty, it's really so much, and it's so pronounced." Ultimately, the differences between them would prove too great, and Gina had to tell Ingrid she was no longer part of the band.

Ana emphasizes that she liked Ingrid and thought she was a great drummer, but to really function, the band needed a connection on a personal and political level, too. In the end, Ingrid was a Raincoat for a brief span in 1980—about the same amount of time Palmolive drummed with the band in 1979. While in the group, Ingrid played gigs across America and Europe, including The Raincoats' first appearance in New York, and on bills supporting a range of political causes in the UK. Her drumming helped to shape some of the stand-out tracks on *Odyshape*. "It was only about one year," Ingrid says, "but it was really such a full year."

SHIRLEY'S ROUGH TRADE BOOKING AGENCY

The year 1980 was full indeed. Shirley started a booking agency.

Between 1978 and 1984, there were four parts of Rough Trade: the Rough Trade shop, Rough Trade Records, Rough Trade Distribution,

LIFE NUMBER 1

and Rough Trade Music. Within Rough Trade Music, Anne Clark ran the publishing and Sue Johnson was the director. In 1980, Sue said to Shirley, "Would you like to start Rough Trade Booking within the company?" At this point, as Shirley remembers, "I was getting all these phone calls asking about booking Rough Trade bands and bands from labels that Rough Trade had distributed." So she started Rough Trade Booking. From that point forward, Shirley not only did the booking for The Raincoats, but also for the rest of the Rough Trade roster, including Cabaret Voltaire, Delta 5, the Red Krayola, The Fall, Pere Ubu, Scritti Politti, This Heat, Young Marble Giants, Essential Logic, Orange Juice, and many more.

"I contracted all the gigs in Europe and the USA, up until the last Raincoats shows in '83." Beginning in 1981, a guy named Mike Hinc joined Shirley at her agency to help with the workload.

Shirley driving the Rough Trade van, 1978

"I remember interviewing him after we planned some really exciting lineups together for 'Rock Weeks' at the ICA where he worked," Shirley says. "I really wanted him to come in and handle the UK booking, and he did." The part of her booking job she loved most was handling dates in the rest of Europe and the States, so she was eager to give Mike the local duties. "Through forming the agency is how I met Carmen Knoebel, Ruth Polsky, Hilary Jaeger," Shirley says, naming key people in the life of The Raincoats yet to come, "and people like Carlos van Hijfte," who'd become the agent for Sonic Youth, another Raincoats connection for the future.

Although she didn't officially start managing The Raincoats until 1980, she took on part of that role from the band's start with promotion. "Starting in about '79," Shirley remembers, "I used to take all of our new releases to John Peel, *NME*, *Sounds*, *Melody Maker*. I'd literally go to those places on a Wednesday and take all the physical stuff there. It was lucky for The Raincoats, because I got the EP to Paul Morley, who absolutely adored it."

In 1984, with the breakup of The Raincoats—what Shirley now describes as the "hiatus," given what would happen in the next decade and the years that followed—she left the agency in Mike's hands. His work primarily involved booking for The Smiths, the biggest Rough Trade group at the time.

ROCK AGAINST SEXISM

On February 14, 1980, The Raincoats headlined a Rock Against Sexism gig, playing alongside Young Marble Giants, Necessary Evil, and Stepping Talk at the Albany Empire. The gig would be the most public expression yet of the band's feminist ethos. "We were all involved in Rock Against Racism," Gina says. "So when Rock Against Sexism started up, we were invited along to a meeting. Rock Against Racism and Rock Against Sexism were always the best gigs to do—they had a platform, it was positive, and it was powerful. What's not to like?"

For the Valentine's Day show that year, billed across London as "The Valentine's Day Massacre," Lucy Whitman (aka Lucy

LIFE NUMBER 1

Toothpaste) created a double-sided handbill. Each of the bands made a statement, and The Raincoats' read as follows:

> We want to be seen to be restoring the balance in a male-dominated culture like rock, by playing our own music in our own way. There is a growing female presence in rock and we want to encourage more girls to play and eventually make a lasting impression on popular music. We work within rock because it is the dominant form, and the most sexist area, and we can be more effective in the end if we confront it on its own ground. We want to show women they don't have to be consumers, and create music that's not based on assumptions of female passivity, especially now when women's control over their own bodies is being attacked by John Corrie's bill to amend the Abortion Act—which comes up for debate again tomorrow (Friday).

Rock Against Racism (RAR) began in 1976, and Rock Against Sexism (RAS) grew out of it. The group that formed RAS was frustrated with some of the positions on gender and sex in the broader RAR contingent. "Bands which were proudly anti-racist," Lucy explains, were often "idiotically sexist and didn't have a clue about feminism." Many of the journalists covering RAR, who wanted to take public action in response to the racist violence of the National Front, "didn't seem to think there was anything wrong with sexism," Lucy recalls, and "thought we were humorless, hairy-legged feminists." Some of the collective's members wanted to do something about it. That meant starting a separate organization. "It became evident that we needed it," she says. While RAS "never attained the massive firepower of Rock Against Racism," Lucy is proud of what RAS did manage to achieve in a relatively short span of time.

In the late seventies and early eighties, the matter of violence against women was quite literally "a matter of life and death," and that sense had only started "to filter into mainstream discourse pretty recently." Lucy explains how many of the members of RAR shared a sense that "sexism is annoying, but racism and fascism are deadly." She felt passionately about speaking and acting against fascism, racism, *and sexism* equally. For a short time, she remained in both organizations, doing overlapping work. Yet as anyone who has given their time to activist work knows, it's simply not possible to do it all. Lucy knew RAR wouldn't fail without her involvement, but the same couldn't be said of RAS, which seemed like the more critical movement to which she should devote her time.

Sexuality was a pressing issue, and members of RAS wanted to "define the right of everyone to determine their own sexuality, whether they be straight, gay, both, or neither." Sexuality, Lucy explains, was tied in with how artists, especially bands with lesbians, presented themselves: "We didn't want to be the objects of anti-lesbian abuse, or heckling, but we also want our audience to know that how we dress, how we look, who we sleep with is really none of their business."

Lucy underscores the immense fear of homophobia at the time, explaining how "punk gave cover to a lot of lesbians, and I know that's true for myself." A certain androgynous look could be written off as punk, when it actually reflected a sexuality or sexual preference. "Punk became the uniform of young lesbians ... disguised but in plain sight," Lucy says, quoting her own words from a television program from the early 1990s. But even in the decade leading up to the new millennium, many people still weren't out because of fear of homophobia. "It wasn't cool at the time," she says. Yet RAS wanted to make society culturally safer and freer for women, regardless of sexual orientation. That kind of change started to take hold with gigs like the "Valentine's Day Massacre" in 1980.

Lucy was keenly attuned to bands that self-identified as feminists, as well as those "blowing up traditional notions of femininity, in their clothes, their lyrics, their behavior." The Raincoats certainly were part of the latter category, and Vicky had been a member of Jam Today, the "archetypal feminist London band," Lucy calls it.

The point of the "Valentine's Day Massacre" was to speak out against traditional constructions of love and romance. It was booked at the Albany Empire in south-east London, a community theatre venue—what Lucy describes as a "lefty, progressive venue" that also had a crucial history in the RAR movement. The National

Front (NF)—the fascist UK political party that rose to particular prominence in the 1970s—began to realize RAR was winning over hearts and minds, so it started staging RAR gig disruptions. Given that some of the celebrated punk bands at the time already had a skinhead following, NF members had a foot in. Often, gigs simply didn't feel safe with NF skinheads "sieg-heiling" in the crowd. There was a general sense of fear in the atmosphere, and a particularly keen sense of women's vulnerability. The Albany Empire was the site of an especially ugly NF disruption in 1978: They burned down the theatre. But it was rebuilt, and playing in the newly renovated space allowed bands to voice a particular kind of *fuck you* to the fascists who'd attempted to destroy it. The "Valentine's Day Massacre" wasn't the first time The Raincoats would play the Albany Empire, and it wouldn't be the last.

With the NF still visibly present and threatening on Valentine's Day in 1980, there was a need for security at the gig. The RAS team knew the Socialist Workers Party had provided security for RAR gigs in the past, so they went to them for help. "They kept the gig safe, but it was a very volatile environment," Lucy notes, describing the atmosphere in which bands like The Raincoats were eager to perform—acts of resistance.

Compared to other women-centered bands at that time, Lucy describes The Raincoats' music as "much harder hitting." Although many songs were markedly playful, they were "really tackling the darker side of sexism and feminism," she says. As Gina emphasizes, "Men have thought for so long that they have a right to sexual assault, and that if women don't respond in a particular way, they can do what they want. This attitude was pervasive, and I think it is still. There was a need to address it, and there's still quite a bit of that same need now."

POLITICS OF REPRESSION

Repression takes different forms depending on geopolitics, insidiously mirroring the modes of expression and freedom it means to snuff out. In the UK in the seventies, the rise of the NF and cemented gender barriers meant that racist and sexist persecution were very tangible and coincided with the continued violent effects of British colonization. The Raincoats recognized the importance of standing against those forms of power within the relative freedoms of London. They'd seen a different form of tyranny in Warsaw, and Ana came of age in the throes of dictatorship fewer than a thousand miles to the south.

With publication of his *Political Constitution of the New State* in Portugal in 1933, António de Oliveira Salazar became the leader of what many scholars have identified as the longest dictatorship in Western Europe. The Estado Novo, as it was known during its forty-plus years of existence in Portugal, arose almost simultaneously with the Francoist dictatorship in neighboring Spain (led by Spanish military general Francisco Franco Bahamonde from 1936 to 1975).

Ana remembers a car trip to mainland Europe her family planned in 1967. "As we were leaving Portugal," she remembers, "I realized that my mother, who was nearly fifty-five years old, could have been forbidden from leaving the country. In order to travel out of Portugal then, she had to present the border police with two documents giving her permission to leave, one from her employer and one from my father."

In the proto-fascist Estado Novo rule, feminism was an alien concept. Article 5 of Salazar's constitution effectively removed women's citizenship rights. As literary critic Ana Paula Ferreira observes, the "demonizing of feminist ideals" quickly became the "*sine qua non* of endorsing the dictator's plans for the moral reconstruction of the Portuguese family."[24] Propaganda routinely depicted women solely as mothers inside their homes; never outside. The dictatorship's philosophy was summed up in the phrase "God, Nation and Family," and propaganda emphasized the importance of a heteronormative household in which wives (and mothers) were subordinate to their husbands. Indeed, the Portuguese dictatorship "upheld and promoted rigidly dichotomous gender roles, both in law and in mainstream culture."[25] The national consciousness acknowledged—regardless of whether all agreed, and certainly they did not—that women were relegated to private, domestic realms

LIFE NUMBER 1

Ana onstage
in Warsaw

under Portuguese law and that their bodies were controlled by the state.

"It was great to come here to London," Ana says, "because people can look different here and nobody abuses them. In Portugal, if you looked a bit different... I used to have really long hair, and a couple of times it happened that somebody would say, 'Are you a woman or a man?' At that point, women started wearing trousers more, and I was wearing trousers, and maybe they thought I was a man because I was wearing trousers but that I also looked like a woman because I had long hair. They operated on stereotypes, and it made me feel uncomfortable."

While Ana was raised in Madeira, far from the center of Portuguese politics and dictatorship (which enabled a certain kind of freedom), she "didn't develop the way kids do now, or even did then in other places," she says. There are nineteen-year-olds she knows now in the UK who are outspoken and political, who feel free to use their voices. Ana never felt that sense of freedom at that age, she says, "Because you couldn't discuss politics properly, you couldn't say certain things. You couldn't be seen as someone getting involved in any kind of action because you would go to prison."

Ana remembers a "list of things you would have to pay fines for, like holding hands in the street—and I mean a man and a woman, I'm not talking about two women or two men. Very repressive. I didn't notice because I was living in it, and that was just life. That was the law, how it was, and it was very difficult to challenge when nobody around you was challenging it. When I was young in Madeira, I just thought, that's how it is. I didn't have information or good newspapers that challenged the status quo." Things changed when she left Madeira but remained within the confines of the dictatorship.

"When I went to university in Lisbon I opened my mind a lot more. I went to university in 1968, when there was a student movement happening in France. And in Portugal, some of it was happening, too." The Paris protests echoed in Lisbon, and the spirit of revolution felt palpable. Demonstrations started taking place in secret, many within Ana's proximity. "My university was opposite the law university," she explains, "so there was a lot happening there, as well. I used to go to all of the meetings because I was absorbing and learning. It felt dangerous because secret police would be there." Ana describes secret police posing as custodial workers and other administrators in the corridors of the university buildings. (As in all dictatorial regimes, Salazar had his own secret police force, which was known by its acronym PIDE/DGS, and tasked with exacting violence and torture upon political opponents.) "There was a meeting one time when metal chairs started being thrown around on the marble floors. I had to climb out of a window to get home. It was heavy."

Meanwhile, Ana was also imbibing resistance music from the radio. She was listening regularly to the program *Em Órbita*, which played contemporary songs that "questioned political, social, sexual situations, sometimes suggesting alternative ways of thinking, being, and living in a freer way." That music—by Bob Dylan, Joan Baez, Jefferson Airplane, Joni Mitchell, Neil Young, The Doors, and others—revealed how there were "two worlds (of the songs and of our reality)" operating parallel in Portugal. Those songs taught Ana that it's possible to question the status quo through song, to use "music as a weapon." And that sentiment spread among those in Portugal acting in resistance. She reflects how "part of the fight against the dictatorship was made by the songs written by various Portuguese artists who, I'm sure, contributed to the success of the 25th of April Revolution." Members of O Grito do Povo, a communist resistance group (just one of the resistance groups among many fighting the Estado Novo dictatorship), taught themselves "protest music serenades" to survive being tortured in political prisons.[26]

In many cases, activists had to use all means at their disposal, including peaceful tactics that nonetheless put their own physical safety at risk. "My cousin was involved in some of the resistance, leafleting. He didn't put a bomb anywhere or anything like that, he distributed leaflets and posters, but he ended up going to prison. I also had another friend who was imprisoned. They weren't doing terrorist things—they were saying what they thought and informing people." Ana continued attending political meetings after her cousin was imprisoned, but "that was all I did, go to the meetings," she says.

The dictatorship officially ended in April 1974. The Carnation Revolution, as it's called outside Portugal, or the Revolução de 25 de Abril as it's known inside the country, set the stage for a return to democracy.

Ana left Portugal and arrived in London on December 13, 1974. In her adoptive city, she'd end up making a home for more than fifty years. Her experiences under dictatorship impacted the art she created there. "Maybe I brought to The Raincoats' work a certain anguish from that time, and a will to break down the walls that had surrounded me," she explains. Her words allude to the "You're a Million" lyrics she wrote while behind the similarly oppressive boundary of the Berlin Wall, traveling back to London from Warsaw in 1978.

FAN MAIL: A LETTER FROM THE MAZE IN NORTHERN IRELAND

In 1979, The Raincoats received a piece of fan mail at Rough Trade from a writer named Jim Kyle. The return address at the top read "Compound 19, H.M.P. Maze"—the H-Blocks in Lisburn, Northern Ireland. The letter had been sent from the feared institution that held political prisoners sentenced for acts of violence during the Troubles.

Dear Raincoats,
After repeated plays of the new album I just have to write and offer some praise, especially after reading the panning that bigot McCullough gave it when reviewing it in *Sounds*. I hope his article didn't discourage you too much as I'm sure anyone who reads *Sounds* regularly knows by now that he allows personality clashes etc. to influence his honesty. Stiff Little Fingers were another among many to incur his juvenile attitudes. As Ana said when replying in *Sounds* it makes one angry to think that someone like him has the power to influence peoples choices.
Anyway back to the album itself, which I think is brilliant. When I ordered it from Rough Trade a couple of weeks ago I also bought the new Jam, Fall, and Banshee L.P.s as they are among my favourites. However although they are very good it has been your album which has dominated the turntable and is what I'm listening to as I write this. A lot of things impress me. The actual music itself is first class especially on the Void and No Looking but I think it is the brilliantly structured vocals that makes it all so special. It's hard to explain in words what I feel impresses me in the album the highest accolade I can give it is that I really enjoy it. The standout for me is the excellent Off Duty Trip. Also your version of Lola would make a great single.
I hope it's not too long before you release something else. In the meantime I think I'll be playing The Raincoats a lot.
Cheerio,
Jim[27]

LIFE NUMBER 1

H.M. Prison Maze was designated for prisoners during the Troubles and held detainees from 1971 to 2000. "The Maze," as it was sometimes simply described, included a series of compounds or cages making up an area known as "Long Kesh," which was opened in 1976, and eight adjacent H-Blocks, named for their shape. It was a maximum security prison that became known globally as a result of the protests occurring there, including the blanket protest and the 1981 hunger strike led by Bobby Sands. The prison was separated into "cages," as they were called by republicans, or "compounds," as they were called by loyalists.

There's very little written information about the names of the prisoners who were interned in the H-Blocks at any given point in time, unless they appeared in the media or have since given testimony to the Prisons Memory Archive. The "Jim Kyle" who wrote to The Raincoats is neither named in existing print materials nor listed as a narrator in any of the post-Good Friday oral history projects to come out of the Troubles and the closure of the Maze. Those whose names don't appear are absent by choice. There was a Jim Kyle interned in one of the republican cages, a prominent member of the Irish Republican Army (IRA), but he was not the Jim Kyle who'd mailed a handwritten letter to Rough Trade in London. Given that the letter writer identified his location as a "compound," and "Compound 19" more specifically—a known loyalist area of the prison—the Jim Kyle who'd written was most likely a loyalist, not a republican.

On Shankill Road in West Belfast, a predominantly loyalist area of the city during the Troubles, the ACT Initiative was established in 2008 as a conflict transformation program designed "to facilitate the civilianisation of the Ulster Volunteer Force (UVF)."[28] Dr. William Mitchell, the director of ACT, remains in touch with many of the surviving political prisoners who were once imprisoned in Compound 19, where he himself was incarcerated for political murder at the age of seventeen. For William, it's crucial to focus on reconciliation, and to address the stifling atmosphere that turned so many young people into violent offenders on opposing sides during the Troubles.

William knows Jim Kyle well, and Jim agreed to have his story included, centering on his abiding love of music and The Raincoats. William can provide all the surrounding details, he says.

"Jim and I were actually in the same cell," William explains. "And my own personal development, musically, was initiated by Jim Kyle.

Because as a seventeen-year-old, in 1976, he lent me an album by Bob Dylan, *Desire*." From that point onward, Jim opened up the musical minds of many prisoners in Compound 19. It's a story, William explains, about difficult stereotypes of young people involved in the stark violence of the Troubles. Like many of their same-age counterparts, the young imprisoned loyalists were beginning to come of age as punk happened, and many saw themselves as part of the cultural revolution taking place in music, despite the very different sides of the conflict on which they committed acts of violence.

"I'd only been in prison about six months, same as Jim, we were arrested the same month in 1975," William says. "Both teenagers. I was seventeen, he was eighteen. Not on charges related, we didn't know each other until we'd come into prison." Thanks to Jim, William came to understand the deep politics and significance of Dylan's music, "this protest singer who, as soon as I dropped the needle on *Desire*, sang, pistol shots rang out in a barroom, enter Paddy Valentine from the end of the hall. It was an epiphany moment, and it literally

Reconstruction of a 1970s cubicle (cell) from the Long Kesh Compounds with the original record player on view (ACT Initiative, Belfast)

LIFE NUMBER 1

changed my world, changed my life. Through his music, I developed an interest in the characters in the songs and became introduced to William Burroughs, T.S. Eliot, Shakespeare, Arthur Rimbaud, all of these people who, as a young man, really fascinated me."

How was anyone listening to records in the H-Blocks? William explains, "You were literally caged," but they could roam freely within the compound and had access to study and educational facilities. There was a markedly large population of very young men, teenagers, and otherwise very young adults, like William and Jim, who'd been recruited during what William describes as "the worst years of the conflict," from 1972 to 1975. And those prisoners in Compound 19 together, around the same age, "were drawn to the punk movement as a subculture, and we looked at it from afar with the disappointment that we couldn't engage in it. But we could listen to it and hear it on albums," William says.

Jim loved punk and post-punk, but he was also a well-rounded lover of music. William describes it, warmly, as a "quite eclectic taste," explaining, "Jim used to religiously get the *NME* and *Melody Maker* and look for mail order opportunities, but of course, Rough Trade was his major focus. And we were this camaraderie, this group of young men. So anytime someone got an album, they shared it. That record player was the only one we had between eighty prisoners," he says as he points at a small suitcase record player behind him on a shelf. The record player "lived" in the study area of Compound 19, and there was a hardback book that sat beside it. If you wanted to listen to a record, you'd put your name in the book and the hour you wanted it.

Jim introduced the sounds of "alternative music," and music that was making a political impact in the UK, "including, of course, The Raincoats," William says. Jim recently reminded William of playing him The Raincoats' cover of "Lola," but he emphasized that what drew him to The Raincoats initially was the *Fairytale* EP, "their first single." But he loved it all, and he sent the fan letter after receiving the self-titled LP from Rough Trade. Throughout his time in the Maze, he kept in direct contact with Sue Donne, who handled Rough Trade mail order. He gratefully recalls how Sue began sending him "freebies" and discounting records for Jim to give a listen to.

Did the records get censored? All the records would be opened and examined, and some things would be censored. But if there wasn't anything obvious—thank goodness for the subtlety of The Raincoats' political interventions—the records would be delivered to the prisoner who ordered them. But not before they'd been desecrated. Jim holds up some examples of records that had come into the Maze. There are large black redaction marks where the guards essentially made scribbles to damage the records. The prisoner's number would also be written largely on the front. "But it actually gives them a kind of authenticity now," he reflects.

Jim would sometimes put on The Raincoats in the evening for everyone—"And you can just imagine some of the criticism he would have got from the older folk," William says. But it didn't deter Jim. The music was that important. He was imprisoned for around four years in total. During that time, he brought the world of Rough Trade to the prison, and he opened the sonic and political minds of many young prisoners in the larger compound with him.

Jim loved music so much, and learned so much about it from the records he ordered and shared with fellow prisoners in the H-Blocks, that he opened a record shop in Smithfield Market in Belfast after he was released from the Maze. The market "was a hard place," William explains, with a long and violent history during the Troubles. "It would get bombed every other month during the conflict," he says, but after the Good Friday Agreement, it became a space of peace. And, thanks to Jim, of music. William used to visit the shop regularly until it closed, and he bought a fair amount of his current record collection from Jim.

What was the shop called? "Jim's Records."

CAROLINE SCOTT, SECOND-WAVE FEMINISM, AND "OFF DUTY TRIP"

Political violence also existed closer to home for The Raincoats. Although the term "rape as a weapon of war" was yet to be coined, sexual assaults perpetrated by members of the armed forces were more common than not. The lyrics of the third track on

LIFE NUMBER 1

The Raincoats, "Off Duty Trip," were written by Caroline Scott, a political activist and ally of The Raincoats. Vicky, who roomed with Caroline, worked on the lyrics with her, then brought it to the group. The song publicized the prevalence of rape and the startling lack of accountability. It's one of The Raincoats' most enduring political statements.

Vicky first met Caroline at either an International Marxist Group (IMG) meeting, or a Troops Out Movement meeting in late 1977. The latter would make sense, given Caroline's long-term interest in republican political activism. Either way, they bonded over their interest in a shared sense of politics and soon moved into a shared flat together in Camden.

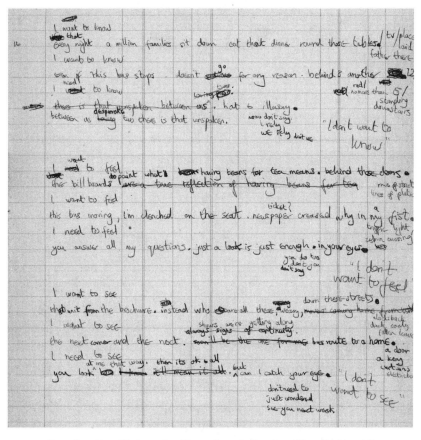

Caroline Scott's handwritten diary lyrics for "Family Treet," one of her songs on *Odyshape*

The Troops Out Movement (TOM) was an anti-imperialist, anti-colonial civil rights organization in England that garnered support from various left-wing and women's rights groups following its founding in 1973. It arose in response to British policies concerning Northern Ireland, in particular the British military occupation of the region, the start of internment in 1971, and Bloody Sunday in Derry the following year.[29] The movement's bulletin, Tom-Tom, *released its first issue in early 1974. It announced TOM's demand for "self-determination for the Irish People as a whole." TOM tied the British military presence in Northern Ireland to the same colonial violence perpetrated by the Commonwealth in various regions of the Global South. The group held regular meetings in London, and many supporters who attended were closely aligned with radical feminist groups throughout the UK.[30] For many aspiring political activists, TOM meetings became places to meet like-minded agitators, especially for young culturally aware feminists seeking community.*

As flatmates, Vicky and Caroline had a lot of time to "chew the fat over issues," Vicky says. For Vicky, listening back to Caroline's lyrics for "Family Treet," on *Odyshape*, is "the crux of it, really." She refers to "family, class, and nation," and as Vicky explains, "It was about how feminism, class politics, and anti-racism intersected—those were our interests." Caroline always wrote her lyrics through a personal lens, illuminating her own pain in relation to the larger political issues she was tackling. Caroline's daughter Frankie smiles and says, "My mum loved writing, she had a way with words." Vicky agrees, "Caroline was a great writer. She had a great grasp of imagery and a lateral way of describing situations. We bounced off each other's shared view of the world, and then she would put it into lyrics. They were always about alienation, really, and that resonated with me."

Vicky and Caroline often discussed sexual violence and the objectification of women in the media. They talked about these issues constantly, and Vicky asked Caroline if she'd help her write a song addressing the problem more directly. "Writing lyrics really wasn't my thing, because I was more of an arranger, a musician, so I was quite happy for Caroline to take over that role," Vicky recalls. "And then this case came up in the press of a British soldier who'd committed a rape but would face no consequences. It was an extreme case, but not *that* extreme," Vicky laments. The news story "became a very visual, immediate thing to put the song around." They wanted to illustrate how the outcome of that case spoke to the wider picture, that this wasn't so uncommon. "Looking back now," Vicky says, "that's hardly changed in forty years. It's all still the same, men being protected by their status and positions of power within institutions."

In 1975, feminist scholar Susan Brownmiller, who started her career as a writer for cultural weekly the Village Voice, *published the groundbreaking book* Against Our Will. *Brownmiller has often said that, at the time of its publication, she believed her book would change minds and radically reframe conversations around rape, gender, and power. While it illuminated the vicious normality of rape, Brownmiller acknowledged to the* Guardian *in 2018 that, ultimately, not much really changed.*[31]

At the time Vicky and Caroline saw the news clipping, the Belfast Rape Crisis Centre advocated for survivors when the law would not, and the politics were not partisan. The women who ran that center attended to rape survivors sympathetic to the IRA or members themselves, and others loyal to the republican cause. Loyalists and British soldiers, or anti-colonial republican paramilitary members—the separatism became unimportant when recognizing the politics of sexual violence during the Troubles, according to Susan McKay, founder of the Belfast Rape Crisis Centre.[32]

After releasing "Off Duty Trip," The Raincoats played a Rape Crisis Centre benefit concert in June 1982 at the Pavilion Theatre in Brighton. The flyer advertising the event depicted three fierce, armed women—an image that has become a common representation of women in revolt. While The Raincoats never wielded firearms, their words and music became cultural weapons.

CARMEN KNOEBEL AND PUNK AS MODERN ART

In 1979, on a routine trip to London, Carmen Knoebel stopped by at Rough Trade. She saw a record "with really nice hand drawings," was intrigued, bought it, and took it home to Düsseldorf—the West

German city where she founded the Ratinger Hof, a venue considered to be the birthplace of German punk. Carmen immediately loved *Fairytale* and went to see The Raincoats perform when they passed through Eindhoven. Ana recalls that gig as one of her most memorable in the long and varied lives of The Raincoats, because it was the first time promoters had a hot meal for them and helped to set up their equipment. "We'd never felt any warmth from a promoter before," Ana says. Carmen met The Raincoats backstage, and the band's indelible connection to modern art was made. "Carmen was the first person when we were on the road who really appeared to value us and treat us with utmost respect and care," Gina emphasizes. "We knew we had found a very special person."

"Carmen wouldn't put on just any gig," Shirley explains. "It had to be music she was passionate about." In the mid-1970s, Carmen needed a way to make money to support her family. Ideally, she wanted to earn a living doing something she loved. She had two children and was married to the artist Imi Knoebel. "He had enough money to pay for his studio and material for his work," Carmen explains, "but I did the rest for money to pay the rent."

She'd worked previously at the Konrad Fischer Galerie, starting when the gallery opened in 1967 with an exhibition of Carl Andre's floor works. "Everyone was standing on them," Carmen laughs. (Andre was accused of murdering artist Ana Mendieta shortly after they were married; it's quite cathartic to imagine his works being trampled.) Carmen understood the immutable link between music and visual art. She organized music shows in gallery spaces, including an early performance by Kraftwerk. That idea—that music and gallery spaces could and should be one and the same—catalyzed the rise of art punk and art rock, including in the identity of The Raincoats. She took the concept further in buying the space that would become the Ratinger Hof with business partner Ingrid Kohlhöfer. Carmen did it in part for the money, but the venue was also founded on her love for music and art. To be clear, there weren't art exhibitions *inside* the Ratinger Hof alongside punk gigs. "The Ratinger Hof itself *was* an art piece," Carmen says.

When she took over the space, the interiors had an old German feel, with "dark wood up half the walls, a place where the older generation went to drink beer" as Carmen describes it. She and Ingrid renovated. Everything went bright white with neon lights. (In the late 1960s, Carmen had been in touch with the contemporary artist Dan Flavin, known for his neon light sculptures. Since Konrad Fischer had been interested in bringing artists from America to Germany, and Carmen was interested in Flavin's work, she brought him over. It was his artistic impulses and esthetic that inspired the interiors of the new Ratinger Hof, the birthplace of German punk.)

"Nobody wanted to come in at first," Carmen laughs, suggesting punters preferred to be anonymous in dark spaces. "To go into the Ratinger Hof meant you will be seen." But soon the venue became synonymous with new experimental sounds. It helped that the band ZK (later to become German rockers Die Toten Hosen) had been rehearsing in the basement long before the renovation, and bands like Kraftwerk and Neu! would come to listen. So naturally, when the space became new again, it wasn't so difficult to convince ZK to venture upstairs. They played their first official gig at the Ratinger Hof. The venue also brought punk artists from the UK and the US, including Pere Ubu, Wire, XTC, 999, Glenn Branca, and Dexys Midnight Runners. To Carmen, Pere Ubu was the real face of punk—"Not the Sex Pistols," she says. She'd spent time in New York throughout the 1970s, where nothing started to get interesting from her perspective until she heard the Contortions and the Ramones, and it all just got better from there.

By 1979, Carmen decided to move on from the Ratinger Hof due to creative differences with her business partner. She started the Düsseldorf-based record label Pure Freude and kept a hand in promoting punk in other venues, including the Okie Dokie in Neuss where The Raincoats made their German debut.

The Okie Dokie became a central venue for punk, post-punk, and other underground artists once Carmen left the Ratinger Hof. Its doors were open from 1979 to 1987, during which time its stage supported a wide range of UK bands that would go on to international longevity, including The Raincoats, Bauhaus, Modern English, Scritti Politti, Killing Joke, and The Jesus and Mary Chain. Conny Plank, acclaimed West German sound engineer and producer for Kraftwerk and Neu! among many others, could be spotted frequently in the audience. While the venue closed its doors in 1987, its name has lived on in the contemporary German cultural memory, with a prominent gallery named Okey Dokey and a music venue and bar Okie Dokie reminding visitors of the name's sonic legacy in and around Düsseldorf.[33]

On April 1, 1980, The Raincoats played a solo show at the Okie Dokie while a "new wave video" program from "DIEGO CORTEZ New York" screened behind them. (Diego Cortez was the alter art ego of James Allan Curtis, a cofounder of New York's Mudd Club and curator of the later 1981 *New York/New Wave* show at P.S.1—later to become the anarchist outpost of MoMA (New York's Museum of Modern Art)—that brought the work of Jean-Michel Basquiat and Keith Haring to public acclaim alongside works by Fab Five Freddy, Andy Warhol, William S. Burroughs, Lawrence Weiner, Maripol, and others. At that point, Basquiat was still going by his graffiti-tag name SAMO. It made perfect sense, in retrospect, that The Raincoats would become linked to the New York City no wave scene before its founding—they'd soon find themselves in the city playing their own gigs at the venues that would make no wave famous.)

The Raincoats had arrived in Düsseldorf earlier that week via train, and Carmen remembers finding herself in a state of culinary confusion—they were all vegetarians. The Raincoats asked Carmen for full use of her kitchen. "This was the first time I had any contact with a vegetarian! Totally new," Carmen laughs. Despite their varying penchants for consuming meat, Carmen became quick and close friends with Ana, Shirley, and Gina, and their friendship would ultimately last a lifetime. Shirley describes Carmen as something akin to a benefactor.

During that first stay in Düsseldorf, The Raincoats went to an art exhibition, a retrospective of the Russian avant-garde modernist Kazimir Malevich at the Kunsthalle Düsseldorf. Ana bought a poster of Malevich's 1930 painting *Peasant Woman* (Крестьянка), which would become the inspiration for the *Odyshape* cover. A German edition of *Sounds* announced the band's new record with a photo of them standing in front of the Malevitch exhibition poster, hanging on the wall above Ana's bed. Naturally, The Raincoats returned to Düsseldorf in support of *Odyshape*, at

LIFE NUMBER 1

the Hansa Palast on October 2, 1981. Tickets and records were provided by Carmen's label Pure Freude. It was a particularly special version of the LP: Ana made a miniature booklet to be included in each of the Pure Freude copies of *Odyshape*, and the colors were slightly different. (When Kathi Wilcox of Bikini Kill made a pilgrimage to Ana and Shirley's West London flat in 1993, filmmaker Lucy Thane captured Ana explaining the significance of the Pure Freude copy of the LP: "The German version is more like we wanted it, because it's silver here [pointing to the type on the back] and the Portuguese version is black." Ana gifted a Pure Freude copy of the record to Kathi that day.)[34]

Düsseldorf series, 1981

The Raincoats have always returned to Düsseldorf, and they meet up with Carmen whenever she's in London. Each time, it's like no time has passed at all. When The Raincoats reunited in 1994, in addition to gigs in the UK and the US, along with a handful of other spots, they did a special, intimate performance at Carmen's fiftieth birthday party in Düsseldorf. Over the years, Carmen dissolved Pure Freude (the last official release was a reissue of an Imi Knoebel flexi disc in 1998), but she couldn't quit the music business entirely.

It was Shirley to whom Carmen turned for advice when she was approached by an American label about a large-scale project that Conny Plank was set to produce. "It wasn't just me helping The Raincoats, it was both ways," Carmen says, referring back to her early financial support of the group. "A special kind of friendship. I trusted Shirley in a way I would not trust anyone else." She remained so close with The Raincoats that her daughters got to know them and fell in love themselves with The Raincoats' cover of "Lola." That song was such a central part of their lives that Carmen's daughter Stella named her first daughter Lola. "It was really and only because of The Raincoats," Carmen says.

August 2024 marked Carmen's eightieth birthday, her and Imi's fiftieth wedding anniversary, and "some other very important dates that all added up to two hundred," Shirley explains. It wouldn't have been a party without The Raincoats there, and Ana, Gina, and Anne [Wood] played another special and private show in Düsseldorf.

What Carmen has always loved, and still loves, about The Raincoats is that, "When you think you have found your way in a song, they make a break and take a different, sharp, direction. It is so unusual," she says, "and don't forget about those lyrics!" In some ways, their music has always been the very definition of punk for Carmen, but also something more. "Something with so much power," she says.

FAN MAIL

In the first life of The Raincoats, they received a wide range of handwritten fan mail, mostly sent to the Rough Trade shop, all now handmarked by Ana indicating that The Raincoats had sent a reply. Many came from repeat writers. Some letters were sent to the entire band, others to specific members. While a couple of the letter writers were famous themselves, most weren't.

Keith, a frequent writer from Manchester: "I like the raincoats [sic]. I wrote the name on a desk at school in a French lesson and a teacher caught me and made me sandpaper it off. (he's a CUNT.)"

Ali in London: "Ever since I wrote to you last, I keep meeting Raincoats fans and they are all waiting for the album and more gigs. Please hurry, we're getting desperate."

Alastair from Aberdeen: "I heard you on [the] John Peel show a while back and thought you sounded fantastic. I eventually tracked down your LP two days ago and it is the greatest thing that ever happened to my life—it's incredible. It has just replaced Velvet Underground *Live 1969* as my favourite lp ever, I especially like 'no side', 'off duty trip' and 'Lola' but all the tracks are pretty orgasmic ... If you are in Aberdeen please come to the address above where a growing faction of the Raincoats Army will be only too willing to take you out to Radars for at least 4 Radarburgers and a least 4 french fries [sic] ... Please, please write back—I'm waiting with bated breath."

Michael from Bristol: "Dear Ana, Do you think you're commercial enough to become famous?"

John from Cambridge enclosed "a 'personist' poem," and explained, "which means it ought to be read over the telephone, but I hadn't the line ... I'll deliver it during my reading at the Poetry Festival on 11th June." The freeform verse included lyrics from various Raincoats tracks off the self-titled LP.

Ali from London, writing again: "It would be best if the band remain mostly unwanted and only cater for a small audience so as not to smooth the rough edges ... Let's have more violin."

Greil Marcus, longtime writer for *Creem*, the *Village Voice*, and *Rolling Stone*, sent a postcard: "Thought you and friends would be interested to know that at his PiL press conference yesterday John Lydon announced The Raincoats were the only group worth listening to—aside from PiL, of course."

Philippa, who gained notoriety for her fandom, and was nicknamed the "Raincoat Humanoid" by the Rough Trade staff: "My boss—who's getting on for 60—said she liked 'Animal Rhapsody.' (Raincoats appeal to all ages ... I'm going to get together an all femal [sic] vocal trio doing all the Raincoats Hits ('shouting out loud shoobe doo') to counter all the female backing oohs and ahs (Harmonies?) that are plastered on everything at the moment. Going to call it summut like THE RAINCOATETTES Tee Hee or even (gasp) Martha Humanoid and the Raincoatellas Tee Hee Hee Ha Ha Ha ... The official Raincoats fan club has just decided to hold a Raincoats Look alike competition. Large furry hats optional." (Teenage Philippa's mom often dropped her off at gigs in a DIY coat she'd made with her own Raincoats design on the back. "I just arrived at exactly the right age," she says now and smiles. Indeed, music became her life: She went on to open Piccadilly Records in Manchester.)

Gary from Bournemouth: "I consider myself a real fan and I appreciate (I think) the word 'feminism.' Thanks."

Clare from Preston, writing to ask questions for her fanzine *Reading for Pleasure*: "All the lads in Preston love Ingrid, they think she's an unbelievable drummer ... Work hard + make me proud of you."

ON FEMINISM

Even when The Raincoats weren't playing official RAS gigs, they were rocking against sexism. But the terms "feminist" and "feminism" weren't always self-claimed ones for every band member. The Raincoats were all feminists in the sense that they were in favor of, and took significant steps themselves toward equality of all genders. Certainly, the music press used the term in identifying them, both in ameliorative and anxious ways. But the terminology also brought tensions to the fabric of the group.

Given Ana's experiences in Portugal during the Estado Novo dictatorship, it shouldn't come as a shock that she already knew about—indeed, lived—feminism and wholeheartedly ascribed to its aims. Yet she often pushed against being pigeonholed under any single label—"feminist," or "queer," for example—while Vicky welcomed the identity of a feminist band. Since she'd joined The Raincoats from Jam Today, she understood feminism to be a powerful descriptor. Ana saw it as limiting. Vicky came to the band eager to discuss feminism and feminist politics. Ana sometimes found that frustrating, given that she wasn't in need of an education. "Sometimes I'd feel like piggy in the middle," Gina laments, wanting to declare herself a feminist while also wanting to maintain the deep friendship and bond she had with both Ana and Vicky.

Ana suggests that the tension she and Vicky experienced during the first life of The Raincoats stemmed from their distinct notions of what makes music political. "She told me my lyrics were too personal," Ana remembers, "and although we were fond of each other to a certain extent, we didn't see eye to eye.

Gina singing in Acklam Hall, 1979

Although some of the songs Caroline wrote, that Vicky brought to us, were obviously political, they were also very emotional songs. To me, everything is political, and you don't need to be overtly political." Vicky often felt that being explicitly political was a way to promote the realities of what feminism promised, but she didn't think it should necessarily be obvious in all The Raincoats' songs. Vicky says: "As a person, feminism informed the way I did everything, whether it was playing in a band or anything else. Yeah, I was a feminist, and when I joined The Raincoats, there was a bit of aversion to using the word feminist. I was quite happy to use the word, and I think I brought that to the group, what we called then a socialist feminist perspective." She continues, "But I have never felt that lyrics have to be overtly political to have an impact, quite the reverse. Nothing is more dull than preaching in a song. There are other ways of putting a point across."

"Writing overtly feminist or political lyrics isn't enough for me," Ana says. "I think it's more powerful when they portray a more personal experience, like Gina's lyrics in 'Feminist Song,' but I don't think Vicky really understood my point of view. Fair enough. Each person has different needs, but I think that was always the big difference there." Moreover, Vicky adds, "The real feminist aspect of the group was that it was non-hierarchical, the fact that we were collaborative and didn't have a leader." Even among feminists, disagreements occur. The fact that Ana and Vicky didn't always see eye to eye, or agree about how to get their respective ideas across, reveals their humanity; they'd had different experiences, and while they saw the world in similar ways, they also saw it differently. "We were all fighting our own ways through the world," Gina reflects, "and we probably could have all been more supportive of one another, but I don't think we even knew how then."

The disagreements surrounding feminism in the early Raincoats years reveal the true democratic nature and freedom of the band: They could disagree and still make the powerful, experimental music that has been preserved for all time on their releases from 1979 to 1983.

Says Gina, "The Raincoats have always been out on a limb, at odds with the world, not fitting in anywhere really, and that was both very powerful and very difficult. I wanted to belong but I knew I needed to fight for the right things, to do with the way we dressed, the way we made the songs, the way we did the artwork, and the way we did 'business.' It was all very important to be done just as we wanted it."

ON MISOGYNY

Although The Raincoats might not have always agreed on the manifestation of the "feminist" ethos within the band, they were united in their opposition to sexism, misogyny, and the patriarchal impulses that ran rampant in the seventies and eighties (and into the present).

In 1979, The Raincoats were pelted with beer at a Manchester gig at the Russell Club, one of the famous (or infamous) "Factory" nights put on by Tony Wilson, Rob Gretton, and Alan Erasmus of Factory Records. Despite the fact that women worked to make that club run, and female artists sometimes performed on stage, the atmosphere wasn't necessarily a welcoming one. Ana remembers that gig as "particularly hostile."

In November 1981, at a Birmingham Town Hall "Jobs for Youth" show, The Raincoats were blitzed with objects by misogynist punters. "I'm not going to have things thrown at me," Ana says defiantly. "I don't know why we were asked to play—maybe because we were political, it was for 'Jobs for Youth,' fighting against Margaret Thatcher's policies." (Thatcher had been elected prime minister in 1979, which began more than a decade of Conservative policies in the UK.) Yet opponents to Thatcherism fighting against Conservative politics weren't necessarily aligned with feminism (and, in fact, often weren't). Ana's sentiments hearken back to Lucy Whitman's thinking around the creation of RAS. "It was full

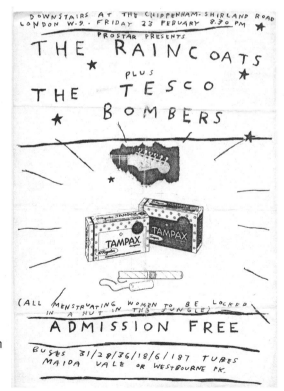

Flyer for a Raincoats gig at The Chippenham with a playful take on sexism

of fifteen-year-old boys, full of testosterone," Ana says, describing the show. "They started shouting at us and then started throwing things, such as tomatoes." Ana had her suitcase of instruments open up on the stage, and one of the tomatoes struck it. The mark is still there. "The second night was even worse," she says, "because they came equipped, knowing we were playing again. They threw Zippo lighters, tomatoes, and coins at us." It was a wake-up call to The Raincoats, who realized punk venues were not a so-called "marketplace of ideas" where egalitarian, determined, and smart voices have the ability to win out. "You can't feel the presence of people who are actually enjoying what you're doing. You're just feeling the nasty presence, which is a shame," Ana laments. That second night, the teenage misogynists booed and continued to assault the band. Gina was keen to skip her songs, so the set went very fast. "It was scary and I didn't want to stand at the mic and sing my heart out to lighters and objects flying at my face," Gina says.

After a series of shows in the UK with The Slits, Delta 5, Young Marble Giants, and The Pop Group, The Raincoats traveled to Paris to play on March 26, 1980 with The Slits. The five of them—Ana, Gina, Vicky, Ingrid, and Shirley—were walking back to their hotel together when the danger of being a woman on a street at night reared its wretched face. "This car drove up alongside us," Shirley recalls. The Raincoats immediately hailed a taxi "to protect ourselves," Ana explains, when the driver of the unknown car became violent. "This guy tried to pull Vicky into the car," Shirley exclaims, still horrified at the memory. "She spat at him, and we were pulling her, and he was talking in French to the taxi driver, trying to get him on his side. We managed to persuade the taxi driver to believe us, to take us away from the situation because Ana speaks some French, but *Vicky was about to be kidnapped in a bloody car!* Just some guy driving up." Vicky also remembers the horrific incident and says, "We were scared and had to run as fast as we could to get away. It felt like a serious assault, really frightening."

"Italy was pretty bad, too," Ana says, "and Portugal used to be quite bad, as well." Shirley jumps in with a particular memory: "We were in the middle of a park in Rome [in a boat on the lake]," just a couple weeks after the incident in Paris. This time, The

LIFE NUMBER 1

Raincoats were playing with Swell Maps for two nights. They had a bit of downtime. "And these guys encircled us," Shirley says, "throwing big rocks to try to sink the boat. They didn't know who we were—they just knew we were women." Ana quickly follows up, describing various memories in which men on foot and in cars would spit at The Raincoats walking on the street, often before or after a gig. "I think there must be something threatening about seeing women together who look like they decide what they want to look like and do what they want to do and be what they want to be."

"I don't think the misogyny The Slits faced was as commonplace for us," Vicky says. "Just general disparagement from certain quarters, especially from guys who thought we were scruffy, unappealing, unsexy, nonconforming." Yet even the seemingly lesser amount of shit the Raincoats put up with wasn't nothing. Vicky continues, "I do remember being quite shaken by some aggression." She describes a Raincoats tour in the UK where "one of the roadies thought it was really funny to tape phallic images to my amp, so when I came on stage one night and went to turn up my amp, I'd see these pictures. A kind of power play. I'm sure he intended it as some kind of joke, but I did not think it was funny."

The Raincoats' responses to what they faced reveal their lasting influence. Charles Hayward describes a memory from Germany when The Raincoats weren't able to bring their "totally feminist, totally cool" live sound engineer, Martin Harrison. The in-house sound guy condescendingly questioned Ana's requests. Why do it her way? "And she said, just so simply," Charles remembers, "'Because it inspires me.' And how the hell can you argue with that? I thought that then, and I thought it again more recently when my daughter dealt with something similar ... The Raincoats are even bigger than the sound—you don't need to know about The Raincoats to be in a reality where The Raincoats made change and created all the good parts of the reality now, where women have confidence and know they can be loud inside previously male-dominated space. My daughter knows that, and women will continue to know it in the future. That's a testimony to what The Raincoats did."

THE MUSIC PRESS

Writing for *Sounds* on December 11, 1976, after the so-called birth of punk but shortly before the inception of The Raincoats, Vivien Goldman described the relative dearth of female musicians, implying a need for new role models to come forth. Like a directive, she wrote: "When women perform a professional, hard-rocking set, with no concessions to female stereotypes, they're an automatic threat. They're a threat to men because they challenge male supremacy in a citadel that's never been attacked before; they're a threat to women who've perhaps never dared acknowledge that THEY want to be onstage doing the energising instead of watching their boyfriends doing it, in passive admiration."[35]

The Raincoats heeded the call. But in doing so, they also made obvious the pervasive misogyny in the pages of the music press. Nobody cared that the Sex Pistols weren't classically trained musicians, or that the Ramones were mostly three-chord wonders. When reviews came in for Raincoats' albums and live performances, they were often depicted as amateurs who didn't know how to play their instruments rather than experimental artists, breaking down boundaries.

"Male journalists were totally threatened by women performers who were clearly not trying to be attractive, for whom that was not part of their agenda," Lucy Whitman emphasizes.

One of those journalists was Dave McCullough, the writer about whom Ana wrote with aversion in her 1979 tour diary. He trashed The Raincoats in a review of their first LP, titled *Shrieks from the Grove!*, before it had even been officially released. It hardly makes sense to give published space to his language, but it's notable that it wasn't reserved for The Raincoats alone. He also had choice words for The Slits, Kleenex, and other punk bands comprised of women. Ana wasn't having any of it. She drafted a letter to the editor:

> I am writing this letter just to tell you what a bunch of ununderstanding shortsighted unintelligent people (i.e., men, because women seem to have no part in your "wonderful crusade") you have collaborating in the paper of which you are the editor.

Ana on the run at the University of Reading, 1978

What is it there is about Dave McCullough that allows him to have the job and power of using a paper to write to so many people about his lies and misinterpretations of somebody's work and honest commitment? Was it just stupidity that inspired him to write what he did about our record? Or is it revenge for us having refused an interview with him a few months ago?

When he says that our record was lying on his desk for a week without him even noticing it, is he wickedly showing disinterest because he was angry for having not been sent one record except when he specifically asked for one urgently because he wanted to review it?

If he was a good writer, he would have, instead of just politics, talked about our music, and in what way those politics are reflected on it. He did it in the way he accuses us of doing also in our interviews. Well he should know by now that what you read in an interview is what the interviewer chooses (as well as the editor) to put out. Why didn't he say in what aspects those politics are reflected in our music? Is it the words? Has he really heard them I wonder? Or is it the structure of the instrumental and vocal aspects?

I could talk about many more things to prove him wrong, but either you have the capacity to understand what we talk about and how, or you agree with Dave McCullough and my time would be totally wasted.

Do I have to hope for a better "Sounds"?

Ana da Silva of The Raincoats

The *Sounds* editor published Ana's letter. A few weeks later, frequent writer of fan mail Sue Emerick sent a note via the post: "I was really pleased to read your letter of retaliation to Dave McCulloughs [sic] degrading album review, I felt totally humiliated when I read it, so I can imagine how you all felt."

More fan mail echoed Sue's sentiments. Lou Stein from Cambridgeshire wrote: "Dear Ana, I loved your letter ... personally I find Mr D. McCullough as convincing as a Nixon biography. Lots of love and plastic flowers."

The next *Sounds* piece on The Raincoats was a full-page write-up by Vivien, who'd since become features editor. She wrote, "The mere fact that the Raincoats are expressing an undiluted woman's view is a piquant change." To her readers, she posed a familiar question: "But how many women are doing it, being in bands?" The Raincoats told her, at the time, "There's not a single woman drummer to be had ... Women just have to be twice as good and twice as pushy." In closing, Vivien underscored that, simply by existing as a band, "The Raincoats have put their lives on the line; they've got to continue to be twice as good and twice as pushy."

LIFE NUMBER 1

In the present, Vivien recalls getting "quite a few objections" from her *Sounds* colleagues when she wanted to feature The Raincoats and other female-fronted bands. "I always remember two-thirds of the guys were like, 'Why should we cover women?' The line was always, 'Women don't buy music, women don't make music, women aren't interested in music, so why should we cover them?'"

🕺💃

The Raincoats received loads of reviews over the course of the band's first life, and many were great. Some full-page, some blurbs that could fit in the palm of a hand. Ana and Shirley clipped the reviews on both sides of the spectrum and everything in between. Hundreds in total.

But Ana wasn't necessarily clipping because The Raincoats were taking cues from the music press. She was creating an archive, and one without a hierarchy. She pasted fanzines alongside pieces from *NME* and *Sounds*, even tiny runs from distant writers whose zines may have reached only a dozen people—democracy inherent in the archive.

For Gina, it was important to be visible in the music press because "they were kind of the Bible of us, of the young people in the music scene. And in London, that was what we all related to." The papers created a type of sonic community among readers that remains evident in retrospect. It wasn't necessarily about the "truth" of the articles, but the circles they drew among publics through their domestic circulation and export.

Clippings from the music press are vivid reminders that no music news story is ever the complete story; it's a product of the interviewer's questions, the interviewee's mood and memory on the day of the conversation, the editor's excisions and revisions, and final cuts before anything goes to print. In many instances, what appears in print might not be what the writer intended, as Jane Garcia explains of the extensive, full-page Raincoats feature she wrote for *New Music News* in 1980. Her article, which appeared in the July 19, 1980 issue with several of Shirley's photos of the band, was titled "Never Mind the Gannex: The Impermeable Jane Garcia Hangs Out With The Raincoats."[36] Jane mailed The Raincoats a seven-page typed facsimile of the interview she originally sent to her editor with a note:

> This is the full, unexpurgated version of an article I wrote for 'New Music News' on The Raincoats which was sub-edited by necessity but got a bit chewed-up in the process, cutting out what I consider to be particularly important and relevant points.
> As the final printed piece rather shifted the emphases and intentions of the original article, I thought I'd make copies of the original available to anyone who might be interested in reading it.
> 'New Music News' know about this and agree that I should do it because the problem arose out of a misunderstanding over what I particularly wanted left in and what wasn't THAT important. Anyway, it's a bloody good paper, so ... Lots of love from Jane Garcia xxx[37]

But the press is always good for something. In the May 24, 1980 issue of *Sounds*, John Lydon went on a rant about all the "two-faced, greedy, pointless hypocrites who are just long and confused," naming The Clash in particular as a band that "will fit into any mould that will get their faces in the papers ... or their voice on the radio." When he was done, the interviewer asked, *Is there anyone or anything you do respect?* The first four words out of his mouth: "I like The Raincoats." And he didn't stop there. On the cover of *Trouser Press* a month later, he couldn't keep quiet about The Raincoats: "It's all over now ... Rock 'n' roll is shit. It's dismal. Grand-dad danced to it. I'm not interested in it ... I think music has reached an all-time low—except for The Raincoats." Even as recently as 2009, the former Sex Pistol and PiL frontman continued to sing the praises of The Raincoats. Speaking to the *Guardian*, he listed The Raincoats' self-titled LP as the sole record he'd choose to represent "the punk years."

For many young readers, press surrounding The Raincoats sparked their own interest in the band and, occasionally, in writing about music. Shirley refers to Laurence Bell, cofounder of Domino Records, who interviewed The Raincoats when he was only fourteen. Thurston Moore of Sonic Youth remembers being "really intrigued by The Raincoats in the British weeklies," which he and his bandmates would frequently steal from the now-defunct Manhattan institution Gem Spa. And *Rolling Stone* writer Rob Sheffield says steadfastly, "I can tell you the first sentence I read about The Raincoats. It was in this beautiful thing, which is the *Rolling Stone Illustrated History of Rock & Roll*, the 1980 edition . . ."

That Greil Marcus piece he's referring to is what led The Raincoats to ask Greil to write the liner notes for *The Kitchen Tapes*. The rest is history.

"BEAT THE BLUES"

Although The Raincoats weren't always obvious about being political, as Ana emphasizes routinely, *everything is political*. And their vivid presence at left-wing partisan events made clear to anyone where their politics lay.

On June 15, 1980, The Raincoats were part of a large lineup at Alexandra Palace for a critical benefit gig: "Beat the Blues," an anti-Tory festival and rally. The *Guardian* ran a short piece on it the Saturday prior, calling it "Britain's brightest summer festival." Shirley organized the event along with Dick O'Dell, the then manager of The Slits and The Pop Group.

It was important to get news of the festival out to the public because, just a week before it was set to happen, the Independent Broadcasting Authority (IBA) banned radio advertisements for the event. The *Daily Telegraph* reported, "Under the IBA Act, the authority is bound to ban advertisements from any organization whose aim are 'wholly or mainly of a religious or political nature.'" The IBA determined that ads for "Beat the Blues" were of "a whole or mainly political nature" and thus could not be aired.

The Raincoats performed with the Au Pairs, Essential Logic, John Cooper Clarke, The Pop Group, and The Slits. The radio presenter John Peel served as "compere." Digging in with its political position, the organizers advertised that anyone who was "unwaged" could purchase a ticket for half the price (£1.50 at the time).

MINIATURES

In 1980, Ana got tired of answering all the same questions about The Raincoats, so she made a miniature booklet to be sold at Rough Trade. With dimensions of 10.5cm by 7cm, it included drawings and text by Ana and lyrics by the band. An emerald green cover in Ana's handwriting read, simply, "The Raincoats Booklet." Eight pieces of paper were used inside, measuring about 14cm by 10.5cm each, stapled in the middle and folded to create the 32-page booklet. Ana reproduced the pages at Better Badges, accompanied by Marlene Marder from Kleenex who remembered the place as having a bad smell. The booklets were sold at the Rough Trade shop for 20p, and fans could also write with a SAE and payment to purchase one.

In the years since Ana created *The Raincoats Booklet*, it has become a prized and sought-after item. Recognizing the treasure it is, Ana will gift a copy to new friends who voice an interest, or to other artists who've been coveting one for decades (she still has some copies left).

Thurston Moore of Sonic Youth remembers finding a copy of the green booklet at a book fair. "Something like twenty years ago," he says, "and I've always held on to it, it's a pride and joy." When he first met The Raincoats officially, years later, he asked them each to sign it, "and they did, really tiny on the back here." Thurston holds up the book and points to the small signatures. "I'm really an uber Raincoats fan."

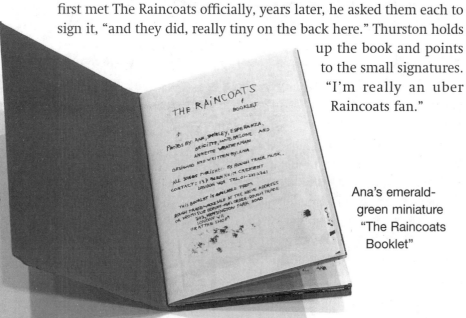

Ana's emerald-green miniature "The Raincoats Booklet"

LIFE NUMBER 1

Tobi Vail of Bikini Kill remembers receiving one in a package from Ana in the 1990s. They'd become pen pals and "being pen pals was a big deal then," Tobi smiles. "We started writing letters back and forth, and she wrote to me at my parents' house." Tobi still has the little green booklet, naturally.

Jane McKeown and other members of her band, Lung Leg, opened for The Raincoats in Glasgow in 1994 after spending years as massive fans themselves. "And then Ana showed up and had a little green booklet for each of us!" Jane exclaims. "I've moved house so many times since then, but that's the one thing I always make sure I still have."

Rob Sheffield of *Rolling Stone* got his personal copy of the booklet in 2017 when he was out to dinner with the band in New York. "Ana just handed me this," he says, referring to the object on display behind him. "I was like, 'You've got to be kidding me! I haven't earned this!'"

Forty years after Ana first made the booklet, the punk artists' literary magazine пионер ("pioneer") published a series of indispensable artist artifacts—Ana's green booklet was included.

There's just something about the miniature form. Ana crafted the folded miniature booklet for inclusion in the Pure Freude copies of *Odyshape*, and in the decades that followed, she reveled in making miniature artist proofs of CD booklet reissues. There's nothing diminutive about The Raincoats, or about their outsized influence. Yet the miniature remains a vital element of Ana's practice, one that speaks to the intimacy of her art.

The miniature is a form that hearkens back to different periods of historical time, from miniature portraiture of the Mughal Empire to a period of American popularity for miniature portraits, largely from the mid-eighteenth through to the mid-nineteenth centuries. The latter, in particular, were designed as markedly personal objects, "intended to be worn or carried, often close to one's heart."[38] The miniature has often been understood as a talisman, an object that "can be easily held and worn." As poet Susan Stewart suggests, "A reduction in dimensions does not produce a corresponding reduction in significance; indeed, the gemlike properties of the miniature book and the feats of micrographia make these forms especially suitable 'containers' of aphoristic and didactic thought."[39] The miniature becomes monumental.

In her book on The Raincoats' self-titled LP for the 33⅓ series, Jenn Pelly also plays on the heightened merit of the miniature. Even before The Raincoats were involved, the 33⅓ series was itself an established study in miniatures: Content-wise, each book focuses on a single album, and the size and shape of them make them pocket-sized, not unlike the copy of Pablo Neruda's *Canto General* that Che Guevara is said to have kept faithfully in his back pocket. In a playful and reflexive move, Jenn draws attention to the miniature nature of "The Raincoats Booklet" by reproducing whole-page excerpts from it, reduced in size, in her 33⅓ book—miniatures within a miniature.[40]

TR3

The Raincoats were always destined for New York City, and the downtown venues were the perfect places for their sound to reach open ears. Their first NYC gig was set for Tier 3, known as TR3, a venue run by Hilary Jaeger.

"I can still feel the excitement of New York in the pit of my stomach," Gina smiles. "We had this idea of what it would be like, and it was even more peculiar and more special than I ever imagined it could be. It was a kind of freedom, New York."

The Raincoats, along with Caroline Scott and Vicky's friend Annie, got picked up from the airport "in a big white van with a hole in the floor," Gina remembers, "and brought to Hilary Jaeger's mom's place on Second Avenue." Hilary and Angela Jaeger, New York City born and bred sisters, had already established roots in the UK before Hilary returned home to start TR3. They'd both traveled to England for school—Hilary in rural Norfolk and Angela in London. In Norfolk from 1976 to 1977 or thereabouts, Hilary was living "without running water or electricity." "It sounds like London squat living," she laughs, but it was a world away from

LIFE NUMBER 1

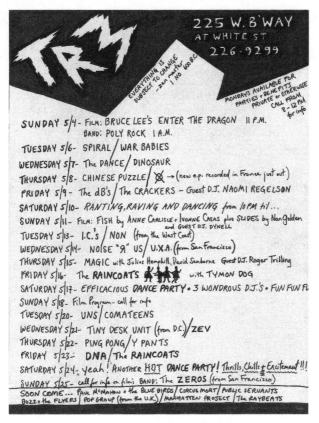

Hilary Jaeger's hand-drawn flyer for TR3 shows, featuring The Raincoats

that community. "I was up in the boondocks! So I'd go down to London to get a sense of the burgeoning punk scene since I couldn't even listen to the radio (no electricity)." Angela went to London in the fall of 1978 to follow The Clash and The Slits. That's when she became aware of The Raincoats and a new model of DIY punk—one that didn't sound like the Sex Pistols or Ramones but took the DIY ethos and made it new. Hilary and Angela were enrapt in the DNA of punk.

Hilary came home to her mom's apartment in the East Village, on Second Avenue and 11th Street overlooking St. Marks Place. "It was a great building," Hilary says, "one of the few pre-war elevator buildings with a view to the north of the Empire State Building and the Chrysler Building." She needed a job after getting back from England, and she heard about a "restaurant-slash-jazz-club" opening in what's now Tribeca (at the time, simply "Downtown"). Sometime around December 1978 or January '79, Hilary started waitressing there. "They were trying to do lunch shifts, but they just didn't have the people coming in. No one was around midday except the people working in the strange factories nearby and the Tombs [the infamous New York City jail] ... it was really dead," she says. When you're filling up a restaurant and music venues mostly with secretaries and jailers, you've gotta start thinking out of the box. "The owners were griping about the money situation, and at the time everybody I knew was in a band and forming bands," Hilary recalls. "So I proposed booking bands and they agreed."

Hilary and Jim Geiger, the future TR3 bartender, started booking bands together. The owners told Hilary and Jim they'd need $500 from each of them up front "to cover back rent and electric," due to the restaurant's financial struggles. Hilary and Jim agreed, paid the cash—for which they were never fully repaid—and the now-famous downtown venue TR3 got started. The restaurant was already named "Tier 3," simply because the space had three levels, but Hilary "started calling it TR3 because I thought Tier 3 was such a stupid name," she laughs.

The space was actually two buildings that had been combined. When you'd walk in, there was a bar to the left that had been salvaged from the Mercer Arts Center. "It was really beautiful, classic," Hilary says.

The Mercer Arts Center, in Greenwich Village, was a performance and rehearsal space structurally adjacent to the Broadway Central Hotel. It was a location synonymous with the burgeoning glam punk scene in the City. The New York Dolls were Tuesday-night regulars, Jonathan Richman and The Modern Lovers frequented the venue, and it's where Suicide played their earliest shows. Eric Emerson and the Magic Tramps were rehearsing there when the structure started to shake. There'd already been cracks appearing in the walls and the facade had been "bulging," according to reports—sure signs of impending disaster. Just after 5 p.m. on August 3, 1973, the adjacent structures started to fall. Emerson and the Magic Tramps reportedly had to

LIFE NUMBER 1

run for their lives. Alan Vega said, "It looked like a bomb had been dropped." After the collapse, new venues like CBGB and Hurrah became central for burgeoning downtown punk and no wave, with subsequent venues like TR3, the Mudd Club, and Danceteria emerging.[41]

Beyond the salvaged bar at TR3, there was a long, low-ceilinged room to the left with a brick wall between—where the buildings had been joined together, and where the bands played. "As many people remember, initially, we didn't have a stage," Hilary says, "and when bands played, people were stepping on their toes." They soon built one, but it was only about a foot off the ground, given the low ceiling. "If you jumped on the stage, you could bang your head," Hilary notes. No big deal. The "sound guy" was also in that area, along with a DJ booth and a mural painted by Jean-Michel Basquiat. There was no separate entrance to the gig area. On the second floor, TR3 had what they called the "disco room" with a DJ booth and some plexiglass. "I remember Cynthia Sley of Bush Tetras telling me they used to wrestle up there all the time," Hilary laughs. The whole space had about 250 capacity, "but people *packed in*," Hilary remembers, "full to absolute capacity for sure." (Cynthia Sley and Pat Place of Bush Tetras both remember playing with The Raincoats at TR3, but Hilary's diary reveals time is playing tricks on them; they actually played with The Raincoats at Brownies in 1996. Nonetheless, Cynthia and Pat gush about how much they loved The Raincoats sound and how important it was to have more women playing experimental music in New York in those days. "That in itself was cool," Cynthia says, and Pat agrees, "We really liked their music, and we really liked them, too.")

    Cultural critic and member of Jim Jarmusch's no wave band the Del-Byzanteens, Lucy Sante, laughs, "TR3 was like our living room!" The entire downtown crowd, and members of all the no wave bands, saw it as a home away from home. In its short lifetime, thousands of people saw American and British musicians who reshaped the sonic history of downtown New York. The Raincoats were scheduled to play two nights in May 1980.

    Hilary first heard The Raincoats when she bought the *Fairytale* EP at 99 Records on Bleecker Street. "After that single came out,

I remember being mesmerized and playing it nonstop," she says. So when the possibility of bringing The Raincoats over from London to play TR3 came up, Hilary quickly made it happen. She received a letter from Dick O'Dell, then manager of The Slits, in January 1980 (at that point, Dick had already helped get The Slits over to TR3, and he and Hilary had become friends). He reported that he'd been at a Slits show, and, "The Raincoats played too with their new drummer, Ingrid ... and it was brilliant. Best show I've been to for ages. Vicky (Raincoats) played violin on 'Adventures Close to Home' and the sound was great (pat on the back)." Dick put Hilary in touch with Shirley, and they went from there.

On Tuesday, May 6, 1980, Hilary sent a letter to London on lined stationery with a grayscale image of an egret in the bottom-left corner:[42]

> Dear Shirley,
> It was good to talk to you on the phone last week—Everyone at TR3 is very much looking forward to hearing the Raincoats at our club. Enclosed is the contract you sent me—I hope everything is in order. Also, I was wondering if the band needs equipment, and if so, what exactly is required. If there is need for a lot or all of their equipment we can either rent it, or perhaps, to avoid that cost—book another band with the Raincoats so that they can share some equipment. Let me know what you think, and if you can call me and let me know exactly what's needed—I can start seeking some of it out. I may be able to borrow a few things as well. The best time to reach me is between 11AM + 7PM NYC time. I will try + call Rough Trade this week, so hopefully we can sort some of this out over the phone.
> I've also arranged for places to stay for the band. I'm still not sure of for how long these places are available—but I myself can offer the spare room here at my mother's place (where I live) for about a week. Please assure The Raincoats (+ you!) that they are most welcome at the places I've found—and that I think they'll find the people they'll be staying with to be most anxious to make their visit comfortable and enjoyable. A couple of them (Amy + Mike) shared their home with the Slits when they were in town and

LIFE NUMBER 1

it worked out real well. As I said, everyone is most enthusiastic about having the Raincoats come to NYC.

The promo stuff you sent was just fine. If there are any posters, badges, promo records etc. available, they would be much appreciated. But I do know the cost of sending these things is pretty high, so perhaps you could bring it over with you, and I could pick them up when you arrive. Of course, these things are not necessary, although a poster or two could help with publicity—it's most a matter of there being a lot of Raincoats fans among the staff at TR3!

Anyway—I'll be in touch again soon—and look forward to meeting you (you are coming over with the band I hope).

My best to everyone at Rough Trade, and to the Raincoats.

Love, Hilary

The plan was for the band to stay with Hilary's mom on Second Avenue. "Everyone from England stayed there," Hilary laughs. "The Slits stayed there. Memorably, Ari [Up] put her head through the glass of the French doors. The Raincoats stayed there at least twice, in 1980 and again when they came back for *The Kitchen Tapes* in 1982. By the second Raincoats stay, I'd moved, so they spent a lot of time with my mom." Ana ultimately stayed in touch with Hilary's mom for years to come, up until her death in 1991. It wasn't so much that Hilary's mom was a fan of the sounds emanating from downtown; she was simply a supporter of both her daughters. "She did it mostly as a favor to me, but I do remember taking her to a show at CBGB, and she came down to TR3 a few times, but no, she wasn't playing Raincoats singles on her own," Hilary laughs. "She was just that kind of mom who would do that for me, and The Raincoats were such likeable people and good guests. I don't think she was aware of how significant it all was, but I don't think any of us were at the time."

Their mom liked a lot of the bands—as people, if not a consumer of their music—who stayed in her apartment, and Angela remembers her mom speaking of The Slits, Delta 5, and Young Marble Giants in particular. "But, you know," she says, "she liked The Raincoats the most."

Corresponding with Shirley across the pond before The Raincoats' first NYC visit, Hilary and TR3 entered into a contract with the band for two shows in May. The plan was for The Raincoats to play the first night with Tymon Dogg and the second with DNA, May 16 and 23. "Joy Division was due to play the next date," Hilary says, thumbing through her diary.

Hilary's diary, Monday, May 12, 1980: "The Raincoats have arrived today. Manny and I drove out to the airport in the pouring, drenching rain, smokestacks and factories enveloped in a wet Queens mist. Gina and Ana are staying here with me. I look forward to The Raincoats being here in the same house." Gina and Ana slept in Angela's bedroom while she was in London, both during the 1980 gigs and again when they came back in 1982 to record *The Kitchen Tapes* (Vicky, Caroline, and Ingrid slept elsewhere). Angela did fly home in May 1980 and made it to one of The Raincoats' gigs, but she didn't stay long and was soon back in London.

The downtown scene wasn't necessarily built on feminist principles, but it was one in which women had outsized power to influence the sounds of the city. From Thurston Moore's perspective, there were dozens of male musicians coming from a background of "learning how to play like Clapton," while so many experimental female artists had no available precursors. While that presented different kinds of challenges, in Thurston's mind, it meant that those female artists were able to take a liberating approach to their instruments, to learn to play them in new ways that ultimately created a new language. That's what he was thinking about when he first heard The Raincoats, and that's why he went to see them at TR3 in May 1980.

Kim Gordon wasn't at the show, a fact she laments. "I should have been there," she says. "I don't know why I wasn't."

But this is all pre-Sonic Youth. In fact, Sonic Youth might not have happened otherwise. Thurston, mesmerized, watched The Raincoats play. Members of his band at the time, The Coachmen, were standing outside TR3 having a shouting match with Michael Gira, who'd go on to form the experimental band Swans. Thurston wanted to see The Raincoats finish their set, but the other Coachmen weren't interested in the music. One of his bandmates, says Thurston, "said something like, 'This is horrible, they don't even play their instruments the right way!' He was jealous they were getting all this attention, and when they ended with their cover of 'Lola,' he complained, 'They can't even play "Lola" for Christ's sake!' He'd come out of this world where you learned to play Kinks songs perfectly," Thurston explains, "as they'd been written, and The Raincoats' way of playing was a *big change*." For Thurston, it was just the change he needed. "After seeing the Raincoats, I left The Coachmen and started Sonic Youth. I can only blame The Raincoats and their 'Lola.'"

By December 1980, Hilary received an eviction notice from the owners and had to close down Tier 3. Hilary and Jim never had an easy financial relationship with the venue's owners. The owners wanted more of the door takings, even though they were getting all the bar money, and then they pushed Hilary to stop booking bands on the weekends and bring in only DJs. It was also difficult competing with tech-laden venues like Danceteria. Hilary and Jim briefly considered moving TR3 to another space, but nothing panned out. Hilary took the record collection from TR3 and left.

HURRAH

On that first trip to New York City, The Raincoats played the club Hurrah just after their TR3 debut, a show booked by Ruth Polsky.

Ruth Polsky and Hilary Jaeger were friends, but more importantly, something like ardent compatriots as two of the only prominent women booking bands in New York City. Hilary remembers the first time she met Ruth. "Why don't you come over to my place on Houston?" Ruth had asked her, adding, "We're both women booking bands, and there aren't many of us." Ruth was really welcoming to Hilary as she was starting up TR3, and a few months later, Ann Magnuson did the same thing for her. "We're some of the only women," Hilary remembers Ann saying. *"I'm doing Club 57, and you're doing TR3. Why don't you come over?" There was an indelible bond among women doing this work and recognizing the need to support one another.*

While Hilary and Shirley were in touch about The Raincoats' travel plans to NYC, Ruth and Shirley were also in touch. The latter were already close; Shirley had been working with Ruth for quite a while.

"I met Ruth because I was working at Rough Trade, and we met just prior to setting up the booking agency. It was really important for me to meet Ruth," Shirley explains, "because she knew Scott Piering, a colleague of mine I shared my office with who was in charge of promotion, and he did PR for a lot of bands." Ruth was a regular visitor at Rough Trade in London, where "she used to arrive in a black cape, quite dramatic!" Shirley remembers. "And from the start she was really keen for The Raincoats to come over to New York."

On May 5, 1980, Ruth handwrote a letter to Shirley on Hurrah stationery:

Dear Shirley,
As you said in your letter, I'll probably be speaking to you before you get this, but anyway at least you'll have the contract in hand ... I've arranged for the Raincoats to borrow equipment from the support act on Weds. (a 6-piece all-women band from Borton who are excellent but have the rather misleading name of Bound & Gagged!), and from Gang of Four on Thurs., which should save a bit of money. I'll suggest to Hilary that she try and do the same thing at Tier 3 ...
One other thing, which I will speak to you about on the phone—as Scott knows, the NY club scene is more competitive than ever. There's one particular place opening next week called Danceteria, booked by Jim Fouratt, whom Scott can also tell you about. I'm quite sure he will contact the Raincoats to play there & offer decent money—but I would ask you not to let the band do it. He's already tried to get Gang of Four there, ostensibly for a "party," but Linda (Neville) quickly sussed out that he was

LIFE NUMBER 1

merely using the band's name to promote the club, and declined the offer. After the Hurrah date, Hilary & I might be able to line up more gigs if the band wants, but it's very important to me that you stay away from Danceteria—NY is different from London, and I do want to have a good relationship with you and the Raincoats. Thanks for understanding.

I do hope you can come with the band, so you can see them conquer New York! Again, I'll be speaking to you to clear up any last-minute details.

Love, Ruth[43]

Shirley emphasizes how Ruth, who tragically died in a car accident in 1986 at the age of just thirty-one, took care of The Raincoats while they were in America: "She made New York such a special place."

The Raincoats took the stage at Hurrah, and an unnamed cameraperson filmed nearly the entire performance on video, illegally of course.

David Bither (who'd go on to head up Nonesuch Records and sign powerful and experimental artists such as Laurie Anderson, Rhiannon Giddens, Caroline Shaw, and Emmylou Harris) wrote a full-page piece for *New York Rocker* on the band's show at Hurrah. He opened with the sentence, "Everything about the Raincoats challenges the heretofore trusty clichés of rock and roll." He spoke with the band, who told him "matter-of-factly," he wrote: "We just make our music. Whatever you do you have to fight. We're very aware of the position we are in and what we're up against and the history of women in the sort of music we're playing—you can't ignore it." Bither followed that quote with, "The Raincoats are musicians who play rock and roll—there are the relevant facts. And the Raincoats' rock and roll is altogether wonderful."[44]

He went to Hurrah to hear them play, immersing himself in the crowd with his notebook. He reported on a punter coming up to him and complaining that The Raincoats "should have learned to play their instruments before they crossed the Atlantic." But he had an answer to that: "The Raincoats sound the way they *want*

Hilary Jaeger with Ana in NYC, 1980

to sound," and quoted Gina and Vicky to support his assertion: "'Within the structure of our songs, everyone is attempting to play in a way that will stretch us, rather than just strumming along,' explains Gina. 'We take risks where other people won't.' 'Sometimes we take risks beyond our capabilities . . .' begins Vicky. '. . . And things just collapse,' finishes Gina. 'Because we don't play in a conventional way, with a conventional sound, we confuse people's expectations.'"

LIFE NUMBER 1

Bither described The Raincoats' sound as "a structured and often complex blend of multiple time changes, haunting gypsy melodies and three-part vocals with interchangeable lead voices." He depicted Ingrid's drumming as having "a graceful artlessness while producing a sound comparable to pounding shoeboxes full of cotton." His analysis concluded with references to The Raincoats' "anarchic quality ... that tends to fray the middle as well as the edges."

By May 24, The Raincoats weren't yet ready to head back to London. Hilary's diary entry reads: "It's been a busy week. The Raincoats have done their three dates. Hurrah two nights and Friday at TR3. They are a lovely and wondrous band and make music as beautiful as they are. And they are really special people. I've come to like them SO much. I'm glad they're staying an extra week. I wish they could stay longer, though I don't think Mom does."

Hilary laughs as she muses about how much her mom really did like The Raincoats but was probably weary after having guests in the apartment for so long. Her diary entries continue into that extra week of The Raincoats' stay in the City:

> They've [The Raincoats] made me feel a whole lot better. The other day I gave them a tour of Loisaida. A real coconut ice sold by an old Puerto Rican guy on Avenue B made with shaved ice and real coconut bits. Yesterday we took a walk to Washington Square and said hello to Manny and his dreads. [Hilary stops and explains how "a lot of West Indians used to play soccer in the park."] Later on they went to see Sun Ra at Irving Plaza and I DJ'd my shift at TR3, then we went to the new club, former TriBeCa, to see 8-Eyed Spy.

In addition to checking out the club scene, The Raincoats stopped at Manny's, the famous Midtown instrument shop adorned with rock star press photos and autographs. There, they purchased several of the international instruments they'd use to make *Odyshape*. According to Gina, everyone "guiltily" snuck all their new instruments from Manny's through customs, although she says, "We were never sure whether we needed to declare the not-very-expensive items we bought."

The Raincoats eventually took their flight back to London, but Hilary's diary entries weren't finished. She wrote once more after they departed:

Oh The Raincoats, The Raincoats! So good to hear live "Adventures Close to Home," "In Love," "Lola," "No Side to Fall In," and "Off-Duty Trip." I love that band and I love them truly. I've gotten to love Ana and Gina and thought I haven't spent as much time with Vicky, I like her a lot. And the three of them together are an incredible trio of women . . . Their music is soft yet strong and determined. Not obsequious or mushy.

INGRID'S NEW YORK AWAKENING

New York City was a place of dreams for every Raincoat, and for Ingrid especially.

Despite being excited about the scheduled gigs, Ingrid says she "always felt like the odd person out" on various tour dates in Europe because, as she explains, no matter where they were touring, "It'd be Gina and Vicky sharing a room, and obviously Ana and Shirley in one, and then I almost always had to share with a sound guy or stay alone." She recalls having no designated place to stay when The Raincoats got to New York; the rest of the band were scheduled to crash at Hilary's mom's place. Ingrid had heard famed music producer Roger Trilling wanted her to stay with him because of how much he liked her drumming, so that made the New York trip feel a bit different than any of the other cities on Raincoats dates that year. She crashed at Trilling's Hell's Kitchen apartment for the duration of the NYC dates. Gina adds that Trilling was a "great supporter of The Raincoats."

How did Ingrid end up the sole Raincoat staying with him in Hell's Kitchen? "I think it was down to Robert Wyatt," Ingrid says, trying to recall how Trilling had heard about her. "He'd told me he really liked my drumming, and that he'd told others, too. And, well, he's just the bee's knees!" Ingrid exclaims, remembering the compliment from Wyatt. Vicky is quick to note that she didn't get

LIFE NUMBER 1

Ironic "Housewives," 1981

a spot at Hilary's mom's apartment, either, although she and Gina often lament that they "didn't take better care" of Ingrid in New York.

In some ways, Ingrid got the best end of the deal because she got to talk with Trilling. She still speaks excitedly about how he managed James "Blood" Ulmer and had connections to Fab 5 Freddy and Herbie Hancock. Trilling made her feel secure in her drumming and in her experimental percussion work. "Roger picked up on and liked my drum patterns," she recalls, explaining how he cultivated her interest in "music based on something called harmolodics," which was James "Blood" Ulmer's "specialty."

Ingrid ultimately negotiated New York City herself on that visit, and it gave her a sense of confidence in her own abilities.

FIRING INGRID

"I never really felt like I fitted in with the band, and I don't think they really felt like I fitted in, either. I'm never mentioned in any write-ups on The Raincoats, even though I'm in some of the photos that are used in the same write-ups," Ingrid laments. "If I'd been a bit older and more assured, I probably would have said something, would have done things differently, would have made sure that I was accepted for who I am ... but not having any kind of ego, and not knowing how to stand up for myself, that was the end."

Gina says, "I think Ingrid coped incredibly well," adding, "She exuded confidence, but probably that confidence is the cover for something else. I do think Ingrid should have stayed in the band."

For Ingrid, there are regrets and lingering frustration. "I did what I did in The Raincoats, and I think—I know—my drumming was pretty good," she says, finding the words that emit a kind of confidence she regrets not being able to summon forth in 1980. "And I suppose, in a way, it hit me a bit harder than I realized at the time, because that was it for me. I didn't want to be involved in music ever again. My kids are musicians, and they've kind of dragged me back in, but I've never played drums again. Now I play bass." Referring resignedly to her past life as a drummer, Ingrid says, "I just no longer have the energy for attack."

LIFE NUMBER 1

ODYSHAPE

By the time The Raincoats' second full-length album began taking shape, Ingrid was out of the band. "We worked on *Odyshape* for a long time together," Ingrid remembers, and they finessed a lot of the music while they were playing on tour in 1980. "'Shouting Out Loud' was something I'd written on my own, the music part, and when I brought it to them, they were quite pleased." Ingrid almost kept the song to herself, a quintessential Raincoats track for which Ana would write lyrics. Gina adds, "The first part of the song is pure Ingrid, her melody and bass line. But as the music shifts, it was written by the whole band, and the bass line was written by me on one wet afternoon meandering around ... it's one of the bass lines I'm most proud of."

"I originally didn't want to bring the song to them because I felt it was different from what they'd done before, so I was honestly embarrassed to bring it," Ingrid says. "I'd had that melody for a few years, actually. I was sixteen when I first made it up, when Palmolive became my idol. But I remember thinking it didn't fit into any kind of music that I knew of, and I had a few things

Rough Trade poster for The Raincoats' *Odyshape* album

– 127 –

like that, but it was one of those situations of just not having self-confidence. So I was surprised when they actually liked it, and I think maybe they were surprised they actually liked it, too!"

But with Ingrid no longer a member, The Raincoats were left to shape the rest of the album without any backbeat. Rehearsals largely involved Ana, Gina, and Vicky. The album came together while the three of them played in the rehearsal basement on Monmouth Road, as well as Vicky's Brixton squat. "I remember Robert Wyatt coming to my squat once to rehearse with us," Vicky says. It had a boarded-up front window, so they used that room as their rehearsal space where nobody could see or hear them from the outside. "It was a dump," Vicky laughs, "but that's where I lived so I could be in the group and not have to make a living, basically."

The lack of percussion opened up new angles of experimentation with the recently smuggled menagerie of instruments from Manny's. "We weren't fighting against drums," Ana says. "We were just three melodic instruments working against and with, and weaving within each other. And then we added most of the drums later." From Gina's perspective, it would have been a very different record had they been working with a drummer for the entire album. "It wouldn't have been what it is, and I think it's the most quintessential Raincoats," she says.

Odyshape saw a kind of instrument-shifting that The Raincoats hadn't done previously, which reflected a desire to push toward new forms of experimentation. For Ana and Gina, it meant learning their own ways to play the balafon, shruti box, and more. For Vicky, it meant adding acoustic and electric guitar and bass to her repertoire. Vicky had played guitar on "Off-Duty Trip," but otherwise the instrument was new to her. "It put me in the same boat as everything else, and it pushed me out of my comfort zone," she says. Ana and Gina also switched instruments on some of the tracks, with Gina on guitar and Ana on bass.

Odyshape had "a lot of stretching going on," Vicky describes it, an apt characterization for a record with that enigmatic title alluding to bodies and shapes. "We were trying to get to a place that seemed perhaps a bit out of reach, which is what makes *Odyshape* what it is." That experimental evolution came naturally for The Raincoats,

Homage to the Beatles in Vicky's backyard

who were never going to replicate what they'd done previously. Pushing boundaries in all senses of the term requires reconfiguring methods of artistic output.

"If we'd made *Odyshape* five or ten years later, we'd have sampled those instruments," Vicky says, referring to the instruments from Manny's and the rapid increase in electronic music technology in the years after *Odyshape*. "But because we couldn't do that, we actually incorporated the real instruments, which of course meant we didn't know how to play the real instruments, and that added to the sound." Vicky remembers that the "slightly Eastern quality" that Ana and Gina brought out affected her violin parts, as well. "There was a feeding of things," she reflects.

Bringing in drums was another matter. By the time they got to the studio, "Robert Wyatt just came in and played along," Ana says. She explains how the song "And Then It's O.K." had a "strange time signature," which meant Wyatt "didn't understand what the timing was and played over it." Richard Dudanski drummed on "Dancing in My Head," and Ingrid returned briefly to record her drum parts for "Shouting Out Loud" and the song "Odyshape." "Ingrid worked that song with us from the beginning of its inception," Gina says. Charles Hayward became the go-to on most other tracks and later stuck around with The Raincoats for live performances marking the release of *Odyshape*. For Ana, "Charles was the right person for the album and the right person to tour with."

For Charles, joining The Raincoats was "a fantastical learning curve," but he knew he wanted to be part of what they were creating. He went through a serious "stripping down of technical considerations," as he describes it, since that was "the last thing on the list for The Raincoats, who wanted to focus on imagination, mood, and atmosphere." Charles had to reimagine what drumming could be. Rather than center his mind on the kinds of rhythms he'd honed, he focused on visual elements of the music. As he saw it, *Odyshape* songs revealed either a "Gina shape" or an "Ana shape," these "different types of modernist shapes that rarely repeat, never necessarily reappear, sometimes overlap, and sometimes don't."

Studio time for *Odyshape* was ultimately a much larger-scale affair than it had been for *The Raincoats* studio album. Beyond the range of drummers, there were a number of session musicians: Dick O'Dell recommended Kadir Durvesh to play the shenai (a type of oboe) on "Dancing in My Head"; Dick O'Dell played ektara in "Baby Song"; and cellist "Georgie" (Georgina) Born played cello on "Dancing in My Head." Charles says he knew immediately that Adam Kidron was perfect for handling the engineering, because he was "a polymath who did wonders in the studio."

On tour dates starting that fall, Charles was on drums for six or seven months, although many of the *Odyshape* songs proved

LIFE NUMBER 1

difficult to replicate live. (Anton Fier of the Feelies and Lounge Lizards actually auditioned for the tour when Charles thought he'd be called back to This Heat, but there was no chemistry between Fier and the band.) Charles recalls audiences being "surprised there was a bloke playing drums," but that's one of the "big things for The Raincoats," he adds. "What's so incredible about them—they were always bringing things from a different perspective, deconstructing all of the strutting that had been going on before, breaking down assumptions. The Raincoats were particularly adept at that, and I knew I wanted to let myself learn how to do that from them."

On the first Rough Trade accountancy sheets for *Odyshape*, Caroline Scott's handwriting across the top of the ledger reads: "the sweetest shape." An initial 9,229 copies were pressed, with 391 set aside for promo.

Odyshape, unlike all other RC records, was actually pressed for US sale through Rough Trade's office in San Francisco.

Odyshape is at once a document of its time yet has a quality free from temporal constraints. "*Odyshape* has this beautifully coherent sound, a sort of punk edge," Charles says to describe it. "But you can still listen to it ten, fifteen, forty years later, and it's not a thing that's stuck in any single time," he underscores. "It stands within and outside time." His love for the record is evident in the tone his voice takes.

Gina believes that if The Raincoats were ever to make another record together, "it would have to be more like *Odyshape* than any of the others ... it is, I think, *the* Raincoats album. We were at our most experimental on *Odyshape*, and that should be at the forefront of our history. I love the first album, but *Odyshape* is where we really, really shine."

The album ultimately offers a powerful design for living, according to Charles. "*Odyshape* is a pattern for being alive as a functioning creative person," he smiles slyly, "if you think you can find the pattern."

ON THE BBC

In 1982, the Open University in Milton Keynes did a series of combined courses and television broadcasts on the subjects of popular culture and women in rock for TV14 and the BBC. One broadcast included The Raincoats playing one song from *Odyshape* and one from *The Raincoats*, respectively: "Go Away" and "No Side to Fall In." (At the very back of the screen in a few shots, behind the drum kit, it's possible to see Duncan McDonald, who played seven times with The Raincoats when they were short a drummer that summer. Shirley chuckles and describes him warmly as "a cute, young boy.")

The Raincoats received a letter in advance of the broadcast from the Open University, addressed, "Dear Sirs." Shirley firmly inked a large "X" through "Sirs" when she opened it.

While the broadcast originally aired in 1983, it would actually repeat on the BBC multiple times into the mid-1980s across the UK, and viewers who hadn't been quite old enough to catch The Raincoats in their first life discovered them anew through the television.

THE KITCHEN TAPES

ROIR A-120
(Pronounced "roar")

The British Invasion Reversed! A real score for ROIR! One of the U.K.'s most eminent/seminal "new wave" bands have selected ROIR and the cassette-only format to present their newest album length material, recorded live at NYC's prestigious avant-garde Kitchen For The Performance Arts in December 1982 . . . For many years, both independent and major U.K. labels have been in the vanguard of discovering new American bands and recording them for U.K. releases, initially available in the United States only as high priced imports. At ROIR we are especially pleased that The Raincoats "The Kitchen Tapes" represents a "hands across the water" cultural exchange that hopefully presages a healthy new collaboration between U.K. bands and U.S. labels.

LIFE NUMBER 1

Gina with the Statue of Liberty, Super 8 camera in hand

That ROIR press release alerted Americans to the cassette-only album, and The Raincoats' only live record, to be released stateside. But it wasn't all coming up roses. Since the release of *The Kitchen Tapes*, the band has hated the album. They have varying issues with it, ranging from the sound quality to the personal circumstances swirling about at the time of the recording. They've come around to it a bit in recent years, though only slightly.

But that's only part of the story of *The Kitchen Tapes* and The Raincoats' first performance at The Kitchen.

The Kitchen was originally named for the nature of the space, a cooking area in the Mercer Arts Center. From its inception in 1971, The Kitchen was conceived as a transdisciplinary, experimental space that was committed to showing community art that "museums couldn't accommodate at the time," Tim Griffin, former Artforum editor and director of The Kitchen from 2011 to 2021, explains. It was ahead of its time, in part because it needed to exist; there was no other venue in downtown New York City filling that role.

After the Mercer Arts Center's notorious collapse in 1973, The Kitchen relocated to 59 Wooster Street in SoHo, former home to the LoGiudice Gallery. Here, it became the center of the avant-garde and experimental music and arts scene in New York. Indeed, as the space welcomed no wave and rock performers, and later hip-hop artists, a lineage emerged that demolished genre barriers. Arthur Lewis, Rhys Chatham, and George Lewis were the music curators. Cindy Sherman's Film Stills had their first showing at The Kitchen, as did Dara Birnbaum's Technology/Transformation: Wonder Woman. "As Laurie Anderson would say," Tim explains, The Kitchen offered artists an opportunity to "enter a space where you were allowed to fail. You could experiment. You could be adventurous. You could go off the rails. And that was an experience to be treasured," both for the performers and audiences alike.

While The Kitchen relocated again in 1986 to a former ice house in Chelsea, it has remained a venue for innovative performance and creative output into the present.

In 1982, The Raincoats were back in America on a wintertime East Coast tour, with stops in Philadelphia, Maxwell's in Hoboken, and the 9:30 Club in Washington, D.C. In addition to the usual suspects, all added session players were in the touring party: Ana, Gina, Vicky, Richard, Derek Goddard, and Paddy O'Connell. Gina's best friend Petra P was also along for the ride. Everyone in the band remembers the freezing temperatures and blizzard in D.C. "We all bought hats because our ears were so cold!" Shirley recalls as she describes a memory of driving by the White House, cloaked in a blanket of snow. They ended the tour back in New York.

Richard had brought Derek in for added percussion—they were both friends of Joe Strummer's, and Derek was a master on the bongos, cymbals, and kalimba. He was "very aware" of "being auditioned," he says, and knew his connections to Richard wouldn't automatically get him a spot in the band. But ultimately, The Raincoats offered Derek a chance to tour with them. "I think they must have thought," he says, referring to his African percussion work, "this is an ingredient we can cook with." He'd ultimately record on *Moving* with the band, too, and remembers an inclusive experience with The Raincoats. "I was very aware of being a twenty-year-old Black man in punk," he says, often experiencing what he calls "a culture dilemma." But with The Raincoats, he encountered a different atmosphere. "The Raincoats never made me feel like I was different, even though I experienced things along the way that were racially motivated."

Meanwhile, Amy Rigby had already befriended The Raincoats after their New York dates in 1980. When they got back to the city in 1982 and needed transportation, Amy came to the rescue. "They needed someone to help them rent a van," she laughs. "I didn't have a credit card—nobody did—but I did have a US driver's license, although I'd hardly driven at all. I'd learned to drive in Pennsylvania, and I'd never actually driven in New York City. But we went up to Midtown to get this van, and I was going to be the one to drive them downtown to The Kitchen. It was like twenty blocks, whatever it was. That was far enough for me—I was so terrified." The building was on the corner of Wooster and Broome Streets, smack in the middle of heavily trafficked SoHo.

"We actually played two shows at The Kitchen in 1982," Shirley says, and explains how Anne DeMarinis was the "brilliant curator" who booked them. (Anne had been in an early lineup of Sonic Youth.) "Then Neil Cooper, who was running ROIR got in touch and said he'd started doing a cassette-only thing with artists."

Neil's wife, Paula Cooper, had already become well known in the New York City art world with her eponymous SoHo gallery, which she'd started in 1968 after working briefly at the Gagosian. Paula's work with minimal and conceptual artists like Sol LeWitt, Donald Judd, Claes Oldenburg, Bernd and Hilla Becher, Dan Flavin, and Lynda Benglis put her on the map early on, and her experiences working with female artists and navigating the misogyny of New York's art world kindled Neil's interest in sonic modes of subversion, experimentation, and resistance. He founded ROIR in 1979 and released a record by James Chance and the Contortions. His label would go on to feature a broad range of underground artists whose sounds influenced artists across genres in NYC, including Glenn Branca, Bush Tetras, Black Uhuru, Einstürzende Neubauten, Lydia Lunch, Malaria!, Mekons, MC5, New York Dolls, Nico, Suicide, and Television. Most of the cassettes were live recordings to avoid violating the artists' studio contracts. Neil died in 2001, and his son Lucas took over the ROIR label.

On the 1982 US tour, "The Raincoats' budget had gone a bit haywire," Shirley explains, "and we were going to need a couple hundred pounds, basically, to all get back home." Neil offered to pay The Raincoats to put out a ROIR recording, and Shirley knew they were going to need that money if they wanted to get home to London. An advance from ROIR could cover the cost of more than a couple of plane tickets. The Raincoats agreed to a ROIR cassette, what would become *The Kitchen Tapes*. After the shows were recorded, Shirley sent the rest of the band back to the UK, and she and Ana hung around NYC until the ROIR advance came through and they could get standby tickets.

But everything was falling apart. "There were six people playing in the band at this time, and I was finding that it was all slipping away from me, from what I thought we were and what I thought the music was," Ana says. "There were songs being played that I wasn't that keen on, and then we had to go to New York and ended with this performance at The Kitchen." Ana reflects that, although The Raincoats really did "split up after each record, in a way," this time it felt different. "I thought, *I just can't do this anymore*, and I told Shirley, 'I do not want to do this anymore,'" Ana says.

For Vicky, the period around *The Kitchen Tapes* was a particularly difficult one, too. Her mum was going through cancer treatment, and The Raincoats' lineup included Vicky's boyfriend at the time, the saxophonist Paddy O'Connell, with whom she recalls having "a very volatile relationship, shall we say." It wasn't easy to be on tour with him, and their alarming accommodations in New York's Alphabet City brought added anxiety. "I remember turning up at an address around there," Vicky says, "ringing a doorbell and waiting to be let inside, and honestly worrying we were going to be stabbed in the street. The streets there felt so unsafe, and when we finally got into the flat, it turned out to be a junkie's apartment, so filthy, and sheets covered in blood. We slept fully clothed on top of the sheets and ran out of there the next morning. It was absolutely horrendous, and I don't even remember where we slept after that, but it all felt so insecure without a place to stay, and there was so much tension." Not a very auspicious setup for recording the band's only live album on relatively short notice. "I remember an argument backstage because there was, of course, stuff going on between us personally, which was not easy. And then, the added tension with everyone else in The Raincoats. We hadn't even recorded yet, gone on stage. But we did end up performing that night in December 1982, and maybe a bit of that tension came through in *The Kitchen Tapes* recording." Vicky refers to The Raincoats having developed "very different musical strands themselves" that were emerging "in rather disparate ways." Many of the songs were works in progress and would ultimately appear on the third and final LP of the band's first life, *Moving*.

Gina has trouble describing the difficult period around the live album and the band's time in New York, and sums it up in a neat metaphor: "There was no more glue to hold us together."

"We all just had a bit of a bad feeling around *The Kitchen Tapes*," Shirley recalls, "and none of us really liked it. Although, it's really just that it reminds us of bad times. And I mean, "The Puberty Song"? What the fuck were we thinking?! It's really that *The Kitchen Tapes* has a bit more baggage than anything else, which may not be so much to do with the actual recording and how it sounds. And, you know, Rob Sheffield loves it, so . . . we all really must sit down and listen to it again."

Greil Marcus, who'd previously written on The Raincoats for *Rolling Stone*, seemed like an obvious choice to do the ROIR liner notes. "He just got it, what The Raincoats were all about, he got it completely," Shirley says.

In March 1995, Neil Cooper sent Shirley a fax with an accounting to date of *The Kitchen Tapes* and to say ROIR was reissuing its early cassettes on CD. "We would very much like to do this with The Raincoats," he wrote. At this point in time, The Raincoats also learned that ROIR had licensed *The Kitchen Tapes* in Japan in CD format without their original permission, with an insert design for which Shirley and Ana have the same reaction: "Hideous!"

Nothing further came of a CD release of *The Kitchen Tapes* in US or European markets at the time (that happened later, in 1998 with the original artwork), and the Japanese copy never really took off because ROIR withdrew the artwork.

༺༻

ROIR had a series of tapes that were sold at major music shops across the US, from places like Tower Records to burgeoning indies. That series of cassettes was crucial for getting The Raincoats into the hands of American listeners. In the mid to late eighties in particular, *The Kitchen Tapes* was the only Raincoats album still being manufactured for sale in the States, where it was possible to buy the cassette right off the shelf. That also meant it would become the only available Raincoats music in the early nineties after Nirvana fans read Kurt's *Incesticide* liner notes about meeting Ana in London.

The Kitchen Tapes also had the rare quality of being the only Raincoats record with the band's faces on the cover. Unless you'd happened upon some press with a photo in it—which was extremely rare to come by in America once the band split up—the ROIR cassette was the only opportunity to put faces to those powerful sounds. "It was a life-changing artifact," Rob Sheffield says of finding *The Kitchen Tapes* one day in 1988 at Newbury Comics in Boston. "And I know life-changing is a much abused term, but I'm afraid life-changing will have to take a little more punishment." He saw the faces of Gina, Vicky, and Ana on the cassette: "The first picture of them I'd ever seen, and it would be the last for many years after that." (That photo, by Eric Watson, was done for a "No One's Little Girl"/"Running Away" shoot earlier in 1982. Eric, Gina explains, "was at Hornsey at the same time. He went on to become a successful photographer and music video director.")

For many Americans who weren't yet of an age to see The Raincoats live in 1980 or 1982, *The Kitchen Tapes* became the only circulating evidence of their music, and the first Raincoats record they'd love and others would covet. All that would change with the eventual CD reissues in 1993, but up to that point, *The Kitchen Tapes* was an underground hit in the States.

MOVING (ON)

As The Raincoats were planning for *Moving*, their singles off the new album were being celebrated. In 1982, pre-Kitchen, "No One's Little Girl"/"Running Away" was released as a 7-inch single. The Raincoats initially recorded "No One's Little Girl" around the time they were making *Odyshape*, but "it just didn't feel right at that time," Shirley says. The Raincoats re-recorded it a year later at the studio of Phil Legg (who'd also formed the band Essential Logic with Lora Logic following her departure from X-Ray Spex), where Gina worked on it with a number of special guests including Tom Morley from Scritti Politti, and from Pigbag, Roger Freeman and Chris Hamlin. "I played several bass tracks, and we had lots of fun," Gina recalls. "And Vicky wrote the looping, beautiful violin part." As Vicky remembers, "I overdubbed all the violin parts to try and recreate the sound of a string section." It's one of Gina's most-loved Raincoats songs.

The Raincoats remake "Lola"

The following year, after some time at Berry Street, the second *Moving* single would be released, "Animal Rhapsody."

As for *Moving*, the most "polished" of the Raincoats records during the band's first life, it's the one that nearly didn't happen. Vicky remembers Adam Kidron being "very instrumental in putting together the album," pushing for "a more polished sound." Unlike previous studio time, The Raincoats did a number of takes while recording the album's tracks, and Adam tried to focus efforts on "getting a good take." According to Vicky, "It was a completely different approach, and I think that does come over on the recording."

The method for *Moving* changed by necessity rather than by choice. What arose from the *Moving* studio sessions was largely the product of a band breaking apart. While a sense of "falling apart" had previously pervaded The Raincoats' sound in a warm way—"Part of the charm," Vicky says—the seams had become threadbare by 1983, and there was very little holding the band together. Earlier on, pre-*Moving*, pre-*The Kitchen Tapes*, Vicky does admit she'd felt some frustration if instruments were out of tune, or if there was a sense of impending collapse on stage at times. "But I just went with it back then," she says. By *Moving*, she recalls a distinct feeling that the ground was shifting beneath them.

And whereas there was once magic produced from the often equivocal dynamic between Gina and Ana, the divide was deepening. Shirley emphasizes that she often saw herself in a role of "containing the fire between them and making it productive, channeling it," but by *Moving* something was changing.

Ana explains how Shirley had to convince her to record *Moving*. "She suggested that we go into the studio and record with each of us directing our own songs. When we'd finished the album and the artwork, I thought that was the end of The Raincoats. I didn't think we could get back together ten years later after anything like that."

The studio sessions this time around were tough for most everybody, and *Moving* didn't exactly emerge into the public in the form The Raincoats had hoped. "It all felt very dysfunctional," Derek says. While The Raincoats would make revisions to the record upon the CD reissue in 1993, they had to live with *Moving* as the band's final LP for a decade.

LIFE NUMBER 1

"When *Moving* was made, we decided we'd each direct our own tracks because we were no longer a democracy," Gina says. "Scritti Politti got to that stage in 1978 or 1979, but it took us until almost 1984 to get there." According to Ana, "By the time of *Moving*, it was everybody moving in different directions, and moving away from each other." She continues, "It's difficult to have really creative people doing things together, because it's very difficult to agree. So there were my songs, and there were Gina's songs. And in a way, it's sort of the same thing as the Beatles. Some songs are completely different John songs, or Paul songs, and some George songs. And that makes it interesting." Artistically, the forms of experimentation that were at the heart of The Raincoats' first life were in some ways "what started to split us apart in the end," Gina says, referring to "little moments of fracture as we were all getting serious about different things."

There were also interpersonal strains that nobody in the band likes to discuss. "We definitely had our arguments," Gina laughs a little bit uncomfortably. By the time of *Moving*, certain personal stressors became pronounced. Vicky and Ana weren't seeing eye to eye, although they rarely had. Vicky remembers how she was becoming interested in "musical progressions," immersing herself in new genres and forms, whereas Ana "had an insistence on experimenting from one position," Vicky recalls, "and I respect that, because that's being very sure about who you are."

Ana talks about Vicky critiquing her lyrics. Gina remembers that flashpoint as well, and feeling increasingly caught in between them because she really respected them both and the positions they were coming from. "There was a real power and joy" in the lyrics Ana created, Gina says, "but definitely a sadness, too, and that's a powerful thing itself. And it can be more subtle, you have to look for it to see it, you have to want to know it's there. With Vicky, she was really interested in putting the politics out there and being clearer about what it was we were saying. That was the important language to her, and she and Ana didn't see eye to eye."

On top of that, there were occasions where Gina and Vicky felt like the two of them were pitted against Shirley and Ana when it came to decision-making for the band. Neither Ana nor Shirley shared that perspective then and still don't today, but for Vicky and Gina, that's part of their experience and their story in the group, especially during the *Moving* period. As Vivien Goldman reflects, anytime you have a band where two people in the group are a couple, emotions run differently, even if nobody intends that. "Just consider how the members of Sonic Youth who weren't Kim and Thurston felt," she suggests. The Raincoats conceived themselves as an equal collective, a democracy, but in practice not everyone experienced it that way.

But it wasn't just personal clashes within the band. Stressors were affecting The Raincoats from all sides. Family members had become ill, romances had become toxic entanglements.

"And I wasn't the right person for *Moving*," Adam reflects, citing his increasing interest in pop and engineering music for radio play. Ana agrees about Adam's interest in popular music, recalling a vivid memory of him "listening to disco cassettes." Shirley says Adam focused on songs that might "be a hit," which were few and far between. He pushed the band to include "Avidoso," one of Richard's songs.

The Raincoats were quickly becoming a powder keg. "Geoff told me once we were more fractious in the studio than any of the boys in the bands, and I think that was really saying something," Gina ruminates. "I think at that time of your life, and ours, we were all just kind of fighting our own way through the world, and you've got enough issues of your own without thinking of everyone else's, but I supposed we all could have been more supportive of one another. I don't know that we even knew how."

In early November 1983, Rough Trade issued a press release for *Moving* that coincided with the release of the album's single, "Animal Rhapsody":[45]

> It's the rainy season ... The album entitled *Moving* will be scheduled for release in the new year and features 50 minutes of 12 original new songs and is The Raincoats third studio album to date. Possibly the most definitive album to date, it's certainly the most unexpected yet accessible, but unfortunately the last.

LIFE NUMBER 1

The future holds a final live performance in Japan with some exciting new projects soon to be unleashed.

Unbeknownst to fans, The Raincoats had already disbanded. The Japan tour never happened. The Raincoats were scheduled for dates in Tokyo, Nagoya, and Osaka as part of Takahashi Festival. It would have been their first time playing in Asia, where they later developed a loyal following. The cancellation fully cemented the end of the first incarnation of The Raincoats. In a fax at the start of 1984, the festival organizers wrote: "We have been working on setting up the schedule for Raincoats Japan tour. But sponsor informed us that the board meeting finally decided not to do this tour. I'm sorry to tell you that we had to give up. We hope for next chance and our future cooperation."

A *Cosmopolitan* article in February 1984 described *Moving* as The Raincoats' "farewell album" and "the best thing they've ever done ... would clearly establish them as the most talented group of girls working together in rock today."

The Raincoats continued to receive fan mail at Rough Trade, some pieces of mail angrily questioning the breakup of the band, others hopeful. Paul from London wrote: "What is the future of the band? Because I hear rumours that you and Gina are splitting up! That would be sad because as long as you and Gina are together it would be the Raincoats as they have always been."

Little did Paul know, time would prove him right. But not for a decade that felt like a lifetime.

"Unfortunately, The Raincoats are 'Moving' on!" the final Rough Trade press release for *Moving* concluded.

Ana, Anne, and Gina, ca. 1995

LIFE NUMBER 2

"We realized eventually that in the United States, that's where we had the most people interested in what we do, and where we had the biggest influence," Ana says. And so, in the rainy musical wilds of America's Pacific Northwest, The Raincoats' second life began.

BEAUTIFUL KAOS AT 89.3 FM

Unbeknownst to the band, their second life was germinating well before they'd even broken up and their first life came to a somewhat unceremonious end. It all began at KAOS, Olympia, Washington's independent public radio station operating in partnership with the gloriously radical Evergreen State College.

Bruce Pavitt, who's perhaps best known as a cofounder of Sub Pop Records in Seattle, developed a lifelong interest in hyperlocal music communities once he made it out to Olympia in 1979. As he saw it, the scene in Washington's small capital city was a place shaped by the influence of The Raincoats. When Bruce left his hometown of Chicago to attend Evergreen and joined the slate of presenters at KAOS, he discovered "the most progressive music policy in America," and what he emphasizes is "an unexplored impact." That story actually starts with John Foster, Bruce explains.

"John was the music director at KAOS, and his feeling was that a community radio station should play music that prioritizes music made by members of the community," Bruce says. "So he instituted a policy that stated eighty percent of what got played at KAOS had to be on an indie label. This is where I got my real education." Bruce started his KAOS show and zine of the same name, *Subterranean Pop*, out of which he eventually formed Sub Pop Records to the north, "and all this flowed out of the KAOS music policy." Bruce got a quick introduction to the Rough Trade bands, which were central at KAOS. "Rough Trade happened to be an indie DIY, of course, but what's also crucial contextually is that they were supporting so much music made by women." In Bruce's KAOS show, he pulled from the station's vast collection that included The Raincoats, Delta 5, Young Marble Giants, and others. "'Lola' by The Raincoats was getting a *lot* of airplay," Bruce says, "and it influenced the culture of the whole community."

As John reflects, "The one thing I can say about Olympia in the late seventies and early eighties is that it was not a bunch of snobby scenesters; folks were very nice. Everyone who participated in the scene, playing or observing, was welcome and accepted for whatever they brought. The Raincoats embodied that ethos to us."

Bruce cites Calvin Johnson and his band Beat Happening as particularly influenced by The Raincoats, thanks to KAOS. Calvin was playing The Raincoats on his KAOS Olympia Community Radio show *Boy Meets Girl*. Fellow Olympia artist and musician Lois Maffeo also draws a connection between The Raincoats and Beat Happening: "It would be pure speculation to say that Beat Happening found inspiration in The Raincoats' music, although sonically, I can see a parallel in the skronky songs of Supreme Cool Beings, whose cassette was the first release on K Records [the label Calvin would later establish in Olympia]." Referring to Calvin specifically, Lois says, "His anti-corporate philosophy and esthetic of both music-making and music-listening are central to the Northwest scene."

Slim Moon, who'd go on to found another influential Olympia label, Kill Rock Stars, remembers Lois's own KAOS show *Your Dream Girl* as a constant source of Raincoats songs. It created a dialogue among a wide and diverse range of female artists, and there was rarely a *Your Dream Girl* show, if there even was one, that didn't feature at least one Raincoats track. Lois frequently drew from *The Kitchen Tapes*, playing "Puberty Song," "Rainstorm," and "No Side to Fall In." As for the latter, Lois was completely taken in by the sound of the electric violin on that track, explaining, "'No Side to Fall In' just starts with that ripping scratch sound and then matches it at the end with the bare chorus of voices singing along with, what, a stick and a can? That combination of wild sound and plain sound was catnip to me! Today!" She also loved "In Love," the first Raincoats song she ever heard when she bought a copy of *Wanna Buy a Bridge?* on vinyl in a Seattle record shop.

Lois regularly featured tracks from *The Kitchen Tapes* for a simple reason: "I was proud to own it," she says. "I'm not a record collector/nerd/jerk in general, but I think I was bragging a little with that. I loved that tape because it was authentic-sounding. It had all the mistakes and out-of-tune moments that only happen on live recordings and I found that really invigorating." For Lois, the cassette was also a prized possession because it "shared songs from my absolute favorite record by The Raincoats—the 'Animal Rhapsody' 12-inch with 'No One's Little Girl' and 'Honey Mad Woman' on the B-side," so she was "delighted to hear live versions of beloved tracks." Lois loves that single so much that, she says, "It's the only record I have two copies of. I wanted to make sure that if I wore the first one out, I'd have a backup!"

As a KAOS presenter, Lois's show was crucial not only in cementing the significance of The Raincoats in Olympia, but illuminating a sonic lineage of which The Raincoats were a crucial part. On *Your Dream Girl* shows, The Raincoats played alongside artists who came long before like Eartha Kitt, contemporaries such as Kleenex/LiLiPUT [due to legal issues, the band initially called Kleenex changed its name to LiLiPUT in late 1979] and Crass, as well as more recent hip-hop and disco artists like Taana Gardner. Lois describes her playlists as "genre-busting." That term, she says, also emerges if you listen solely to Raincoats records. "If you hear The Roches, African electric guitars, eighties NYC hip-hop, nursery rhymes, British pop," Lois reflects, "yep, it's there but it's re-patterned and made into something new. Radically different from pastiche."

Bruce is certain: "KAOS came to shape the culture of Olympia," and "KAOS is ultimately the roots of Raincoats appreciation in Olympia and ultimately the Northwest."

SHAPING SONIC YOUTH

Meanwhile, back in New York (while The Raincoats were in the throes of their first life, knowing next to nothing about developments on America's West Coast), Sonic Youth was forming, indelibly shaped by The Raincoats' ethos and politics.

Sonic Youth certainly doesn't *sound* like The Raincoats. Yet, as Thurston explains, "It's about the approach to the instrument." As he sees it, for The Raincoats and Sonic Youth, "it's an emotional approach as opposed to any sort of traditional technique." When he first saw The Raincoats, he realized their approach was "accomplishing the essence of what I loved about rock 'n' roll. It was all about the joy of being in the moment, this attitudinal idea, and it really stuck with me." As Kim says, "They didn't sound like any of the English punk bands. They seemed confident and fearless, and that's what role-modeling is—it's better than talking about stuff. They weren't ever talking about being feminists—they just *were*."

Kim brought her own Raincoats-like approach to Sonic Youth. "She was coming at it from a totally different approach, being an artist, where the strings on the guitar just related to one another in her own personal way," Thurston explains. "There was no way you could say to Kim, 'Can you play an E or a G-sharp?' Forget about it. And I didn't know how to transpose those notes on an alternately tuned guitar, but with Kim, you might as well have told her to play an X."

As Kim describes it, "There were The Slits, and I really like The Slits and was inspired by them, but then with the development of The Raincoats, they were kind of more like New York in a certain way. Less conventional, but relatable. The Slits were fun, but The Raincoats were introverted, poetic, and I could relate to them." The Raincoats' music was "unconventional and yet familiar," she says, "and it felt like very intimate music."

For Thurston, The Raincoats made it possible to have confidence experimenting with intuitive methods: "There were these levels of how we were each approaching the instruments, but never any judgmental value given to any of them. Rather there was this idea of unity, and that was something that The Raincoats obviously really had." In a place like New York, says Kim, where music was "very dissident," The Raincoats were perfect models.

In nineties press for The Raincoats and the new LP they'd eventually release on Sonic Youth's label at the time, DGC (Geffen), journalists loved writing about how The Raincoats had inspired bands like Nirvana's Kurt Cobain, Sonic Youth, and Bikini Kill. It's difficult to find a review or a feature on the band that doesn't include those references.

LIFE NUMBER 2

BUT REALLY, ALL ROADS LEAD TO OLYMPIA

The Pacific Northwest became ground zero for the birth of The Raincoats' second life, centered on a vibrant new generation of feminist, anarchic, queer musicians. After KAOS playlists had enough airtime to shape the cultural framework of the small Washington city, connections to The Raincoats really became apparent. Fellow West Coaster and drummer extraordinaire Patty Schemel declares, "Olympians *revere* The Raincoats."

According to Lois Maffeo, the "ethos of the music and art scene" in Olympia at that point in time was akin to what The Raincoats revealed was possible: "Make do and make magic out of nothing." Simple enough, right? But as Lois emphasizes, "The scene in Olympia was aware that simplicity wasn't simple"—they recognized the trick of The Raincoats' music.

The Raincoats' songs became part of the fabric of the city and the culture it (re)produced. "The acts of making music and making art were liberating," Lois says. "What were we liberated from? Corporate culture. Patriarchy. Religion. Military. Expectations. And many of us heard the sound of those expectations being dissected and the sound of that freedom being enacted in the music of The Raincoats. The arrow flies from 'No One's Little Girl' to Riot Grrrl pretty swiftly."

Like Lois, Jean Smith of the Vancouver band Mecca Normal was also taking cues from The Raincoats. Although Jean was based in a city a few hours north of Olympia, her two-piece band with David Lester would, like Beat Happening and so many of the Riot Grrrl artists to come, become abidingly linked to Olympia and K Records. "Listening to The Raincoats freed me from many previously held limitations," Jean says. "That they were women made that freedom tangible. Visceral. I could hear their like-minded affinities and encouragement, yet their approaches were all very different. They seemed to be functioning based on working fully with what they had at hand, giving it everything in terms of creativity, confidence, and vulnerability." Jean underscores that she and David are a bit older than the Riot Grrrls who emerged out of Olympia in the early nineties; Mecca Normal's music was important, like Lois's KAOS show, in making Riot Grrrl possible. "The Raincoats allowed me to take inspiration, to build and maintain confidence, and some years later, to inspire the cofounders of Riot Grrrl," says Jean, "along with The Raincoats and all those other women-fronted bands that energized a social movement that, to this day, still shows signs of being ongoing as opposed to over, in the way that rock historians like to nail things down."

Carrie Brownstein and Corin Tucker of Sleater-Kinney, who were some of those original Riot Grrrls in Olympia (with the bands Excuse 17 and Heavens to Betsy), confirm Jean's words. "I always liked how The Raincoats felt deliberately and dangerously strange," Corin says, "and that gave license to a lot of bands in Olympia, including Sleater-Kinney, to forgo traditional instrumentation. We didn't have a bass, and often we were playing dueling melodies. The Raincoats deconstructed all these entrenched, codified ideas about music and yet remained very appealing and clever." Carrie agrees: "I love the artiness of The Raincoats combined with this intellectual quality. The music showed a real openness to experiment within the band that I really related to, and that avant-garde element was something that really influenced Sleater-Kinney."

As any fan knows, the band name Sleater-Kinney originates from Sleater Kinney Road that runs through Lacey, Washington, adjacent to Olympia. "We didn't relate to that meat-and-potatoes punk rock and were always striving for something more experimental," Carrie says, "so The Raincoats were very influential to us in that way." Corin adds, "I don't know if they were trying to be ugly, with a sort of dissonance, but to us, there was something so charming about that, and that charm had teeth to it. It was a kind of cloaked weaponry that Sleater-Kinney was really into." She continues, "With Sleater-Kinney, we wanted to say, 'Come a little closer, and out come those teeth,' and The Raincoats did that, too. I feel like bands in Olympia wouldn't dare be as weird as they actually were without The Raincoats, because otherwise people are too afraid to do that stuff. But The Raincoats sounded fearless."

There was also an indelible Olympia connection for G.B. Jones, the Toronto-based musician, filmmaker, and visual artist who'd formed the all-female band Fifth Column, coined the term "queercore," and cofounded the zine *J.D.s*, which ran from the mid-1980s into the early 1990s. She started hearing about The Raincoats from trusted sources who'd been over to London and back. In 1980, like Lois, she got hold of the Rough Trade compilation album, *Wanna Buy a Bridge?*, designed for North American listeners, and heard "In Love." That same year, G.B. formed Fifth Column with Kathleen Pirrie Adams and Janet Martin. They met Caroline Azar in the washroom at a Slits show in Toronto and quickly added her as the singer. And in Fifth Column, G.B. remembers, "Everyone loved The Raincoats." Fifth Column was looking to other women in bands "for ways to be a female musician in the public sphere, but not go back to the old ideas about how women presented themselves in the media from the past, and The Raincoats allowed this dialogue to happen." The Raincoats taught them how to be taken seriously, to avoid being judged on looks, and to have the freedom to experiment with music.

She continues, "The Raincoats were absolutely essential for rethinking what a female band could be in the eighties and the entire sense of experimentation ... rewriting what makes a band, what a song can sound like, what kind of image a woman can have in the media, and even what labels you can put your music out with and what that means for yourself. The Raincoats made that possible." Fifth Column didn't *sound* anything like The Raincoats—Fifth Column was interested in musique concrète, reading software, and trying to sound like different machines. But it was The Raincoats' play with new percussive instruments, and even non-instruments like clocks and objects as percussion tools, that made an impression. "How can you reword and rework the entire idea of what a song can be?" G.B. asks. The Raincoats demonstrated a way of doing that and paved the road for artists following in their footsteps.

G.B. made cassette compilations, started writing a zine called *Hide* with Caroline Azar, and began trading with Calvin Johnson in Olympia. Early Fifth Column records got distributed in the Pacific Northwest through Calvin, and an indelible link was formed. G.B. maintained a long-term connection with K Records, the label Calvin would form and through which Fifth Column would ultimately be distributed, and her friends in the Pacific Northwest made sure her queercore zine *J.D.s* got circulated widely. But before all that happened, The Raincoats became a different kind of "Seattle Sound." Eric Erlandson of Hole calls the band "an integral part of the Northwest's musical playbook."

In 1983, Calvin wrote one of the first US Raincoats cover stories and interviews in *OP* magazine, in which he asked Ana what she liked to have for breakfast (she wasn't keen to answer). John Foster of KAOS was a cofounder of *OP* with Toni Holm, Dana Squires, and David Rauh. The magazine was short-lived—only twenty-six issues, one for each letter of the alphabet—and the founders wanted more Raincoats. Dana, who also served as art director for the magazine, says: "They were an influence, as they sounded like they were doing what they needed to do ... sounded natural." Bruce Pavitt remembers Dana's love of The Raincoats in particular. "I very specifically remember her reproducing the *Odyshape* cover," he smiled. He also describes *OP* as an influential magazine that did in print what KAOS did in sound, ultimately reaching a bigger audience. "KAOS DJs wrote for *OP*," he explains, and, "Both KAOS and *OP* began getting international recognition."

As a fan and interviewer of The Raincoats, Calvin would ultimately be the one to introduce The Raincoats to one of the artists who permanently put Olympia on the feminist map. Tobi Vail, cofounder and drummer of Bikini Kill, "first heard The Raincoats in September 1984 because Calvin put them on a mixtape for me," she says. She was fifteen years old.

She knew Beat Happening as a local band and had gone to see a few of their shows, but she also associated Calvin with his day job: He drove a shuttle from Evergreen State College to downtown, and that's how Tobi got to a lot of gigs. She'd also listened to Calvin's KAOS show and was eager to know more about some of the female artists he'd been playing. Tobi spotted him one day in downtown Olympia. "I ran up to him on the street and said, 'You just played this song on the radio, and you said the band was all girls, and they weren't singing in English. Who was it?!'" Calvin assumed it was Shonen Knife (an all-female Japanese pop-punk band from Osaka, who'd ultimately be released in America on K Records), but Tobi

LIFE NUMBER 2

insisted it wasn't and that she needed a mixtape. It turned out the band was the female-fronted French group The Calamities, who recorded a single eponymous LP on Posh Boy Records (a Hollywood label linked to the rise of the early-eighties punk scene in Orange County). Calvin's mixtape included The Raincoats' "In Love." Tobi fell in love with The Raincoats.

She started hanging out at Calvin's apartment where she could listen to his Raincoats records, and a couple years later got her own KAOS show. "The reason I did it was because, that way, I wouldn't have to bother other people to tape me records," she remembers. "I could hear all the music I wanted and listen to *The Raincoats* [album]." KAOS was the only place in town besides Calvin's apartment with an original copy. "I immediately started listening to that record. It got stuck in my head, it lasted, and there was more and more to discover," Tobi says. The song "The Void" would become her anthem of sorts, shaping her musical sensibilities as she formed bands that included the Go Team (with Calvin) and, soon after, Bikini Kill. "I was *obsessed*," she admits.

Tobi didn't actually own the record herself for several more years—British import copies from 1979 were extremely hard to come by. "I'd never seen it in a record store here *ever*," she remembers, initially assuming it was because Olympia was "pretty isolated, and the record stores here had a limited selection of punk and post-punk." When she went on tour to San Francisco in 1987, she thought she'd find it, but nothing. "As a kid in the United States, it turned out you could only have that record if you happened to be alive and buying music when it came out in 1979." Tobi introduced her friend Kurt Cobain, who was about to become known worldwide as the frontman of Nirvana, to The Raincoats. They'd listen to them together on the cassettes they'd recorded from Calvin's vast collection. She eventually got her own copy when Kurt and Nirvana went over to Europe. "He brought me some Wipers records from Germany, too," Tobi recalls.

Meanwhile, in a more roundabout way, Calvin was also the link between Kathi Wilcox of Bikini Kill and The Raincoats. Around 1984 or '85, Kathi's stepbrother gave her the *Fairytale* 7-inch EP. He was a student at Evergreen and lived across the hall from

Calvin, so "he was familiar with the music scene and bought all these records," Kathi remembers. She wasn't even in high school yet. Eventually, her stepbrother wanted to listen to his vinyl on cassette, so he brought the goods to her and asked if she'd make cassettes of them all; the upshot was she could keep the vinyl. *Fairytale* was in that stack. "Suddenly *I had the Raincoats!*" Kathi says. "I didn't have any frame or reference for understanding their music, but that record hit me the hardest when I got into high school and was really trying to wrap my mind around what music *was*." It gave Kathi a way to completely recalibrate her thinking about songs—how they're made and what they can do. When she eventually met Tobi, they came to one another as Raincoats fans. Kathi didn't have the self-titled LP *The Raincoats*, and Tobi didn't have the *Fairytale* EP, so they shared their records.

Carrie Brownstein of Sleater-Kinney confirms that the apartment complex where Calvin and Kathi's stepbrother were living was a Raincoats hotbed. "I definitely first heard The Raincoats in the Martin Apartments in Olympia, around 1994. *Everyone* was looking for those records," she says. "They were just something you were searching for. And if you had a Raincoats record, you definitely showed it off in your apartment!"

"I didn't know then, but it seems like lots of encounters people were having with our music was through tapes, and people making tapes of tapes of tapes," Ana says. "In Portland, Olympia, I heard from Calvin of K Records that he was doing that kind of thing, and Rob Sheffield in New York, as well."

Kathleen Hanna of Bikini Kill eventually made her way to Olympia to attend Evergreen State College. It was there—thanks in large part to the ethos of a city inspired by The Raincoats—that she learned without a doubt "punk is NOT a genre," Kathleen declares. "I was already open to the idea that punk wasn't a genre—it's an *idea!*—but listening to the bands on K Records, and listening to The Raincoats, made me know that punk doesn't have to be this in-your-face aggressive, fuck-you music. It can be this really complicated, nuanced thing." What punk meant, Kathleen learned from The Raincoats, "was that we could do whatever the fuck we wanted, and what felt important was making the kind of music we wanted to make."

She learned new forms of political defiance through song. "The Raincoats always felt way more confrontational to me than just loud, fast, in-your-face punk music, because their songs are falling apart and coming together at the same time you're listening to them." She realized that resistance music need not be overt, with objectively political lyrics. "I remember thinking, when I first heard 'The Void,' *Oh wow, this is a whole third option.*" Until then, Kathleen thought protest music needed to be "really didactic, really obvious."

Meanwhile, for G.B. Jones and the group of artists that would become known as "queercore," listening was key as The Raincoats' music revealed new layers of metaphor and meaning.

J.D.S AND THE RISE OF QUEERCORE

One of the most fascinating aspects of the Raincoats influence on the queercore movement of the eighties and nineties is that it was completely unbeknownst to the band as it was happening. Especially in North America at that time and in the years that followed, there was a significant overlap between the punk and queer communities. And for a lot of the queer female artists in particular who wanted to see themselves in the musicians from whom they found inspiration, The Raincoats laid a foundation.

Of course, stateside, nobody knew The Raincoats personally, and there was very little personal information published about them in the press. So queercore artists had to look for signs; there was an intense desire to find likeminded musicians while working hard to avoid exposing them to homophobic violence. For artists like G.B., it was critical to avoid doing anything that would unintentionally out another queer artist who wasn't open about their sexuality or didn't openly identify as part of the queer community. But "there was a network of people who talked," G.B. says, and amongst themselves, they wanted to know who else out there was like them. "We'd say, quietly to one another as part of the queer underground punk community, this person is queer, and that person is queer, too." For anyone who wasn't around then or wasn't aware, you've gotta think back to the critical question of safety at the time. Remember Lucy Whitman of Rock Against Sexism recalling how dangerous it was to be openly gay even in London? On either side of the Atlantic, an openly queer identity could be life-threatening, and the importance of establishing safe spaces (that's an anachronism) was paramount. Yet it was also crucial to create a community in which artists could find kinship and sonic role models among those with whom they shared experiential knowledge of maintaining an underground sexual identity.

G.B. coined the term "queercore" in *J.D.s*, the zine she co-created with artist Bruce LaBruce. In their zine, the term got its start as "homocore," and *J.D.s* published a "Top Ten" list of homocore songs for listeners in the underground queer punk community. G.B. compiled the list and several songs made it because they offered a way for readers, despite their geographic location, to become part of the same network that G.B, and others established years prior: those in the know about queer artists making waves and pushing boundaries. By the second issue of *J.D.s*, The Raincoats' "Only Loved at Night," a song Ana wrote, featured prominently.

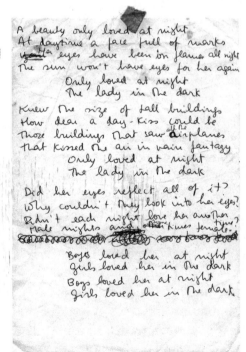

Ana's lyrics for "Only Loved at Night"

G.B. kept a keen ear out for what she describes as queercoding, or secret references to queer identity and queer love. Without even having to pause in reflection, G.B. recalls that "Only Loved at Night" "was even more overt than other songs we included on that chart," referring to the song's "whole sections devoted to the female protagonist and her relationship with another woman." Being direct in those days simply wasn't feasible due to discrimination and violence, G.B. stresses. Instead, artists were forced to speak in literary language that could be parsed solely by others in the know. Gina reflects on how several of Ana's songs dealt in subtle yet beautiful and meaningful ways with "issues of sexuality and gender," and says, "People who listened and cared really got it ... and all that was happening when homosexuality and gay marriage were still criminalized," both legally and socioculturally.

"Only Loved at Night" was not only added to the zine's "Top Ten" in Issue no. 2, but it remained on the list throughout the life of *J.D.s*, introducing queer readers in the US, Canada, UK, Japan, Germany, Australia, New Zealand, and beyond to the music of The Raincoats.

Many of those zines made it to London, and filmmaker Lucy Thane and the rest of the self-named "queercore militia" found power in the music of The Raincoats. It was Lisa Cook of London queercore band Sister George who first gave Lucy a Raincoats tape, and she remembers a special kind of power and allure in the underground nature of The Raincoats' presumed queer identities. "The Raincoats weren't out there saying, 'Oh we're queer,' but I think everyone smelt it," Lucy says, "so they didn't actually need to say it, and it's not like they've ever hidden anything. That would be a whole other thing, and that's not what it was. It was more the kind of thing where once you officially name it—once you say 'queer'—it kind of disappears in a way or doesn't have the same power," she explains. Thus, it was important that none of The Raincoats were going out of their way to make that self-identification publicly. "It's like the fairy tale trope in a way, where naming it is at once so powerful, but it's double-edged," Lucy suggests, because once you say it, the power starts to dissipate.

"I never declared my sexuality publicly," Ana says. "I don't know if it was right or wrong. When you're playing, people ask all these stupid questions that try to put you in boxes, like, 'Are you a feminist? Are you this or that?' So I never declared it because I didn't want the story to become all about that."

The upshot is that The Raincoats opened the world to queercore musicians, filmmakers, and visual artists in new ways. Lucy herself would go on to immortalize a diverse range of female artists within the queercore community in her 1997 documentary *She's Real (Worse Than Queer)* after first becoming inspired by The Raincoats herself.

Meanwhile, many fans of The Raincoats and *J.D.s* in the UK and stateside became part of a globally disparate queer punk underground community through zine culture. Raincoats music and other songs on the *J.D.s* "Top Ten" offered a critical way for them to reframe the destructive narrative surrounding their identities: from homophobia to joy.

As G.B. emphasizes, *J.D.s* and other circulating queercore materials provided information that readers "simply could *not find* in mainstream media at all, in any way." Any sense of joy among members of the queer punk underground was not mainstream news; if homosexuality was represented in the news at all, the language and images were discriminatory. "This was during the AIDS crisis," G.B. explains, and describes memories of "Ronald Reagan standing up and laughing at people dying of AIDS, so you couldn't find anything positive in the mainstream media about any kind of queer community." The kind of news queer punks needed to survive came from zines like *J.D.s*, and it became a form of news that could travel into urban, suburban, and even rural geographic regions. G.B. proudly recalls how *J.D.s* established networks among queer communities in Olympia, Toronto, San Francisco, and London, as well as smaller towns around the globe. "It hooked up all these queer kids," she says, "and I think it was so amazing, because instead of a queer community in one geographic place focused around a bar or a bathhouse, it was all connected through music and wasn't limited in that spatial way." *J.D.s*, and the queercore movement it developed, opened up possibilities for queer artists who finally had the courage to make their art public. "And I think that's why people felt this excitement about seeing a band like The Raincoats in *J.D.s* and finding out more about them—it's like a lifeline, this sense of 'Oh my God, there are other queer women doing amazing work, experimenting with music, and experimenting with their image and media.'"

The effects of *J.D.s* remain salient in the present. Even in the decades following the rise and fall of what G.B. and others officially term queercore ("Anything after 1995 is something else," G.B. says), The Raincoats' music has continued to serve an anthemic purpose for queer artists of younger generations. In the 2020s, Honey Birch (Gina's daughter and a recent London art school graduate) explains how many of the queer friends they made in art school were fans of The Raincoats. "It's really music that speaks to queer artists *now*," Honey says.

ROSELAND

While the foundations for The Raincoats' second life were being laid in America, Ana and Gina were pursuing new creative outlets in England. "It wasn't like I thought, *oh, let's get another band*," Ana says. More simply, she started writing songs on her own, "some quite idiosyncratic stuff." Since she'd enjoyed playing with Charles Hayward so much, she thought it'd be worth giving a new

Roseland cassette design

band a try. Along with Charles, she added two other musicians, Helen Ottaway and Sarah Homer. Roseland was born. After some rehearsals in southeast London, "We only played a couple of gigs," Ana says.

When Ana asked Charles to join Roseland, he was so eager that he designed a drum kit specifically for the band. It was a 16-inch small bass drum—"Like a kid's bass drum," he describes it—a set of smaller toms, quiet cymbals "more like pencil than paint," and very small gongs. He wanted to create a kit where "the whole junket was more like a drawing than a painting," speaking the language of The Raincoats, which blends visual and sonic elements. He made a point of picking up odd and left-behind instruments, those that had been largely discarded or set out for resale "in secondhand markets after the Second World War." Being part of Roseland gave him an opportunity to engage in sonic experimentation that drew on what The Raincoats had developed, and he reveled in looking for unique instruments—"Without even necessarily knowing if they were instruments," he says—and collecting them for Roseland.

The music, in Charles's memory, had a "manipulated complexity of multiple part lengths." It was about "letting Ana be Ana," and over a very short time, the band "became more and more Ana without it going through The Raincoats filter," he says. There was no studio recording but Roseland did make a tape. "A sort of demo," Ana describes it. Shirley took the photos and Ana did the cassette design.

The sound was different from The Raincoats, and Ana "loved playing with them." Charles was on his specially made drum kit, of course, Helen was on a Yamaha DX7, and Sarah on bass clarinet, which Ana says she found to be "the most beautiful instrument, although Anne Wood [who'd later play with The Raincoats herself] said it was the way Sarah played it." Ana played guitar and wrote the songs, so the dynamic was also distinct from what she and Gina were doing together in The Raincoats. "But then it just fizzled out. Nobody said they didn't want to do it anymore, it just fizzled out because everyone had their lives," Ana recalls.

Some of the Roseland songs ultimately ended up on Ana's first solo record, *The Lighthouse* (2005). Although, for quite a long time,

LIFE NUMBER 2

Ana wasn't thinking about making another record. She started working in her cousin's antique shop where, she says, "Sometimes I'd maybe think about writing some lyrics." But for the most part, "I gave up that kind of thing," she says.

DOROTHY

The Dorothy seed got planted while Gina and Vicky were still in The Raincoats, perhaps as early as *Odyshape* when they were both listening to more reggae, dub, and funk. "I really remember it starting with us doing some work together on one or two cassette machines, sampling some music, but this was before samplers," Vicky explains. "I was still in my squat, and I moved out in '83, so it was sometime before that." For Gina, the first inkling of Dorothy emerged one day when she was jamming. "It was with Paddy, actually, and I remember just finding out I could do crazy stuff on the guitar, and I felt really free," she says, "because I suppose The

Dorothy music video, Super 8 film still

Raincoats had an identity, which felt contained to a degree, and then suddenly I realized there was something else." Dorothy took hold in the late 1980s after Gina concluded nearly a year with Red Krayola in Germany.

In the earliest Dorothy recordings, Gina and Vicky created music that sampled dialogue from film noir, with spoken word extracts from female stars like Lauren Bacall, Joan Crawford, Marlene Dietrich, Veronica Lake, and Gene Tierney. Gina was especially interested in Cindy Sherman's *Untitled Film Stills*, which grappled with the politics of the femme fatale. So the film noir samples seemed like a perfect addition to Dorothy, a connection to that past while critiquing it in the present. It was all part of a concept Gina and Vicky wanted to create with the band. "We were playing around with stereotypes and commenting on the politics of glamour," Gina explains.

"And then we were told we had to replace everything because we couldn't clear the copyrights," Vicky sighs. "And we did that all quite well, too! A shame," Gina laughs. They remember Noel Watson, DJ and producer from Belfast, helping them to redo the sampling with clips they could use.

"We had this idea that we could really do something pop, but neither of us were really naturally inclined toward the pop thing," Gina says. "In a way, Dorothy was almost more of a reaction against The Raincoats. We did it a bit mischievously, and when we weren't doing it with any big studio involved, it was funny and fun. But when the big studio was involved, it all got taken a bit too seriously."

Dorothy signed to Chrysalis, and it wasn't the right fit for what Vicky and Gina wanted from the project. "The first Dorothy music video, which I didn't make, I really wanted John Maybury to make," Gina says. (The painter turned music video director was famously described as bringing the auteur theory of filmmaking to the music video with his film for Sinead O'Connor's "Nothing Compares 2 U," which won best video at the MTV awards.) "I loved that Sinead O'Connor video, but he turned us down, and I felt quite devastated because I'd set my heart on him."

But with Chrysalis having an eye toward profits, Dorothy's first music video shoot put a damper on Gina's burgeoning interest in

LIFE NUMBER 2

returning to filmmaking, as well as the entire musical project. "It was a horrible day, and I really didn't enjoy it at all," she says. "It was suggested that Tim Pope do it, and I didn't like him, the producer, or the makeup artist. They picked me up, all these guys, and put me in the back of the car while they drove for miles and miles, chatting and smoking. I wish I'd done a runner!" Gina jokes, but underscores the experience was an example of the sexism she thinks is pervasive in the music video industry. "I've never felt less like somebody than I felt making that video. And you can put that in the book." In 1991, the *New York Times* cited Robert Longo—famed artist and music video director for bands including New Order, R.E.M., and Megadeth—discussing how difficult it was for women to break into and be seen as equals in that world centered on MTV. "It's almost impossible for women," he was quoted as saying.

Gina shot the second Dorothy music video herself. "That Dorothy video I made is ... quite peculiar," she laughs. "I don't know what we were thinking it was going to look like, but it was really a bit of fun to make with those back projections."

The theme arose from their interest in mid-century cinema, thanks to Cindy Sherman, and all the gender-based tropes that went with it. Given their interest in classical Hollywood film noir, it made perfect sense to create a rear-projection driving video.

You know the visuals: two people seated in a car's interior, a famously fake-looking background designed to give the appearance that the occupants are en route to a destination. It's what you've got in the Humphrey Bogart film Dark Passage *(1947), or scenes where Janet Leigh's driving fearfully down the California highway in* Psycho *(1960), or as Grace Kelly's getting to know Cary Grant while driving them along the French Riviera in* To Catch a Thief *(1955).*

While Gina downplays the quality of her first attempt at a Dorothy video, that work ultimately rekindled her interest in the moving art form she'd once loved. It also led to her directing music videos for dozens of new Rough Trade artists in the 1990s and 2000s, including The Raincoats on their DGC debut to come.

Vicky and Gina also recorded a full Dorothy LP, never to be released. "A bunch of heads of the record company got changed," Vicky explains, "and if you don't have a hit with your first singles, they don't bother with your album. So three strikes and you're out, and we were out."

"But we really should get it back and put it out," Gina says to Vicky. "We should," she agrees.

COLLEGE RADIO

As the 1980s marched onward, the KAOS ethos made its way to nearby college radio stations. Patty Schemel remembers recording tapes of The Raincoats off KEXP-FM, the University of Washington's college station (which would later be the first in America to play both Soundgarden and Nirvana). Patty barely got a signal from where she grew up in the small Washington town of Maryville outside Seattle, so her cassette recordings of The Raincoats were fuzzy with radio static.

Sheri Hood, who'd later become the US manager for The Raincoats in the mid-nineties after managing bands such as Stereolab for the record label 4AD, became a fan herself of the feminist punk band while DJ'ing on her college radio station at Rutgers University. "There was one DJ in particular who was a huge Raincoats fan," Sheri remembers, who brought the band's music to the station. She immediately found it to be "richer" than existing punk, with "such a strong presence of the strength of women." For Sheri, "to be able to hear The Raincoats, their strength, the power ... that is empowering as a woman."

Around the same time, music journalist Rob Sheffield was playing Raincoats music as a DJ on his college radio station, New Haven WYBC. "There were all these women running things and making their voices heard," Rob says of the station at Yale. Otherwise, he suggests, you wouldn't necessarily hear a lot of music like The Raincoats on the radio. He reflects on the elements that made it so alluring to American audiences reaching for their own sense of the alternative. "It's really dizzying, it's really uncertain, constantly teetering on the brink of collapse," he says. "There are vocals where they're almost laughing, gasping for breath. I can't think of other music where you hear the singer just gasping for breath between words. It creates such a powerful, and yet really welcoming, sound. There's such a warmth to it, despite the abrasiveness." And, Rob adds, "It was funny! It's hard for me not to keep going back to that word, funny." He describes the playfulness of the music and the manner in which it was recorded, with Ana and Gina often "shouting back and forth to one another." Gina's frequently playful lyrics in particular used humor to address the discomfort and the absurdity of modern life.

College radio in America was critical for getting noncommercial music onto the airwaves and into the ears of young listeners and outsiders. The Fortnightly College Radio Report praised the Raincoats' *Odyshape*, leading to its continued play on stations long after the Raincoats' first life ended. "There's probably never been a record quite like this one," the report read. "Intelligent lyrics, involving personal and romantic observations and vocals of surpassing subtlety. Also, instrumental tracks that—while they are in no way mainstream music—still tantalize and ring true. *Unquestionably the music of the next century. And if everybody got it now, we'd be there, wouldn't we?*"[1]

GINA AND FILM

Post-Dorothy, as time rolled into the 1990s, Gina threw herself into filmmaking. She fell in love with the medium in her early days at Hornsey and later enrolled in a film course at the Royal College of Art. She went onto direct music videos for lauded indie bands, from New Order to the Pogues, Daisy Chainsaw to the Libertines.

How'd she end up behind the camera? Before starting at Hornsey back in 1976, Gina had imagined an enormous, spacious studio area where she'd be painting larger-than-life canvases. Instead, she arrived and was shown up "a little rickety staircase with a small desk." She was disappointed, but her creative impulses weren't dampened. She headed to the "4-D department, where they had video," she explains, "and that's when it really started for me." She'd read about American artist Dan Graham's installation work and his explorations of cybernetics and embodiment through videography. "People videoing each other rolling around on the floor, essentially," Gina laughs. It was that kind of conceptual cross-disciplinary creative impulse that led to Gina's experimentation with pieces at the intersection of video and performance art.

Gina at The Marquee, 1978

LIFE NUMBER 2

That impulse was set alight with the arrival of Derek Jarman at Hornsey. "He showed his Super 8 films, and I kind of fell in love," Gina says. "That splotchy brilliance, the smudginess that Super 8 has. Seeing those was my first spiritual experience." The first time Jarman showed his work, Gina was running late. She walked into the library—"Not a traditional library," she quickly clarifies—and saw the room "full of people lining the walls. People sitting on the floor, people lining the wall standing up, and the bright light of the Jarman Super 8 projection." Her memory also goes immediately to the performance-based film work Jarman was doing at the time, with "people dressed in these amazing costumes with mirrors flashing into the lens, and hitting the sunlight." Gina found it to be a beautiful kind of "otherness," a world where the romance of creativity came alive. "I remember feeling like I'd got into heaven, like I'd finally arrived at my Catholic childhood vision of heaven, come to fruition in Derek Jarman Super 8s."

Gina got her own Super 8 and started shooting. "Those rich and beautiful colors that come through, I just fell for it. And it seemed like a medium that was going to be very accessible, but it turned out not to be so cheap! It was like getting a drug addiction, spending *all the money* on film processing," she laughs. "I did become a bit of a Super 8 addict." During her Super 8 addiction, Gina made a range of films, including *3 Minute Scream*, which would eventually become the face of Tate Britain's *Women in Revolt!* exhibition nearly fifty years later.

Her music video career started with films she made for Dorothy, but in terms of paid work, Gina's first commission involved videos for karaoke club backdrops. But don't worry: She could never go so commercial. While she was creating karaoke films, she was directing dozens of women, in black and white, burning their bras and rejecting stiletto heels.

Since her Raincoats days, Gina remained close with Geoff Travis, who catalyzed her music video career. While Gina was enrolled at the Royal College of Art, Geoff was getting Rough Trade going again. He called her up and asked if she'd make a music video for the female-fronted UK rock band Daisy Chainsaw, touring Europe with American bands Mudhoney and Hole. Gina directed a promo video in 1991 for their first single "Love Your Money" and another the following year for their follow-up "Hope Your Dreams Come True." (While The Raincoats would soon be described in newspapers across the US and UK as the godmothers of Riot Grrrl, Gina was directing the music videos that would bring the sounds of Daisy Chainsaw's KatieJane Garside—who Courtney Love described as "one of the first true Riot Grrrls"—to TV audiences globally.) She also directed additional music videos for Factory Records, Flying Nun, and Rough Trade, featuring bands like New Order, Girls In The Garage, Cortney Tidwell, The Veils, The Long Blondes, Garageland, Palma Violets, Dee Dee Ramone, and the Pogues. "Geoff put a lot of film work my way," Gina says.

RIOT GRRRL FAIRY GODMOTHERS

In Olympia and elsewhere in the US, Riot Grrrls were finding the confidence to unleash their sonic power, thanks in part to The Raincoats. Riot Grrrl was a movement, a genre, a community, and so much more that began in the early 1990s and catalyzed a wave of overt feminist politics on stages across the country. Finally, the Riot Grrrl artists insisted, *women to the front!*

And Riot Grrrl wasn't just rising in America. In a UK parallel akin to the simultaneous transatlantic rise of punk in 1976, bold, loud, feminist artists were emerging in England and Scotland. Anjali Bhatia cofounded British Riot Grrrl band Mambo Taxi in 1991 with Ella Guru, Delia Sparrow, and Andrea Stallard. She left Mambo Taxi in 1993 to form a new British Riot Grrrl band, Voodoo Queens, with Ella Guru, her sister Rajni Bhatia, Steffi Lucchesini, and Anjula Bhaskar. Later, Mambo Taxi would open for The Raincoats at their first reunion gig at The Garage in 1994. She recalls being "so nervous to meet The Raincoats because Gina and Ana were absolute legends in my eyes, the two true godmothers of Riot Grrrl."

Without The Raincoats, Anjali might never have picked up the drumsticks that gave her the confidence to form Mambo Taxi. She first heard "No One's Little Girl" on John Peel's radio show and was immediately hooked. She got a copy of *The Raincoats* on cassette. "It's one of those experiences where you remember exactly where you were, and for me it was sitting on the pavement in East London with my sister." Anjali was "blown away" by Palmolive's drumming and the way every part of the drum kit felt essential. "The way she did her paraddidles on the times!" Anjali exclaims. "I'd never heard paraddidles like that before." It was then, at the end of the eighties, that Anjali started to play drums. "I'd never even picked up a drumstick, but my friend who'd given me the *Raincoats* cassette handed me a pair of drumsticks, and that was a life-changer."

"With The Raincoats," Gina explains, "we didn't quite know where to look for that kind of influence ourselves, so we looked in jagged places, and I think that's what made the records perhaps seem odd, so different." She cites various visual artists, ranging from Dada sculptors to Ana Mendieta, as well as The Slits, reggae, dub, and experimental rock. But Anjali interjects to simplify things: "The Raincoats are the mothers of invention of the *entire scene*. It was so clear, listening, that there was never a fear of experimenting, about always questioning what you're creating and how you're doing it. And that's what I found so influential and still do." Delia Sparrow of Mambo Taxi agrees. "Bands like the Runaways were competing in a men's world but The Raincoats were making their own world."

"For me," Gina jumps back in, "the Riot Grrrl thing was completely brilliant because in The Raincoats' early times, I often felt like, *What the hell is going on? Who am I? What am I doing? Oh my God!* And as time moved on, I almost forgot about The Raincoats, but when Riot Grrrl happened, it was so enriching for us. We were so nurtured by it and fed by it, and so in awe of the Riot Grrrls and what they were doing, with different motivations and inspirations." Gina looks at Anjali and smiles, "I'm talking about you lot!" For Gina, the post-Raincoats "girl bands" in the mid to late eighties never offered the same kind of experimental, feminist space that The Raincoats and their Rough Trade peers had. "It felt distressing and disappointing," she says. "But then when Riot Grrrl happened, and of course it was fractured, and it wasn't the cozy tea party I like to imagine, like some people think it was for us in the early punk days—it was something completely new."

Not all the Riot Grrrls were, well, girls. Jon Slade of London's Huggy Bear was, he ventures to guess, the biggest fan of The Raincoats in his band. He wasn't old enough to see The Raincoats live the first time around. "But I heard about them as this really important reference," he explains. And, from that point, he started looking for them *everywhere*—quite literally. "At shows around in the crowd, at Notting Hill Record & Tape Exchange—The Raincoats' stomping ground—I was always looking for The Raincoats!" he exclaims. Both in the flesh, as well as on vinyl or cassette. "But there were no Raincoats to be seen, and it was even hard to hear The Raincoats," Jon laments. Their records had gone out of print, and nobody was letting go of used copies. He'd often venture to the home of music journalist Everett True (aka Jerry Thackray) to listen to Raincoats records, *Odyshape* in particular. "My favorite Raincoats for a *long time*," he says of the second LP. Until he found his own 7-inch copy of the *Fairytale* EP in the upstairs "collectible" area of Notting Hill Record and Tape Exchange, that is. His favorite had to become the object he owned.

For Jon, it's essential to highlight the distinctions between the "American independent music" that Riot Grrrl grew out of, and the media-identified Riot Grrrl bands in the UK. Those British Riot Grrrls, including Huggy Bear in particular, "had a feeling of abandonment" when they got grouped in with the American Riot Grrrls. "There was a feeling that we should become more British," he explains, "so we made a point to start looking at things that were or had been around us to take inspiration from." Namely, he says, "THE RAINCOATS!"

The Raincoats were so often "lumped in" with other female-fronted or all-female bands like The Slits, Delta 5, and the Au Pairs, Gina explains, that it resulted in them feeling a sense, at times, of being pitted against one another. "We all fought that, and we fought the idea that we were similar just because we were all female. But there were so few women in punk that it seemed an inevitability. Riot Grrrl changed all of that."

And it wasn't just in England that The Raincoats were having that impact. Their music and ethos spread to other parts of the UK. The Glasgow band Lung Leg shared something important when

LIFE NUMBER 2

they got together to make music: a love of The Raincoats. They took so much inspiration from The Raincoats, in fact, they made it a point of covering "Fairytale in the Supermarket" at every gig. "They were so sophisticated compared to us," Lung Leg bassist Jane McKeown says, "and we were so scared to play, but we looked up to them, so we did it!"

"Now, this is just such a great Glasgow story," Jane continues. "I walked out of my flat one morning and bumped into our manager, and he was with Steve Shelley." It was 1994, after Steve Shelley of Sonic Youth had become the new, albeit temporary, Raincoats drummer. Steve, as it turned out, was in Glasgow to play a gig with The Raincoats that night. "I didn't even know they were playing!" Jane exclaims. "I just went BERSERK! And I was like, *Oh my God, I have to go, I have to get tickets!* And then, next thing I knew, The Raincoats were asking, 'Well, do you want to play tonight, too?' They asked us to open for them! We hadn't practiced at all beforehand but obviously we said yes, absolutely. I think they took pity on us," Jane laughs, "because they invited us to play more support gigs with them after that."

The Scottish indie pop band bis were also Raincoats fans and dying to play with them. In what Bis drummer and keyboardist Amanda MacKinnon (aka Manda Rin) calls a "bonkers" and "absolutely crazy" fact, The Raincoats opened for her band in Glasgow in 1996.

For the record, Bis wasn't a Riot Grrrl band, and Lung Leg didn't initially call themselves Riot Grrrls. But parallel to bands like Mambo Taxi in London and Bikini Kill in Olympia, Bis released records on Olympia label K, and Lung Leg were taking a DIY approach, creating their own zines, and making music overtly about female equality. Raincoats-inspired stuff. So, by default, Lung Leg became Glasgow Riot Grrrls. They were routinely booked with the self-proclaimed English Riot Grrrls. "So when people said to us, 'You're Riot Grrrls!'" Jane remembers, "we thought, yeah, we're really happy to be part of that and really proud of that legacy."

For Anjali, while there was certainly a sense of power and community among Riot Grrrls, the making of the Riot Grrrl generation in the UK felt stifling at times. It seemed crucial to "have a particular opinion on certain topics," she explains, "and if you didn't, you feared being politically ostracized." Yet as Gina and Anjali ultimately agree, the Riot Grrrl bands were able to form a movement with political power. "And The Raincoats made that movement possible," Anjali tells Gina. "You didn't need slogans, you didn't need overt political language. Just by existing, and doing what you did, and making what you made, The Raincoats were the fiercest statement, and one that made it possible for all of us a decade later."

The power was flowing back in the opposite direction, too. "I remember so distinctly going to see Huggy Bear and Mambo Taxi with Ana," Shirley says, "and it was the best thing we'd seen since The Raincoats ended. It really felt like, wow, something is finally happening again after this horrible time for music after '84 when there was just nothing that excited us, nothing that made us feel anything."

On February 26, 1994, *Melody Maker* called The Raincoats "proto-Riot Grrrls," and *NME*, *Rolling Stone*, *Billboard*, and others followed suit. The phrases "godmothers of Riot Grrrl" and "godmothers of grunge" began to stick. *LA Weekly* called them "Riot Moms," while the *NME* used "grandmothers of invention." Keep in mind, they were in their thirties and forties at this point. *Billboard* saw The Raincoats as near-supernatural beings, "impermeable to time." No matter which seems most fitting, nearly a decade after they'd called it quits for good, The Raincoats had become Riot Grrrl fairy godmothers and Riot Grrrl royalty.

ANA AT THE ANTIQUE SHOP

After the "fizzling out" of Roseland, Ana largely shifted away from music. She became an antiques dealer of sorts, thanks to her cousin Manuel, who got into the business with a stall in London's King's Road market area (then Chenil Gallery). Ana initially sold antiques at that stall, nicknamed "the box shop." Manuel focused on ornate and elaborate wooden and lacquered boxes with intricate inlays. Some were Georgian and Victorian sewing boxes, others writing boxes and tea caddies.

Ana in Manuel's antique shop, surrounded by santos, 1993

Manuel eventually opened an antique shop at 53 Ledbury Road, just a short walk from the Rough Trade shop on Talbot Road and from Ana's flat. "The style of a lot of things was really Indo-Portuguese," Ana explains, made in India according to Portuguese taste but influenced by local esthetics. "They were a marriage of Indian and Portuguese styles created in the Portuguese colonies in India, like Goa, for example." She highlights the "Catholic figures" that Manuel sold: large, wooden polychrome busts, sitting atop metal skirt-like bases. "People would often get them and hand-sew dresses for them," she says, using her hands to depict how the bottom part of the forms essentially were voids, waiting for adornment.

The dolls with the "cage" skirt design, Manuel explains, are called santas *(or* santos) de roca, *while those with a whole body were known more simply as*

– 175 –

santas or santos. They were typically made in Portugal by local craftsmen, primarily for wealthy residents with chapels in their own homes, while the faces were often crafted to mirror those of the owners. They also appeared in city churches, where they were made by professional sculptors. Their production began in the eighteenth century but occurred primarily in the nineteenth, and those from the nineteenth are known to be more sophisticated in detail and with brighter colors. Some would be used in processions from country churches, where people would pin money onto the dresses, most likely in exchange for religious favors. Men typically crafted the heads and arms while women made the dresses. Years later, many ended up for sale in antique shops.

Those polychrome figures would play their own small role in Ana's musical reawakening about to come.

KURT LOVES THE RAINCOATS

Before Nirvana became Nirvana, Kurt Cobain was listening to The Raincoats thanks to Tobi Vail. "When Kurt and I were friends and hanging out, we listened to The Raincoats so much," Tobi says. "We'd make each other tapes."

Patty Schemel says it definitively: "Kurt loved The Raincoats." She remembers listening to The Raincoats, The Vaselines, and Marine Girls with him long before she became the drummer of Hole and before Kurt began dating Hole's lead singer, Courtney Love. It was a shared reverence, and when Patty later moved in with Kurt and Courtney in Los Angeles during her Hole days, she remembers a turntable setup with records in front, stacked in two rows designed for flipping through. "*The Raincoats* record was always in the front," Patty says. "He'd walk by and flip through the records, and if someone had moved it, he'd put it back out in the front." Kurt would receive more records than anyone might know what to do with from record companies, artists. "But *The Raincoats* always had to be in the front," declares Patty.

It was an Olympia thing, says Bruce Pavitt, who signed Nirvana to Sub Pop in 1989: "Kurt was always more Olympia than Seattle."

LIFE NUMBER 2

Indeed, despite Nirvana's historic association with Seattle, Kurt almost always identified the group as "Nirvana from Olympia, WA."

"I remember Kurt discovering The Raincoats and being interested in them," Kim Gordon says, "and that was sweet because Nirvana had such a loud sound that had become mainstream—they were *rock* with millions of fans—so I think it was surprising to Nirvana fans when Kurt talked about The Raincoats, because he was embracing something that was so soft . . . he wasn't afraid to be vulnerable in that way, and maybe it made it OK for other boys to feel that way."

There was an enduring link between Kurt's love for The Raincoats and the egalitarian politics of Olympia that also gave rise to Bikini Kill and other Riot Grrrl mainstays. Referring to Kurt's deeply rooted feminism, Bruce says, "I really think that Kurt, retrospectively, can be seen as a visionary in so many ways." While The Raincoats were ingrained in Kurt's thinking, his intellectual connections to Olympia were distinct from the other members of Nirvana. As Bruce explains it, The Raincoats simply weren't in the same orbit as bandmates Dave Grohl or Krist Novoselic, or for other quintessential Sub Pop bands like Mudhoney. Michael Meisel, Nirvana's longtime agent, confirms it: the band was "Kurt's thing."

FINDING ANA

In the summer of 1992, Jude Crighton was working in the Rough Trade shop on a fairly quiet midweek day. Delia Sparrow, who handled Rough Trade mail orders by day and played in UK Riot Grrrl band Mambo Taxi after hours, was also at work. Jude's Rough Trade business partners, Pete Donne and Nigel House, would ordinarily have been there, too, but they'd gone to see a cricket Test match between England and Australia. "Kurt and Courtney walked in, and Delia and I said, 'Oh!' We knew who these people were!" Jude recalls excitedly.

Jude remembers both of them looking "quite nondescript, like any music fans who'd walk into the shop at the time." But of course, Jude and Delia knew all about the success of Nirvana's

Jude Crighton and Pete Donne (right and center), working in the Rough Trade shop, 1979

Nevermind, Hole's *Pretty on the Inside*, and the relationship between the two artists that had become notorious in the music press. They immediately walked over to the 7-inch record rack. Rough Trade had been working with a German guy in the nineties who recorded bands and "produced these really high-quality 7-inch picture sleeves," as Jude describes them. But in her memory, the first interaction she had with the famous couple wasn't a good one. Courtney was angry to see the bootlegs, and Jude watched her as she flipped through and pulled out a Nirvana record. Courtney turned to Jude, as Jude remembers it, and said something like, "This is my husband's record! Why are you selling it?"

"She claimed royalty rights over them," Delia remembers. Jude laughs, remembering how Delia was "really inclined to argue with Courtney," but Jude quietly calmed Courtney. Rough Trade had around six copies of the Nirvana 7-inch, so Jude told Courtney to just take them if she liked. Courtney acquiesced. Kurt still hadn't said a word.

LIFE NUMBER 2

Very quietly, he turned to Jude, "Do you have a copy of the first Raincoats album?" The record had been out of print for years and was only "circulating hand to hand," Jude remembers. "But I can tell you where to find Ana," she replied to Kurt, "because she might still have one she can give you." She drew a rough map for Kurt and Courtney to get from the Rough Trade shop on Talbot Road to the antique shop on Ledbury Road, less than half a mile away. Before they left, Delia remembers, "they signed all the Nirvana and Hole stock we had in the store." Jude adds, "We heard Kurt might have had his own copy of *The Raincoats* originally but lost it in his breakup with Tobi Vail."

With Jude's directions, Kurt and Courtney set off to find Ana. They turned onto Ledbury Road and began walking ever so slightly uphill toward Manuel's antique shop where Ana was behind the counter. It was a less than ten-minute walk in a summer on record for being particularly temperate and without much rain.

"I probably should have called Ana to tell her they were coming!" Jude laughs. Ana laughs, too: "I didn't even know who they were!" They seemed different from the typical antique shop clientele but, Ana remembers, "Kurt really liked the religious female figures from the churches," referring to the *santos* dolls. "He seemed enthusiastic about buying one," she says, but Courtney dissuaded him. "'We'll think about it,' she told him." (In his liner notes to Nirvana's *Incesticide*, Kurt was still thinking about the Portuguese saints. "I arrived at this elfin shop filled with something else I've compulsively searched for over the past few years—really old fucked-up marionette-like wood carved dolls (quite a few hundred years old). Lots of them ..." he wrote. "They wouldn't accept my credit card but the dolls were really way too expensive anyway."[2] Patty Schemel would later describe Kurt's interest in those kinds of polychrome figures, referring to his "collection of mannequins, dress forms, and various anatomical dolls" he kept stashed in an attic.[3]

After Kurt pondered the *santos* dolls, he asked Ana about the self-titled LP. She told him she didn't think she had any copies, but they exchanged contact information and Ana promised to let him know.

Meanwhile, Pete and Nigel returned to the Rough Trade shop after the cricket match. "Hey, do you know who came into the shop earlier and what they were asking for?" Jude said to them. They all wondered if Ana was going to have a copy of *The Raincoats* to give to Kurt. Jude knew her copy, which she'd had since 1979 ("Well, Ross's copy!" she laughs) was in Australia. But Pete still had a copy and offered it to Ana to send to Nirvana's management. Ana adorned it first with one-of-a-kind art before posting it. "The connection was made," Jude smiles.

In December 1992, Nirvana's compilation album *Incesticide* hit shelves, and the American CD booklet featured Kurt's writing about his trek to find Ana:

A while ago, I found myself in bloody exhaust grease London again with an all-consuming urge to hunt for two rare things: back issues of *NME* ... and the very-out-of-print first Raincoats LP ...

In an attempt to satisfy the second part of my quest, I went to the Rough Trade shop and, of course, found no Raincoats record in the bin. I then asked the woman behind the counter about it and she said "well, it happens that I'm neighbors with Anna [sic] (member of The Raincoats) and she works at an antique shop just a few miles from here." So she drew me a map and I started on my way to Anna's [sic] ...

I politely introduced myself with a fever-red face and explained the reason for my intrusion. I can remember her mean boss almost setting me on fire with his glares. She said "well, I may have a few lying around so, if I find one, I'll send it to you (very polite, very English)." I left feeling like a dork, like I had violated her space, like she probably thought my band was tacky.

A few weeks later I received a vinyl copy of that wonderfully classic scripture with a personalized dust sleeve covered with xeroxed lyrics, pictures, and all the members' signatures. There was also a touching letter from Anna. It made me happier than playing in front of thousands of people each night, rock-god idolization from fans, music industry plankton kissing my ass, and the million dollars I made last year. It was one of the few really important things that I've been blessed with since becoming an untouchable boy genius.[4]

LIFE NUMBER 2

As soon as she saw it, Ana drafted something to Kurt:

Dear Kurt,
I am writing to you to say how thrilled we all were with what you wrote in the American version of "Incesticide." Shame it didn't come out in the English version, as your story was all connected with London.
I'd hoped you'd send the booklet of "Nevermind" and Hole's "Pretty on the Inside" back to me, signed and maybe a thanks note but I was totally surprised by you mentioning anything at all in your booklet, let alone the amount of space you devoted to it and I'm still quite shocked at how much it meant to you. At times like this, it feels it was really worth doing what we did and the reason I say this, is, not because you sold as many million as we sold thousands, but because I like your work (I've been listening to it quite a lot) and what you stand for, I mean your position towards the prejudices (about sexuality, colour and women) that you talk about in the booklet. I also think it was great to talk about the people and things you've found rewarding in your career, etc life and music.
There are no words to express how happy all this has made me (and the other Raincoats). Also, since you seem to enjoy it when you can have some positive influence on something, I'm letting you know that we've been asked to release that album and I think your interest in it has been a key factor in their decision helpful to us. We're still in negotiations about that, but I take this opportunity also to ask on behalf of the whole group if you'd write a piece for our booklet. Obviously this would mean a lot to us. We want to release it in the states and here (At least).
~~The company will only be able to release it here and in Europe, so we'll have to find something in the U.S.A. (any ideas?), etc.~~
For now, I hope everything is going well with your group, Courtney and the baby. Are you recording anything at the moment? Your voice is especially beautiful, intimate and warm in quiet bits so, please, do more of those!
I'll make a tape for you with some early stuff (end 70's, early 80's) some of which you might have not heard—things I got at the

Rough Trade shop that only came out in small numbers—others
you probably will have heard but . . . "nevermind."
　Lots of love
　Ana (as in Nirv<u>ana</u>)

Ana redrafted portions of the letter several times, and in a subsequent copy told Kurt she thought he would "make a great lullaby singer for Frances."

About a year after Kurt and Courtney's visit, Ana documented her recollections of meeting them in the antique shop and seeing the *Incesticide* liner notes:

Well, what he wrote there made me feel really good (I still do) and not because he is famous, but because he writes great music and is an anti-sexist anti-homophobic and anti-racist person and because his voice is angry and tender. End of story? Not quite.

As Ana's entry foretold, the connection with Kurt would soon bring The Raincoats back together, back into the studio, and back onto the stage. The Raincoats reformed in 1994 and later signed to Nirvana's record label DGC, due in no small part to Kurt's fandom. It didn't take much for the music press to turn this connection into vaunted lore.

"Prince Charming revives Sleeping Beauty," Richard Boon (one-time manager of Buzzcocks and founder of the UK record label New Hormones) began an article in *Puncture* magazine. "Surely we all know this fairytale by now. How Saint Kurt on a schedule break in London tracked down Portuguese-born former Raincoat Ana da Silva to her early-nineties job in an antique store, expressed a fawning enthusiasm for her group's past work . . . and suggested, maybe they should get back together?"[5]

But first, the fairy godmothers of Riot Grrrl had more magic to make.

LIFE NUMBER 2

HOLE PLAYS LONDON

"Ahhh, yes, the 'only-females allowed' show with one of my all-time favorite bands, Huggy Bear," Eric Erlandson says. "Funny, 'cause last time I checked, I'm a man. And there were two blokes in Huggy Bear, aw well! A fun experiment that failed."

On March 24, 1993, Hole played Subterania on Acklam Road, with Huggy Bear supporting. "Beneath the Westway, Portobello!" Lucy Thane exclaims, remembering the show while drawing attention to its palimpsestic location—Subterania used to be known as Acklam Hall, where The Raincoats and so many other West London punks had taken the stage years before.

A 600-capacity venue—small and intimate, as far as many venues in London go these days—it's about a half-mile walk from Ana and Shirley's flat, and not much farther from where Gina was living at the time. In other words, right in the middle of The Raincoats' stomping ground. Hole was in London to do a live BBC recording in advance of their new album, *Live Through This*, which was set for release in spring 1994, with Courtney Love on vocals and guitar, Eric Erlandson on guitar, Kristen Pfaff on bass and background vocals, and Patty Schemel on drums.

Liz Naylor, Bikini Kill manager and founder of UK queercore label Catcall Records, organized the gig as a women-only show—in line with the ethos of Riot Grrrl, and in part a response to the Bikini Kill–Huggy Bear tour where the misogyny of male concertgoers was often on display. The idea was for a gig space where women wouldn't need to push their way to the front; they'd already be there, safely. The aim was for women to feel like they were a critical part of the performance. The idea harkens back to some of the Jam Today women-only shows in the 1970s that Vicky participated in before joining The Raincoats. While Eric's memory of the gig underscores how this idea didn't take off in the nineties, it represents a kind of thinking innate within the Riot Grrrl scene—an ethos made possible by the influence of The Raincoats, who were there to experience it for themselves in the nineties at Subterania.

Ana and Shirley, separate from Lucy, were all near the front—*grrrls to the front!* To Lucy's surprise, Hole started to play a cover of

The Raincoats' "The Void" when she spotted someone who looked like Ana da Silva standing in front of her, very near the stage.

Shirley remembers the gig like it was yesterday. "When they started playing 'The Void,' I remember turning to Ana and screaming, 'The Void! The Void!' and Ana was like, 'What? What?' She didn't recognize it," Shirley laughs. "Well, she changed the words!" Ana insists, but laughs all the same. "She had a kind of rap going, talking about revolution. It's not that I don't like the idea of a revolution, but I didn't recognize it as 'The Void.'"

Suddenly, Lucy noticed the woman who resembled Ana yell out, "I wrote that! That's my song!" Lucy poked her on the shoulder and inquired, "Is this really your song?" The woman said it was, and Lucy asked if the woman would be willing to appear in the Bikini Kill film she was making. The woman said yes. "And that's how I met Ana!" Lucy says. "Isn't that just adorable?"

"I didn't know she was there!" Eric says. "We had just recorded 'The Void' for the BBC session and then played it live at that show. I don't think we ever played it again after that."

Two days later, on a Friday night, Ana sent a handwritten letter to Courtney that read in part:

I enjoyed it a lot the other night and I was VERY pleased about you covering 'The Void' (I wrote that one myself).

THE BIKINI KILL PILGRIMAGE

"The Raincoats were mysterious, well, they still are," Liz Naylor says. "And Kurt Cobain, Tobi Vail, Kathi Wilcox seeking them out ... It makes them part of some kind of fairytale, doesn't it? You have to find them, if they're really there at all."

Finding Ana wasn't just a turning point in Kurt's story. She was also the subject of a pilgrimage for members of Bikini Kill less than a year later. Liz was prepping for the Bikini Kill–Huggy Bear UK tour and getting ready to put out the split LP *Yeah Yeah Yeah Yeah/Our Troubled Youth* on Catcall in the UK (and Kill Rock Stars in the US). She tagged along with Jenny Black to Gina's place in

LIFE NUMBER 2

Polaroid of Bikini Kill's Kathi Wilcox with Ana, snapped on Ana's flat balcony, 1993

Westbourne Grove to talk about the upcoming Bikini Kill tour. Jenny was already planning to interview Gina anyway. "'These gigs, this music is going to change the world!' Gina said something like that," Liz says, describing Gina's unabashed enthusiasm. "And then I started pushing to get them to come to the Bikini Kill–Huggy Bear Conway Hall gig in London on March 3, 1993." It didn't take much convincing; Gina, Ana, and Shirley were almost always up for going to a gig (they were then, and they still are today—especially if it means supporting other women artists). "There was something in me that made the obvious connection between The Raincoats and Bikini Kill. I saw that lineage then, and I still think it's there. I could draw that line," Liz adds.

That year, members of Bikini Kill stayed at Liz's flat in London but were on a mission. "It was this case of a younger generation coming over and seeking," Liz explains, noting how Kurt's "story has been written about a million times. Everyone knows that one." But Tobi and Kathi engaged in a quest that Liz describes as a "lineage of clear feminist politics." Bikini Kill saw that "there was something right about going to pick up that connection again" in tracking down The Raincoats for themselves.

The Bikini Kill obsession with "finding a Raincoat" elevated Ana and Gina into mythical characters. "I know I'm talking about this pilgrimage, making them sound like part of some *ancient* fairytale," Liz laughs, "but they [Tobi, Kathi] were talking about them like they were some ancient oracle! You'd have thought they were ninety, one hundred years old, but they must have been what, *maybe forty* at the time?" Liz laughs harder as she describes Tobi, Kathi, and sometimes Jon Slade roaming around West London, hoping to happen upon a Raincoat.

"Tobi and I were *obsessed* with The Raincoats at that point, and we *really* wanted to meet them—that was one of the goals of going to England," Kathi explains. "We just kind of hounded anybody who we thought might know The Raincoats and were like, *you have to introduce us!*" Kathi credits Liz with the eventual meet-up, along with some help from Lucy Thane, who was following Bikini Kill for her documentary. "I think Liz sort of reached out to Ana, or to someone who knew Ana, and said, 'These girls want to come over and meet you.' I don't think Ana and Shirley knew we were bringing a film crew!" Kathi laughs. Kathi felt really nervous, especially since she considered Tobi to be the "Raincoats expert." But Kathi made a point of letting Ana know at least one clear thing: "There was an obvious lineage between us and The Raincoats," Kathi says. "I told Ana The Raincoats had influenced our band, and bands have since told us that they were influenced by our band. A lineage of inspiration," she describes it.

It's important to be clear that there wasn't a sonic lineage—it wasn't about *sounding* like The Raincoats, but rather a shared ideology and ethos. "Our band was all about trying to get permission," Kathleen Hanna explains of Bikini Kill, "and seeing and hearing

LIFE NUMBER 2

The Raincoats made me realize how you give people permission. That's such a big part of their band, and it has always been a big part of Bikini Kill—giving permission." Kathi emphasizes how Ana understood that kind of lineage deeply. She later wrote a note to Kathi that said, simply, "Keep up the courage, Kathi, you are our daughter."

While Liz remembers Lucy's near-constant presence on the UK Bikini Kill tour as "really stressful, like, *Oh fucking Lucy's turned up again with another camera*," Lucy not only made a much-loved documentary in the end but also managed to capture the afternoon in full where Kathi visited Ana. Only a few minutes of the footage made it into *It Changed My Life: Bikini Kill in the UK*, but she kept the full hour of film for posterity.[6]

In the footage, Ana and Shirley are sitting around a small kitchen table with Kathi, drinking glasses of orange juice and smoking cigarettes. It's a tight shot; Lucy's on the other side of the table in the small room, out of frame. Ana's talking about gigs she remembers, and Kathi asks if she has any photos. "Yeah, yeah," Ana says, knowingly. She and Shirley both stand up from the table, walking toward their living room where Ana's archive is lovingly kept. Ana grabs an *Odyshape* LP and brings it out to Kathi at the table. Shirley follows behind with *The Raincoats* LP. "This is the best one," she says to Kathi, who replies, "It *is* the best one. I've never heard that one [gesturing toward *Odyshape*]." Meanwhile, Ana has gone back into the living room and brings out a binder of clippings and fanzines while Shirley explains that they hadn't actually listened to *The Raincoats* themselves in years until they heard there was interest from record labels in doing CD reissues. "It was like two o'clock [in the a.m.]," begins Shirley. She tells Kathi that Gina and Vicky came over, they put the record on "full-volume," and started dancing around to the music. "Jude from Rough Trade, who lives next door, she told us the next day she'd heard it all," Shirley laughs.

Ana places the blue binder on the table and says to Kathi, "It's a bit boring, but when I had the patience I put this together." She opens it up to a copy of *Live Wire* No. 18 at the front. "This was the first thing that ever came out about The Raincoats." Kathi flips through and stops on an original advertisement for the *Fairytale* EP. "This single is *so good*," she tells Ana, then can't help but stare down at the table where *The Raincoats* is sitting. "We should listen to this record. Can we listen to it now?" Ana replies, "Yeah," and asks Kathi if she wants her to "Stick a tape in? Have you got this?" Kathi looks up excited: "No, like record it, make a tape? That would be great!"

"Have you heard this, Lucy? 'Fairytale in the Supermarket'?" Kathi says to Lucy. Ana starts the record, drops the needle on the first track, and then picks it up and restarts it. A more "formal" interview commences for Lucy's documentary, and Kathi asks Ana how the band started and how they all met. "Well, it all starts with me and Gina, really," Ana says.

They talk about "Adventures Close to Home" when it starts playing, and Kathi says she thought it was a Slits song. Ana explains that Palmolive brought it to them, so it was ultimately both a Slits and Raincoats track. Kathi asks if they're still friends with The Slits; Ana says she sees Viv and Tessa around sometimes but not often.

They discuss rampant sexism and dealing with misogynist sound engineers, the unfortunately shared idea they've both heard that "girls can't play."

"One thing I thought was similar between your group and ours, not musically, is that you switch instruments, because we used to do that a lot," Ana tells Kathi. "I played bass occasionally, even played violin, and drums one time or a few times. It reminded me of us, having really good fun. Even if it doesn't sound very good technically, if there's something else there, that becomes more important."

Kathi asks Ana why The Raincoats broke up.

"We were pulling in different directions, basically, and we were all starting to want different things from the group, and we decided to split up. Then we had all these songs, and it was a shame if we didn't put them on record, so Shirley had this idea that we go and record this record [*Moving*] ... We thought the only way of doing it was each person having the responsibility for their own songs, the last word. It ended up working really well, better than before,

LIFE NUMBER 2

but that was it anyway. We did another two or three goodbye gigs and that was it really."

When "The Void" starts to play, Ana jokes with Kathi, "It seems to be popular on the West Coast."

Kathi asks Ana what she's listening to these days, and whether she wants to play music again, to which she replies, "I lost touch with a lot of what was going on, although everybody says nothing was going on. I think since Kurt came to see me, I started going more to Rough Trade, and recently, Judy [sic], who's one of the partners at Rough Trade, gave me singles of Bratmobile and Bikini Kill ... I've got to get you to sign it, actually," Ana says to Kathi of the Bikini Kill record.

"I can't wait to see in ten years all the crazy girl bands who are doing what they're doing because of us, and we're doing what we're doing because of you," Kathi tells Ana before Lucy's camera dies.

The footage starts up again at a branch of Dunkin' Donuts. Tobi's there. The premise is that Tobi is now interviewing Ana, but the filming opens with Ana asking Tobi who her favorite drummers are. "I don't know anything about drumming. I'm kinda sick of drumming and want to play guitar now," Tobi replies. She talks about her new band The Frumpies (with Kathi, Billy Karren of Bikini Kill, and Molly Neuman of Bratmobile) and says, "We're gonna record a bunch of singles and record a Frumpies album in August and in September we're gonna go on tour. There's one song on *Bikini Kill* that's a Frumpies song, it's 'Safety First.'" Ana listens intently.

"Maybe we should talk about Donut Nation," Tobi laughs nervously. "It's twenty-four hours where people can hang out ... There's this particular one called Winchell's where we hang out with Bratmobile, Witchy Poo, and in D.C. there's like Slant 6, Cupid Car Club, but it's a thing. And in the UK there's a thing called Donut Republic, which is entirely different and this is the basis of it, but you can't really come here twenty-four hours a day so you have to come in the daytime. The bands that are into it are Huggy Bear, Blood Sausage." Ana doesn't seem sure what to say, but smiles as Tobi speaks.

Tobi and Kathi sign the Bikini Kill 12-inch at the end, and Tobi tells Ana not to read it until they leave:

From Tobi:
Donut Nation Girl friend
Raincoats equalled something lifeforce-ful transforming the void (!!!) etc. truth <heart> TOBI

From Kathi:
For Ana, you are my girl
Super hero-girl
Love xo Kathi Wilcox

Looking back, Ana says, "I don't think I had ever had a Dunkin' donut until then. I remember me and Shirley sort of looked at each other ..." She laughs.

Kathi wrote in her diary after the Dunkin' meetup and recently dug out the entry, which read in its entirety: "I bought donuts for everyone: Ana had a lemon filled, Shirley a maple frosted, and I got strawberry frosted." Kathi laughs, "I'm glad I recorded these important details for future generations!"

Shirley vividly remembers going to see Bikini Kill in London, with Huggy Bear as support, the night before Kathi and Lucy came to their flat. "It was in Kentish Town," Shirley says. "And it had only been nine years since The Raincoats had last played, but it felt like so much longer. Suddenly there were all these really politicized, powerful girls doing their own fanzines with a decidedly feminist agenda in this clear DIY way, and it felt so exciting, like a return to 1978, '79 again in a way. Ana and I still think about when we first heard from Kathi that The Raincoats had influenced all of it, and it's still just, *my god!*"

Lucy keenly remembers Ana's presence in all the 1993 Bikini Kill footage, and not just at the flat Ana and Shirley shared. "Ana was at *all* the gigs. She was a total fangirl," Lucy says. "I think she actually held the microphone at quite a lot of the Bikini Kill events for me, because I had all this borrowed equipment and I needed help. And she was there, with Shirley, to hold the mic and be a Bikini Kill fan."

ROUGH TRADE REISSUES

A 1986 letter from Rough Trade to The Raincoats explains the dearth of any vinyl or cassette copies of their music lingering in London shops or elsewhere:[7]

> Dear Shirley, Ana, Gina, Vicky
> This is to inform you that Rough Trade are deleting your record(s) RT013 'Fairytale,,,', RT 094 'No One's . . .' RTT153 'Animal Rhapsody', Rough 003 'The Raincoats', Rough 013 Odyshape, and cassette COPY 003 from our continuous-manufacturing and accounting programme.
> We are taking this step because the movement of the product in the market is virtually nil and we are confronted by serious storage problems. Further, the accounts department has its hands full dealing with the market life of active product.

With renewed interest in the band in the nineties, The Raincoats needed to get their music into shops, and CDs were the logical answer. "I'd been thinking about how everything was now on CD, and nothing of ours was on CD, and our albums were out of print. So I went to see Geoff and Jeannette, who'd literally just got the label back," Shirley recalls. "Geoff said, 'It's brilliant you've come in today, because I've just got backing from Martin Mills,' and he said they were going to do some licensing deals and reissue back catalogue. It all sounded great."

Jude frequently interacted with shoppers coming into Rough Trade looking for The Raincoats "because of what The Raincoats represented," she says. Often, it wasn't even that they'd even heard the music. "Fans were passing on information to other fans, especially women," Jude recalls. The same people buying music coming out of Olympia—music licensed from K Records and

Kill Rock Stars, especially—were also asking about The Raincoats, with whom "The Raincoats just meshed so well," Jude explains. "We heard from young women in particular listening to the Raincoats on archive copies or tapes, or just hearing *about* the Raincoats, and being inspired by them, saying, 'We can start a band, too, because we've got the same spirit.' It wasn't about making the same music, the same sound. It was about *the spirit*." So, with the consumer shift to CDs, Rough Trade knew it would do well to consider Raincoats reissues.

On May 1, 1993, The Raincoats reached an agreement with Rough Trade Records to reissue the first three albums on CD. Shirley then sent a handwritten letter to Cathi Gibson at Rough Trade Music: "Currently there is interest from Geffen to simultaneously release in USA which may put back releases by 1 to 2 months (but who cares if *they* want us!)." The CDs were originally slated for UK release on September 27, 1993, but the release was delayed with Geffen's interest pending.

Meanwhile, The Raincoats had to sort some logistics. "Vicky hadn't had anything to do with us professionally since 1984, but we had a meeting together, the four of us—me, Ana, Gina, and Vicky—and we agreed to do the three albums on CD with Rough Trade, and to have a party in London for the release," Shirley explains. Vicky was clear that The Raincoats were part of her past; she wasn't interested in getting back together, even for a one-night party to celebrate the reissues. She'd since founded the successful dance label Fresh and had no plans to look back. But she gave the others the go-ahead.

Ana, Gina, and Shirley agreed that, together, they'd go into the studio to digitally remaster the three albums in preparation for the CD reissues. They listened to the records and decided to add "Fairytale in the Supermarket" to the reissue of *The Raincoats*. Since they wouldn't be reissuing the *Fairytale* EP, they wanted to find another way to get that single into the ears of nineties listeners (all subsequent pressings of *The Raincoats* have included "Fairytale in the Supermarket" as the opening track). They decided to keep

Odyshape exactly as it was originally released, but things got a bit tricky with *Moving*.

In the mastering room, Ana, Gina, and Shirley felt concerned about "Avidoso" and "Dreaming in the Past," two songs on *Moving* written by Richard. Ana describes them as songs that "didn't feel like The Raincoats." A third song, which had also appeared on the record originally, Vicky's "Honey Mad Woman," was cut. Vicky decided she didn't want the song on the CD reissue, Shirley says, and "No One's Little Girl" was added since that had been a popular and well-known song for the band, as well as a single around the original *Moving* release. Vicky adds, looking back, that she may have agreed to the excision "due to a lack of confidence in myself." But Richard's songs posed more complications.

There's always the beauty of hindsight, and it felt particularly important in 1993 to think about how The Raincoats were being framed and packaged to new audiences who hadn't bought their records the first time around.

The Raincoats cut "Avidoso" and "Dreaming in the Past" when they reissued *Moving*. "The thing that happened with Richard's songs is really one of the only regrets we have, where we'd do it differently if we were to do it again," Shirley regrets, adding, "I think we are absolutely sorry that we didn't discuss it with Richard." Gina sighs, "I sang on 'Dreaming in the Past' and was very close to Richard. I am sad that it is not on the album in retrospect. I wish I had been more considered in my thinking."

Richard wasn't informed ahead of time; he realized only after buying the *Moving* CD for himself. Ana, Gina, and Shirley all ruminate on how they might have kept "Dreaming in the Past" even if they wanted to remove "Avidoso," given the emotional significance of the former (a deeply personal song for Richard, which he wrote in the wake of his sister's suicide). But there's no digital whiteout for the past.

It never got easier between them in the years that followed. Shirley and Gina remember being at the Rough Trade shop on Record Store Day 2015, when Richard played with the 101ers and launched his memoir *Squat City Rocks*. Standing outside the shop, Gina told Shirley how upset Richard was about the *Moving* reissue, and Shirley agreed they needed to find a way to resolve it. "We always tried to be fair to everybody, and this issue with Richard's songs on *Moving* and changing Ross's original words to 'Life on the Line' are the two things I really regret, that we just didn't handle properly."

Richard describes it as a "thorny topic," recalling a bit reluctantly how upset he was back in 1993. And when he saw the new CD insert, he even thought he'd been "airbrushed out" (four paper doll figures were cut down to three, a design necessity in shifting from LP to CD). He finds solace thinking Geffen must have had a hand in the revisionist history. "I can imagine what might have happened," he says, "but I don't really know. When big record companies get involved . . . marketing and PR people at Geffen . . ." (All the creative decisions were actually made by The Raincoats through Rough Trade alone, and the CDs were licensed to Geffen, but Richard assumed the decision had come from the major American label.) He continues, "I really don't want to point any fingers . . . it's a hard thing, because of the friendships . . . Sometimes it feels like an Orwellian rewriting of history, especially because of the happy times I remember being with the band, being a Raincoat. It's a minefield."

DGC REISSUES

While Shirley was discussing Rough Trade CDs with Geoff, Kurt Cobain was pushing his A&R guy at DGC, Ray Farrell, to make The Raincoats part of the newly formed "indie major" label's reissue campaign. Ray had a very strong relationship with Kurt, and Kurt had Ray's ear. "He was the type of person who didn't like discussing his own music, but was really into talking about records," Ray says. "He knew I'd worked at SST and Rough Trade in San Francisco years before, and he was *really* into The Raincoats."

"To have this interest from Kurt, and his label . . ." Jude muses. She knew it could launch The Raincoats into a kind of popularity they'd never known before. Ray didn't really need much nudging. He was already a Raincoats fan himself.

LIFE NUMBER 2

When The Raincoats first came to underground prominence in the UK, Ray lived in the Bay Area and joined the early *Maximum Rocknroll* radio team (pre-zine). He moved into a management role for Arhoolie Records, and later to Rough Trade's San Francisco office. When the *Fairytale* EP came out in 1979, he was importing music from Rough Trade UK to sell at Rather Ripped on the north side of UC Berkeley's campus. The store prided itself on offering difficult-to-find records, including UK imports from what Ray calls the "really groundbreaking" Rough Trade roster. "Rough Trade would sell directly to American record stores," he explains, "and I brought in a lot of imports, including The Raincoats."

Fast forward a decade. Ray's working for SST and decides to follow Sonic Youth over to DGC. Geffen was "moving into the A&R realm," he begins, "and wanted me to find releases that had kind of disappeared from the alternative world so I could put together reissues." Ray was eager to introduce a new generation of listeners to underground UK punk, especially early Rough Trade stuff. He started off with a Pere Ubu box set—the first attempt at excavating "disappeared" sounds for DGC. It was a natural direction for Ray to take at Geffen, Thurston Moore suggests, given that "Ray was really anomalous at DGC, a total longstanding indie guy who was all of a sudden in this corporate world. But he was nobody's dummy," Thurston emphasizes. "He knew what was going on and did take advantage of the situation, realizing he could put these records out and get them into these distribution streams that they'd never experienced before." Ray's move from SST to DGC gave him a budget that allowed risk-taking and experimentation in a way he hadn't known before. "Things were flush, so he could get away with a lot," Thurston laughs, "and Ray really could have his way."

Ray reports, "Kurt brought The Raincoats to me ... well, *back* to me." Kurt's enthusiasm drove the reissue project to the finish line, and the three Raincoats LPs became the second set of reissues in Ray's new role with Geffen. "What cemented my enthusiasm was the fact that Kurt was really interested in The Raincoats, wanted to do liner notes for the reissues, and wanted to talk about whether The Raincoats could join Nirvana on tour. All of that pointed to the idea that The Raincoats albums *needed* to be available in the States because of the legacy the Raincoats represented," Ray declares. He ran with it.

In the early nineties, Ray was keenly aware how The Raincoats were role models for up-and-coming female artists. The Raincoats "represented a very unique form of communication through music," he explains, "that they did it their own way, didn't become—or want to become, some female version of the Ramones or anything like that." There was just *something*," Ray continues, that "came about from their own creativity." It was a sensibility that's difficult to put into words, one that's part of an enigmatic Raincoats vocabulary.

Kurt certainly wasn't the first musician to find inspiration in The Raincoats and seek a wider reach for their music. But he did have a kind of power that queercore artists, musicians on K Records and Kill Rock Stars, and other Riot Grrrls didn't have at the time: He was the voice behind DGC's best-selling album of all time. Nirvana's *Nevermind* (1991) sold ten million copies in the US alone and twenty-five million worldwide before DGC would be reabsorbed into Geffen Records in 1999. The "indie major" didn't last even a decade, but it resurrected The Raincoats in America while staying afloat with Nirvana profits.

Large-scale ads in every magazine DGC record buyers might pick up announced the reissues. "THE LONG LOST LEGACY," they read, with quotes pulled from Kurt's *Incesticide* liner notes. His words were used strategically; they offered readers a chance to take part in the same London quest Kurt had embarked upon to find Ana simply by heading out to buy a Raincoats CD.

The marketing campaign highlighted connections to Nirvana and Sonic Youth, promising new liner notes from Kurt and Kim, while the photo from *The Kitchen Tapes* lured in American listeners who'd known the band only through that live cassette. With those ads, DGC fixed The Raincoats in time, as if they were still the young women who'd played The Kitchen in 1982 in order to buy plane tickets home to London. The label also touted The Raincoats as a "new DGC band," as though they were just getting started.

LIFE NUMBER 2

The CD reissues took on different lives between the UK and the US. In America, they became a near overnight success, on sale in every record store across the country. Other bands on DGC who'd been looking for their own copies of Raincoats albums got a chance to nab them from the Geffen offices on Sunset Boulevard. Before the CD reissues, Patty Schemel had combed secondhand shops for copies of Raincoats vinyl but never found anything. Her luck changed with the DGC CDs. She remembers going into the Geffen building in Los Angeles to see Hole's A&R person and heading straight for the music closet to "basically take all of the CDs," she laughs. "I grabbed all of The Raincoats!"

The DGC reissues also got The Raincoats onto mainstream American radio. While their music could be heard on the KAOS airwaves in Olympia and across college stations on the East Coast for years, it was DGC that brought their music to a broader public. As a division of Geffen, DGC was set up in part to highlight "alternative" music and artists who might not otherwise be suited to a major label. But what came with the "indie major" status of DGC was a whole new radio staff. "They had great people who were completely different from the Geffen staff," Ray says, explaining how radio employees ensured DGC's "alternative" sounds were all over the radio.

"Ray had been working at SST all those years, this vanguard label that was all of a sudden being shown some respect by the big corporations [like Geffen] because of the influx of college radio people at the major labels," Thurston says. He's referring to a general shift taking place: Underground music was becoming commercially viable. And with that shift, presenters who'd been on college stations were moving into corporate work. Those recalibrations allowed Sonic Youth and other bands to stave off the presumption that signing to DGC was "selling out," Thurston says. "You had this dynamic of college radio people saying, 'No, it's cool, you'll be safe as long as we're here because we know what we're doing.'"

Those commercial (alternative) stations were then amenable to playing tracks from reissued Raincoats CDs, because "they were in 'Nirvana World' and 'Sonic Youth World,'" Ray clarifies. It wasn't that The Raincoats sounded like either band—Nirvana and Sonic

Youth occupied two distinct sonic worlds themselves—but the Raincoats narrative had become interwoven with the oxymoronic marketable underground. "Maybe Nirvana opened the door for everybody's ears to become wider," Ray reflects.

Vivien Goldman sighs, "It took a guy to reintroduce The Raincoats, but you know, I've never been a separatist myself, and he was part of a generation that was raised when people had heard of feminism and it was possible for the punks of this generation to be supportive of one another, and for the she-punks to rise." She thinks for a moment before concluding, "Really, a bit of a halcyon moment."

LINER NOTES

The Raincoats asked a range of musicians to write liner notes for their CD reissues in 1993. Kurt and Kim were already up for it; no need for additional correspondence there. Kim still feels strongly about *Odyshape* and the liner notes she wrote back in 1993: "*Odyshape* is very, very modern, contemporary, ahead of its time ... it still sounds so fresh and forward-thinking."

Aside from Kim and Kurt, Ana, Gina, and Shirley discussed a list of other potential writers and sent them requests through the post and via fax.

Ana drafted a note to Courtney Love that Shirley faxed to LA, but she never received a reply. Her letter read:

> Dear Courtney
> I hope all is well with you and that everything is going according to your wishes in relation to your new album. I really like the single and judging by that the album should be great.
>   As I must have told you I didn't realize you also liked our music as it was Kurt that talked about it when you came ~~to the shop~~ to see me. So it was such a nice surprise to see you do the Void at the Subterranea. Also somebody sent me a tape of the Peel session which I didn't realize was going to include that song. Shame I missed it on the day. We all heard it together and really liked it. Thanks.

LIFE NUMBER 2

May 26, 1993

To: Ana Da Silva c/o Rough Trade, 071/221-1146
From: Michael Meisel

RE: RAINCOATS COMPILATION
KURT COBAIN'S LINER NOTES

I know a lot of coolies who suck and feed off the fact that they know about and (supposedly) enjoy unknown, obscure bands of present and past. These coolies thrive on their own little discoveries like those tiny fish who attach themselves to bigger fish and parasitically feed off the hosts' droppings and burnt coffee.

The Raincoats were not very well known in the states -- I don't know about The U.K. and Europe. In fact, I really don't know anything about The Raincoats except that they recorded some music that has affected me so much that whenever I hear it I'm reminded of a particular time in my life when I was (shall we say) extremely unhappy, lonely, and bored. If it weren't for the luxury of putting on that scratchy copy of The Raincoats' first record, I would have had very few moments of peace. I suppose I could have researched a bit of history about the band but I feel it's more important to delineate the way I feel and how they sound.

When I listen to The Raincoats I feel as if I'm a stowaway in an attic, violating and in the dark. Rather than listening to them, I feel like I'm listening in on them. We're together in the same old house and I have to be completely still or they will hear me spying from above and, if I get caught -- everything will be ruined because it's their thing. They're playing their music for themselves. It's not as sacred as wire-tapping a Buddhist monk's telephone or something because if The Raincoats really did catch me, they would probably just ask me if I wanted some tea. I would comply, then they would finish playing their songs and I would say thank you very much for making me feel good.

Kurt Cobain

Kurt Cobain's faxed liner notes for the 1993 reissue of *The Raincoats*

The reason I'm writing to you, though, is that we'd be very happy if you would write something for the liner notes for the re-release of our 1st album—whatever you feel like—our music, the group, a song—anything. It can be any length you like. We're also asking Kurt and a few more people to do something. We'd love to have it by the end of June, but the sooner, the better, so we can plan everything well and with no rush. It's due to come out on the 23rd of August in two formats—LP + CD. Later we'll release the others as well. We'll have a party to celebrate and if you're here, we'd like you to come to it. Don't know yet when. Wishing you well and good luck, and I wait for your answer. Love Ana.

P.S. See you at the Grand on the 15th of July.

Ana also handwrote note to Tobi Vail, which she sent by post. It wouldn't be the last time Tobi would be asked to be involved with The Raincoats:

Dear Tobi

Thanks very much for your card. It was very nice to have met you all and therefore I'm pleased to hear that you might come here in the summer. There is another reason why I'm pleased about that. As I probably told you, we're re-releasing our records and the first one is scheduled to come out on the 23rd of August on Rough Trade Records. We're planning to have a party to celebrate, so we thought we'd play a few songs for fun. We're all around except for Palmolive and therefore we'd like you to play the drums for us, if you're in London, and if you'd like to do it, of course.

I would also like to ask you another favour, which is if you and Kathi (and the others if they want to) write something for us to put in the first album. Since some people (including you) seem to find our contribution inspirational, it would be interesting to know how. We'd need this as soon as possible—late June the latest. It can be any length and about one thing. Please let me know about all this and when you're coming over as I would like to meet you again anyway.

Lots of love

Ana

LIFE NUMBER 2

When she didn't get a reply, Ana wrote to Tobi again. This time Shirley faxed it for speediness, and in case Tobi hadn't received the first letter:

> Dear Tobi
>
> Thanks very much for your card. I was really pleased to receive it. I really enjoyed your gig at the "[blank space]" so it was nice to hear you might come back in the summer. I'll be away visiting my family from the 18th July to the 5th August. I hope I won't miss you.
>
> As you might know we're rereleasing our records starting with "The Raincoats" (our first one) in August. We're doing it on CD and vinyl. As I've heard from Kathy and [blank space] you have liked that for a long time and this is why I'd like you to write something about it to put in the booklet. Anything. Either about a particular song, the whole album, whatever. It has to be very soon. Please let me know as soon as possible if you will do it anyway. Thanks. Love to you all.

Tobi's reply came too late. In November 1993, she wrote a five-page letter to Ana on lined notebook paper:

> dear Ana,
>
> I have been meaning to write to you FOREVER and only am just now actually doing it for many reasons. I was on tour this fall with my other band, the FRUMPIES, where me + Kathi sing + play guitar. We toured the west coast and the midwest mostly + some of the East coast. This was with HUGGY BEAR ... me + Kathi decided after it was over that it was one of the hardest things we'd ever done + are looking forward to our less-upfront RHYTHM section stance, which brings me back to BIKINI KILL! Things are looking up for us. The main reason I haven't written yet it because I've been totally depressed + freaked out at the possibility of B.K. is coming to an end. But we've just recently decided to get together + start practicing together in January + if all goes well we could tour both the U.S. + Europe this spring ...

I've made you a tape + am sending you a catalog for our label Kill Rock Stars + so let me know if you'd like to hear more of anything. I recommend Bratmobile, Heavens to Betsy + Unwound but I don't know what you've already got or what your tastes are so I've made the tape as a kind of sampler. Also, I want to apologize for not writing anything for your liner notes. At the time you needed them I was totally unable to write anything. I've always made a fanzine—Jigsaw—and have always found it relatively easy to write but when we started getting known other peoples perceptions of me started to affect me too much. I lost my confidence. I'm just now realizing how useless that is and I regret not realizing it in time to write the liner notes. It was such an honor to be asked, I can't express what it meant to me. The same goes for being asked to play the drums with you all ... what I would like to do tho is to get together + play with you for a possible project if we get back to the U.K. this year. Would you be interested in that? Meeting you at the time I did [at Dunkin' Donuts] was a bit too much for me I think and so I hope I didn't blow it by being too nervous and withdrawn ...

The Raincoats first L.P. is maybe what I consider to be the best record ever in this one sense. It totally changed my life and meant everything to me for such a long time. It was also the soundtrack for a broken hearted time of my life that ultimately was the time right as we started BIKINI KILL. I've been on a huge campaign to get everyone I know to listen to the record for as long as I've known about it, so when you said it was getting re-released I was so excited. There are so many questions I want to ask you ... [*Tobi asks about how the Raincoats' punk scene got started and who was involved, and notes that there was nowhere in the US to read anything about this.*] I got the *Wanna Buy a Bridge* compilation before the Raincoats LP and it totally re-organized my whole idea about punk rock ... Basically I just wanted to write + maybe get a correspondence going. What have you been doing? Have you seen the rough edit of Lucy Thane's film? Did the Raincoats play after all? Did the re-issue come out + if so how can I get a copy for my sister?[8]

LIFE NUMBER 2

While Ana was contacting Americans, Shirley was getting in touch with London-based Riot Grrrls. Anjali and Delia of Mambo Taxi agreed to draft something. Shirley also wrote to members of Huggy Bear. Niki Elliott replied on August 10, 1993:

> To Dear Shirley
> Yr postcard to these quarters ruled on its arrival and I want to confirm the yeahness of our answer to you. We would love to write the sleevenotes for "Odyshape." All of us are thrilled at the prospect of translating, our heartbeats exposed, the importance and specialness of the Raincoats bold and darling sound.
> The deadline is approaching fast . . .
> I must now, this afternoon, finally consult the other Bears on their ideas. Their insistence on writing, in full, the true excitement of the Raincoats sound is resoundingly emphatic. We think still today the Raincoats crossbow could so easily take out the youths unblinking eye
> So—
> I'm going now to the furnace of Huggy Bear life. We will beat out gold for you.
> Much love and respect
> Niki Elliott
> XXXXXXXXXX[9]

After Shirley received faxes from Geffen with Kurt's and Kim's liner notes, Ana wrote to each of them, thanking them for their words.
To Kurt, she said:

> I'm writing to you just to thank you very much for the liner notes. I hoped to have a CD to send to you but as the release date has been postponed, there aren't any around yet. So, I just send you this letter for now. We really liked the piece you wrote and we certainly must have that tea.
> We don't know yet when our Raincoats celebration party is going to be, but when we organize it, I'll let you know, just in case you're around. It would be absolutely fantastic if you could be there, but life isn't that easy, so . . .

To Kim, Ana wrote:

The reason I asked you was that I thought that you might have understood what we were doing, and because you are the co-creator of some of the best music ever made. It's so beautifully composed, creating all sorts of intense feelings—"music that hits you, music that feeds melancholy, it grows, your mind grows, the day grows . . ." You prove what a rich mode of expression music can really be and how much that richness can be shared and experienced by the listener."

[In an earlier incarnation of the letter draft from August 1993, Ana wrote, "I really love 'Dirty.' I'd take it to a desert island, in fact when I went to see my parents in this small Portuguese island by Madeira which is where I come from, I took a tape of it and walked the beach early in the morning (quietness, warmth, blue, yellow) with it playing in my Walkman."]

RAINCOATS LINER NOTES

I missed The Raincoats' notorious Tier 3 gig on their first visit to N.Y.C. ('79 or '80). Tier 3 was a small cool club I went to religiously to witness the downtown N.Y. whatever (8 Eyed Spy, Theoretical Girls, Y Pants, DNA, etc.) and the much anticipated English groups (Pop Group, The Slits, A Certain Ratio, etc.). Those nights were mysterious, lonely, and exhilarating. I loved The Slits because of their boldness and that they actually had commercial songs but it was The Raincoats I related to most. They seemed like ordinary people playing extraordinary music. Music that was natural that made room for a cohesion of personalities. They had enough confidence to be vulnerable and to be themselves without having to take on the mantle of male rock/punk rock aggression...or the typical female as sex symbol avec irony or sensationalism. It was, of course, their personalities that created the music -- and it showed post-punk music to have yet another different face...one that could be defiant in its spirituality without being corny. I finally did see The Raincoats but it was much later and they had two male drummers and were more slick. I worshipped every second of it.

Kim Gordon
Summer, 1993

Kim Gordon's faxed liner notes for the 1993 reissue of *Odyshape*

LIFE NUMBER 2

Anjali and Delia Sparrow wrote the liner notes for *Moving*. "Writing those notes reminded me of the first time I heard The Raincoats, in the late eighties, and the influence it had on me. The idea that music can be raw and vulnerable yet so strong and powerful. That had a huge effect on my own musical career," Anjali says.

Anjali sent her liner note draft in nearly illegible handwriting on three pieces of pocket-sized paper:

> I dumped my boyfriend and stole his drum kit. I'd never really played the drums before + was struggling but determined to slice those skins. A friend of mine lent me a tape while I was at the first stages of drumming independence (ie hitting 3 different things at once) and he insisted that I listen to the tribal tom tom + skreeching (sic) sounds of the Raincoats. This was my first introduction to the band.
>
> I can remember vividly trying to emulate the particular drum beats, but also being inspired by the raw ranting of their songs.
>
> Many years passed. I remember rummaging through my flatmate's tapes and coming across one entitled "The best of the girls"—a handmade compilation of female bands and singers ranging from the 50's to the 90's. There was a song on that tape that had me mesmerized, resonant violin which veers around a melodious bass and guitar. I was enticed by the different sound of the Raincoats, perfect to light up any rainy day . . .
>
> and I'd managed to achieve something similar to that wonderous [sic] tom tribal Raincoats sound.[10]

Delia handwrote the first draft of her liner note on spiral paper, roughly torn at the top. She added a quick note to Ana, letting her know she'd highlighted a sentence that might not be necessary. "Should maybe be cut out?" she asked. Her draft read [with the highlighted sentence represented in strikethrough]:

> How do you explain love at first sight? How can I put into words how much I like The Raincoats without falling into a sea of superlatives?

I can write about how I first heard them—on a compilation tape with "In Love" shining out from all the other songs. I can tell you how ecstatic I was when I found the album that I still can't remember the name of (the one everyone remembers as "the one with the singing children on the front").

I can tell how Nigel from Rough Trade record shop gave me a white label of "No One's Little girl" that had been stored in the vaults (well—the toilet cupboard) and how he regreted [sic] it when I made him listen to it all day.

Musically I think they sit proudly between the Velvet Underground and The Beatles—they make me wish every band had a violinist.

Maybe their music touches me more because they're female, but I think it transcends that. No journalist could get away with the "not bad for a girl band" tag that's so often relied on.

~~I think the fact that they're female adds to their music + definitely their lyrics but I don't think they're missing anything by not being male.~~

Anyway—whatever I say—however I say it—I love them + I don't care if it's sycophantic because it's true.[11]

Shirley typed up a draft for the official CD reissue and cut the small portion Delia had identified for excision. The note eventually got the title "Letter on the Underground . . ." (inspired by Mambo Taxi's song "Poems on the Underground," which was taken from an initiative in which the London Underground displayed poems in tube trains).

Each of the three "original" Raincoats—Ana, Gina, and Vicky—also wrote a liner note themselves in 1993: Ana for *The Raincoats*, Gina for *Odyshape*, and Vicky for *Moving*. Ana's was a brief history of the band, beginning in 1976 before reaching the lineup that would record *The Raincoats*:

> So with this line up in 1978, all women for the first time, we got serious. Shirley started organizing us, and we recorded our first

single with Rough Trade. It's hard to describe the influence which affected us—they were so many: things, people, musicians. We certainly wouldn't have sounded as we did if we hadn't heard and loved the Velvet Underground, if we hadn't been touched by the courage of punk and its irreverence to rules, which was really empowering to us as women, and if we hadn't been open to each other's individual inputs. We came from very different places and backgrounds and it was the mixing of those differences that characterised our work. When we finished putting our songs together we went on a five week tour of England. At the end of the tour we went into a studio, played the set pretty much live, with very few overdubs, and finished this album in 3 weeks. So here it is, put it on, whack it up ... and ...

Reflecting on *Odyshape*, Gina wrote:

The excitement of the first album was over and we took some time off from doing Raincoats stuff. After Palmolive left the band we had to search hard to find another drummer to replace her, as she had been so energetic and spectacular. We auditioned lots of people, until we found Ingrid, who was very young but had a strong powerful style of drumming ... Our style of writing had changed a lot from the way we used to work on the first album. I supposed we had developed musical skills and we pushed them to see where they could take us. I think we always took punk philosophy very seriously and we rejected the traditional forms of rock music that in fact most bands didn't ultimately reject ... I think this album is the most experimental of our records and in a way the most dangerous in the sense that we really pushed ourselves ...

Although Vicky wasn't interested in being part of a Raincoats resurrection, she'd been a crucial component of the band's first life, as reflected in her own recollections for the *Moving* insert:

Writing about the third and last Raincoats' album now, the temptation is to talk of differences, rather than the elements that united us to produce our sound, for despite all the different directions there definitely is a sound, in my opinion, unlike any other ... More than ever 'Moving' was the result of a myriad of influences and styles and the formula, or lack of one, was stretched to breaking point on this album. Trying to contain influences as diverse as Chic, African music, Abdullah Ibrahim, kunk, Cajun music and the ever present reggae along with the continuum of guitar-based post-punk was a difficult act to pull off, and, in the end, pulled us apart. But in the meantime we created something with ever-experimental textures, which veers from the edgy sound of the fiddle and penny whistle on "Balloon" and "I Saw a Hill", to the smoother sound of acoustic piano and sax on "Rainstorm" and "Dance of Hopping Mad." The music on this album sounds like no other, and it is for this that I would like us to be remembered, not for the spurious 'women in rock' tag where the short entry into the history of punk usually stresses some media-concocted image of fanatical feminism and dowdy thrift shop clothing (it's all absolutely true!) at the expense of what we created together, and, I hope, the importance we hold for the next generation of women attempting to make their mark in a largely uninterested market place ...

YUGOSLAV WARS AND BOSNIAN WOMEN'S AID

While The Raincoats were preparing their reissues, a genocide was taking place less than 1,500 miles from London, and an international criminal tribunal was preparing to prosecute sexual violence against women as a form of attempted annihilation. The Iron Curtain had fallen with the abolition of the communist regime in Poland in June 1989, and the remaining satellite and bloc countries followed; the USSR was dissolved. The repressive Warsaw where The Raincoats introduced punk was at last free in terms of its government structure, but Yugoslavia, the socialist authoritarian dictatorship to the south, originally an ally of Stalin in the early days of the Cold War and later a "neutral" federation, remained a socialist republic on the brink just as Kurt and the soon-to-be Riot Grrrls were discovering The Raincoats for themselves in America's Pacific Northwest. With the start of the Yugoslav Wars in 1991, and coordinated acts of sexual violence against women perpetrated as a method of genocide, DGC artists wanted to help the survivors by supplying monetary aid.

It made perfect sense for The Raincoats to become involved in a women's aid effort in the former Yugoslavia, even if they didn't know it at the time; their music had briefly been part of underground life in southeastern Europe after their visit to Warsaw.

In the late 1970s and early 1980s—some of the most repressive years in Poland and the Soviet Union—Yugoslavians, despite being under a somewhat similarly structured socialist dictatorship, enjoyed relative freedom. The Yugoslavian alternative music magazine *Džuboks* (also written as Џубокс, or the phonetic "jukebox") thrived. In 1981, *Džuboks* included an anonymous feature on The Raincoats and their recently released album *Odyshape*. Similar to the title of the magazine, the band's name was written phonetically in a language known then as Serbo-Croatian: рејнкоуте (RAYN-COHT), rather than the Serbo-Croatian translation for raincoats, кабаница. The magazine itself, and its use of language, was an act of rebellion like the work of many of the artists who appeared inside its pages. It described The Raincoats' "strange rhythms" and "unreal voices" that brought a "combination of complexity and constant tension." The feature lauded the band's work on *Odyshape*, a record illuminating The Raincoats as an avant-garde ideal, an album against which there was "nothing to compare." A large photograph of Ana, Gina, Vicky, and Ingrid from their 1980 trip to New York City appeared below the text.

Džuboks was founded in the Socialist Federal Republic of Yugoslavia (SFRY) in 1966 and was the first music magazine to appear in any of the communist countries in the East. It was also one of the rare publications that began its multi-decade run with a female editor-in-chief, Višnja Marjanović. Speaking in 2018 about the cultural impact of Džuboks, Marjanović described her work as "scandalous," "revolutionary," and "unusual." The magazine routinely sold out and was popular among university students.

The band's appearance in *Džuboks* wouldn't be the last time The Raincoats' music was to be relevant to politics in Yugoslavia. On January 18, 1994, Shirley made a note that she'd given the go-ahead to include a Raincoats live/unreleased track on the compilation album *DGC Rarities Vol. 2* to benefit Bosnian Women's Aid. Myriad news articles about the genocidal rape camps in Bosnia were appearing in the Western press at the time, and Ray Farrell immediately points to the benefit show Nirvana played on April 9, 1993 at the Cow Palace in San Francisco for the Tresnjevka Women's Group in Zagreb, a nonprofit organizing assistance for rape survivors. Krist Novoselic of Nirvana had traveled through the former Yugoslavia, and news reports suggested that, with familial ties to Croatia, he was keen to put Nirvana's fame to good use.

The Yugoslav Wars began in SFRY in 1991 with the breakup of Yugoslavia and the emergence of individual republics that had been part of the socialist state, including Bosnia and Herzegovina, Croatia, Macedonia (now North Macedonia), Montenegro, and Serbia. The conflicts resulted in the rise of ethnic nationalisms, and Bosniaks (Bosnian Muslims) were targeted for elimination. The Bosnian genocide was perpetrated through mass executions and sniper shootings during the Siege of Sarajevo, but this particular genocide also opened the eyes of the international community to the eradication of a population through carefully engineered mass rape. Islam is patrilineal, which means a child must have a Muslim father to be born Muslim. Attempting to ethnically cleanse the population of Bosnian Muslims, Serbs set up rape camps in which Bosniak women were raped repeatedly to impregnate them with Serbian Christian fetuses. Data collected by the International Criminal Tribunal for the Former Yugoslavia (ICTY) suggests that anywhere from 20,000 to 50,000 women were subjected to this form of violence, recognized as torture and genocide by the International Criminal Court.

There are no specific details of The Raincoats track that would have been included on *DGC Rarities Vol. 2* (which ultimately wasn't released), but Ray suggests it could have been "Babydub," an extra track that arose out of Gina's song "Babydog"—an at once emotional yet playful narration of her experiences with miscarriage.

LIFE NUMBER 2

The possibility of a Bosnian Women's Aid benefit CD serves as a stark reminder of the geopolitical climate in which The Raincoats were re-forming, writing songs, and recording a record. The cause also recalls The Raincoats' "Off Duty Trip" and their earlier benefit shows for rape crisis centers and Rock Against Sexism—bleak dispatches about sexual violence in times of war and peace.

MEASURING THE HALF-LIFE OF "THE VOID"

Shortly after the 1979 release of *The Raincoats*, the Rough Trade shop received a fan's letter asking for clarification about "The Void":

> Dear Ana, Gina, Vicky
> I am writing to say . . . am puzzled by one of your songs: "The Void." What is "the void"? Perhaps the song is supposed to be equivocal (though I suspect not). But what makes this song stand apart from the others is the way it has been written. Songs like Black and White/ In Love/ No looking seem to capture an experience which is then communicated to the listener. But the void seems so remote, almost "abstract." Perhaps you could enlighten me?

When Hole were invited to do a Peel session for BBC Radio 1, they decided to cover the song. "I think Courtney came up with the idea," Eric says. Patty also remembers Courtney wanting to do a cover—something in addition to the new songs coming out on *Live Through This*—and one from the first Raincoats record. It seemed like an obvious choice since everyone in Hole loved *The Raincoats* and had their own connections to it.

Eric remembers Courtney consciously seeking out songs that were favorites of Kurt's, as well as those "beloved by the Olympia scene." Eric had his own interest in The Raincoats' music from his pre-Hole retail work at Licorice Pizza, the small LA record store chain. Once he started hanging around Kurt in 1991, he reconnected with The Raincoats' music and realized the extent of the band's second life upon relocating to Seattle in '92.

If Patty had been able to make the final decision about which Raincoats song to cover, she'd have wanted to play "No One's Little Girl," she says. "The best Raincoats song to me is 'No One's Little Girl' from *Moving* ... that violin part! I love it. And I want to just shout it out loud!"

But back when Hole was in Europe in 1993, "Kristen Pfaff had just joined the band, and we had a few club shows in Europe," Patty says. The band stopped in France, and Patty remembers "a quick little trip to the UK to play new ideas for *Live Through This* that we were planning to record."

"We had just performed our single, 'Beautiful Son,' on the TV show *The Word* the night before," Eric remembers, "and I had the silly idea of asking a record company handler to find us some ecstasy, so we could celebrate. He took Patty, Kristen and I out to a London techno club, and you can guess the rest of the night from there." They barely slept and had to record their Peel session the next morning. "Courtney took one look at us and rolled her eyes," he says. "She was all business, for a change, and we were a glorious mess. We decided to cover 'The Void' right then, and scrambled to learn it ... I love Kristen's backup vocals on the song. I think that was the only time we used her vocals. Recording while coming down off of E. Talk about the void!"

Both Eric and Patty agree Hole's cover of "The Void" wouldn't have been possible without Kristen Pfaff, who died tragically of a heroin overdose just over a year later. "It's such a cool song because the bass does the melody," Patty explains. "It's built on that Gina Birch bass line, and Kristen Pfaff was such a good bass player that she could do it and could learn it in a second." Kristen's voice comes in to do the vocal counting, making a Raincoats' time signature her own.

With their cover of "The Void," like other covers Hole played, Courtney would "have me Led Zeppelinize them, take a clean, minimalistic song and transform it into heavy rock, like a vulgar American bastardization of the British esthetic," Eric says. Patty describes the sound as Hole "putting our own style on it, but leaving some of that Raincoats 'voice' in there." Patty also wanted to find a way to put her own percussive viewpoint into the cover.

"There's a section where Palmolive goes into half time, it goes to a fast part, and I didn't do that so I could make it into my own idea of a Palmolive part." It wasn't about *improving* on Palmolive's drumming, Patty emphasizes, but about interpreting the song anew. Patty quickly recounts an experience when Hole was playing at the Chicago music festival Lollapalooza in the nineties and Siouxsie Sioux came to watch. Afterward, she gave Patty one of her favorite compliments she's ever received: "She said, 'I haven't seen somebody play drums like that since Palmolive.'"

Nirvana also played a cover of "The Void" at a Geffen-only show in June 1993. "Three of us DGCees saw Nirvana play the *In Utero* album in sequence at their practice room, Jukebox City," Ray recalls. "They finished without announcing a song that I thought might be a Raincoats song, then I second-guessed ... maybe it's a Hole song. When they finished, Kurt asked me if I liked it. I said, 'Yeah, it sounds like Sabbath playing The Raincoats.'" It was, in fact, a cover of "The Void." Ray continues, "Kurt looked at the band and said, 'See, I'm not the only one that thinks we play everything like Sabbath.'" That session, of course, wasn't recorded; it exists only in the memories of those who were there. But while The Raincoats were on tour in the US the following year, Ana briefly chatted with Ray in person and he mentioned hearing that Nirvana cover. Ana wrote about it in her diary:

> The Void (he heard Nirvana do it in rehearsal and there was an argument about who would cover it, Nirvana or Hole.).

On that same tour, after The Raincoats learned of Kurt's tragic suicide, Ana dedicated the song "to Kurt forever." At most Raincoats shows since then, Ana has reminded audiences of the dedication in perpetuity.

CD DESIGN

Once The Raincoats had plans to reissue CDs with Rough Trade and DGC, they needed to reimagine the vinyl sleeve artwork in CD form, which meant creating booklet inserts. Just like before, Ana, Gina, and Shirley collaborated. They dug out the large archival portfolio in which they'd been storing their originals and got back to work.

All the original artwork for *The Raincoats* was there, and the front and back of the sleeve could be resized with the CD jewel case in mind. But they'd need a lot more material for the booklet. Ana sketched out a rough design they could work from. They went back through their stacks of photos, looking for the perfect images from which to create art-board mockups of the multi-page booklet.

They photocopied dozens of images, and Ana handwrote lyrics to include as visuals. More photocopies. Lots of physical cutting and pasting. Ana also turned back to *The Raincoats Booklet* she'd made in 1980 and did some photocopies for the CD insert. The same process was repeated for *Odyshape*, but Ana ultimately decided to include some original new artwork. She painted a blood-red face, in profile, with a green background and jet-black frame. In that same jet-black paint, she handwrote song titles. That painting would become the back of the insert booklet, the first thing buyers saw as they opened the jewel case.

For *Moving*, they referred back to the original artwork, but Ana redrew the text and made cuts to the original image of the four figures on the cover. She experimented heavily with the size of the font, wanting to get it right, and designed the back of the CD with a new photograph by Shirley: an extreme close-up of a rose bush with a bleeding and broken stem with thorns.

GETTING THE BAND BACK TOGETHER

They never thought they'd do it. Not in any lifetime. It was a monumental decision brought on by Kurt and excitement over the reissues. In so many ways, the reformed band was a fairytale brought to life, but it would also become a tinderbox.

"We always hated the idea of reforming," Gina told Richard Boon in 1996, and Ana explained how she'd received a call from a journalist "who was saying it cannot work, anybody reforming."

Yet they both emphasized that band reformations are never just one thing, and, according to Gina, "It was a case of being mad to do, madder not to," given the interest from Nirvana and all of the Riot Grrrl bands.

In the present, Gina reflects a bit differently and says, "We'd had a long break from it, and it felt exciting, in my memory, to think about doing it again." She wished Vicky would have agreed, too—"Even just one show, but I know she was busy doing her own stuff, and she'd got her own label and become quite successful doing it. And I knew she hadn't picked up her violin in years, and she told me she didn't even think she could play the violin anymore, just didn't want to pick the bloody thing up."

Ana remembers, "When me and Gina got together after ten years of not working together, it felt really good. I still remember that moment of being in Gina's basement, her with her bass guitar and me with my guitar, going through the old songs. They felt alive, and they still made sense." So they agreed: They'd reunite for at least a celebratory gig when the CD reissues came out.

THE RAINCOATS NEED A VIOLINIST

As usual, The Raincoats were going to need a drummer, but by 1994 they were also short a violinist. And The Raincoats wouldn't be The Raincoats without a punk on violin. Gina was connected with Jocelyn Pook, now a lauded composer for film and television, and asked if she'd consider playing "just one show," an upcoming reissue release party at The Garage in London. Jocelyn was unable to commit and instead suggested a friend named Anne Wood in her string section. "It's just one gig, they said!" Anne laughs. She'd go on to become the violinist in The Raincoats from 1994 to the present—more than thirty years.

Anne's first meeting with the band was at Gina's place. She went over "so we could suss each other out," she remembers, then laughs, correcting herself, "Well, maybe so they could suss *me* out as a working session musician." She played with them a bit and they asked her to play The Garage. "Soon after that, Kurt invited the band to come on tour with Nirvana," Anne remembers, "and the rest is history!"

While The Raincoats had experienced their fair share of revolving drummers, they'd been steadfast with the violin. They'd need someone who could really become part of the band, as Vicky had been. Anne was the perfect match.

Like Vicky, Anne was classically trained. She originally took "the route that many classical violin players take," receiving training designed to place her with an orchestra. "And I knew I *never* wanted to do *that*," Anne laughs. Instead, she started "getting involved in lots of alternative stuff in London," including "fairly left-field theatre, music, and a lot of improvising." For Anne, her Scottish heritage was important and she was interested in traditional Scottish and Celtic folk music. When she left college, she led a musically varied life in the London scene in the eighties and nineties. There were "all these different scenes that had nothing to do with each other," Anne remembers, and she'd "pop into one and come out to go into another." The experimental theatre scene was "totally unrelated to the folk music scene," she says, "and then there was a whole improvisation scene that had nothing to do with either of them." She looks back on herself then as "a bit of a chameleon, jumping between different musical worlds." But one thing is certain: Before she joined The Raincoats, Anne knew she wasn't a "full-on classical player" because she never felt at home in a symphony orchestra. She'd already begun the process of learning to play a kind of punk violin as a session musician for bands such as Massive Attack, and when performing for experimental theatre and dance productions.

Getting ready for The Garage, despite her variegated background, was a new experience for Anne. "Shh," she says and laughs; she didn't start out as a fan of the band. "I didn't really *get* The Raincoats until I played with them. It was then, *from the inside*, that I became a fan." She was aware of them, but was still in school during the first life of the band and wasn't so keen. Yet when The Garage rehearsals started, Anne was completely hooked. "As soon as we started playing together, it was like I suddenly got it. It all just exploded, and I exploded with them," Anne gasps. "Like I'd touched a place really deep down within me that could finally just be released." Before that rehearsal, Anne never expected her time with The Raincoats to be the incredible thing it was, that it became, and that it remains.

THE RAINCOATS NEED A DRUMMER

By 1994, replacing a drummer was old hat for The Raincoats. For artists outside the band, the "drummer problem" didn't seem like a problem at all. "The Raincoats always had different members on drums," Kim Gordon says, "and I admired that kind of flexibility. I mean, I'm sure it was out of necessity, how things happen that people come and go, but I thought it was cool." Patty Schemel agrees, referring to the "always interesting revolving lineup of drummers."

Shirley remembers asking Richard Boon about his favorite drummers: "He said Ringo Starr, Moe Tucker, and Steve Shelley of Sonic Youth." They weren't interested in asking Ringo (an interesting counterfactual to consider!). But Shirley did get in touch with Tucker, and Gina had several phone calls with her. Ultimately, Tucker was too busy working on a project with John Cale at the time. They were eager to ask Steve if he'd want to do it since all of The Raincoats were fans of Sonic Youth.

Steve already knew Ray Farrell—as Kim explains it, when Sonic Youth moved from SST to DGC, they basically brought Ray along with them. "Ray's definitely the reason I got the call to do the shows," Steve says. When Shirley got in touch with him to ask, "he was really up for it as a side project," she recalls.

By this point, Sonic Youth had released many of their best-known albums, including *Evol* (SST, 1986), *Sister* (SST, 1987), *Daydream Nation* (Enigma, 1988), *Goo* (DGC, 1990), and *Dirty* (DGC, 1992). The band was on a temporary hiatus; Kim was pregnant. In other words, Steve was free to join The Raincoats on the "limited run."

He'd first heard The Raincoats when he was growing up in Michigan, where someone had put "In Love" on a mixtape for him—one of the tracks on the *Fairytale* EP that was also featured on the *Wanna Buy a Bridge?* compilation album. But he didn't become fully enamored until he got hold of the records for himself. "It was at Kim and Thurston's place on Eldridge," Steve says, referring to their apartment on a Lower East Side street that ran parallel to the Bowery. "They had the *Fairytale* single there, and I was making mixtapes, so I put those songs on all my mixtapes."

Before Steve headed to London in 1994 to meet The Raincoats in person, he mailed them a quick note with some music from his Hoboken, New Jersey indie label, Smells Like:

> Hi ana, gina & shirley,
>   here are a few things I thought might be good to send off and give you a chance to have a listen. the two singles are on my record label here that I run in my spare time. the cd is something I worked on w/ jad fair and tim foljohn. I thought it'd be nice for you to hear some of my playing outside of Sonic Youth. hope you enjoy the music. I'm looking forward to coming over and playing w/the raincoats. I'll speak to you soon.
>   best regards,
>   Steve[12]

The music he sent over included a single from the band Blonde Redhead (one of the first releases on Smells Like), while the CD he references is the product of short-lived project Mosquito, a collaboration from 1993 to 1994 among Steve and two former members of the band Half Japanese, Jad Fair and Tim Foljahn. Steve would later release additional music from Fair and Foljahn, including solo projects and Two Dollar Guitar (Steve's band with Foljahn).

On February 9, Ana wrote to Steve, less than a month before The Raincoats were set to take the stage at The Garage with Steve on drums—their first show in a decade. Steve needed the setlist since he hadn't had a chance to rehearse with The Raincoats in person yet. Ana's handwritten letter included sketches of eighth notes and a drawing alluding to the self-titled LP. It read:

> Dear Steve
>   Hope all is well with you. I thought I'd send you a list of the songs we've decided to do. If anything gets changed, I'll let you know.

From 1st	Fairytale in the supermarket
	In love
	The Void
	You're a million
	No looking
	No side to fall in
	Adventures close to home
2nd	Shouting out loud
	Odyshape
3rd	Balloon
	No one's little girl
	Ooh ooh la la la

We haven't touched the last three yet. Anne is great. She's also playing guitar on Adventures . . . + Odyshape. The three of us played a radio session and it went really well. The rehearsals are sounding good, so I feel very positive about it all. And we can't wait for the drums!
   P.S. Thanks for the CD + 2 singles
   Love
   Ana

THE GARAGE, 1994

The Raincoats hadn't played together since February 1983. It was supposed to be a one-off gig, a party. Steve flew over from New York. "I'd always stay with Gina and Mike," he remembers, "in a basement room full of records." It was right around where the band would practice at Westbourne Studios. Steve was there for just a few days before The Garage party happened.
   To play with The Raincoats—to get it right—Anne had to "relearn to play the violin, start all over." Not even arranging for avant-garde theatre could have prepared her for the type of playing she'd be doing. "With The Raincoats, the sound is *something else entirely*. I don't even know how I make those sounds!" she exclaims. "Something takes over."

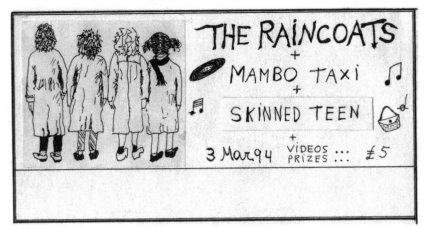

Flyer for the first Raincoats reunion gig at The Garage, March 1994

Steve says, quite definitively, "I think it was harder than drumming in Sonic Youth." He explains, "Being a drummer, a lot of your life depends on organization, so it was interesting to suddenly be in this much different situation, in a working band that was not your band, where their method of organization was ...different." He laughs and continues, "I'm treading lightly here, but it's a completely different situation with them [The Raincoats], because their organization is really about a lack of organization, and trying to move rhythmically between them," referring to Gina and Ana. "They're old friends who are excited to be present for new generations, and for themselves, but their styles are also completely different." *How?* After much pause, Steve decides how to put it: "Gina is earthier and Ana is spicier, and I mean that in the most flattering way for both of them."

Anjali and the other members of Mambo Taxi got a call from Shirley, asking if they'd open for The Raincoats. "It was us and Skinned Teen," Anjali remembers, "and I remember getting a feeling of how George Harrison must have felt the first time he was asked to play with Ravi Shankar! I was so nervous, so excited." Delia adds, "I was also DJ'ing."

Huggy Bear wasn't playing, but band member Jon Slade wouldn't have been anywhere else. "I'd never actually seen a Raincoat until 1994!" he exclaims. He remembers being "knocked out" by their reunion show that night. "I'd been sniffy about bands reforming previous to this, but I did *not* feel that way when I saw The Raincoats. If any band was going to reform," he insists, "it always should have been The Raincoats, and I was all for it. That night at The Garage, I felt like I was observing something really special."

Lucy Thane actually opened the night with the premiere of her Bikini Kill documentary, including some of the footage she'd shot at Ana's and Shirley's flat. On a 16mm projector, Lucy screened *It Changed My Life: Bikini Kill in the UK* to an audience of Raincoats fans and Riot Grrrls. "They asked me to premiere the film at this reunion gig," Lucy remembers, "and well, I was a bit drunk, and I was really nervous, and I dropped the projector on Ana's head. Ana was very gracious about the whole thing. She and Gina are just fucking lovely women." The audience ate it up with anticipation before The Raincoats took the stage.

Gina remembers the emotion Anne brought to the stage that night. "She was quite a mad performer compared with Vicky, and she was flying all over the stage!" Anne's fierceness drew on the intensity coming from the crowd that night. "When we played, it really hit a lot of people hard, because they'd been listening to the records and didn't think they'd hear us play again. Some people were crying," Gina remembers. "It was a very emotional, very heartening evening, and it felt incredible."

The Raincoats hadn't been sure how many people would come out, if anyone was still interested. As it turned out, The Garage went beyond capacity that night with a crowd that included new fans, old fans, and friends who were all thrilled to see them. Carmen even traveled from Düsseldorf.

From that night onward, Anne realized the band "went into a different zone" while performing, and that The Raincoats were far "more demanding" than any other band with whom she'd played. It wasn't possible to just play what was written: "With the Raincoats, it's easy enough to learn the shapes of the songs, but they turn strange corners ... it's a Raincoats violin sound which is like no other sound I make. It's radical sound production." Playing with The Raincoats taught Anne "to become a proper punk."

NIRVANA TOUR

The Raincoats got handpicked by Kurt to tour with Nirvana in 1994. It could have changed everything, and it's one of the most tantalizing what-ifs to come out of the myriad tales of The Raincoats.

Russell Warby, Nirvana's UK agent, first got in touch with Gina. "For some reason," she remembers, "a phone call from Russell came through to me in an edit suite where I was editing a music video for the Pogues. I was amazed and surprised, and forwarded Shirley's information to him to take things forward." From there, Russell called Shirley. "We thought, *blimey*, tour with Nirvana?! But obviously Kurt revered the band, so of course we agreed to do that tour," Shirley says. "And they made it all really easy; they said they'd carry all of our stuff in their truck and we could use their backline, and they told us they'd pay six hundred quid per show, which was just *unheard of* in those days." Shirley admits she had some reservations. "I was worried it was going to be like Birmingham and Manchester, all these young boys throwing tomatoes again."

"There was a thing I'd do with Kurt," Ray recalls, "where I would ask him if there were bands that he'd like to see on tour with him. The Meat Puppets had requested it, and he really wanted to work with the Meat Puppets as well as The Raincoats." It went even further after Kurt played a key role in the DGC reissues of their music in America. "He would have bumped anyone else off the list," Ray says, meaning the Nirvana tour lineup, "if he could get The Raincoats on it, in order to accommodate them."

Shirley phoned up Anne and told her Nirvana had asked The Raincoats to tour with them. "Obviously, that was pretty bloody special, and she asked me if I wanted to do it," Anne remembers. "Of *course* I wanted to do it! Next thing I knew, we had the tour with Nirvana booked before we left for the US dates on the East Coast with Liz Phair. The plan was to immediately go and join Nirvana afterward." For Anne, the tour was also exciting because of Nirvana's recent experimental use of classical stringed instruments. "Kurt had been doing a lot of unplugged stuff with a cellist in there, so I thought, this is just *perfect*. I can't wait to meet these guys."

Breakfast with Steve Shelley at Gina's kitchen table

"It'll be a limited thing," Steve remembers Ray telling him about The Raincoats dates, "and it'll all basically be warm-ups until we do this tour with Nirvana, six to eight weeks of shows. Of course," Steve continues, "the dates with Nirvana kept getting delayed, postponed, we'd hear that Kurt overdosed, or the tour was canceled, the tour was back on ... I got the sense that this whole project was wrapped around Kurt in a way, and Kurt wasn't really present in my life. I mean, we played shows together, but their career took a much different tangent, so it's not like we were hanging out at Maxwell's together. It was weird to have Kurt sort of—not in a malevolent way—dictating your movements while he's dealing with the issues he was going through at the time. It was affecting us. So my life in The Raincoats felt like it was about waiting on Kurt."

It's not clear how the other members of Nirvana felt about The Raincoats, or plans for including them on the tour. "It was really just Kurt's thing" is all anyone will say.

By January 28, 1994, Nirvana confirmed its UK dates for spring with The Raincoats, and with Sebadoh also supporting:

27 March, Manchester, G-Mex
28 March, Glasgow, SECC Hall
30 and 21 March, Birmingham, Aston Villa Centre
1 April, Cardiff, International Arena
3 and 4 April, London, Brixton Academy

"Wembley Arena on standby for at least one extra London show," a fax to The Raincoats read. Soon after the announcement, a tour poster plastered around the city showed all the dates sold out. Shirley faxed Steve on February 7, confirming the above dates and apologizing: "I'm sorry I didn't get back to you in time about bringing your snare over with Nirvana. I guess you'll have to bring it now. The situation for the tour is that they are carrying our gear, so we'll be travelling light ... It's likely that there will be one or two extra London shows as the tickets sold out really fast, but I'll let you know as soon as they are confirmed."

Around 4 March, 1994, Kurt overdosed in Rome and remained in a coma for a short time. The tour had to be rescheduled. Nirvana's management sent out a press update that assured readers: "Press speculation can now cease. Kurt is restored to full health and is looking forward to touring the UK ... Nirvana would like to apologize for any inconvenience and distress caused to their fans. They understand the disappointment that all this has caused, however they have promised to give their British fans the show of their lives." The rescheduled dates were:

12 and 13 April, Birmingham, Aston Villa Centre
14 April, Manchester, G-Mex
15 April, Glasgow, SECC Hall
17-20 April, London, Brixton Academy
9 May, Cardiff, International Arena
10 May, Dublin, "venue tbc"

The tour was never to happen, but that part of the story is yet to come. Paul Smith, founder of record label Blast First (who would later release Raincoats material in the UK), says he was excited to "see The Raincoats back on the cultural map, but personally I was glad the Nirvana dates never happened." Their sound, Paul says, "was unlikely to have translated to stadiums—as Kurt noted, The Raincoats' sound was an intimate experience, and Nirvana were by that time a full-on blockhead-rock audience act, with the dull thud of Foo Fighters looming on their horizon."

A PEEL SESSION

Before Kurt's death, and with Steve still in London after The Garage gig, The Raincoats recorded a Peel session on Tuesday, March 29, 1994.

"Peel sessions are so strange," Steve begins, "because as an American, you'd just fantasize about Peel sessions and think, 'I'm gonna hang out with John Peel!' But you get to the studio [in Maida Vale], and it's this faceless place with these engineers who seem like they're stuck in this gig even though they're talented engineers, dealing with a different band that comes in every day who are often the worst people in the world, and they have to record them while they're just waiting for pub o'clock. You think you're gonna be there hanging out with John Peel, Siouxsie and the Banshees, The Birthday Party, and it turns out it's just this little efficient studio with the ethos of 'let's get this done.'" One of the reasons Steve knows some background on Peel sessions is from his time with Sonic Youth, a band that "always went in totally unprepared," he laughs. "So I know what it's like to look at these engineers who are looking at you like, 'Ugh, I'm never gonna get to the pub.'"

On April 14, 1994—fewer than ten days after Kurt took his own life—The Raincoats sent a note to John Peel to be read before their session played. They asked him to read this dedication on the air: "Kurt Cobain gave so much life, inspiration and liberation in his music, and he gave us a new life. This session probably would not exist without his love and enthusiasm and we dedicate it to him." Shirley sent the letter the week The Raincoats were supposed to open for Nirvana.

TOURING THE EASTERN SEABOARD

When The Raincoats left London in late March 1994 to tour America, they were still under the impression these shows would be warm-ups for the forthcoming Nirvana dates. Ana kept a tour diary, like she'd done back in 1979, with entries from everyone traveling with the band. Aside from The Raincoats (Ana, Gina, Anne, and Steve), the entourage included Mike and Petra P. They all flew into New York and went back to Manny's, just as they'd done in 1980, this time to buy "leads, stands, and picks," according to Ana. They also took some extra days in NYC to catch some art exhibitions.

Ana wrote briefly about visiting the DIA Center for the Arts to see Katharina Fritsch's *Rat-King*, Ann Hamilton's *Tropos*, and Dan Graham's *Rooftop Urban Park Project*, the latter on the building's roof. They ate at the Empire Diner, Gina introduced everyone to Michael Shamberg of Factory Records' New York arm, and Ana "saw a ROIR Raincoats cassette in a shop."

From there, they rented a van to play a few shows at iconic venues, including the Middle East in Boston, Maxwell's in Hoboken, and the 9:30 Club in Washington, D.C. They drove between cities with Steve at the wheel.

Gina wrote about the April 5 show at the Middle East, where she and Ana were pulled away to do a college radio interview that didn't go too well. The station cut off "Don't Be Mean" about halfway through the song, and then it offered a call-in contest to listeners to name the original violinist in the band. "'Kimberley' won," Gina wrote, irritated. She also reflected on how she'd "played badly," but enjoyed the show "in spite of that" given the eager crowd.

They drove to Hoboken from Boston and Ana's diary entry reveals a marked anxiety. "Everybody had pizza but I felt like a washing machine going berserk inside my chest. Water started pouring. No reason for it except tiredness. This never happened to me before." She writes about stopping into the record store Platters: "Didn't buy anything but saw 'Moving' on wall for 14.99." After the sound check, Ana wrote about sitting with Ray Farrell to talk:

LIFE NUMBER 2

Chatted about CDs. (They sent out 6,000 of 1st and 4,000 of 2nd + 3rd—no returns); MTV (situation not too promising to show video of Fairytale); Nirvana (will it all happen after all? maybe 3 months? ie tour in U.K. . . . about whether we want to do more stuff, etc.

Ana observed, "People seemed to have really enjoyed the gig," and she noticed "somebody was wearing our blue/window badge. Shirley had given it to him in Rough Trade." She also noted the guest list: "Michael Shamberg (loved the gig) + Miranda."

The Raincoats made a stop at WFMU to play a live set on Irwin Chusid's show, and he wrote in the diary:

An historic occasion—which I'll never forget! People say "Don't ever change." You haven't! You sound as great and as vital as ever. Please come back and make sure you continue making records. The world needs The Raincoats!

It wouldn't be D.C. without some Dischord artists in the audience, and The Raincoats got some of the all-time greats. Slant 6 opened for The Raincoats—yet another Riot Grrrl connection—and naturally remained at the venue to see The Raincoats play. All three members (Christina Billotte, Myra Power, and Marge Marshall) signed the guest book and posed for a photo. Ana saved her two "one drink on the house" tickets and pasted them into the tour diary on top of that night's setlist. They covered Alternative TV's "Love Lies Limp" in the encore, one of Gina's personal favorites.

Looking back now, Anne remembers audiences of "a different generation of fans, a mix of this younger generation and older generation coming together, and everybody seemed to know the songs and were buzzed about the gigs." It felt unexpected, the sheer numbers in the crowds and their love for the music. "I think it surprised even The Raincoats," Anne says, "because they'd only played America a few times." Of course, The Raincoats had taken on a new stateside life entirely, unbeknownst to them. There were Riot Grrrl fans and self-proclaimed Riot Grrrls in the pits, along with everyone who'd latched on to anything blessed by Nirvana.

NEW YORK WITH LIZ PHAIR

After D.C., The Raincoats made it back to New York, ready to play two shows with Liz Phair.

Liz came to the shows as a fan of The Raincoats herself. "I was introduced to The Raincoats by John Henderson, owner of the indie label Feel Good All Over," Liz remembers. She'd been subletting his back bedroom in his Wicker Park apartment in Chicago, in 1992. "One of the perks, or price, of the deal," she says, "was that he played his favorite music day and night. Luckily, he had excellent taste." Liz reflects on how John's recorded collection expanded her sonic horizons, in part because he owned a Raincoats record. "The Raincoats made such an impression on me that their songwriting style and spare, spontaneous performances still influence my studio production goals today. I'd never heard women sound so innocent and so expert simultaneously," Liz says. "I got the feeling that they were a bunch of girlfriends who were sick of hearing their brother's/boyfriend's/neighbor's band rehearsing and figured they could do better. I could relate."

When her album *Exile in Guyville* came out in 1993, Liz says she was "gobsmacked to learn" she'd be playing with The Raincoats in New York City. Gina adds of *Exile in Guyville*, "I loved this record a lot and knew every note by heart."

"It was an intimidating venue for me to tackle," Liz continues, explaining that she still felt "green as a performer." And when it came to having The Raincoats on the bill, "technically, you could say they opened for me," Liz remarks, "but that's not how I viewed it. From the beginning of my career, I've known that concert lineups are a reflection of local market share, not a measure of quality, cultural impact, or skill. Every artist experiences a variety of performances on the road, from opening slots to headlining gigs, sometimes back to back. That night was the first time I cared more about the musicians watching me backstage than the eyes and ears of the audience."

The anticipation of the two-night bill would turn to tragedy before the first night even started. Ray Farrell came in during the sound check to deliver startling news: Kurt Cobain died.

LIFE NUMBER 2

The Raincoats underneath The Academy marquee with Liz Phair, 1994

Nobody needed the update that the tour was canceled. Shirley returned all their unused tickets; they needed the money to cover the costs of present expenses they'd no longer be recouping with the Nirvana dates. "The Nirvana–Raincoats tickets ..." Gina sighs. "We wish we hadn't got the money back. That's a lot of money now!"

Ana wrote in her tour diary contemporaneously:

We found out about this from Ray as we finished our soundcheck for the 1st Academy gig with Liz Phair (the first group was Versus). It's a tragedy for a lot of people and we felt that the warm relationship that had developed between us had actually not been consummated in terms of us actually meeting and getting to know Kurt and each other. The tour we were supposed to do together in the UK could have been rewarding and warm. My thoughts also go for Courtney and little Frances bean. Our gig was clouded by this and lots of the words in the songs had different meanings from the usual. We're a million to come we're a million to go. I dedicate The Void forever to Kurt. Talked about him during the gig. Liz Phair also dedicated a song to him. The audience's thoughts were also for him. We played well and I wish a small fantasy of mine had turned into reality—that Kurt would have come to NY to see us. I think he would have liked us as we're playing well and delivering something strong. Bye, Kurt.

"It was a really odd day," Steve reflects. "It all felt like this false climax, and I felt like the air was just taken out of our sails. We'd been sort of waiting on Kurt, and all of a sudden, that was it." Steve felt so much of The Raincoats' second life was wrapped up in the upcoming tour with Nirvana, so the news of Kurt's death is the one day of the tour he remembers in detail. "I guess it was unspoken," he says, "but it felt like that was going to be the end."

Gina tries to remember some of the good things from that night, including how much she loved *Exile in Guyville*. She recalls wanting to be able to sing "Flower" with Liz, one of the songs from that record, and she and Ana sang it together with Liz during the encore. But the gig was tough, and Gina has tried to suppress some of those memories: "We had been so excited to play with Nirvana, hear them every night, scared their audiences would hate us, but knowing we would have had the most incredible time getting to know all of the band, with Kurt at the heart. It was beyond heartbreaking news that Kurt was gone."

"When I was singing some of my songs, I was thinking of Kurt," Ana says. "And I knew 'The Void' was his favorite song. I dedicated it to him forever, that night. Some of the things about him—his sadness, his desperation—I felt some of that sadness when I was singing the songs." Ana went back to the hotel room and "just started crying, there on my own, because it was such a great loss. Why him? Why anybody, but why somebody who brings so many people so much help in a way through their music, in a way people listen and identify, or maybe just don't feel so alone . . . He was so poetic and so full of ideas."

Steve Shelley reflected on the immense loss in the tour diary, too:

> a sad and hyper-surreal night. black friday. and now everything has changed.

Ray, too, wrote in the diary after the show:

> This has been a wonderful and inspirational week. It's great to see the Raincoats after all this time and even greater to see the crowd's reaction. You've also helped keep my spirits up in this rough week. I sincerely hope that we can work together again.

Amid the grief and thoughts of endings, the tour also marked the beginning of another intersecting Raincoats story. Opening that night at The Academy was Chan Marshall, aka Cat Power, playing her first solo gig. "There was this young woman there who was petrified, but she was really great," Steve remembers. "Just after she'd finished her sound check, we were all going out for a bite, and because she looked so terrified, I said, 'Why don't you come with us?' She came along, and I told her if she ever needed someone to play with to give me a call because she sounded really great. It was Chan Marshall, and of course, the rest of that connection is history." Steve went on to be heavily involved in playing and releasing Chan's music. Gina laughs, "I think all those guys, Steve, Chan's guitarist, and I can't remember who else was with them, just fell in love with Chan Marshall that night."

Chan wrote a full-page, stream-of-consciousness tour diary entry that ends, "i am glad i made memories here i am not sure why i am still here." Ana snapped a photo of Chan as she was writing in the diary, with an unlit cigarette in her mouth. Below the entry,

Ana made a personal note for herself: "Chan Marshall used to be in Cat People." (Chan was originally in a band called Cat Power, and soon began using the band name as the solo stage name under which she'd become known.)

Liz also wrote two full pages, in large cursive handwriting:

> Oh my god we should have sound checked! But in the grand tradition of rock
> > To ~~suck~~ rock is holy
> > To suck is divine
>
> I can't recall my proverb. Wow. I wonder where you will take this diary—now to Detroit, now to Japan. What does it feel like to play again after 10 yrs? It was one of the best shows I have ever watched. Raincoats are in my opinion the most beautifully creative arrangements that have ever graced vinyl. Diaries are so brilliant. They give you something to do as the head cools down post performance. My friends have arrived so I am going to go enjoy them. I hope you can tell how much it meant to me to play with you and though I am a shitty correspondent, if we ever get a chance to hook up in any capacity—I will be there in a heartbeat.
> > All my love
> > Liz xxxooooxxx

After the second Academy show in NYC, Gina wrote about how well the gig had gone, and about eating Ukrainian food after getting turned away from John Lydon's NYC party:

> What a buzz. We were on form from a week of touring and the crowd was right with us. Didn't feel like a support slot at all. Very warm feeling Raincoats seem to bring this out of people ... tonight's gig had a lot more Raincoats fans there. Great gig. After there was an interview with intense Lydia then an attempt to blag our way into John Lydon's party unsuccessfully. Didn't look much cop to be honest so we went to the Kiev—the real Ukrainian thing with scowling waitresses + amazing menu. They eat blueberry pancakes with garlic sausage and eggs!

LIFE NUMBER 2

Ana also reflected on the second night in NYC and the end of the tour. In addition to continuing to dedicate "The Void" to Kurt, she wrote, "I've dedicated 'You're A Million' to Shirley and Shirley was very touched by this when I told her on the phone to the UK." She also reported that Mike videotaped the second New York gig (the tape, unfortunately, is now MIA) and listed some of the people who'd attended one or both nights, including "Kim + Thurston," Sharon and Craig of God Is My Co-Pilot, Francis Ford Coppola, and Dan Graham. Her final words:

> The mini tour was such good fun and it was so great to play so well and feel so comfortable doing it. It's exhilarating—it's difficult to explain. It's very sociable also.

Steve didn't have the last words in the diary, but in some ways, he had the final words to sum up the tour:

> i never would have thought that someday i would be playing with the raincoats. it's still hard to believe that this happened. and i'm proud that geffen has reissued all of the raincoats cds. a ~~minor~~ major triumph for a major life!

Reflecting on her memories of seeing The Raincoats take the stage before her on April 8, 1994, Liz says, "The band I saw perform was confident and impressive, different from the unstudied, insouciant musicians I first encountered on their album *The Raincoats*," which she describes as their "electrifying debut." Yet The Raincoats were not a band of the past. Indeed, they were a very present influence on the female artists like Liz and her contemporaries. Fifteen years after their debut LP, Liz insists, "Their impact on alternative music was reflected everywhere in the music a lot of us were drawn to, and their poetic, dynamic and wholly original compositions shone even more brightly. Their lyrics of female disenchantment was going mainstream."

The Raincoats' music was so important to Liz that she wanted to make the inspiration part of her own music's visual esthetic.

"I made an allusion to their self-titled album artwork on my second album, the *Whip-Smart* cover," she reveals, referring to a small figure on the bottom left of the sleeve. "A riff on Chinese Cultural Revolution propaganda."

REMEMBERING KURT

After returning to London, Ana wrote her thoughts on Kurt's untimely death for a tribute in *Melody Maker*:

> It only takes a quick read of Incesticide's liner notes, to know what a humane person Kurt really was. He looked and therefore he saw things that most people seem more comfortable hitting on the head—he embrassed [sic] difference and had a dislike for the previlege [sic] of a small portion of our society. He believed in beauty and was gifted to create it. He wanted to make a difference and he certainly made it. It's a terrible shame his gifts and rewards weren't enough to destroy the walls that kept him imprisoned.
> 'When I looked at the streets/ and when they looked at me/ The void/ The void could only stop being/ When I ... 1, 2, 3 3, 2, 1 1, 2, 3 3, 2, 1 nil' These are the words to one of our songs 'The Void' that Kurt liked. We've dedicated it to him forever and will never forget what he did for us.[13]

Ana also felt she should reach out to Courtney but wasn't sure what to say or how. Ultimately, she turned to a form in which she felt comfortable, a handwritten letter:

> Dear Courtney
> I've been meaning to write to you, but it's difficult to know what to say. I would like you to know, though, how so deeply sorry we all were and are about what happened. First my thoughts went for Kurt and to how depressed he must have been to end his own life and leave everything behind, mainly you and Frances, but also his music and what he had to say. My thoughts so soon went

LIFE NUMBER 2

to you and your daughter and the great sense of loss, despair, frustration and anger you must feel about it. And this really breaks my heart. I've thought so much about the whole thing since he died. We found out about Kurt's death after a sound check in NYC and that put ~~a very~~ such a dark and heavy cloud over the evening and somehow so many of our own lyrics seem to speak about things so relevant to the moment. I have dedicated "The Void" to him forever as I know he, too, liked this song.

We meant to write to him to put his mind at peace about the tour—we didn't have any resentments at all towards him about it. Of course, we would have loved to have done it, but the only thing I feel really sad about is his death/absence and, at the time of the cancellations, I only had the wish he'd get better—tour or no tour—as people like Kurt are scarce and because he made a difference in the world we live in. I really wish he had listened to the voices of respect and love that so many people had for him and not the negative voices that seem to have haunted him.

We're sending you our Peel session, that we dedicated to Kurt. I think of you when I heard "Shouting Out Loud," which we also played in the session.

I'd like you to know that I have very warm feelings towards you ~~both~~ and Kurt and am very thankful for everything he did for us. It didn't only help us do what we're doing, but gave us some sense of value of what we had done, that it had actually been meaningful and therefore worthwhile, something I hadn't been aware of at all before. I thought we had been kind of forgotten. I started listening to contemporary music again after buying "Nevermind" and "Pretty on the Inside" and that has given me a lot of joy.

I would write more but I think I'll just say that I hope you and your daughter can give and receive from each other the love you both need, and find there some comfort.

I hope to meet you again, but, for the time being, if you need anything, just let me know.

Lots of love
Ana
(The Raincoats)

EXTENDED PLAY

Kurt's death shocked and saddened The Raincoats, but they wanted to try to keep going. Shirley had the idea to put out a Raincoats EP from the Peel session. Steve was on board with his label Smells Like in the US, and Shirley approached Paul Smith at Blast First about the UK release. "I was delighted to be asked as a long-time fan," Paul says. "Blast First was all about bands that had created their own soundworlds, whether it was Sonic Youth, Sun Ra, Suicide, or fellow travelers UT, and The Raincoats had most certainly done that."

Smells Like got started because Lou Barlow of Dinosaur Jr. sent Steve a cassette with two songs he liked, which he wanted to release as a 7-inch single—the songs "Loser Core" and "Really Insane." Steve remembers they were trying to think of a name for the label. "Nirvana mania was going on, and a buddy of mine jokingly shouted, 'You should call it Smells Like Records!'" referring, of course, to Smells Like Teen Spirit. "Everybody was laughing at the silliness of it, and somehow, that unfortunately stuck," Steve laughs. Ultimately, the Nirvana connection would take on more meaning in the label's release of a live session recorded with plans to be Nirvana's tour support.

To do the EP, Shirley had to get a release of the BBC tapes. She wrote to Steve on May 8 to explain an ongoing delay with the BBC and to discuss plans for summer rehearsals and gigs:

> A few things—<u>1st</u> I am waiting to get hold of the BBC tapes—I have sent them all the clearances and licensing forms—so now it's just a question of getting the DAT! As soon as I have news I'll let you know. Ana is doing the artwork right now and will have it finished for Tuesday afternoon. I'll check what they normally send to USA—or you let me know what's preferable.
>
> Also, we need to make a letter of agreement for 'The Raincoats' licensing the tapes to 'Smells Like Records'.

Shirley suggests Steve plan to return to the UK in July to start thinking about the new Raincoats record.

LIFE NUMBER 2

By August '94, nothing was yet written in stone for a new record, and Steve wasn't going to be able to continue playing with The Raincoats—he had to return to Sonic Youth. They were writing and recording for *Washing Machine* (DGC, 1995) and preparing for the Washing Machine Tour the following year (a tour on which The Raincoats would open for Sonic Youth in London). Shirley wrote Steve on August 23 to finalize the Smells Like licensing for the CD *Extended Play*. The deal they'd worked out was exactly what The Raincoats had enjoyed during their relationship with Rough Trade in the late 1970s and early 1980s—a fifty-fifty profit share. Simple, straightforward, fair.

A FETE WORSE THAN DEATH

With Steve unable to remain a Raincoat, the band was in a very familiar predicament: They needed a drummer. Joe Dilworth came in for a few shows and they lucked out with a new live sound engineer, Steph Hillier, who'd end up joining them for all future shows through the nineties and into the 2000s.

"I met them because I'd been doing live sound for Bandit Queen," Steph says, referring to the Riot Grrrl-adjacent band on Paula Greenwood's Manchester indie label, Playtime Records. "And The Raincoats did a show with Bandit Queen, so that's how it started. Then, one day when I was doing some festivals, I got a call from Shirley asking if I was busy that day." Steph laughs, "I *was* busy that day, but it ended around two, so I dashed down on public transport to Hoxton Square and made it for the sound check by the skin of my teeth." The Raincoats needed Steph to do live sound for The Fete Worse Than Death.

The Fete Worse Than Death was an event to support emerging artists, a type of gig The Raincoats knew well from their days supporting Rock Against Sexism and playing the "Beat the Blues" festival. Yet it was much more than a showcase to fund young British artists and their practices. It was an event that cemented a nascent connection between The Raincoats and the art world.

This "hybrid pop culture extravaganza," as it styled itself, was put on by Factual Nonsense, the curator Joshua Compston's gallery in Shoreditch, East London, which would ultimately become the name of Compston's company and an art movement unto itself. One of Compston's often quoted adages reads: "My guns are directed at modern culture. It needs to be massively reinvented." It was an idea to which The Raincoats were never strangers.

Today, the Paul Stolper Gallery describes Factual Nonsense as a "crazy powerhouse of ideas" and the Fete as "an anarchic swipe at the notion of a traditional village fête." It featured a range of emerging artists such as Tracey Emin, Sarah Lucas, Gillian Wearing, and Gavin Turk, and also "included some of the biggest, yet still then unknown, stars of the art world, including Damien Hirst and Angus Fairhurst, who dressed as clowns producing the first spin paintings at the fête (for sale at the princely sum of £1)."[14] Fashion designer and legendary performance artist Leigh Bowery performed with his punk band, Minty, only six months before his untimely death.

The Raincoats played alongside other musicians, including The Flying Medallions and Armitage Shanks, performance artists Gavin Turk and Cerith Wyn Evans, and video works by filmmaker Thomas Gray.

In 2014, to mark the twentieth anniversary of the Fete Worse Than Death, the keepers of Factual Nonsense decided to put on a more clear-cut benefit event titled "A Fete Worse Than Death" to support struggling East End galleries that were interested in cultivating spaces "where artists themselves can come together and run things themselves, do things on their own terms, making things happen (if they still want to that is?)." The promotional materials for the benefit stressed that, in 2014, "things aren't looking to good in the East End, what with developers grabbing everything, with the swing of the wrecking ball getting closer, with the urbanists and the Foxtonists [a reference to the controversial London-based estate agency Foxtons] and those indulging in the business of making money out of artists without really showing that much consideration for the artists making the art—and the apathy, the apathy is the big killer." What all artists needed, the promoters suggested, was something The Raincoats brought to their communities in the late 1970s and into the future: "a bit more of that spirit of the visionary."[15]

Joe accompanied The Raincoats from one type of radical art space to another. Less than two weeks after the Fete in '94, he traveled with the band to Düsseldorf to play a special and intimate show for Carmen Knoebel's fiftieth birthday.

TIM/KERR FAIRYTALES

As contemporary interest in The Raincoats continued to grow, the American indie label Tim/Kerr, cofounded by Thor Lindsay and Thomas "Tim" Kerr IV, was keen to do a "greatest hits" record. Vinyl only, the Portland-based label released the compilation *Fairytales* in 1995. It included tracks from the first three albums. The plan seemed predestined, given that Tim/Kerr was known for releasing music by some of Kurt's favorite bands such as the Wipers and Daniel Johnston, and had even done a 10-inch vinyl collaboration between Kurt and William S. Burroughs.

Shirley was keeping Ray updated since DGC was involved in the "T.K. Records Compilation," as she frequently called it. In May 1994, Shirley wrote:

> Ana has completed the front cover—just needs back/label finishing—and this depends on track listing which we hope to sort out in the next 24 hours. Please let me know what else you need and when. (If you have an idea for tracklisting let me know.)

A couple months later, Shirley gave Ray another update:

> Ana has been liaising with Thor Lindsay about artwork and the possibility of a metallic blue vinyl. Here is the title and tracklisting—can you fax me any relevant details from DGC which need to be on the label and sleeve.

Shirley contacted Thor in October 1994 to let him know she'd received the proofs for the record, but some changes were necessary. Rather than a matte finish, the sleeve should have a glossy finish. The inner sleeve should be typeset in a different location, and the red color should become Pantone 205, a deep pink. The label, likewise, should be changed to Pantone 205 with the track timings in white. Shirley also advised of track-listing corrections:

1. Fairytale In The Supermarket (not Fairytales In . . .)
8. No Side To Fall In (not No Side To Fallin)
12. Overheard (not Overhead)

Shirley also shared a publicity blurb from Chris Sharp, then at Rough Trade, for the promo:

'Fairytales' is both a perfect introduction to the thrilling blend of beauty and daring that is The Raincoats sound, and a convincing explanation of their continued high critical standing. From the early dissonant joyous leaps of 'In Love' and 'The Void' to later instinctive explorations like 'Only Loved at Night' and 'Rainstorm,' 'Fairytales' is the story so far of a genuinely original group, whose honesty and imagination shines through every song they have recorded.

By 1995, the record was finished and was ready for release. On February 7, 1995, Ana wrote to Thor, and Shirley faxed it out that same day:

Dear Thor
    Hope everything is going well with you. Our plans are: Heather is coming on the 24th of April. We'll be rehearsing for about 10 days, then leave to N.Y. and record during Mary. When that's done, Gina and I will probably go to LA to meet the DGC people. We've only met Ray. We're really excited about doing this record. If by any chance you go to NY at that time, we must meet.
    The sleeves of the black vinyl records you sent were bashed, so I wonder if we could have a few more of those and also when the blue ones come, it would be great if they were packed in a way that wouldn't bash them . . . Thanks for having done our compilation and I hope it does well along with the other stuff on the label. I think the label is great, adventurous, and a provider

of good music. [Ana asks for some additional Tim/Kerr releases and lets Thor know that she and Shirley now have a fax machine.] Please keep us 'faxed.'

Six weeks later, Thor replied via fax:

Dear Ana,
    Please forgive the delay, there really is no excuse. I thought your package had been shipped already. The paperwork was misplaced in our shipping department, and on following up I just discovered our error. I have expedited the shipment to you, and I apologize again for the delay. Thanks for letting us share this project with you. I feel honored. I have included some of our current releases. I hope you enjoy them. Good luck on the upcoming album, and we will keep you posted on reviews of "Fairytales." Please stay in touch.[16]

The director of business affairs at Tim/Kerr got in touch with The Raincoats in February 1996: "Unfortunately it did not do as well as we had hoped but we're not giving up yet ... In any event, we look forward to releasing the next Raincoats album on vinyl."

That same year, as the correspondence alludes to, Tim/Kerr played the important role of distributing *Looking in the Shadows* on vinyl in the United States. DGC wasn't in the vinyl market; they wanted to sell CDs with an eye firmly toward the largest possible profit. That wasn't what vinyl pressings were doing for any labels in the mid-nineties. But The Raincoats wanted their new record on vinyl in America, and as a label committed to independent artists and the preservation of material culture, Tim/Kerr was heroic. Naturally, Rough Trade pressed the vinyl record for the UK market.

NEGOTIATING A GEFFEN PRODUCTION

By May 1994, Kurt, one of The Raincoats' biggest supporters associated with DGC was gone, yet Ray was still interested in bringing The Raincoats into the DGC fold.

"We had not thought of doing another record," Ana says definitively. "We weren't *really* a band at the time—me and Gina had just done a few gigs that were supposed to be for the tour with Nirvana ... So when we were asked to do an album, I had a few songs I'd written and played with Roseland, and Gina had a few as well, so we thought, let's give it a try."

Gina agreed, and when the thought of a new album came into view, she was really excited. "It all seemed like a mad offer, a series of mad offers! Tour with Nirvana, make an album on DGC. But why would we ever think of throwing that away? We started to take it really seriously and knew we wanted to do it, and Ray Farrell was saying things to us like, 'Oh, you're going to sell millions! It's going to be this, it's going to be that'—all these ideas of how brilliant it'd be. So for a while it was really exciting."

Ray wanted DGC to move forward with a new Raincoats studio album "because Kurt had encouraged it," but the process was markedly different from the band's Rough Trade days. The Raincoats would have to jettison their commitment to the DIY ethos and comply with DGC norms: hiring a New York-based law firm, shockingly high budgets, complicated negotiations, impersonal communications.

With Geffen involved, there was also a need for a US manager. As early as August '94, Ray brought this up with Shirley, but she tried to head it off. Ultimately, the issue had to be addressed. Ray suggested The Raincoats work with Sheri Hood. Sheri was based in New Jersey and had already done US management for British bands, including the Cranes, Slowdive, and Stereolab—she had that 4AD connection. For DGC, US management was a necessity if The Raincoats were going to do a record and tour in the States.

Back in London, Shirley felt diminished, with an ache in her heart. Sheri assumed it was all kosher—she'd done this before—but soon realized there were significant feelings at stake; this was more than just a business arrangement. The first time Shirley and Sheri spoke was on December 8, 1994, and Sheri talked with Gina and Ana after the New Year on February 7. It was clear to Sheri that London was The Raincoats' center, both literally and metaphorically. She understood she'd be handling US matters—working directly with Geffen, setting up the touring team, working on budgets—but that she didn't have the same degree of input as Shirley. There was never a question for her that Shirley was the *main* manager, but the situation felt fraught and fragile on both sides.

Sheri and Ray were in what seemed like constant contact as the DGC negotiations were taking place. "There were *lots* of meals with Ray," Sheri laughs. And Ray was, she emphasizes, "the biggest support The Raincoats could have within a label." He was able to push internally at Geffen in ways that other A&R people wouldn't have been able to at other majors, and certainly in ways Sheri herself couldn't. In the end, he got the contract through. But before that could happen, some practical matters needed to be resolved.

THE RAINCOATS NEED A (RIOT GRRRL) DRUMMER

Ahem. The Raincoats needed a drummer.

It was Ray's sense they needed a Riot Grrrl. How better to bring the band firmly into the politics and spirit of the nineties female-fronted music story?

Ana got in touch with Tobi Vail first. "They asked me if I wanted to play drums with them," Tobi says, "and I remember thinking *I do not know how to do that!* I'd never learned anyone else's songs. I'm also a four-four-time kind of drummer, and their songs are . . . not that at all! So I didn't think I'd even be able to do it." Shirley remembers thinking Tobi "was a bit freaked out, and said something like, 'Oh God, I don't think I could do this!'" As a riotous Raincoats fan, it's a little surprising Tobi declined the offer, but as she explains it, "I still would have *no idea* how to play that music. I'm a pretty straightforward minimalist, rock 'n' roll drummer. I know I'm good, but I don't know how to do that."

Once Tobi turned her down, Ana reached out to Delia Sparrow of Mambo Taxi. "Ana asked me to drum in The Raincoats," Delia says, "but at the time I'd never drummed in a band and I didn't have the confidence, so I turned her down. It's one of my I-wonder-ifs."

Tobi recommended Heather Dunn, former Tiger Trap drummer extraordinaire who was touring with Lois Maffeo at the time. "Heather was one of the best drummers I could think of at the time," Tobi says. Ana remembers Kim Gordon also recommending Heather.

Slim Moon of Kill Rock Stars also takes credit for Heather. "It sounds like I'm bragging," he laughs, "and really the person who should brag is Ray Farrell, but Ray called me and said The Raincoats need a drummer and asked about women drummers. I suggested Heather, and she ended up playing with them, so I have this teeny part of the story." Jon Slade heard The Raincoats had asked Tobi and Molly Neuman of Bratmobile. Heather remembers getting a call from a DGC rep who told her, "We're looking at Tobi Vail and Molly Neuman, but do you want to go over to London and audition for The Raincoats?" Molly says she definitely wasn't asked.

Ray was set on finding a female drummer who was in "the same sphere of musical influence" as Riot Grrrl. "I don't know that Heather would have called herself a Riot Grrrl exactly," Sheri says, but there's no doubt that anyone associated with the Riot Grrrl movement "worshipped The Raincoats," she adds. Ray had seen Heather playing with Lois on more than one occasion, and each time, he became more impressed. "Part of it was that it wasn't like anything I'd seen before from a drummer," he explains. "She was having *fun*." Heather was also drumming on a range of Lois's songs that "weren't straightforward, weren't four-four signature time, and even when they were," Ray says, "Heather found ways of adding these little elements in." He thought if The Raincoats were into her playing, she could work really well with the band.

Heather got the call in 1994 while recording with Lois. "She's incredible," Heather says of Lois. "While I was playing in Tiger Trap, I was a fangirl of Lois's shambly music. When I had an opportunity to move to Portland after Tiger Trap broke up, Lois asked me to play." Although she was already drumming with one of her idols, Heather was especially apprehensive about auditioning for The Raincoats. "I don't know if it was because it was Geffen," Heather says, "[but] "I was super nervous. Being such an indie rocker, I thought, *Should I even try to do this?* Would it even be OK if I was on a major label?" She remembers discussing it with Lois, and later Tobi, who invited Heather over to listen to Raincoats records. At that point, Heather thought, "*OK, this is awesome.*" Tobi encouraged her to do the audition, and Heather promised, "I'm gonna go for it."

Unlike Lois and Tobi, but akin to Anne Wood, Heather wasn't among the "original Raincoats superfans." As a result, she was worried she wouldn't be able to play the songs in the same way Tobi or another drummer would. On top of it, she knew Steve Shelley had joined the band for their 1994 tour dates. "Could I really fill those Sonic Youth shoes?" she remembers fearing. "It was just mind-boggling, and even the amount of the ticket over to London was *so much*, the definition of 'big money' at the time." But she did it. Ana and Shirley met her at Heathrow and Shirley drove the three of them back to their flat.

"I was a little weirded out by them," Heather laughs, explaining that it was because she knew how much older they were than her. "I'm using 'weird' in an *ultra-loving way*," she says, "now that I'm fifty. But being a twenty-year-old kid then . . . and I knew they were being called the grandmothers of Riot Grrrl, but they *did not* seem like grandmas, *not at ALL*." Back at the flat, Heather got the sense "we were trying to get a vibe on each other, figure one another out," all while she felt extremely uncomfortable. "It took us a little while to warm up, in part because I had this sense of 'here I am, the dumb, young American.'" But they became fast friends, and Heather immediately fell in love with "their cute and dreamy little flat off Portobello Road, right by the market and the Rough Trade shop!" She got an inside look into the way The Raincoats experienced family life and went about their everyday lives.

They immediately jumped into rehearsals. Heather had practiced some of her new favorite Raincoats songs before she got to London, but Ana or Gina would say, "We don't really do *those* songs anymore . . . we do *these* songs." Heather tried to listen and play to the beats of the band. She felt like she'd become part of a Raincoats fairytale she knew about from Lois, Tobi, and other friends in Olympia and Portland. "Being behind that drum set with them in person, in front of me, it was just like, *Wow, this is a dream come true and it's actually happening, mind-blowing*." She wasn't sure about the impression she'd made on them when she returned to Portland, but for Heather it felt like "a magical ten days."

Shortly after she got back, Shirley called to let her know they were going to have a Raincoats discussion. The waiting was painful, but Heather jumped back into her work on the West Coast and tried to put it out of her mind. She didn't know what to think. She felt pretty certain Molly Neuman wasn't going to head to London to play with them, and Heather knew Tobi had already declined. She'd also heard Geffen wanted "a woman drummer who was current, a kind of Riot Grrrl who had been playing with other women." So in that sense, she thought she stood a chance of getting the job—"But it really could have gone either way," Heather says. More time passed, and then she got a transatlantic phone call. The Raincoats wanted her to return to London for some live gigs and to record the LP that would become *Looking in the Shadows*.

On September 28, 1994, Shirley wrote to Ray confirming plans to go ahead with Heather on drums:

> Ray: Heather left yesterday and I just want to let you know that we all love her and her playing. I've discussed the situation with her and she definitely wants to play with us. So that is resolved. All we have to do now is discuss the fine details which are mainly to do with finalizing the contract and working out cover to records.

Ray knew Heather was apprehensive about her own abilities as soon as she got the go-ahead. "She was very nervous that this was even the situation, as if she didn't deserve it," Ray says. In a lot of ways, Heather was the best person for the job. "Heather was a perfect fit in terms of her enthusiasm ... the dynamic she brought was *fun*, and she brought Ana and Gina together in that they *laughed*," Sheri remembers. "And she brought that spirit of *oh my GOD THE RAINCOATS*, we're gonna do this, let's fuck shit up!" Sheri laughs. "I know she became a liability later on," Sheri continues, referring to issues such as Heather showing up late for rehearsals, forgetting her drumsticks, and other related antics. "But she also made them *come alive*."

"She was twenty-one going on ... thirteen at that time," Ana says. "We are quite open to some craziness, but it was a bit too much. I always had to bring drumsticks and a drum tuner because she'd forget to bring them. I love her, and we've seen her since and we're friends, but back then, it was all just a little bit too much!"

Tensions would manifest once Heather got back over to London, but first, The Raincoats needed to confirm a producer for their Geffen album.

JOHN CALE

John Cale initially agreed to produce *Looking in the Shadows*, and The Raincoats even got to the point of sorting out a production budget with him on board.

Cale is best known as the cofounder, with Lou Reed, of the Velvet Underground in 1965. Cale gave the band one of their most distinctive sounds with his viola, and that sound inspired The Raincoats to add Vicky to their lineup in 1979. That connection alone would have been enough to get The Raincoats interested in working with Cale. But in his post-Velvets years, he made his name as an innovative and experimental producer on records as wide-ranging as the Stooges' self-titled debut (1969) and Patti Smith's *Horses* (1975) to those by Jonathan Richman and the Modern Lovers, and the Happy Mondays on Factory Records. He could go seamlessly, it seemed, from lo-fi punk to acid house. By the mid-nineties, he'd worked with Siouxsie and the Banshees on a comeback album and had produced personal music with Lou Reed.

Behind the controls, he seemed to understand the divergent needs of experimental and pioneering artists, and he wasn't one to kowtow to corporate desires. Music critic Amanda Petrusich wrote that "Cale has always thought of art as fluid rather than static—he has rarely been satisfied by recapitulations of the status quo."[17] Who better to help bring The Raincoats back to life?

"The Raincoats really wanted John Cale to produce them, and I wanted John Cale to produce, too, and we actually got him to agree," Ray says. But when he asked trusted confidants if they thought it was a good idea, "I got drastically different responses," he says. "One person told me it's really chaotic, and if the band doesn't know exactly what it wants and is ready to fight for it, this could end up being a disaster." He also heard from a musician who'd worked with Cale recently: "As long as you have a good engineer, you'll be good. He really doesn't get that engaged." But another said, "Just be prepared for the possibility of drama." While Ray was excited at the prospect of potentially getting Cale on board, he wondered if it was going to make for a difficult recording session. "I thought, well, I'm still gonna give it a shot," he remembers. He contacted Cale, who indicated he was "really interested." Soon, Cale's engineer did most of the talking for both of them. He told Ray they had a New York studio in mind, and that Cale "really likes The Raincoats' music" and wanted to find a way to work with them.

By January 1995, Cale provisionally agreed to produce *Looking in the Shadows* for $20,000—nearly a third of the budget The Raincoats would be getting from DGC.

The plan was to have The Raincoats meet in New York, where they'd record. Cale insisted on New York—nowhere else would do. Logistically, it seemed like it might get too complicated, especially with Ana, Gina, and Anne in the UK. While The Raincoats had a long history with and connection to the city, logistics were raising eyebrows. Every time Ray got Cale pinned down to a schedule, there'd be changes due to Cale's other commitments. "He'd say, 'Oh, I've got to take four days off to play a festival in Spain,' and here I'd be, paying for The Raincoats' hotel rooms in New York while John Cale is over in Spain. I thought if we agreed, he might not come back when he said he would, might not ultimately finish their release," Ray explains. "So I thought we really couldn't do it. I'm sure The Raincoats would have loved to have been in John Cale's discography of the productions he'd done, but ultimately the logistics stopped me from moving forward with him."

Meanwhile, Ana and Gina were also having second thoughts. They took the Eurostar from London to meet with Cale in a Paris café. When they showed up, he'd set aside only twenty minutes for them—there wasn't time for more than a quick tea. He insisted they'd need to do the album on his schedule, and he emphasized that The Raincoats would need to come to New York; he wouldn't produce the record in London. "We had both been huge fans, but he was cold, wasn't particularly nice, and didn't seem interested," Ana remembers. "He didn't want to do it, so we didn't want to do it," Gina says, and Ana adds definitively, "If you don't like me, I don't like you. That's my motto ... He wasn't for us."

"It was disappointing," Ana reflects. "I love the Velvet Underground, and it would have been a nice thing to do, but ..."

Shirley remembers when Ana and Gina returned from that Parisian jaunt and reported the brevity of their meeting. "It just wasn't right," she says. "It was really disappointing because he was a big hero, but better to go down that route at that point and be disappointed early than end up somewhere else."

By April 8, plans for John Cale to produce had been scrapped. Shirley reached out to PJ Harvey to see if she was interested, but while they waited for an answer, The Raincoats went to meet with Paul Tipler at the legendary Blackwing Studios. Sheri was already familiar since Stereolab had made a name for itself there, and Shirley faxed a note to tell her they "also met Tim from Stereolab."

Shirley was also looking into other options. "Ana, Gina, and myself were really impressed at that time with PJ Harvey's *To Bring You My Love*, which was produced by Flood." She sent a fax to Flood's agent. "He was unfortunately involved in another project, but his agent worked with Ed [Buller]," Shirley says, "and suggested Ed. And I'm so happy we had that opportunity."

As Ray remembers it, "Ed Buller's name came up because he was very quick in the studio." Ed says Steve Mackey put his name forward to Ray. Ed had been a member of the Psychedelic Furs and had become a prominent producer of Britpop bands Lush, Pulp, and Suede. As the bassist of Pulp, it made perfect sense Mackey would have suggested Ed.

Although Ed had never met Ana or Gina, he says knew of them, "obviously," noting the "buzz about them because Kurt Cobain had said things in the press." Ed was nervous about producing their new DGC album, because it "wasn't the sort of thing I'd normally get asked to make," he says. It became his "first experience working with two leaders of a band, and two *really strong women*." On the whole, it was an interesting learning experience, but Ed remembers how the record was "a little tricky to make."

The Raincoats entered into a production agreement with Ed for his production services on July 1, 1995. They'd have three weeks to do the album in Trident Studios. Finally, with a producer on board, the full DGC contract could be executed.

DGC CONTRACT FOR LOOKING IN THE SHADOWS

The DGC contract was signed after more than a year of discussions and negotiations. It's sixty-one pages in total, novella length compared with the three- or four-page contracts The Raincoats had entered into with Rough Trade.

The Raincoats would also sign a contract with Rough Trade for the UK and Ireland in June 1996; DGC had the rest of the world. Before that happened, Shirley had two meetings with Allison Schnackenberg, now head of A&R at Rough Trade Records. "We decided to work together shortly afterwards when Ana and Gina met with her too," Shirley says. Allison would become their A&R person in the UK, an incredibly enthusiastic supporter of the band.

By February 1996, Shirley's concerns about working with a major label became clearer. She jotted down worries about having to hire "an outside agent" for PR and told Ray The Raincoats were meeting with Savage and Best. Around the same time, she learned DGC was thinking about "Pretty" and "You Ask Why" as singles, what she described in frustrating terms as "the two more different songs on the album!" Meanwhile, in the UK, Allison told Shirley, "I myself am chanting 'Love a Loser' somewhat like a mantra in the hopes that my positive energy will descent [sic] upon Geffen's meeting" about selecting a single. Ultimately, they wouldn't take the band's suggestion or consider perspectives coming from Rough Trade. In April, *Billboard* described the band as "DGC's Raincoats."

None of these issues are surprising to anyone familiar with the story of bands moving from indie to major labels. As Patty Schemel says, labels like DGC were "not even thinking about rolling out the red carpet" for any bands that weren't earning them millions. "There were some nice and interesting people at DGC, but if you weren't in a band that was *really* going to sell, you didn't get that sort of Nirvana attention." The marketing focus was solely on what could sell, not on what the band wanted. That perspective would become increasingly clear to The Raincoats—and especially frustrating to Shirley—in the months that followed the execution of the DGC contract. Yet early DGC frustrations were tempered in the summer of '95 with a renewed joy around European touring and the prospect of recording new music.

ZÜRICH

The friendship between The Raincoats and Kleenex/LiLiPUT, forged in a van and on British stages in 1979, remained strong into the 1990s and beyond. On April 28, 1995, Marlene Marder wrote to Shirley to invite The Raincoats to perform in Switzerland that summer:

> Dear Shirley
> I hope you are all well.
> As I said on your Tel machine short, I heard this song of the BBC Session "Old & Grey" (or whatever the new title is) on Swiss National Radio. Great. Well, my question: do Raincoats again play live? If yes I would like to invite them to Zürich, 'cause we have this week 'bout women in rock music, with exhibitions, concerts [. . .][18]

The song Marlene refers to as "Old & Grey" was "Don't Be Mean," which would become the single from the band's DGC album *Looking in the Shadows*.

Ana remembers being excited to see Marlene again and to be back in Switzerland. For Gina, the chance to travel to Zürich was also a way to remake the 1979 tour on her own terms. "I'm normally really friendly!" Gina says, "but I don't think I was on that tour, I couldn't be. But when we went back to Zürich in the nineties, I got on so well with Marlene. So I got to try it again!"

Gina, "Don't Be Mean" single, 1996

MORE ARTWORK

After The Raincoats officially reformed in 1994, they picked up where they'd left off on their collaborative artwork design process for *Extended Play* (1994), the Smells Like–Blast First record that featured Ana's painting of a yellow lemon amid a black painted background. "I was collecting lemon paintings at that time," Gina explains, "and was especially keen for a lemon to be on the cover, so Ana painted one for it." Photos by Gina, Martyn Goodacre, and Alison Wonderland were also used in the inner sleeve design. For Tim/Kerr's *Fairytales* compilation (1994), Ana sketched windows, a visual trope that placed the compilation album in dialogue visually with The Raincoats' 1979 *Fairytale* EP.

Gina did the artwork for the first *Looking in the Shadows* (1996) single, "Don't Be Mean" b/w "I Keep Walking," which was released solely by Rough Trade; the band maintained the same creative control over the design that they'd enjoyed for so many years with the UK indie label. Joe Dilworth, Stereolab drummer who'd played

LIFE NUMBER 2

Ana, "Don't Be Mean" single, 1996

with The Raincoats in a few shows, was also a photographer. He took a series of portraits of Ana and Gina with flowers in and near their mouths, often obscuring their faces. Markedly saturated, bright yellow and green backgrounds. Those images would become the centerpiece of the 7-inch sleeve.

As Joe remembers it, "Those photos were really directed by Gina." He explains how he'd been "doing a lot of experiments with color," and Gina wanted him to capture images that were "beautiful, but also violent." Joe's brief, he says, "was to capture them being hit in the face with the flowers, at the point of contact." Joe cross-processed the film to get that particular look. He knew Gina pretty well at this point, so he had a good sense of what she wanted. "And she trusted me to have a go at it," he says. There are also standalone images of flowers on the back of the 7-inch sleeve, still lifes. "We tried putting the flowers down and shooting out of focus," Joe recalls. (The intense, saturated feel of the images speaks to the work Joe had been doing as a music photographer up to that point, and his experiments with color. His work is perhaps at its most recognizable in oversaturated shots he did for My Bloody Valentine in 1988 for their *Isn't Anything* album.) "Oh!" he says, remembering something else. "I also took Gina and Mike's wedding photos. But those were a bit more straightforward." Gina adds, "Fantastic photos taken on Joe's amazing Russian camera."

Ana also began work on a design for *Looking in the Shadows*, but that process would become a very different experience than previous ones.

DESIGNING LOOKING IN THE SHADOWS

The DGC honeymoon didn't last long. As autumn of '95 approached, Ana was under contract to design the record artwork and Shirley the cover photography, with Gina as music video director.

On October 16, Shirley sent the following to the Geffen Records art department:

> Briefly Ana's design is based on an 8-page full colour booklet which has a very specific concept, the Greek myth of Persephone, the goddess, queen of the underworld, who ate pomegranite [sic] seeds. The cover has a close up photo of a mouth with one single seed on the lip. The colours are rich and warm with the single seed being the strongest colour, red. The lighting is very shadowy and there is a thin veil of translucent silver fabric.
> The next two pages will contain details of songs and some lyrics on a photograph stretching across both pages of silver and gold fabric with 6 objects, some veiled and others on the surface. The objects are a clock, a train, a hand, a baby, a crystal, a pillar which make reference to songs, lyrics and the theme.
> The centre pages, which will be shot by Maria, contain a double page spread photo of Ana and Gina wrapped with the gold and silver fabric.
> The following two pages have details of the recording and band set into gold and silver fabric with shots of the whole band, shot by Maria.
> The last page of the booklet has an image of the mouth similar to the cover, it is unveiled and there are several pomegranite [sic]

LIFE NUMBER 2

seeds with honey like substance on the lip. The same image will be used for the back cover.

The disc itself will have a red image of a split pomegranite [sic] the seeds visible, with track information etc set into the red and silver of the disc.

The images will be shot by two photographers, the mouth, objects and pomegranite [sic] will be shot by Shirley, and the images of Ana and Gina, and the whole band by Maria. The mouth/object shots are planned for October, and the band shots for 5 November.

Artwork will be designed by Ana with digital imaging by Nick Clark, supplied on whatever disc format is required. Laser prints of the mouth and objects and pomegranite [sic] can be sent this week.

Geffen sent official contracts for Ana and Shirley to sign in which Ana's name was spelled incorrectly, written for "Anna da Silva." Ana was glad to be working on the sleeve design, but it was painfully clear she didn't have the creative freedom, or respect, she'd always enjoyed with Rough Trade. After the design contracts were executed, Geffen initially allotted a portion of the budget to Shirley for the cover photography and to Ana for the sleeve art (and to Gina for the "Don't Be Mean" video to come later), but ultimately decided that Ana's front cover idea had to be scrapped. "They said they'd just released a record with another red cover," Shirley sighs, "so we decided that I would reshoot the front cover with the memory dress, and the split pomegranate remained on the back cover and on the label."

More frustrations ensued. "The dreaded Geffen came back and said, 'OK, you've got this budget for photography for band portraits,' which had to be used or it wouldn't be available to us for anything else, so I said, 'Let's look at people's portfolios,'" Shirley says. "But there was nothing interesting in the portfolios they sent over, as far as I could see." She decided to try something else. "We all loved Maria Mochnacz's images of PJ Harvey, so we got in touch with her and set up a session, which was marvelous. I still have some Polaroids from that." Maria was a longtime photographer, music video creator, and PJ Harvey friend and collaborator.

To The Raincoats' relief, Geffen agreed. So there was a silver lining: The Raincoats made this connection with Maria, who'd ultimately introduce them to one of their favorite drummers. But that story comes after the *Looking in the Shadows* photo shoot.

THE MEMORY DRESS AND THE FLESH DRESS

Despite the initial concerns around the marketing of *Looking In the Shadows*, Maria Mochnacz's photo shoot produced several magical images that are among the most enduring in The Raincoats'

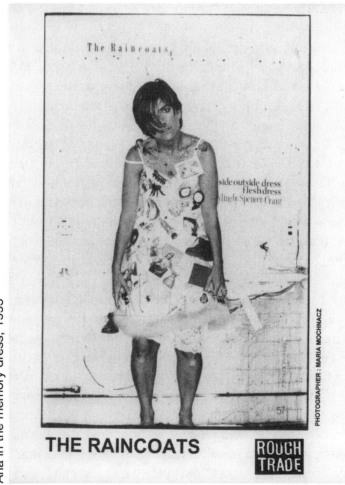

Ana in the memory dress, 1995

archive, namely those of Ana in a memory dress and Gina in a flesh dress. "These dresses were proposed by Maria," Gina explains, "and we agreed that one of us would be each of her ideas. I liked both of them, and Ana preferred the memory dress."

The memory dress is, in essence, just what it sounds like. Ana and Gina gathered photographs and objects that were important to them to attach to a sculpted metal form made by Spencer Horne and Craig Sheppard of the Handsome Foundation, who'd later play a key musical role in Gina's life. Family photos, empty eggcups, train tracks memorializing Ana's fascination with the ones that had run behind her early London flat, a copy of "The Raincoats

Gina in the flesh dress, 1995

Booklet," and various clocks set to different times. Meanwhile, for Gina's dress, Maria cut images of women's flesh from fashion magazines, brought them to The Raincoats, and Spencer and Craig constructed her attire. Gina was, quite literally, covered in ripped and fragmentary images of the flesh of women—a statement on the male gaze and the objectification of the female body. To this day, the memory dress survives and hangs above a stairwell in Ana and Shirley's flat. The flesh dress has been lost to time. "It was just a bit fragile," Gina laughs.

At the end of the photo session, PJ Harvey stopped by to pick up Maria for dinner. "We thanked her for sharing Maria a little bit," Ana says with a smile.

On January 22, 1996, Maria mailed a package with the photographs and a handwritten letter to Shirley, Ana, and Gina:

> Here are B/W copies of the prints I am sending to Jim Merliss as requested (I'm sorry that it's taken me this long but as I said on Anas phone message—I had to git it around some things) [sic] So you have copies so you can go DONT USE THAT ONE if you feel the need—but I like them—Especially LOVE the ones of the 2 dresses layn out together they look great (Polly's seen them all + is jealous!—always a good sign!!) So have I got that message across the 2 dresses are my personal favourites! (use them for something BIG)—do like the band ones too tho! Especially the top one (I know Anas face is a little too dark but I got it right for Jims copy)
> See you soon
> love you Maria X[19]

If PJ Harvey was jealous of the dresses, Maria was obviously onto something.

Shirley photographed the memory dress on her studio wall, and that print was the image used for the *Looking in the Shadows* album cover. It would also appear on all DGC advertising and on merch sold to fans at shows. Ana sketched out a design for a T-shirt and faxed it over to the production company. In the note attached to the design, she detailed the need for a very specific pink color

LIFE NUMBER 2

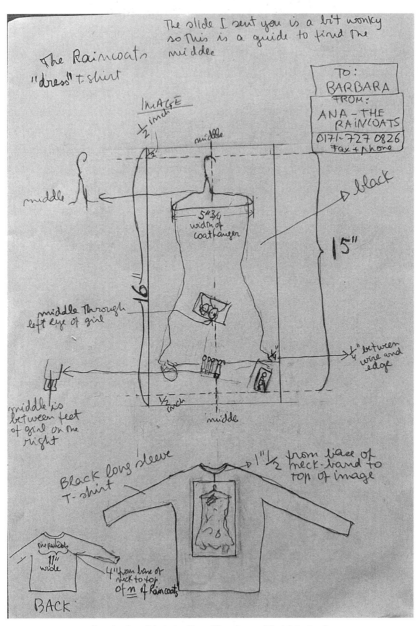

Ana's *Looking in the Shadows* T-shirt design

for "The Raincoats" font. It would be the dark pink splash on the bottom of the eggcup, hanging on the memory dress. Maria's band portraits were used for the CD booklet and publicity.

The concepts of a "memory dress" and "flesh dress" have a range of origins, from so-called low art and "women's work" to pop and fine art. The combined existence of a memory dress and flesh dress trace through-lines across these histories, marking Looking in the Shadows *as a time-crossing and genre-bending artwork. Textile artist Jenni Dutton cites the "domestic" origins of the memory dress, an object often made to wear from family quilts, darned in private homes by women of centuries past. Dutton highlights diary entries about memory dresses on westward journeys from days of the North American "frontier."*[20] *A similar but distinct form of the "memory dress" became a component of mourning in Ireland and regions of the UK, where hospitals and other sites of death have hung memory dresses sewn largely by women marking the deceased's memory.*

Indigenous artists have also reimagined the memory dress in response and resistance to "frontier" histories steeped in colonial violence and the genocide of Indigenous peoples. In Ottawa, on unceded Anishinaabe Algonquin territory, a 2015 exhibition showcased a collectively made piece of clothing in the Memory Dress Project, designed to collect shared histories across geographic space. The artists included objects that ranged from depictions of family traditions to large-scale collective memories of violence perpetrated in residential schools for Indigenous children established by the colonial Canadian government.[21] *Other similar memory dress projects and exhibitions have arisen in the years since in Indigenous communities.*

Flesh dresses, much differently, have their own—and significantly more recent—origins. As the Center for Feminist Art at the Brooklyn Museum explains, there has long been a gender-based assumption about "women's work," that sewing to make clothing could not be considered "fine art" since it "was associated with the domestic and the 'feminine.'"[22] *From the 1960s onward, feminist artists of varying backgrounds and experiences have "sought to resurrect women's craft ... as a viable means to express female experience, thereby pointing to its political and subversive potential." Enter burgeoning ideas for the flesh dress alongside a pointed desire among artists to push back against the misogyny of the "high art" world. The lineage starts with dresses literally made of flesh.*[23]

In 1982, Linder Sterling wore a dress of offal—a "meat dress"—on stage at the Haçienda in Manchester, UK, from under which she eventually revealed a 12-inch dildo, to protest against misogyny and what she perceived as the casual showing of pornography in the venue space. Lady Gaga would do a repeat decades later, wearing a dress made entirely of raw beef to the 2010 MTV Video Music Awards. The details of the dress were inspired by makeup artist Val Garland's flesh dress "back in the 1980s," a garment constructed with flattened steaks, bacon, and pork chipolatas. Garland told the BBC she made the dress to push boundaries and to "be like some kind of warrior."[24] Around the time Garland was constructing her dress, and shortly after Linder wore hers, visual artist Jana Sterbak coined the term "flesh dress." She made headlines with a display at the National Gallery of Canada. The piece was titled Vanitas: Flesh Dress for an Albino Anorectic, 1987, with textures of meat and its "bloody appearance" on full display. As art historians have crucially pointed out, the press largely misunderstood Sterbak's work. It was in fact part of a genealogy of feminist art depicting the gendered body and the pervasiveness of the violent male gaze.

Iconic feminist art critic Lucy Lippard has tracked this lineage of resistance, and in 1991, art critic Sarah Milroy wrote that the mere creation of a flesh dress represents an act of "female disobedience." In "conjoining these two signs" of dress and meat, she suggests, the artist "commits a major gender infraction, naming the equation between meat and women, both objects for male consumption, that patriarchal society would prefer to leave unspoken (and therefore more pervasive)."[25]

That day in 1995, when Maria Mochnacz photographed Ana and Gina in the memory dress and flesh dress, The Raincoats became part of these lineages of resistance.

RECORDING WITH ED BULLER

But before the artwork could be sorted, The Raincoats had to record Looking in the Shadows.

"Trident Studios was very posh," Ana reflects. "Rough Trade wasn't paying this time, so it wasn't Berry Street. This was Geffen. Quite glamorous. People like David Bowie and Blondie recorded there."

The songwriting process that brought The Raincoats into Trident wasn't so different from what it had been in the past, especially on *Moving*—there were Ana songs and Gina songs. But the ultimate product did reflect a starker distinction between the music the two frontwomen created, and their increasingly divergent directions. "We really do think quite differently," Gina explains. Those differences always shaped how they wrote songs, created visual art, and engaged in the world. But by the mid-nineties, as they'd grown and become more confident in themselves, the differences were more pronounced than ever. "I think a bit more laterally, and Ana thinks a bit more vertically, in a deeper way. We have very different ways of seeing things, and that could make Raincoats albums really interesting," Gina says, "but it could also lead to tensions."

Ed explains that he saw it quite clearly: "There were Gina songs, and then there were Ana songs, and trying to figure out how to record those, and then mix them for a single album, was a real lesson for me in producing. I don't think you could have two more different musicians working together. Well, except that they both wanted to avoid commercial radio play, and there they both are, recording a record on DGC," he laughs. Given Ed's "fiscal responsibilities" to Geffen, he initially thought it would be impossible to deliver an LP that illuminated The Raincoats' "musical poetry, where everything around them is secondary," while meeting the terms DGC was expecting. Ultimately, Ed says in no uncertain terms, a label like DGC is in it for the money. It was rare, or even unheard of until The Raincoats, for Geffen to sign "a band that just doesn't give a crap about any kind of commercial success." He remembers trying to "push the songs so they had some shot at radio without compromising what the band wanted."

From Ed's perspective, *Looking in the Shadows* "wasn't a normal record in the sense that there's no inherent hierarchy to the instruments with The Raincoats, and a lot of spoken word aspects to the vocals were very important. A drum kit that's usually bashed like crazy might be kept very quiet compared to a vocal, even a whisper. The music is naturally incongruous, so as a producer, you can't trust yourself when you're mixing it, and it's all a bit anxiety-inducing."

But ultimately, working with The Raincoats taught him a lot about producing and about "a reverence to a very specific and different kind of storytelling."

Gina remembers having fun at Trident, but quickly adds that she's the kind of person who tends to "deal with pain with a bit of humor." The relationship among The Raincoats was fractious to say the least, and it had become tenser with Sheri over in London during the recording sessions. Gina was also working out some of her personal losses through song in that studio. Most notably, "Babydog" was about the pain of the miscarriages she'd been experiencing and of a stark childlessness. (Gina would eventually raise two daughters with her husband, Mike, but after years of loss.) "There was some absurdity to it, in addition to the pain, so I wrote that story as a song. I mean, it wasn't necessarily autobiographical," Gina laughs. "I didn't get a dog then, but I've got one now, after my children have gone!" The song depicts a woman bringing a dog into her life when she can't have a baby. "I don't want to make too big a deal of it," Gina says, "because I have my two daughters, who could not be more wonderful or bring me more joy."

"Gina's song 'Babydog' was hard to record for me," Ed says, "because I didn't realize what it was about, and then Gina told me just before she sang it. That was tough, and there were quite a few very emotional moments—for both Gina and Ana, and for me. And just the idea that this memory and experience were being committed to tape, and for DGC..." Ed sighs. "Gina is a bit more obvious about these things, though, a bit more open, whereas I think Ana was a bit more private. So I felt a bit intrusive at times even just being there. But I had to be there, of course, so I wanted to make sure they were happy with how it was going."

Like *Odyshape* and their self-titled LP before it, The Raincoats added a couple of interesting session musicians to their studio time for *Looking in the Shadows*. "I told Gina they should get Pete Shelley to do some backing vocals," Heather recalls, and that did come to pass. The Buzzcocks frontman, as well as Simon Fisher

Turner, sang on "Love a Loser," the penultimate track on the LP. "I had spent a very fun and drunken evening with Simon Fisher Turner and Pete Shelley," Gina explains, "and I must have relayed the story to Heather of our escapades."

Meanwhile, Heather was immediately uncomfortable in the studio, because the first thing Ed wanted her to do was play a click track. "I was like, *what*?" she remembers. "How is this something for The Raincoats? How is this a Raincoats record when I'm playing a click track?" (A click track is basically a metronome that sounds, in regular time, over the studio speakers or through a musician's headphones during a studio session. The aim is to keep recordings to a standardized rhythm, to prevent a song from sounding fragmentary, disorderly, or untidy. But of course, all you need to do is return to *The Raincoats* or *Odyshape* and listen to the erratic heartbeats that Palmolive's and Ingrid's drumming brought to the songs to see why Heather was reluctant.)

Heather had never recorded a click track before, even though she'd made a couple albums—but none on a major label, and none in a slick studio like Trident. She'd been working with musicians who were influenced by those early Raincoats recordings, not making marketable music for DGC to sell. In Tiger Trap and with Lois, Heather learned there's a feminist politics to sonic disorder. So sitting down to play a click track "just felt really weird," she remembers, and in opposition to the DIY, experimental nature that seemed to define The Raincoats and artists they'd influenced most heavily. Although some of the songs on *Looking in the Shadows* had a more polished sensibility, there was nonetheless a vulnerability and interiority that made an irregular heartbeat seem natural.

For a number of Ana's songs, in particular, Heather describes an intense "sparseness and solemnness" that simply didn't seem in line with use of a click track. "It felt like we were somehow going through the motions, through a cycle, not like we were experimenting, inventing or creating anything new. And this was *The Raincoats!* Plus there was a *dude at the controls*," Heather sighs.

"It was a more produced album, more produced than their others, because Ed was a producer," Shirley says, alluding to the fact that Geoff and Mayo hadn't really done this for a living when they "produced" the early Raincoats records.

Ana enjoyed working with Ed, but it was a much different experience than the first albums all around. "I remember there was one song where Ed said, 'You should take one verse out to make this shorter,' and I had to say, 'No, I'm not taking it out,' and we had to really have a bit of a fight about it. He was thinking about how to make it more like pop, and for me, I thought this doesn't make any sense. I couldn't even consider it because then the song wouldn't work, it would have lost its meaning. So I stood my ground and we recorded the whole thing." Ana suggests Ed was tasked with making some of the songs "ready for radio play," but that never mattered much, if at all, to The Raincoats.

There were also "a lot of overdubs," Ana says, "and I preferred to just have everything ready and to go and record it." She refers back to the "live" quality of their Berry Street recordings. "But I do really like the album," she says. "It's the least successful of all of them, I suppose, because it's the fourth. People always like the first ones better."

ED'S MOOG

Although the Trident experience wasn't what The Raincoats might have orchestrated themselves, there were more than a few upsides. And one of them was Ed's Moog. He brought it to the studio, as he often did when producing albums. He can't remember if it ultimately features on *Looking in the Shadows*, but he remembers it as a source of joy for Ana and Gina alike.

"One of the most important things that happened for me was Ed's Moog synthesizer," Ana says. "It had nine boxes, twelve boxes—I can't remember—but it was big enough to cover a normal wall, well, *almost*," she laughs. "It was completely out of my understanding of possibilities. I couldn't go there, and I didn't know how to. We used it in five songs on the album. On 'Truth is Hard,' there's a bubbly and rhythmic sound he put in, and I loved it. So the Moog gave me a taste for electronic analog sounds," Ana says.

When The Raincoats went back to America to tour *Looking in the Shadows* in 1996, Ana discovered a sampler, and it got her thinking more about the Moog and electronic music.

"The Moog became a bit of a talisman for me," Ed explains, "because I felt it was becoming a bit like the obelisk in *2001: A Space Odyssey*. Just having it around made people jump around. It's just this thing. Even though it rarely got used—was it even used once on The Raincoats' record?—it acted as a presence, and you can feel its presence on the record."

Shirley confirms it: "Ana was already impressed with Ed, and felt at home working with him. But when he brought in his Moog, that was another step! And it was a *massive* influence on her future work." Ana couldn't get the Moog off her mind. "I knew I'd have to sell my soul to be able to afford something like it," she laughs. "I'm exaggerating of course, but it showed me how experimenting with a synth is really just trying things, and you have to go slowly, but in the end it does what it does." Magic. After The Raincoats returned from their 1996 East Coast US tour, she bought an electronic equipment magazine and learned about the Yamaha QY70 sequencer. "This instrument was the size of a VHS cassette but had loads and loads of digital sounds. It had a tiny keyboard, and you could record the songs inside. I bought it, and I composed in it," Ana says.

It became a lifeline of sorts for her. "My mum was quite poorly at the time, so I used to take it to Portugal with me, to Madeira. While I was sitting with her, I'd write songs, and it's where I wrote the song 'Hospital Window.' When I came back, I bought a Roland digital recorder, and I'd record onto it and put my vocals in. This became *The Lighthouse*." Ana's first solo album—and her first recorded music since *Looking in the Shadows*—gave her a new kind of musical life. "Just that sequencer, and the Roland recorder and microphone—that was it. I did it slowly as I got inspired. For me, it was like digital punk!" Ana exclaims. "It was this instrument that cost £300, which is not a lot for what it did, and I had a whole band or orchestra and nobody disagreeing with me!"

As more time went on, Ana discovered small modules and realized she had the patience to teach herself to use them. She started collecting them, and with oscillators and filters, writing more songs. Eventually, those tools became central to her collaborative work with Phew, the Japanese electronic artist with whom Ana would release the record *Island* in 2018.

Vice Cooler, who became a touring drummer with The Raincoats in the mid-2000s, cites both Ana's and Gina's interests in modular synths and samplers as evidence that they'll always stand out from the crowd of their Rough Trade contemporaries. "Most people who don't start with that stuff feel threatened by it because they don't fully understand it, so their instinct is to fight it or trash it. But their instinct is always, 'A new thing? I want to know about it and I want to know how to use it.' They're never intimidated," he adds. "They always want to open up any curtain to see what's behind it, and to take part in the unknown. They're always moving forward creatively."

All made possible, perhaps, by Ed's Moog.

When Ray Farrell sent The Raincoats his notes on the *Looking in the Shadows* studio tape, he put a damper on the use of that Moog, mistaking one type of synth for another. He sent a fax: "Enough with the theremin, already."

FROM FAN MAIL TO PEN PALS

After the 1993 CD reissues, The Raincoats began receiving fan mail again, but this time from many of the musicians they'd inspired. While Ana always tried to reply to fan mail during the band's first life, in this second go-round, Ana often became pen pals with the writers whose letters she received. "Being pen pals was a big deal then, and especially being pen pals with Ana," Tobi Vail says of the correspondence they shared across the Atlantic. Through letters, the two eventually became close enough that, when Tobi brought her mother Beth to London, everyone stayed with Ana and Shirley. "All those letters are somewhere, I know," Tobi says, referring to the mail she collected from Ana over the years. And Tobi wasn't the only member of Bikini Kill to start a Raincoats correspondence. Ana also managed to get a pen pal relationship going with Kathi

Wilcox after the visit with Lucy Thane. In January '95, Kathi wrote to Ana on stylized stationery in pink typewriter ink, letting her know she and Tobi were now sharing a P.O. Box in Olympia where Ana could post letters to both of them. She also informed Ana about upcoming Bikini Kill plans and works in progress:

> Dear Ana,
> Have just returned from Washington, D.C. where I spent November and December making a super-8 movie with a friend of mine and trying to get thrugh [sic] the holidays ... If this silly film turns out at all, I will send a video copy along for you and Shirley.
> What news? It's been ages since I've been able to write to anyone at all, and now that I'm back in Olympia and Bikini Kill is practicing again after our post-tour break, I'm trying to see where everyone has been, what events have transpired, etc. This last B.K. tour of the U.S. was long and taxing and amazing, the first full state tour we've done since 1993 or so. We've got these new songs we want to record sometime this winter and are hoping to tour Australia and Japan this spring. None of us has ever been anywhere except Europe (and I went to Morocco once), so it's an exciting prospect.
> We have a couple shows coming up in March with a band from Oregon called Team Dresch; they have a record out on Kill Rock Stars or something I think. Anyway, it should be interesting to see how we do playing closer to home with so much new material. Tobi is busy making another Jigsaw fanzine and working at Kill Rock Stars doing mail order, etc. Billy and Kathleen both live in town now also, so it's much easier to coordinate. Kathleen is putting together some kind of Variety Show Cabaret type event this month and she wants me to do something for it, but of course I don't dance or do tricks of any sort so am at a loss for ideas. Maybe I could show one of my little movies in the corner or something. Will let you know ... KISSES!!! Kathi Wilcox[26]

Meanwhile, Ana shared correspondence with members of God Is My Co-Pilot, the no wave queercore band that formed in 1991 and who first met The Raincoats at one of their Liz Phair gigs in NYC.

LIFE NUMBER 2

Both Craig Flanagin and Sharon Topper, the openly queer couple who formed the group, wrote in Ana's 1994 tour diary as fans. Like other queercore artists, they'd discovered The Raincoats and a kinship in their music. Sharon mailed a package to Ana at Rough Trade in the summer of '94, full of band merch with a handwritten note on God Is My Co-Pilot stationery (screen-printed in red and yellow ink with a line drawing of an elaborate flamenco dancer and a slogan at the top: "fly the friendly thighs"):

> Raincoat Girls!
> So so sorry we couldn't come + support you on your UK tour. It made me <u>very</u> sad—it would have been such great fun. Another time? Soon? I hope so . . . Here's a photo of us romping on Brighton Beach before our show. We loved playing England (see photo!) Here's a copy of our latest CD. It will be out in the U.K. on <u>vinyl</u>! (Thanx to Soul Static). Hope you like it. Please keep in touch.[27]

Craig wrote to Ana from Portugal in 1997. He had more to say than a mere postcard would allow, so he scrawled a longer note on paper and created a telegram-like package on the back of a postcard from Guarda, all folded up and taped:

> So it was after this Lisboa show that people were having us sign things, and a girl gave me a CD + said "write to Ana" and I did, & she said "how did you know how to spell it?" and I said "I know a woman from Portugal named Ana" & for some reason she said "who?" and I said Ana da Silva and she said "you know her? Wow she is so cool" and I thought I should send Ana a postcard and say hello so I am. We played in Guarda @ an improv festival, and we played a rock show in Lisboa, & then we came to Eviceira for a couple days. Is this still your right address? Best wishes to you—En, espero todo e bom! hi from Sharon, too.[28]

Ana also had a pen-pal friendship with performance artist Kazuko Hohki of the playful Japanese experimental band Frank Chickens, a female-led group bridging theatre and punk. It started when Ana ran into Kazuko at a 1996 book event and didn't have as much time to chat as she'd have liked. Ana drafted a note to her on the back of a Frank Chickens newsletter:

> Dear Kasuko [sic],
> I'm writing to you to apologise for the other night at Mark P.'s book launch. Our friend arrived and the conversation I was having with you got interrupted and later when I went looking for you, I had no luck. I would have liked to talk to you and I hope you didn't think I was rude.
> I saw Frank Chickens a few years ago and remember having enjoyed the gig, so hopefully will see you again soon. P.S. Got your number from your management. Love Ana (The Raincoats)

LOOKING IN THE SHADOWS

The new LP got slated for release on March 12, 1996. In advance, *MOJO* gave it four stars and printed, "all-girl monolith back for the Mac generation."

Meanwhile, Shirley got to work trying to reignite The Raincoats' connection to indie labels that better reflected their ethos. She drafted a form letter that she'd fax out discriminately:

> Dear [blank]
> I am enclosing a cassette of 'Looking in the Shadows' by The Raincoats, the first album they have recorded since 1984. The album was recorded in August 1995 and produced by Ed Buller. The band signed a recording contract for 2 albums firm with DGC this summer. Geffen have rights to release and market the album for the world except the U.K. and Ireland and we are currently interested in locating an independent home for the band. Sheri Hood, who comanages The Raincoats with me will be in London during the week of the 20th November and we will be arranging appointments ... I will call you in a couple of days to check receipt of the cassette.

LIFE NUMBER 2

Tapes were sent to Roger Shepherd of Flying Nun, Paul Cox of Too Pure, Gary Walker of Wiiija, Laurence Bell of Domino, Nick Evans of Elemental, Allison Schnackenberg at Rough Trade, Ian McClaren at Beggars Banquet, Saul Galpern at Nude, Steve Lamacq at Deceptive, Ben Wardle at Indolent, Andy Childs at Rykodisc, Simon Harper at 4AD, Paul Smith at Blast First, Daniel Miller at Mute, and Tim Kelly at PLR. Shirley's personal notes indicate interest from some of the labels she contacted, including Roger Shepherd of Flying Nun, who'd requested a proposal. Domino, Rough Trade, Nude, and Rykodisc had also indicated interest.

"But ultimately it wasn't a great time," Gina says, recalling the anxieties rising around *Looking in the Shadows*. "Whether it would have done better under different circumstances, I don't know. But Geffen dropped us." Shirley says that Ana and Gina did initially want a one-album deal with DGC, but she insisted on a second option with a view toward future financial compensation.

Shirley confirms that, as it was for Gina, it was a terrible time for her, and she felt that everything she stood for and all of her values were being challenged, not only by Geffen. Gina offers a euphemism: "Just a tiny bit of a rift."

"There was this idea that we had to have the same number of songs, that somehow that would make everything fair and balanced out, but it didn't," Gina says. She gets a bit anxious as she recalls the tensions she felt at the time, as though things were breaking down in a way they hadn't before, even when the band dissolved after *The Kitchen Tapes* and *Moving*. "There were a lot of things going on," Gina explains, adding she was feeling "quite out of control of any of it."

Their friends recognized how difficult relations had become, and how emotions were running high all around. Shirley felt like the Geffen machine didn't respect her or what she'd helped build with The Raincoats, and, for the first time, she felt lost in the struggle to reconcile the differences between Gina and Ana. For Gina, in a decision-making group of three where two are a couple, it was really hard, and she often felt left out, or as if her voice didn't carry equal weight. They all felt hurt, and despite being empathetic people, it became difficult to step into one another's shoes. Even in the present, it's almost too much for The Raincoats to discuss their memories around *Looking in the Shadows*. Nearly thirty years have passed, but the wounds run deep. "This was the first time we had a relationship with a major label, and this was a whole different kettle of fish," Shirley says. "I would never, ever do it again. It caused a lot of pain, angst, and grief for me personally ... I wish I'd never suggested we do it."

The tensions from the DGC Records days aren't the center of the band's legacy, and they're not how any of The Raincoats want to be remembered. But they're a small part of any honest story of the band; The Raincoats are, after all, human beings with emotions, stressors, and periods of sadness and grief in their lives. The band's larger legacy has always outpaced momentary difficulties that disrupted their transcendent atemporal rhythms.

Meanwhile, on the outside, *Looking in the Shadows* brought joy. Teenagers who'd first heard The Raincoats on the CD reissues waited in line at music stores to buy the album (including this author). Steve Shelley even remembers getting a copy direct from DGC. "We were so proud that there were people of our ilk on this not very cool major label," Steve says. "Back then, it was really, really unheard of that such creative people would wind up on a major ... we dealt with all kinds of things with Geffen, but to look back now, I can say that they did some cool stuff, and it's pretty great."

MORE FAN MAIL

In 1996, Anita Chaudhuri, working on the women's desk for the *Guardian*, interviewed Gina and Ana about the "resurrection" of The Raincoats upon the release of *Looking in the Shadows*. Unbeknownst to the band, more than twenty-five years earlier Anita had posted fan mail to The Raincoats. "That was the only fan mail I ever sent!" Anita exclaims.

In 1980, Anita sent a letter of four tightly written pages to Rough Trade with the return address given as "Dumpsville,

Glasgow." In it, she discussed her love for the label's female-centered bands and complained about the monotonous "androids" who used to be her friends, succumbing to peer pressures to look and act a certain way:

> I've reached the ultimate in tedium ... Ten year old boys stand in cliches outside the "hip" record shops of the week, in their denim jackets with "Sex Pistols" patches sewn on the back by loving mothers. Or if they're really sussed then they wear Crass T-shirts and UK subversive armbands. I feel very ill. Excessive crows clad in parkas + black and white mini dresses are also beginning to annoy me ... They all look stupid in exactly the same way.[29]

The letter ends, "Pass on enclosed letter to Raincoats. Thank you!"

Anita sent another five-page letter to The Raincoats. She described their cover of "Lola" as "better than the original, perhaps because it's from a woman's point of view," and continued, "I suppose I'm a feminist in the mere sense of the word. But I'm opposed to women's lib and all that bollux ... It's my belief that anyone worth knowing despises the typical girl." She urges The Raincoats to play Glasgow.

"I wasn't somebody in the habit of sending people letters," Anita says, but explains how she was in a difficult place emotionally at school—"doom and gloom, not fitting in, and being the only mixed-race kid apart from my sister." Against that background, she fell in love with The Raincoats in 1979. She thought, *Why not write to them?* She'd already mustered up the courage to go into the Glasgow record store Listen to buy *Fairytale* in 1979, "which was quite intimidating," she says, "not very girl-friendly." But she got the EP, played it constantly, and saw a kinship between herself and Ana. "She actually used her real name," Anita explains, "and if I didn't say this to them in my original letter, I should have. That name made me feel immediately like there was a connection, that there was someone who I could see myself in." Anita refers to the Portuguese colonization of Goa, the southern state on the Indian subcontinent, where a lot of Indian people have the same surname da Silva. "I was desperately trying to find some pop cultural figure that I could identify with in music, and there weren't many. If you look at Poly Styrene, for example, she's actually half Somali, but she never talked about that fact and chose a stage name that didn't reveal her real name or ethnicity." In Glasgow especially, Anita laments how there were so few people of South Asian descent that she felt "really in the minority." Lack of representation mattered and "had an effect on how you perceive yourself as a woman," Anita says, "because we need to see ourselves. And Ana da Silva did that for me."

Frustrations with music journalism kept Anita away from sonic subject matter—until, that is, she was assigned The Raincoats feature in 1996. She showed up to meet Ana and Gina, "and I think they were suspicious of me," she laughs, describing the leather jacket, miniskirt, heavy makeup, and heels she was wearing. (Anita would quote Gina in the *Guardian* as saying, "Punk polarised perceptions of female sexuality . . . You had women who used overtly sexual imagery—like Siouxsie Sioux, experimenting with heavy make-up and bondage—then you had the very asexual approach of dressing in bin liners and old boots, which was basically us.")[30]

"When I showed up, before we started talking, they sort of challenged me and one of them asked me something like, 'What do you know about The Raincoats, anyway?' So of course this was a gift!" Anita smiles, recalling her fan mail decades prior. "My abiding memory of that meeting, and that article," Anita says, "was actually a bit of discomfort, having to reconcile who I was when I'd written to them back then, and who I was at that time."

Anita also remembers the strange realization that Kurt Cobain was being credited with "discovering" The Raincoats. "I almost felt a little bit of a sense of outrage!" Anita says, laughing lightly. "It was like, wait a minute, they're not *yours*!"

THE RAINCOATS ARE ON MTV!

Two Raincoats music videos exist, both directed by Gina: for "Fairytale in the Supermarket" and "Don't Be Mean." With Gina already directing films for other bands and her own projects, she was eager to make the music videos that would be visual representations of

LIFE NUMBER 2

Raincoats music in the nineties. Ana and Shirley agree wholeheartedly that Gina was, hands down, the right person for the job. While "Don't Be Mean" fitted squarely into the MTV trend of music videos for new releases—it was a single from *Looking in the Shadows*—the video for "Fairytale" took viewers back to the very first Raincoats EP. It helped bring the song back into the spotlight alongside the CD reissues that included "Fairytale" as the first track on *The Raincoats*.

"For the 'Fairytale' video," Gina remembers, "I was thinking quite a lot about past, present, and future. I had a slightly romantic notion of that, but I also had this idea of archaeology, a digging up of the past." She discusses the end of the video, where characters literally excavate instruments and records long buried in the ground. "The whole thing of us realizing that we hadn't been buried and forgotten, that was part of this idea, too," Gina explains. "Because once The Raincoats were over, I think we were all in the mindset that it was done, it was part of the past. That's it. And pre-internet, I had this idea that maybe someone might have found one of our records buried in a box, or in their grandma's attic, what have you."

She made the "Fairytale" video knowing that Vicky and Palmolive (who'd originally recorded the song with The Raincoats) weren't going to be interested in participating in the filming. But Gina wanted to find a way to include them. "That's where I got the idea for the masks," she says, describing various moments in the video where child actors dance around with masks of the earlier Raincoats on their faces.

It was also a difficult time in Gina's personal life, something she documented sympathetically in the *Looking in the Shadows* song "Babydog." But it showed itself in another form in the "Fairytale" video. "I'd already had a lot of miscarriages," Gina says, "so I was trying different things to deal with it, and putting little bits of autobiography into the film." She'd been having a recurring dream "that I'd find a baby in the cupboard covered in cobwebs," and it made sense to introduce that image into the realm of "Fairytale," along with a sequence involving a disappearing baby. The little girls in the film "doing the funny walks," as Gina describes them, also reflected on questions of motherhood, childhood, coming of age. "I still don't know if those little girls were past, present, or future," Gina reflects. "In a way they're future, but they're also past."

She also brought in a circular rotunda from which Ana remakes the window drawing that originally appeared on the cover of the *Fairytale* 7-inch EP in 1979. The "Fairytale" video ultimately collapsed Raincoats' temporalities, illuminating time as something creative, playful, laborious, and haunting.

With the music video for "Don't Be Mean," Gina took a completely different approach. It was "quite a bit more poppy," she laughs. "That one wasn't deep in reflecting my personal traumas. The psychological trauma of that one is all in the lyrics!" Gina emphasizes that the video was about having a little fun and paying homage to some of their idols. "Ana had seen Patti Smith spit the flower petals from her mouth, and she had that in a song. I always liked the image, and Ana wanted to do it, and I wanted her to do that." The video also reflects Gina's playfulness as a film director and artist. She was weighing options to reflect shifts visually between interiority and exteriority: The Raincoats, who star in the video, carry a large board with them painted the same color as an inside wall—they quite literally carry the inside into the outside. "I really liked the transition and think it was quite funny," Gina says. "Maybe a bit clunky looking back, but I like it."

They filmed the exteriors on Westbourne Grove, where the lyrics to the song are set. Gina had lived near there for twenty years at this point and knew most of the shopkeepers, all amused by "the goings-on with the video shoot," she says. Gina waited for some passersby to happen along and asked if they'd be part of the video. "I also arranged several interesting-looking people to be extras," she recalls, and, "Dick O'Dell happened to be passing by, so he was pulled in to make an appearance." Gina hired the marching band made up of three little girls to march and play on the sidewalk—"An obvious nod to my 'Fairytale' video," she explains—and got her best friend, who was pregnant at the time, and a few other pregnant women to march around the interior living-room scene. "Maybe my traumas were coming out in that video after all!" Gina quips, but there's always an edge to her laughter.

Gina's friend Simon Hilton co-edited the "Don't Be Mean" video with her, and he was responsible for a sharply quickened pace at the end (she'd found Simon's enthusiasm, ideas, and commitment to be amazing). That change in rapidity was perfect, mirroring the surreal time signatures of The Raincoats' music and the way their energy permeates the atmosphere around them. "He stayed up *all night* working on those edits," Gina says. "He was *a man obsessed!*" Simon also directed and edited films for John Lennon, Yoko Ono, Paul McCartney, George Harrison, David Bowie, Nick Cave, Oasis, Led Zeppelin, Pink Floyd, Iron Maiden, Manic Street Preachers, Depeche Mode, Kylie Minogue, and Supergrass, among others. "He's worked with a lot of interesting people, and he was nothing if not mega committed to what he was doing for The Raincoats!" Gina exclaims. "The editing is really what makes it sing."

Although recording *Looking in the Shadows* was a difficult time for all involved, the music videos are still a source of joy. When Shirley and Ana drive by the filming spot, they both exclaim in unison, "That's where we filmed 'Don't Be Mean!'" The group's friendships weren't wholly fractured, which was a good thing since The Raincoats had committed to some upcoming tour dates.

TO PORTUGAL, THEN BACK TO AMERICA WITH PHIL STAINES

It was obvious to everyone that The Raincoats couldn't keep Heather on, so once again, they needed a drummer. They had gigs planned in the UK and Funchal, the capital city of Ana's Madeira, in the spring of 1996. Another set of dates was planned for America that fall. They'd be revisiting East Coast venues from the 1994 tour and playing some new ones. Their US dates started at the 9:30 Club in Washington, D.C. and ended at Brownies in New York. In between, they stopped at the Trocadero in Philly, Tramps in New York, and the Middle East in Boston. Steph Hillier was with them the entire time to do live sound.

As a sound engineer who happened to be female, Steph dealt with a lot of misogyny in the music industry, but it was thanks

SHOUTING OUT LOUD

Amp settings for *Looking in the Shadows* songs

in part to The Raincoats' groundbreaking effect on early-nineties female-fronted bands that Steph was often hired for the live jobs. Without realizing it, The Raincoats had given Steph a fruitful career. "I think female bands at the time wanted a female sound engineer," she explains, "so I did get asked to work with a lot of those bands. I think I did about 950 gigs in one year, and that meant working more than every night." Most of the bands were Riot Grrrls, or saw themselves operating in similar ideological circles. It would only make sense, then, that she'd ultimately join The Raincoats on tour, engineering their live sound for future generations.

But for other new additions to the touring party, the link isn't as clear. "It's an absolute mystery how I ended up joining them," Phil Staines says of becoming the temporary drummer. "Word of mouth, I wouldn't have been answering an ad or anything. All I know is, I was given directions to a place in West London, and there were Ana and Gina. They gave me a copy of *Looking in the Shadows*, and I started playing with them right away." He knew how lucky he was; he'd previously lived in Vancouver, where much of the Raincoats excitement that began in Olympia had made its way north into the hip Canadian city. "All my friends in Vancouver were listening to The Raincoats."

For Phil, the world of The Raincoats was "a very otherworldly one" to enter. "The music was so intricate," he explains, "so unlike anything I'd done before." He originally started drumming with Thee Hypnotics, a garage group that released its debut LP on Sub Pop in 1989. They toured with acts such as The Damned and The Cramps, and had connections to Lords of the New Church (*yep, indeed, the old Raincoat Nick Turner*) and Dead Boys. "With Thee Hypnotics, we were the antithesis of what The Raincoats were," Phil begins, describing "four guys in tight leather trousers and Lycra shirts." But immediately, he knew he'd fallen into something really special. "The Raincoats genuinely *rocked*," he says. "When it all came together on stage, it was just like, *wow ... wow ...*"

At the gig in Portugal, the band stayed with Ana's parents. Mike accompanied Gina, and Ana's family was happy to have them on the island. A few months later, they headed back to America. Sheri joined some of the tour dates.

In Boston, the atmosphere turned strange. Palmolive (at this point having dropped the pseudonym and going by Paloma McLardy) came to see the show with her son. They were deeply involved in an American evangelical church,[31] and Paloma's son started speaking to the crowd while The Raincoats were in the dressing room. Ana remembers hearing later that he'd made homophobic statements allegedly rooted in Christian ideology. Others at the venue also recalled the tense moment, wanting to feel excitement that Palmolive had appeared in the space, compressing Raincoats time, while contending with discriminatory ideas that pierced the hearts of queer fans. Phil remembers Palmolive's son being quietly removed: "It was one of those situations like, 'Look, please, this is not the right time for this.' I think Gina was especially shocked to see Palmolive as part of this Christian, born-again, fanatic thing." Gina explains, "I think I was most surprised when Paloma said Sandy, her son, wants to be a preacher and Macarena, her daughter, wants to marry a preacher. Not what I expected to hear from a founder of The Slits!"

That last Raincoats show of the US leg took place at the famed venue Brownies; from 1994 until the end of the decade, it was the most-loved venue in New York City for indie rock. The Raincoats show included a double bill with Bush Tetras, a fellow band that found an underground audience in downtown New York during the days of TR3, Hurrah, and Danceteria. Phil had been borrowing drums throughout the US tour dates, so he played Bush Tetras drummer Dee Pop's new drum kit that night. It would be the last time The Raincoats would appear in Manhattan until they returned for a monumental gig at New York's Museum of Modern Art (MoMA) nearly fifteen years later.

When Phil left the band, he'd just been accepted to film school and knew, "It was my time to move on." Yet he's gone to Raincoats gigs since and hasn't been at all shocked to hear they sound just as brilliant as they ever did. "There will never be any band like them. I consider them a national treasure," Phil says. "And I'm not being sycophantic for the sake of being sycophantic. I know my stuff, and they're truly a one-off."

JEAN-MARC BUTTY TAKES A PJ HARVEY BREAK

By November 1996, The Raincoats found themselves in a familiar situation: they needed to find a drummer. They had a gig in Manchester in about twenty-four hours' time. Jean-Marc Butty, as it happened, was on a break from touring with PJ Harvey.

"One of the great things about doing that photo shoot with Maria Mochnacz, besides having her photograph Ana and Gina, was that unbeknownst to us, Maria was friends with Jean-Marc and told him he really should play with The Raincoats," Shirley says. "We knew Heather wasn't going to play with us again. She was a ... wonderful nightmare," Shirley laughs. "Phil was actually booked to come back and play with us, but he just couldn't turn up. Here we were, about to play, and he couldn't come. So we called up Jean-Marc and said, 'Are you doing anything tomorrow?' When he said no, we said, 'Can you come play with The Raincoats in Manchester?'"

"I'd just moved to London and was looking for a band to play with," Jean-Marc recalls. "I saw Maria, who I knew through Polly Jean, and she mentioned The Raincoats." At the time, they were holding auditions. "After my audition, they told me they didn't want to play with me, and now afterward they've denied that!" he laughs, his soft-spoken timbre still coming through. He's referring to some months prior, when The Raincoats were initially planning their *Looking in the Shadows* tour—just after Maria had photographed Ana and Gina for the album cover. Phil ended up on those tour dates with the band. "But it's a funny story," Jean-Marc continues, "because some time later, I got a phone call from Gina, on a Friday evening, and she said, 'What are you doing tomorrow?'" Jean-Marc had just wrapped up the 1996 PJ Harvey tour, so he was free for the time being. "Gina asked me to come to Manchester and play, and I told her I didn't know the songs. She said, 'Oh, just come, we'll work it out.' So that's how it went."

"Memory's a funny thing," Gina says. "I remember Jean-Marc was working with someone I knew called Ken in a project called White Hotel. After he auditioned with us, Jean-Marc wasn't sure that what The Raincoats were doing was for him, but I think later he reassessed."

Regardless of how it happened, the day after Gina's phone call, Jean-Marc got into a van with The Raincoats. Shirley drove. "I spent the whole time on the way, a four- or five-hour drive, just listening to the songs, trying to learn them." It all did come together, as Gina had promised. After Manchester, Jean-Marc continued drumming with them on dates in Leeds, Cambridge, Norwich, London, and Oxford. But it only took one gig with The Raincoats for Jean-Marc to realize he'd entered into a dream. Playing with them, he says, "was complete freedom," a kind he'd never known before.

"With The Raincoats, it is never about putting on 'good' shows—now, they want to put on a good show, but more, they want to share something that's completely remote from the preoccupations of other bands," he explains. "And that's something that's refreshing, that is freedom."

Because of their unorthodox and anomalous methods, Jean-Marc found The Raincoats to be "very mysterious at the beginning ... it's like a very fine line you have to walk between chaos and perfection, and it's a very delicate thing, how it holds together. And it *does* hold together."

Jean-Marc knows his fair share of bands made up of formally trained musicians, and that's not what The Raincoats have ever aimed for—and it's something that remains beautiful and unique about them, from his perspective. "Sometimes you learn more by watching someone who doesn't know how to play technically, and especially someone who is playing your instrument," he explains. He immediately perceived The Raincoats as artists who powerfully eschewed traditional methods. "They didn't have formal technique and didn't want it," Jean Marc reflects, "because they found a way to be challenged by something else that's very strong, that almost cannot be named, and that's part of their beauty."

The Raincoats taught Jean-Marc a new way to create sonic art, and it remains one of the most challenging things he can recall in his career. "Trying to learn the songs is more like trying to learn a story," he explains, emphasizing how it also depends on the way the band wants to craft the narrative at any particular moment in time. "There are moods, ambience, and sections and pieces fitting together, and it's extremely complicated music," he says. But perhaps not for the reason some people would expect. Jean-Marc unknowingly refers back to what so many other drummers have described in their own ways—a complete opposite of attention to a time signature. "The music is not set on a definite number of bars ... it is not like anyone else writes music," he declares.

Those shifting non-time signatures makes the band's approach beautifully alien, in Jean-Marc's eyes. "It is like they are coming from a different planet," he says. "They're using the same instruments as other people, but they're using them with different words, which they've invented themselves, and which are completely purposeful and meaningful. The Raincoats are never just talking for talking, but they're saying something in their own language, and they've never cared what *anyone* thought. It is always an attitude of 'this is who we are, this is what we do.'"

"We love how Jean-Marc plays," Shirley says. Talking to Shirley in the present, it seems obvious Jean-Marc could have been in the band all along. His own poetic way of speaking, and his interest in the unconventional and the experimental, have made for a perfect marriage. But like all great things, it couldn't last. Jean-Marc moved to New Orleans and later Toulouse, and eventually he had to rejoin PJ Harvey on tour.

ANOTHER ENDING

On July 14, 1997, The Raincoats received a termination agreement from Geffen via fax. The label paid a flat $46,000 "as advance against any royalties ... earned pursuant to the Recording Agreement." That was that. There wasn't going to be another LP. Not that The Raincoats wanted it, either; the DGC experience hadn't been the stuff of fairytales for any of them.

As Sheri suggests, Geffen was never the right fit for a Raincoats reunion, at least not one that would keep them together for subsequent records. "After *Nevermind*, labels signed so many bands—just in case—and took on so many A&R people. So, on the one hand, what a gift to be a band where you otherwise might not have been on a major label, but on the other, in a way, you're kind of set up for a fall," Sheri says. "You never felt like The Raincoats were set up for a fall specifically, but the machine runs in a certain way. I think about my furnace: I was told you don't want a furnace that's too big for your place. It's not that it overheats it, it's just that it's too much. You need something that's the right size. So Geffen might have been the right size in that sense they weren't *massive*," Sheri explains, alluding to other majors, "but they had a certain approach ... I don't know how many of the bands they signed were supposed to come out on the other side and actually recoup."

Molly Neuman of Bratmobile sighs. As someone who was among the original Riot Grrrls and has been involved in the music industry from the inside, her perspective is striking. "What was anyone really thinking with The Raincoats getting signed to a major record company; did we really think they were going to be superstars?" She rolls her eyes. "It's so telling about the music industry machinations. The Raincoats are such pure artists, so it's like, what are they going to do—write a hit to meet someone's gatekeeper standard? Is that really the formula we want? Get the fuck out of here, that's just crazy. But the nineties were so embarrassing like that."

THE HANGOVERS

The second life of The Raincoats had come to another end, but Gina had an eye toward more music in the USA. "When the second album option wasn't exercised," as she remembers it, Gina started her own band and her own label. Her new band The Hangovers—a play on post-Raincoats life—actually had its roots back in the early nineties, when Gina met Craig Sheppard and Spencer Horne of the Handsome Foundation, the pair who'd made the memory and flesh dresses. While directing music videos, she met the "brilliant creative duo." They immediately took on an important role in Gina's cinematic work: "They styled and sourced clothes for many of my music videos, and I was thrilled when they created an art performance piece at the ICA and they asked me to make the music for their show, titled *The Fear Show*. It felt like all the music just flowed out of me."

When she attended that live event, she found it "beyond thrilling," and it got her thinking about a new music project of her own. "Many of those songs became those on the first Hangovers' *Slow Dirty Tears* CD," she says, referring to The Hangovers' release on her own label, Smoke Records. "Craig gave me some lyrics from the show to play with, which became the center of the song 'Hello Moon,' but the other lyrics are all by me," Gina notes.

Gina's first experience as a solo artist proved enlivening, and by 1997, The Hangovers were catapulted into the American and British indie rock worlds. To form the band, Gina drew on various musicians she'd met as a Raincoat. Joe Dilworth (of Stereolab) played drums, on bass was either Mary Deigan (of Voodoo Queens) or John Frenett (of Moonshake and Laika), Ida Akesson on sampler and keyboards, and Simon Fisher Turner guested on a couple of tracks. Gina was on guitar and vocals.

They got signed to Kill Rock Stars in the US, and Gina toured there twice with two different Hangovers lineups. "I felt, you know, like The Hangovers represented me more in a way than anything else, because I really felt like I could just be myself. It was all very low budget, but it was just beautiful," she says. "My exuberance sometimes felt stifled in The Raincoats. It was not always the place to express my darting thoughts and feelings," but The Hangovers made this kind of work possible. Gina continues, "Later, I realized I could be my more complete self and be in The Raincoats, too. It was only then I felt truly creatively fulfilled."

As for Gina's personal connection with Kill Rock Stars, it became an indelible one. "Slim and I got on like a house on fire!" she exclaims. "Going over there and doing The Hangovers, staying at Slim's house, I loved it all. And I loved Kill Rock Stars and what they were doing."

LIFE NUMBER 3

The third and present life of The Raincoats is the longest one as far as linear time goes, but it's also the most nebulous of them all. It's filled with ebbs and flows, and germs of offshoot lives that only become possible when the mythologies of a band start to become its legacy, all while opening possibilities in the present.

The Raincoats with Jean-Marc Butty in 2012

FLIGHTPATHS TO EACH OTHER

Back in 1994, Glasgow indie band The Pastels—Stephen, Katrina, and Annabel (Aggi)—collaborated on a gallery exhibition that centered on art and design by musicians. While the title of the exhibition came from a Pastels song, it illuminated global connections among sonic artists working across geographic space and time. "It was really ahead of its time," Annabel Wright of The Pastels says. The exhibition came at a time when The Raincoats were distracted by tour planning and the death of Kurt Cobain, but in retrospect, it was a prescient art show. With the inclusion of The Raincoats, the show *Flightpaths to Each Other* laid the groundwork for Raincoats performances to come in the twenty-first century, where the band convincingly erased the line that was often drawn between musician and artist.

The Glasgow exhibition was scheduled to run at Glasgow Art School from September 21 through to October 7, 1994. Katrina Mitchell had been in touch with The Raincoats previously to gauge their interest in taking part, and plans were made to display Ana's album artwork. In mid-September that year, Katrina wrote with an update:

> I'm just writing to let you know what's happening with the exhibition—it's going up in Glasgow Art School for 3 weeks ... it'll be called "Flightpaths to Each Other." I'm sorting out a list of contact addresses of bands in the exhibition to leave on a table for people to pick up—do you want a Raincoats address included on that?[1]

The exhibition connected The Pastels, The Raincoats, and a wide range of other bands that understood being a musician was, ultimately, about being an artist. In *Flightpaths to Each Other*, The Pastels and The Raincoats were placed side by side with Teenage Fanclub, Galaxie 500, Stereolab, Huggy Bear, Daniel Johnston, Swell Maps,

Cornershop, God Is My Co-Pilot, Voodoo Queens, Lung Leg, Orange Juice, Silver Jews, Saint Etienne, and more.

While Katrina's correspondence focused on the exhibition, her letter also praised The Raincoats:

> It was really great to see the Raincoats in Glasgow—it was my favourite show of the year so far, + it'll take a bit of beating!

Stephen Pastel was at the gig in 1994, too, July of that year. It was the same show where Lung Leg opened for their heroes. Shirley and Ana became friends with Stephen, and he'd later help organize Raincoats shows in Glasgow, including a particularly memorable performance at the Centre for Contemporary Art (CCA) in 2016. "This notion that everything you're doing as a musician is in the service of a total art performance—that's the central inspiration The Pastels drew from The Raincoats," Stephen explains, "and something that has kept them going themselves for decades. With The Pastels, we tried to have a totality approach: The art would be the music, us as people, and even the clothes we wore. We wanted everything to be connected, a whole, and we drew inspiration from The Raincoats to do that."

Since the days of *Flightpaths to Each Other*, The Raincoats have always been destined to blur the line between music performance and art-with-a-capital-A, as Annabel describes it, what's traditionally shown in museum and gallery spaces. "Not just any band could do that," Annabel declares, as she characterizes The Raincoats' music as being "like brushstrokes."

While the exhibition itself occurred temporally during the second life of The Raincoats, its existence foretold the third life in which the band proved, once and for all, that punk is an art form.

ROBERT WYATT'S MELTDOWN, 2001

Following The Raincoats' breakup at the end of their tour in 1996, there were no more gigs. Anne Wood wasn't expecting to do anything more with The Raincoats, but then she got a call from Shirley.

LIFE NUMBER 3

Anne Wood onstage with The Raincoats in 2009

The Raincoats had been invited to perform at Robert Wyatt's Meltdown music festival. It would be the final show for which Steph Hillier would engineer the band's live sound—she made a special trip from Berlin for the event. While at the time it seemed like an ending, a cap on The Raincoats' live legacy, it would actually mark the start of a new beginning in the twenty-first century.

As Anne explains it, part of the shift that ushered in The Raincoats' third life was based on space. Unlike in the years before, Raincoats music in this new incarnation would rarely, if ever, grace the rooms of the clubs and venues in which they'd performed so frequently in the past. Instead, The Raincoats became the soundtrack to art galleries, museums, and performance art spaces. Beginning with Robert Wyatt's Meltdown, there was a shift from "real rock 'n' roll alternative spaces, something like The Garage in London, smoky and sweaty and pulsating evenings in the US, like a human beehive," Anne says, to something else entirely. Back then, she continues, "Those venues felt like they suited the band. But when we started playing museum spaces, gallery spaces, exhibitions, the sound becomes really different." She could never see Ana and Gina returning to the old music haunts. "It's one extreme or the other with The Raincoats," Anne laughs. "CBGB or MoMA, nothing in between!"

Wyatt had known The Raincoats for decades—he'd played on *Odyshape* and was part of the Rough Trade circle. He never was one for the touring circuit, but in 2001, he was invited to curate something special: a Meltdown festival. Sean O'Hagan, writing for the *Guardian*, described it as a "long overdue canonization of sorts" of Wyatt's work and legacy that "reflects his abiding interest in jazz of the experimental variety, past and present cutting-edge music from across the globe, and left-wing politics." Wyatt, in a conversation with O'Hagan, discussed the lineup he'd curated: "My inspiration is anything that will help get rid of the cold chill of loneliness of being on the wrong planet."[2] Enter The Raincoats.

When Shirley's call about Robert Wyatt's Meltdown came, Anne was ready to shift back into her Raincoats brain. She never expected Ana and Gina to play together again. It took something as distinguished as this curated event to do it.

Naturally, it was Jean-Marc who got the call to play drums. After some time away from The Raincoats, it seemed like the start of an eternal return; all of the strange atmosphere came back to envelop him once more, and then for years to come. "When I started playing live with The Raincoats again in the 2000s," Jean-Marc says, "it was *still* like they were from another planet, with their own language, still making things new ... their music is like a dialogue—very sincere, very free, no rules—that always walks a very fine line between the chaos and perfection I saw back in the nineties."

After the Meltdown, Anne would receive a Raincoats call "maybe once a year going forward," and suddenly there was a real sense that The Raincoats were back. "There was no grand plan as far as I know," Anne says, "and surely if there was a grand plan, Ana and Gina would have had different grand plans to one another!" And it wasn't just a sense that The Raincoats were back on the map again for other people. They were putting themselves back on the cultural map of the new millennium, and that cartography traced an entirely new set of spaces. "It was like, The Raincoats have woken up again!" Anne exclaims, as if the band had been a powerful sleeping giant, just waiting for the right nudge.

NO MORE FAN MAIL

The new millennium changed the nature of fan mail. Rough Trade wasn't getting many handwritten letters anymore, and postcards rarely arrived. Instead, fans got in touch online.

"When MySpace appeared, I made myself a member," Ana says, "and there were all these people writing and saying how much The Raincoats meant to them, how the music had helped them go through school, through life. How they didn't know what they would do without The Raincoats music ... I didn't actually know who liked The Raincoats before that, except people who wrote letters."

LADYFESTS

In 2000, the first Ladyfest took place in Olympia, Washington (where else?). It was advertised as "a non-profit, community-based event designed by and for women to showcase, celebrate and encourage the artistic, organizational and political work and talents of women." It promised to "feature performances by bands, spoken word artists, authors, visual artists, and more!!!" and to include "workshops, panels, and dance parties." All promotional materials noted it would be "a woman-run event, but all are welcome to attend."[3] The festival lineup included Sleater-Kinney, Bratmobile, Gossip, and more. Tobi organized the event with her sister Maggie, and they got in touch with Gina to see about bringing her and Ana over for it.

Gina performed at the inaugural Ladyfest in Olympia. "After being with Kill Rock Stars," she explains, "I was invited to perform at the first Ladyfest 2000," and, "it was amazing." As she recalls it, "The whole of the small town seemed to be taken over by women of all shapes, sizes, colors, and creeds, with all sorts of skills—from music to comedy to art to becoming a mom ([with] the 'Hip Mama' workshop), and I was about to become one, too."

At the time of the first Ladyfest, neither Gina nor Ana were thinking about another Raincoats life. (Yet, as it had done in the past, the city of Olympia was laying the foundation for another Raincoats life before Ana and Gina even knew it.)

After the first Ladyfest, the idea sprouted, and since 2000, Ladyfests have been held in cities across North America and Europe, as well as in South Africa, China, and New Zealand. Like in Olympia, as solo artists, Ana and Gina played several of the festivals that took shape, including in London 2002 and Madrid 2005. At that Madrid Ladyfest, Molly Neuman remembers seeing Ana play a solo show. Tobi was also playing in her then-current band Spider and the Webs, as well as Molly's former Bratmobile bandmate Allison Wolfe in Partyline. At the end of the night, along with the contemporary feminist Spanish band Hello Cuca, they all got up on stage together with Ana and sang a version of "Fairytale in the Supermarket." As Molly puts it, "It was one of those incredibly existential moments."

Given that they were the godmothers of Riot Grrrl, The Raincoats seemed destined to headline one of the festivals. News soon swirled around another possible Raincoats reunion, with press reporting that The Raincoats had only played together a couple of times since their breakup in 1996, most notably for Robert Wyatt's Meltdown. On an early April day in 2007, Ana and Gina headed north for Ladyfest Leeds.

This incarnation of the festival included more than a hundred events, including twenty-five bands and nearly fifty performance artists working in other genres. The Raincoats were at the very center of it all. Both Gina and Ana were interviewed at the time and gave the following quotes to the music press[4] before they took the stage:

GINA: "We are really excited to play Ladyfest in Leeds. It is a brilliant idea and all the Ladyfests we have been involved in have been great so far ... a mixture of film, art, poetry, humor, and music, and lots and lots of women doing their thing! Vive les femmes!"

ANA: "An event like this does the most important thing: It's INSPIRATIONAL. And it doesn't stop with the final performance. It will ripple forever and enrich life itself."

As of 2024, Ladyfests are still being planned, and festivals continue to inspire female and nonbinary artists to take the stage.

PERFORMANCE ART, GIRL MONSTER, AND CHICKS ON SPEED

Raincoats appearances have always been performances, illuminating the deep and intertwined connection between music and art. Ask anyone who has played with them or seen them more than once: No two shows are alike, and the unexpected is a given.

"Performance art" has always been transdisciplinary, from Dadaist Cabaret Voltaire events to early twentieth-century Surrealist and Futurist performances uniting visual art, literature, drama, and music. By the mid-twentieth century, modes of performance art existed largely under the umbrella of the "happening," a term coined around 1957 by the artist Allan Kaprow after becoming involved with Fluxus group members George Brecht and John Cage. Kaprow's "happenings" occurred at art galleries in New York, often on stages with audiences in observation. They were marketed as art events in which audiences could witness "something spontaneous, some-

thing that just happens to happen," but they were in fact "tightly planned," as Tate Modern explains.[5] In nearly all their incarnations, "happenings" involved artists playing musical instruments to the sounds of spoken word or singing. While "happenings" were both reimagined by artists in the decades that followed and eschewed by others as too mainstream, the idea of performance art grew and took on greater political significance. Art historian Catherine Spencer suggests happenings, and performance art more broadly, became a mode of feminist communication in the 1970s and beyond.[6]

The idea of sonic performance art catalyzed Chicks on Speed, a multidisciplinary group of artists speaking through music, dance, visual art, design, and fashion. Alex Murray-Leslie moved from Australia to Munich to attend the Academy of Fine Arts, where she met Melissa Logan, who'd come from New York. They founded Chicks on Speed and worked together at Seppi Bar, which Alex had set up a few years before as a performance space that could double as a way of making money to fund her work. It was the spot where Alex and Melissa would introduce feminist art to the Riot Grrrl crowds of Munich, a place Alex describes as "an illegal bar in Munich, behind the art school, very much in the spirit of Dada." She's referring to the Cabaret Voltaire in Zürich, which opened in 1916 as the First World War was raging. Considered to be the first art bar where musicians, writers, visual artists, and dancers could perform, it's also the space that precipitated Dada—or the earliest "happenings," which weren't yet named as such. Carmen Knoebel reformulated the idea again decades later through the Ratinger Hof, and Chicks on Speed wanted to create something similar in the 1990s, where feminist role models could take center stage.

Chicks on Speed often covered songs by female bands of the past, considering that practice "a way to extend the feminist histories and bring them into the now, take feminist meaning from the past and make it relevant again," Alex explains. Chicks on Speed initially covered Delta 5's "Mind Your Own Business" (1979) and Malaria!'s "Kaltes Klares Wasser" (1983). "But it was really The Raincoats that became a group to look to and to see that there are role models out there, because otherwise you feel a bit lost as

LIFE NUMBER 3

a young woman at art school," Alex remarks. At Seppi Bar, they "played, of course, The Raincoats, The Slits, and all those 'girl bands' that had been around first." And both founders of Chicks on Speed actually discovered The Raincoats themselves through their shared love of Riot Grrrl musicians.

"I was really into Riot Grrrl in the nineties," Alex says, "but I didn't know about The Raincoats! I discovered The Raincoats through Riot Grrrl and realized, *oh*, Riot Grrrl is clearly based on The Raincoats! That's where things became really exciting for me. And that connection simply is not spoken about enough, that much bigger trajectory." Discovering that lineage led to Alex's interest in using hers and Melissa's newly formed Chicks on Speed record label to bring the good news, so to speak, to the nations (in 2005, the label would release Ana's first solo album, *The Lighthouse*). "It was the realization—the *hey, wait a second!*—that there's this immense history that we didn't really know about and had just discovered ourselves, and knew it was important for everybody else to know," Alex says. Chicks on Speed asked The Raincoats to play their release party at the Volksbünhe theatre in Berlin on November 29, 2003, and the relationship between the two bands grew.

Alex put together a 63-song, three-disc CD compilation titled *Girl Monster* that featured The Raincoats' "Shouting Out Loud" and Ana's solo track, "Full Moon." For Alex, it was a way of presenting "a generational history of feminist music." The Raincoats weren't just central to the compilation because their music appeared on it; they also played a key role in making it possible.

"I relied on The Raincoats to create *Girl Monster*," Alex says, explaining how Shirley, Ana, and Gina connected her with most of the women whose music she wanted to feature. "The Raincoats inspired the compilation, and then they made it possible." Alex describes in-depth phone calls with Ana and Shirley, and the friendships they helped Alex to form with Vivien Goldman, Julz Sale of Delta 5, Ari Up and Viv Albertine of The Slits, Marlene Marder and Klaudia Schifferle of Kleenex/LiLiPUT, Gudrun Gut of Malaria!, and more. The compilation became available on Chicks on Speed Records in September 2006, linking original contemporaries of The Raincoats with Riot Grrrl and adjacent artists including

Peaches, Björk, Juliette and the Licks, Bikini Kill, Le Tigre, Lesbians on Ecstasy, and Robots in Disguise.

The compilation included a large fold-out zine, "An Introduction to the World of Girl Monster," with a cut-out image of the performing Raincoats as the first thing the reader sees. When the compilation came out, Alex and Melissa heard from "a lot of young women who said, *Oh my God, thank you for doing this! We didn't know about that music, and this history is really, really important.*" For Alex, "it was this epiphany moment." She and Melissa realized they were doing something The Raincoats had already done, but for a new generation in the 2000s. "So The Raincoats became true mentors for Chicks on Speed," Alex declares.

The Raincoats also inspired an even more powerful "Girl Monster" at the Donaufestival (aka Donau) in the Austrian city of Krems. Chicks on Speed organized an entire series under the umbrella name "Girl Monster," a new "culture-animating platform" to include readings, musical performances, and workshops. The name referred to the larger collective, as well as to every individual—they were each Girl Monsters themselves, as well as crucial components of the larger whole. The Raincoats closed out the festival on stage with dozens of women dancing, singing, and playing instruments in a euphonic cacophony. "That was the very first 'Girl Monster Orchestra,'" Alex says, in which all the artists together created a real-time "graphic composition," illuminating "the true energy of these girl monsters."

At Donau, The Raincoats cemented themselves as practitioners of a type of performance art few musicians have been able to replicate. "They're in it for the long run, and they're real artists who are constantly reinventing themselves," Alex explains. For The Raincoats, "it's not about repetition ... they know that once you've done something, you move on and learn to do it another way." Not only have The Raincoats demonstrated how to "make it new!" in a way that speaks to the modernist poet Ezra Pound's directive, but they've turned that slogan into a kind of feminist "sacred obligation." Each show, especially in the new millennium, has been about experimental process; they're performance artists above all. "The Raincoats' music," Kathleen Hanna of Bikini Kill says, "is an art form. They're all artists first." Anjali Bhatia of

The Raincoats play Donau Festival in 2009

Mambo Taxi and Voodoo Queens agrees: "True artists, constantly inventing and reinventing without being tied to any traditional idea of genre." In the third life of The Raincoats, and at Donau in particular, Gina and Ana achieved something they'd wanted since their early days at Hornsey: to be seen as artists for whom music is a form in which they create.

Looking back, Vicky recalls how, unlike in other bands "where someone would say, 'I'm the bassist and I'll play this song this way each time,' we never had that in The Raincoats. Every time we played, we'd be starting fresh, playing in a slightly or wholly different way." Even in the seventies and eighties, the aim was a type of performance art. Geoff Travis ascribes it to the tension that always existed between Ana and Gina. "They never get complacent," he says. "They're always ready to interrogate what the other thinks, and even when it's slightly uncomfortable, that contrast between those two ever-strong individuals makes the music."

While there's no single definition for what ultimately makes something "performance art," the definitions supplied by self-proclaimed performance artists appear as if they've been conceived while listening to The Raincoats. In the 1979 debut issue of *Performance Art* magazine, Laurie Anderson described it as something that rebels against the "linear and narrative," that is "freer to be disjunctive and jagged, and to focus on ... ideas, collisions." In that same premiere issue, Joan Jonas said it's "a ritual, a myth in pictorial form." And as if presciently seeing one of Ana's chair drawings that would later appear on We ThRee merch (the label The Raincoats would eventually found), Stuart Sherman explained: "What I do can be called 'performance art' only insofar as a chair can be called a 'chair.' Therefore, by way of definition, I refused to remain 'seated.'"[7]

The artist Johanna Linsley was at Donaufestival when she was asked if Girl Monster is political. She replied: "Is the revolution a party? Possibly," she wrote, in answer to her own question, explaining how "Girl Monster totally rocked in terms of super-exciting reconfigurations of identity. Queer, female, genderqueer, ethnically and racially progressive. And in terms of opposition, the message is anti-war, anti-globalization, anti-authoritarian."[8]

QUEER STORYKEEPING:
THE BFI LESBIAN AND GAY FILM FESTIVAL

The Raincoats' legacy as multidisciplinary artists in the annals of revolutionary history would continue to evolve after their "Girl Monster" appearance. Nazmia Jamal (Naz for short) became a programmer of the London Lesbian and Gay Film Festival in 2008 at the British Film Institute (BFI). She knew she wanted to feature The Raincoats, but she was nervous to ask them. Naz wasn't sure "if they'd be up for being in a gay film festival because," she says, "the way they move in the world is not like, 'we're a gay band,' or 'we're a queer band.' And while nobody would deny Ana and Shirley's relationship, it's also something very private, and I understand that. But I *really* wanted them in the festival and I also *really* wanted them to like me!" Naz exclaims.

LIFE NUMBER 3

Naz first heard The Raincoats in 1996 when she was in school in the Welsh valleys. She'd started a fanzine with one of her best friends, Maddie Hunter, who made her a mixtape with "No One's Little Girl." That mixtape also introduced Naz to Bikini Kill's "Rebel Girl." As Naz explains it, "Riot Grrrl and The Raincoats came to me at the exact same time." She got interested in feminist and queer activism and contacted the organizer in advance of Ladyfest London in 2001, which she'd read about in *DIVA* magazine. She ended up curating a portion of the event. It was there she met Gina, and Naz later DJ'd Ladyfest Spain in 2005, where Ana played and appeared on a panel with Tobi Vail and Allison Wolfe. By the time the planning for the BFI Lesbian and Gay Film Festival was underway, Naz felt a burgeoning friendship with The Raincoats, but she was still nervous about all of it.

Despite her concerns about The Raincoats' interest in appearing at the BFI, she decided to phone up Shirley and ask if the band had any visual works in progress they could show. She tried to keep in mind something Maddie had told her—that she'd first set actual eyes on Ana and Shirley at a gay pride parade in the late nineties (as opposed to a Raincoats gig), and that they were "really open and proud of who they were." Shirley immediately gave a provisional yes to Naz's BFI invitation and agreed to talk with Ana and Gina about material. Gina directed a work-in-progress edit of a Raincoats film, which included a collection of interviews and the live footage that the three of them had been producing together since 2007 (with the intention of releasing a DVD for Rough Trade). It was titled *The Raincoats, Fairytales—A Work in Progress*.

The screening and a live performance took place on March 28, 2009—Naz's thirtieth birthday, which also happened to be Gina's daughter Honey's birthday, too. "I had a lot of anxiety around the questions I thought they'd get, about sexuality," Naz says, "and at one point I was really worried I'd broken The Raincoats!" But of course, she hadn't.

The BFI program notes, written by Naz, described the cinematic work like this:

> Made up of rare archive footage, much of it unseen, and a series of new interviews with people who knew the band in the late

seventies as well as artists and musicians who have been affected or inspired by their work, The Raincoats, Fairytales—A Work in Progress documents how Ana and Gina, along with their manager Shirley O'Loughlin and the various musicians who flowed in and out of the band's many formations, created a sound that, while inspired by punk and rock music that had come before, was uniquely and uncompromisingly powerful and female, and which has held a fascination over all those lucky enough to have stumbled across it ... The Raincoats inspire in their fans a kind of generous enthusiasm and genuine respect that is rare and difficult to explain.[9]

The Raincoats, Fairytales—A Work in Progress appeared between two events tracing queer histories across time and space: an in-depth film on Stonewall and the origins of "the modern gay movement" in New York, and *Deep Lez*, a retrospective of "maximalist" artist Allyson Mitchell's work.

It all took off from there. Naz's work in the interlinked worlds of visual art and film made The Raincoats visible to new audiences in a way they hadn't been before, and her friendship with the band deepened. "Ana and Shirley are kind of like my mums at this point, they've taken me in!" she laughs. Naz also feels a sense of generational responsibility for their stories and histories. "I hold the queer stories ... the queer daughter often gets to store the stories in their family," she says, emphasizing that queer women can be left without the same generational legacy as women who have taken traditional paths, and had children. For Naz, there's a particular urgency to keeping the stories of "queer women focused on their legacy," and the keepers must share experiential knowledge. "I think if it was left solely to straight feminists to worry about The Raincoats, it wouldn't happen in the same way. It's an intentional creation of a family that Ana and Shirley do, a particularly queer thing to do, to *choose* a family. And Gina has done that in a particular way, too."

LIFE NUMBER 3

THE RAINCOATS KIND OF NEED A DRUMMER: ADDING VICE COOLER

Since 2009, Vice Cooler ("VC") has become a fixture behind The Raincoats on the drum kit, often alternating with Jean-Marc when the latter's schedule doesn't allow for a Raincoats show. VC's first Raincoats gig was for Girl Monster. He went on to play with The Raincoats on their first-ever dates in the Pacific Northwest and West Coast in 2011, and in a range of gigs from 2016 onward. He started out a fan himself and became a friend.

In the early aughts, VC was spending a lot of time with label owners Upset! The Rhythm (or UTR for short) and fellow musicians Chris Tipton and Claire Titley in London. "Chris was a massive ambassador for underground music in London at the time, and all the artists would stay with him." VC notes UTR's work with twenty-first--century indie artists and bands, such as John Maus, Trash Kit, and Deerhoof. Each time VC found himself in London, he'd stay with Chris and Claire, who were big Raincoats fans, loved Ana's and Gina's solo work, and had known Kim Gordon "forever," VC says. He thought it was probably a pipe dream, but he felt like he could tell Chris he wanted to play with Ana or Gina. It happened. "I kept coming through London, and Chris kept setting it up so I could play with one of them, and I became friends with Ana, Shirley, and Gina that way."

From the moment he met Ana, VC was amazed at the way she and Shirley integrated themselves into the music community at any given show. "They were really engaged with everyone in the crowd, socializing, enjoying multi-generations of creative people who they'd inspired, [and who were] saying, 'I love you! I love The Raincoats!'" At this point, The Raincoats didn't need a drummer (imagine that!). But VC's drumming did take a more obvious Raincoats turn when a small label wanted to do a Rough Trade tribute on vinyl. Spoiler: It never happened. *But*, when the label asked VC if he wanted to be involved, he immediately said he wanted to do something off the *Fairytale* EP. That unfinished project brought Ana and Gina together into a small practice studio with VC to record a new version of "Fairytale."

"I was touring, but I had a day off in London and wrote Ana to ask if I could do this tribute and if she'd possibly want to play something with me. She said they had a rehearsal space with a small recording area and drums," VC remembers. Perfect. Ana quickly followed up and said Gina was up for playing "Fairytale" or something from the EP, too. "I was like, *no way*, FUCK YEAH, that's great, that's incredible!" VC exclaims. As soon as he heard Gina was coming, he asked if they could also play "In Love." They met at the studio where The Raincoats had been rehearsing since the nineties. "We cut it in like thirty minutes, and I later got Anne to do violin on it backstage at the Knitting Factory in New York," VC says. He holds on to those recordings for dear life. He always figured they might be never-released mixes, but he doesn't care; they're recordings of him drumming with The Raincoats on early Raincoats songs. "I wouldn't let those go for anything," he declares, noting he never expected to have any more official Raincoats work.

Then circumstances changed and, you guessed it: The Raincoats needed a drummer. "All of a sudden, out of the blue, Shirley wrote me and said, 'Hey, Jean-Marc can't make it to Donau. Would you like to drum at the show?' I was like, uh sure, *of course!*" VC exclaims. Being immersed in Girl Monster, VC realized the Raincoats "are a magnet for cool things happening at random." Each time he's played with them since, "there's something I never thought in my life would happen, and it's always something amazing. Their momentum is life-enhancing."

Anne laughs warmly as she remembers VC joining The Raincoats. "He came in as quite a young fan, and a *real* fan! He couldn't believe he was playing with The Raincoats and was really happy to be there."

For VC, playing in the live Raincoats lineup required a new kind of thinking. Playing parts written by another drummer—multiple other drummers in The Raincoats' case, including Palmolive, Ingrid, and Richard—requires a delicate approach. "You want to honor the original sound while also interpreting it," he explains. And The Raincoats give him "a lot of freedom" to hit that sweet spot where interpreting another musician's work turns it into something new and personal. "They're not the type of band that ever wants something played the way it was once," VC says. "It's about 'how do we want to do it now to keep it new.'"

Kim Gordon remarks on how she has "known VC since he was, like, sixteen years old," mentioning how the band XBXRX would come through Northampton, Massachusetts (where Kim was living at the time), touring in VC's parents' station wagon. "They'd stay with us when they came through, and now he lives about five minutes from me in LA," she says. "And he was perfect to join The Raincoats. XBXRX was maybe the fastest band I've ever heard, and VC has this multitalented DIY esthetic. He makes videos, takes good photographs, plays multiple instruments. Totally makes sense he'd play with The Raincoats."

For VC, joining The Raincoats as a touring drummer has been his own fairytale. "I was a kid who wasn't born when the first Raincoats record came out, but grew up listening to that record and their others. I was a fan, and somehow now I've ended up in the fucking band! It doesn't make any sense, but it's the most ... fucking amazing thing," he says, barely finding words to express his own continued disbelief.

GAY ICONS AT THE NATIONAL PORTRAIT GALLERY

"A gay icon is acknowledged to be a historical or public figure celebrated by many in the lesbian, gay, bisexual, and transgender communities."[10]

National Portrait Gallery

The Raincoats continued to cement their legacy in museum spaces. As Naz remembers, "Someone from the National Portrait Gallery got in touch with me because they were doing a *Gay Icons* exhibition, and they wanted to get in touch with The Raincoats. So we curated a slightly different event there where Ana made artwork— enough prints to put on every seat in the theatre." Ana recalls how some of the drawings were objects, some were abstracts, but all were "icons" in some sense of the word. According to Gina, "I remember Ana said, 'A window can be an icon!' and I thought, *yes, it can*, and that's so lovely, because it shows how Ana never does the expected, and how her mind works in ways that are quite unique to her."

Gay Icons ran at the National Portrait Gallery from July 2 through October 18, 2009. The space on St Martin's Place in London is often regarded as the first art gallery devoted to portraits of "historically significant people," and the definition of who fits within that category has rightly shifted since its original opening in 1856. The face of the *Gay Icons* exhibition was a Jill Furmanovsky black-and-white portrait of k.d. lang, shot in a nondescript hotel room hallway in 1992. The exhibition promised an exploration of "gay social and cultural history through the unique personal insights of ten high-profile gay figures, who selected their historical and modern icons." The "chosen icons," the gallery text read, "who may or may not be gay themselves, were all important to each selector, having influenced their gay sensibilities or contributed to making them who they are." The selected icons ranged from early-nineteenth-century writers and composers to twenty-first-century athletes and activists.[11]

Sandi Toksvig, who chaired the selection committee, chose that k.d. lang portrait and wrote, ". . . it is her androgynous good looks and tendency to strut on the stage which warms many lesbian hearts."[12] Ana was a fan of k.d. lang, too. Before the first three Raincoats albums were reissued, Ana wrote a fan letter to k.d., telling her, "I used to be in a group called The Raincoats," enclosing a copy of *Odyshape*, the only record for which she had extras on hand. She ended the letter saying, "I think you're very important to a lot of people (women especially) and I wish you can do what you want in the way you want and need to do. The world is now ready for you. Stay courageous and cheeky." With that k.d. lang portrait framing the walls around them, The Raincoats performed at the *Gay Icons* exhibition as part of the *Icon-i-coustic* series accompanying still images in the gallery space.

By way of inclusion in the exhibition itself, The Raincoats were invited to reflect on their own icons. Gina made a film in which she discussed her icons, who included visual artist Tracy Emin, English children's author Enid Blyton, and iconic fashion designer

Vivienne Westwood. Ana's drawings, placed on every single seat in the audience (everyone got to take home one of Ana's icons) were her response to the invited reflection. Some attendees got drawings of radios, some of Ana's guitar. Others received drawings where the language stood out most, such as lines from the song "You're A Million," which read "My feelings were killed by laws. The walls that surrounded my city," illustrated by hearts encased in barbed wire. Shirley invited "three beautiful queer friends to make performances," she says, "which we planned, discussed, and prepared together." By way of introduction, Shirley explained how her friends' work was designed to "actually embody some of my iconic moments, inspirations, and moments of being." Anat Ben-David sang "Blue Moon," Shirley's favorite Elvis song, Stuart McKenzie wrote a poem about his father, and Susanne Oberbeck (aka No Bra) sang "Pale Blue Eyes" with The Raincoats, Shirley's favorite Velvets song.

For Ana especially, the performance marked the public embrace of an identity that was vital to so many listeners of The Raincoats, if not central to Ana's own performance. "I've never declared it, being queer, publicly," Ana confirms. "I've never wanted people to see me as just one thing, or to see the music as just one thing. I didn't want people to have an idea of these things and ever see it as a negative ... But as time has passed, these things have become important to me, and important to other people."

The Raincoats played a ten-song set that ended with what reviewers called "the queer cover of The Kinks' 'Lola.'"

"I remember saying to Gina, 'You're a gay icon now!'" Shirley exclaims, "and Gina really embraced that."

Queer icons at the National Portrait Gallery, queer icons close to home.

The Raincoats' status as queer icons extends to more private realms. As Gina's daughter Honey reflects, "Ana and Shirley have been huge queer influences in my life. I never perceived The Raincoats as a queer band until I got older and realized a lot of people, a lot of my friends, who listen to their music are queer.

But Ana and Shirley have always been important queer role models for me, queer icons ... They're officially my sister's godparents, but really, they're mine, too, because they're my queer godparents. I came out when I was fifteen, I think, and had my first girlfriend at sixteen, and they had so much joy for me, seeing this kid they knew since I was very small, and probably obviously gay from a very young age. I feel like I've had a few queer punk icons in my life that influenced me, but they're the first two, and they've introduced me to others, like Naz, another queer icon in my life."

Honey continues, "It became so important for me to see that was possible," referring to Ana's relationship with Shirley. "I appreciate them so much for that. For showing me that's possible."

As queer icons, Ana and Shirley proudly link their own work back to activists who came decades before the National Portrait Gallery recognized crucial gay icons, as they playfully but fearlessly shout, "We're here, we're queer, and we're not going shopping!"

Those words became a rallying cry in response to Clause 28 of the 1988 Local Government Act, which was designed to prevent localities in the UK from "promoting homosexuality." Activists stormed shopping centers, held protests and marches, and fought against de jure *discrimination. In the late eighties, LGBTQ activists weren't able to stop the passing of the Clause, and it became enshrined in British law until the early 2000s.[13] The phrase remains part of a queer rights lexicon, giving voice to heroes of the past while keeping their message alive in the present and future.*

THE LENGTHY HALF-LIFE OF "LOLA"

The Raincoats' "Lola" got an early start in sonic history when Thurston Moore went to see the band play at TR3 in New York City in 1979. In a recent conversation with Gina, the two discussed Thurston's memories of that night. Gina and Thurston both laugh, and he says to her, "I knew right then that was the end of my days playing with that band. You broke up the Coachmen [his first band, which he was still in at the time] and there would be no Sonic Youth without you playing 'Lola.' Thank you very much."[14]

LIFE NUMBER 3

For the most part, if you ask The Raincoats how they decided to cover "Lola," they say it was just a song Palmolive brought to the group, that she liked the Kinks. But it quickly took on a life of its own, the song's themes assuming a mischievous, subversive overtone in the hands of The Raincoats. As G.B. Jones remembers, "That cover of 'Lola' kind of alerted everyone in the queer community to think, *OK, possibly, they're also members of the community and they're out there.*" In that regard, it launched The Raincoats into the heights of queercore royalty.

For Patty Schemel, her love of the first Raincoats LP came through "Lola." Like other queer artists who identified a personal connection with The Raincoats after hearing that song, Patty found a sense of self in women who also shared her "secret." "Everybody loves *The Raincoats*," she says, "but for me it was really because of that cover of 'Lola.' As a kid—as a girl—who fit that stereotype, that cliché of being different in a little town, I was searching for *anything* that aligned with my secret—that I was gay." At the time, Patty didn't realize there was an entire zine scene of queercore female artists finding the same connection themselves, but it was the reason she was originally drawn to The Raincoats; they made her feel like she was going to be OK in a world that otherwise told her she wasn't.

Kathi Wilcox echoes G.B.'s and Patty's readings of the song. "Their cover of 'Lola' is pretty clearly queer-centered," Kathi says. "I mean, that's how it reads to me when I listen to it now, and when I listened to it then, as a queer-positive song. The song is already queer anyway, but they turned it into a lesbian song. It's not like you could find anything out about The Raincoats and their sexuality back then, and it was very difficult to get personal information on any bands back then. But it's clearly a queer-positive, lesbian song." That kind of bravery gave Bikini Kill and other Riot Grrrl bands a sense of empowerment around sonic activism, to address sexuality and freedom. The Raincoats gave permission to make what Kathleen Hanna of Bikini Kill calls "protest songs."

Kathi continues, "The Raincoats stepped out of this orbit, neither male nor female—another kind of being! They taught so many women that there are other ways to play music or be in a band without having to perform any version of gender. They weren't trying to be feminine or not feminine, and it didn't feel like they were trying to occupy any kind of particular gendered identity—they were being themselves and showing you that you were also free to be yourself."

Adam Kidron initially tried to push The Raincoats to record their cover of "Lola" as a single, but nobody in the band was interested; they wanted their singles to be music they'd written themselves. In the present, they experience a range of emotions when they acknowledge the continued power of their version of "Lola."

Shirley happily acknowledges how "it has become an LGBT anthem," while underscoring that's knowledge she only acquired relatively recently. At gigs in the early 2000s, she says, where "the audience embraced it in that incredible way," they began to realize its cultural power. That legacy now, of course, resonates wholly with the band. "It's part of us," Shirley says, and Ana agrees. "Feminist and political," Gina adds, ruminating on the impact of "Lola" across nearly five decades.

Just as musicians in the eighties and nineties saw queer undertones in the Raincoats' "Lola," so, now, does the next generation. Volkswagen recently used the song in a European commercial. The short film depicts a young girl of color wanting nothing more than to learn to play the drums, ultimately discovering a kit in the back of her family's Volkswagen, all while The Raincoats' "Lola" plays. According to Shirley, it was the first time Davray Music Ltd, Ray Davies's publishing company, permitted The Raincoats' cover to be used in this way; it was time, at last.

Honey Birch also points to the massive impact The Raincoats' "Lola" has found on TikTok. Videos abound with queer and trans women dancing freely, in fashions of their own making, while singing along to the cover song. In some videos, teens come out as queer or trans while "Lola" plays in the background. Steph Phillips of Big Joanie, who does double duty as a writer and journalist herself, reflects on the way the import of the song has changed over time, with different meanings for different people. It went "from a feminist reframing of a Kinks song," she says, to a track that's "eliciting an interesting conversation about trans identity."

LIFE NUMBER 3

AT THE CINEMA

Although movie soundtracks—as records unto themselves—gained in popularity in the late 1960s and into the seventies, it wasn't until the eighties that they really took off. By the nineties, films *without* a soundtrack became anomalies. But The Raincoats couldn't feature on just any soundtrack; a newfound interest in André Bazin's auteur theory (the notion that a filmmaker is the writer, director, and all-encompassing "author" of their work) that originally defined the French New Wave saw The Raincoats emerge in cinema.

French feminist auteur and frequent contributor to the illustrious journal *Cahiers du Cinema*, Mia Hansen-Løve included three Raincoats songs on the soundtrack to her cinematic debut, *All Is Forgiven* (2007): "No Side to Fall In," "The Void," and "No Looking." More than a decade earlier, fellow auteur Jon Sherman contacted Gina about featuring "No One's Little Girl" in his directorial debut, *Breathing Room* (1996). From there, Shirley contacted Chrysalis, who had publication rights for the song, and ensured it found its way into the film. Quite naturally, as any Raincoats fan would expect, the filmmakers who've been keen to feature Raincoats music are all auteurs—writers and directors of their own work, a relative rarity since the nineties. Kanchi Wichmann's epic queer feature *Break My Fall* (2011), honored by the British Film Institute as one of the ten best lesbian movies of all time, put The Raincoats' "Off Duty Trip" front and center. Another fellow auteur, James Gray, licensed "Fairytale in the Supermarket" for his personal coming-of-age film *Armageddon Time* (2022), and that song also appeared in *The Hunt* (2020).

And when Mike Mills got in touch about using "Fairytale" in his own autobiographical feature, *20th Century Women* (2016), he mentioned to Shirley that one of the characters (played by Greta Gerwig) was actually going to put the 7-inch EP on a turntable. "Fairytale" wouldn't serve solely as soundtrack, but as diegetic sound with a visual component to match! Shirley asked Mike if he had one of the original 7-inch EPs to use in the scene. He didn't. She got his postal address and sent some out to him.

Beyond soundtracks, but firmly on the silver screen, nearly any American millennial moviegoer you ask—who wasn't yet old enough to discover The Raincoats via Kurt Cobain but was of an age to go to movie theaters as the 2000s approached—first heard the band mentioned in *10 Things I Hate About You* (1999). The now cult classic was a modern adaptation of Shakespeare's *The Taming of the Shrew* with a relatively straightforward plot: Patrick (played by Heath Ledger, in the role of Shakespeare's Petruchio) attempts to "tame" the feminist "shrew," Kat Stratford (played by Julia Stiles, in the role of Shakespeare's Katherina Minola), in exchange for a fee paid by Kat's sister's admirers, by proving they're likeminded and compatible. Patrick shows up at a gig where Boston female-fronted indie band Letters to Cleo are performing. Patrick says to Kat, playing his role perfectly, "They're no Bikini Kill or The Raincoats, but they're not bad."

As far as connections between The Raincoats and visual art go, consider cinema one of those arms.

WE THREE

After the DGC debacle, The Raincoats weren't keen on making another record. Yet as interest in their music persisted—and grew—in the new millennium, they wanted to celebrate their records with anniversary reissues. So they formed their own label: We ThRee.

The bedrock of We ThRee came about in 2008 as Shirley was reflecting on her own mortality and the legacy of The Raincoats. She was going through treatment for breast cancer and started talking with Ana and Gina about "pulling ideas together" for a legacy project. "Coming out of that discussion," Shirley says, "I just thought, right, maybe let's just do everything we can now, because I don't know how long I've got. Let's just do it. It was also coming up on the thirtieth anniversary of *The Raincoats*. So I went to see this guy at Cargo, Craig Gogay, and he was so into it."

Cargo has been an indie distributor in the UK since the 1990s, helping artists to get their music manufactured on vinyl and CD, into retail shops, and ultimately into the hands of buyers.

LIFE NUMBER 3

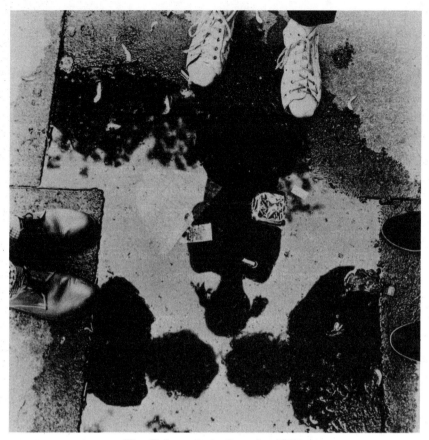

The Raincoats in the rain, 1981

"Craig offered us a manufacturing and distribution deal," Shirley explains, "which was brilliant—an eighty-twenty deal. They pay manufacturing costs up front. So I went back and talked to Ana and Gina and said, 'Well, let's do our own label! I mean, what is the point of us giving fifty percent of our profits to someone now?'" Shirley knew Geoff was interested in reissuing Raincoats releases on vinyl through Rough Trade, but it was time for The Raincoats to take their DIY approach to its obvious conclusion. Ana, Gina, and Shirley would become We ThRee, stylized as "WE 3" on sleeves and merchandise.

"We own the music," Shirley said to Ana and Gina, "so let's do it." Portia Sabin at Kill Rock Stars had also approached Shirley, "because she was keen to put out *The Raincoats* through Kill Rock Stars in the States, which made absolute sense. We'd do everything on We ThRee here and license to Kill Rock Stars in the States," Shirley explains. At this point, Shirley was on a "let's do it!" thing, meaning she was thinking big, about how to really *do it all*. The Raincoats wanted to tour, and Portia said Michelle Cable at Panache could put some dates together. "So We ThRee did its first licensing deal with Kill Rock Stars for the US for five years," Shirley says, and they renewed the contract in 2017. They now export themselves to the US market.

In 2010, We ThRee also licensed the first three Raincoats albums to P-Vine Records in Tokyo for individual CDs and a box set.

The Raincoats had become an official business partnership in the early 1980s with Ana, Gina, Vicky, and Shirley as the partners. By 2008, it was technically still in existence. Although Vicky wasn't interested in being part of The Raincoats anymore, she was legally still one of the partners of the company. With plans for We ThRee taking shape, it was necessary to revisit the original agreement. "So in 2009," Shirley explains, "We ThRee signed an agreement with Vicky for her to give us permission to release the early recordings, and she also made an agreement saying that she was no longer a partner in The Raincoats and hadn't been in the partnership since 1984." That meant Vicky was still a partner in The Raincoats (the original entity) and would continue to receive her equal share of profits from the band's first life, but any Raincoats music made after 1984 would be owned by Gina and Ana alone (with musicians like Anne and Heather paid as session musicians). "Vicky retired, really," Gina laughs.

Shirley admits, "I did kind of persuade Ana and Gina to do We ThRee, but they were really into it, and I think they've become more so. What We ThRee has done since then is to reissue *Odyshape* in 2011, and we do new editions for new anniversaries. We did a gold edition of *The Raincoats* in 2019 for the fortieth anniversary with fine-art-quality prints of drawings by Ana and Gina included, and I think that's our favorite of the ones we've done. Finally we've got a gold record!"

They also handled merch. Ana made Raincoats T-shirt designs with line drawings of a record, a window, and two chairs. "Naz got one of those chairs as a tattoo," Ana smiles. Sometimes Gina would sell her Raincoats art bags, sculptural pieces unto themselves. "I knitted and felted bags, which I then appliquéd with lettering and symbols from Raincoats songs," she says. Often, it'd simply be The Raincoats selling the merch themselves, or having friends do it. When VC started playing with the band in the 2000s, they'd get his friends to (wo)man the merch tables. And of course, The Raincoats have been making their own badges since 1979.

Beyond providing a framework for a new Raincoats life in the twenty-first century, We ThRee also brought the band back into Ray Farrell's orbit. He now works for Orchard, The Raincoats' digital provider.

KILL ROCK STARS AND THE RAINCOATS REISSUE IN AMERICA

From its inception as an Olympia label, Kill Rock Stars (KRS) was connected to The Raincoats. "The Raincoats are the godmothers of the Kill Rock Stars sound," cofounder Slim Moon says.

In 1986, Slim moved from Seattle to Olympia, where he met "the high-schooler Tobi Vail, maybe the youngest person in the scene," Slim laughs. "And she made me a mixtape, and one of the bands on the mixtape was The Raincoats." When Slim went to parties DJ'd by Sub Pop cofounder Bruce Pavitt, he heard The Raincoats, too. The Raincoats were omnipresent in Olympia.

When he started thinking about creating a label, he wasn't immediately making plans to release music by The Raincoats or bands so obviously inspired by them; he wanted to release spoken word 7-inch records. Along with Tinuviel Sampson, he formed KRS, and it all started out modestly. The first release was in 1991—a Slim Moon/Kathleen Hanna 7-inch single, "Mean" b/w "Rock Star." It came with an insert that offered a kind of manifesto for the label. On one side, Slim scrawled:

> We are trying! Everyone I know is locked up in destructive and self-destructive trips that are built to perpetuate. Why is power

so important? Why do we think our idols are so important and powerful? Why do we have to be abusive to feel powerful? ... Kathleen has put together a list of ideas of ways to work against whatever makes us mean and want to be somebody at somebody else's expense. It is printed on the other side of this insert, along with her address. Thank you for purchasing "Rock Star" b/w "Mean." It is intended to be the first of a series of spoken records from KILL ROCK STARS.[15]

On the other side, Kathleen wrote her own manifesto, which could have emerged from chats with The Raincoats:

BURN DOWN THE WALLS THAT SAY YOU CAN'T ...
RECOGNIZE VULNERABILITY AND EMPATHY AS POSITIVE FORMS OF STRENGTH.

The second release was a spoken-word 7-inch featuring Stacey Levine and Peter Toliver. Yet very soon, KRS became a label releasing artists who cited The Raincoats as a key influence. The first KRS comp was the label's third release, featuring tracks by Bikini Kill, Mecca Normal, Nirvana, Courtney Love, and Bratmobile. Within a year, KRS had released the first Bikini Kill self-titled EP, and their split LP with Huggy Bear, *Yeah Yeah Yeah Yeah / Our Troubled Youth*. That split LP is the record Tobi and Kathi brought to Dunkin' Donuts to gift to Ana.

The business plan for KRS was akin in many ways to that of Rough Trade, something The Raincoats would have approved of: putting musicians first without focusing on finances. For KRS, like Rough Trade, the aim was never to make a lot of money but to ensure meaningful music entered the world. For the first decade and a half of KRS, the label defined itself with the following words: "Unlike all major labels and many indie labels, profit is not our primary motivation. Kill Rock Stars is dedicated to releasing high quality, meaningful recordings in a manner that is fair and respectful to the artists."

KRS was, at its heart, a label that emerged from "the time and place of The Raincoats," Slim explains. "So, it's easy for me to say The Raincoats are the godmothers of the Kill Rock Stars sound."

He continues, "The sensibility of the label from the start, and the artists we wanted to work with, was very rooted in a DIY punk history about breaking the rules of rock 'n' roll and about saying 'anybody can do this.'" Slim alludes to some of the male-fronted punk bands. Rather, like The Raincoats, "lots of the Olympia bands played their instruments really weirdly, or differently, or had more or fewer instruments in the band than most people thought rock bands should have. And we learned from The Raincoats that *you can do that*. The Raincoats broke the rules." For fifteen years, Slim oversaw the label that would release music by diehard Raincoats fans, including Mecca Normal, Lois, Bikini Kill, Sleater-Kinney, and more. During those early years, both Tobi and her sister Maggie worked at the label, and their connection with The Raincoats became a direct line in addition to the one Gina had established with The Hangovers.

In 2006, Slim decided to step away from Kill Rock Stars, and his wife Portia Sabin took over. That meant Portia became in charge of all relationships KRS had with artists. Just a few years into her KRS tenure, Porta wanted to release something from The Raincoats. She communicated primarily with Shirley, "who made life much easier," Portia says. "I basically just said, 'Whatever you guys want, we'll do it.' Shirley told me what they wanted to do and we did it."

Portia knew reissuing The Raincoats' self-titled LP made sense for the label. "The Raincoats were one of the most obvious bands to be a Kill Rock Stars band," she says. "Slim created something really special, a label that was extremely feminist from the jump." And by 2000, she says, "Fifty percent or more of the Kill Rock Stars roster was bands of entirely women or with women in them. The whole ethos of the label was so feminist that of course The Raincoats would become a perfect fit." Portia underscores that KRS has always worked with the definition of feminism that The Raincoats instilled: "Feminism is *not* just 'oh there happens to be a girl in the band,' but the idea that women are able to play music, to play it however they want without being put in a box."

In July 2009, Portia emailed Shirley to let her know everything was coming along great for the anniversary reissue of *The Raincoats*.

Naz wrote digital liner notes that appeared on KRS promo mailings and on the website:

> The Raincoats, seminal post-punk band, 'godmothers of grunge' and inspiration to a generation of riot grrrrls, formed in the late 1970s when Gina Birch met Ana da Silva, becoming one of the most important underground bands Britain has ever produced. Ana and Gina, along with the various musicians who flowed in and out of the band's many formations, created a sound that, while inspired by punk and rock music that had come before, was uniquely and uncompromisingly powerful and female, and which has held a fascination over all those lucky enough to have stumbled across it.[16]

The track listing was the same as the 1993 reissue, with "Fairytale in the Supermarket" first on the record. It was released on October 13, 2009, and in support, The Raincoats made plans for a few shows in America: two on the West Coast and one in Brooklyn.

"If I had been really smart," Portia says, "when Shirley and I were talking in 2009 about the self-titled record, I would have been like, 'Hey, how about the other Raincoats records?' But obviously I didn't think of it at the time, and one of the downsides to being an artist-friendly label is that you let artists do what they want, and Shirley didn't approach me again about reissuing any of the other albums."

Carrie Brownstein of Sleater-Kinney wrote a review of KRS's *The Raincoats* reissue for NPR's blog "Monitor Mix," urging readers to buy this record that had just become available to American fans for the first time on vinyl since 1979. Carrie wrote how the band "always inspired a sense of wonder and a sense of worship," especially in Olympia where "all of my major and most informative musical discoveries took place." She continued, "In that dreary-weathered town, lit up with bright, unceasing ideas and enthusiasm ... The Raincoats didn't so much intrude on my world as make it shimmer. To hear the band's songs for the first time was to light a sparkler in a room, each song a tiny, magnificent and uneven torch. The music had shape and then was shapeless, wonky edges with pure, glowing centers. I would listen and think, '*How?*'"[17]

LIFE NUMBER 3

Slim returned to KRS in 2018 and Portia stepped onto other music avenues. By the time the fortieth anniversary of *The Raincoats* rolled around, the label was celebrating its own thirtieth anniversary. They pressed 100 limited-edition pink vinyl copies of *The Raincoats* for the shared commemoration. In choosing *The Raincoats* as one of the KRS thirtieth-anniversary limited edition pressings, Slim and the team wanted "records that were emblematic of our label identity," he says. "Some of the things we do are cool and we stand by them, but they're not *dead center* to our identity. But *The Raincoats*—that is. And it's just something we're particularly proud of and feel particularly aligned with." And it wasn't just another reissue of *The Raincoats* from KRS that invoked the band in the label's own thirtieth anniversary. In 2021, the label released *Stars Rock Kill (Rock Stars)*, a thirtieth-anniversary celebration of the label covers of KRS releases by artists in the roster.

Slim approached artists about covering bands that he considered integral to KRS in ethos and sound. "Jen Cloher knew immediately she wanted to cover The Raincoats' 'Fairytale,'" Slim says, and while Mirah took a little bit of time to decide what she'd want to do, "One day it just showed up in our inbox, along with a video of how she did 'In Love' with very unusual percussion that was very much in the spirit, creativity, and originality of the Raincoats original." The comp had sixty-three digital singles, three of which were covers of Raincoats songs: Jen Cloher and Hachiku covering "Fairytale in the Supermarket," Mirah covering "In Love," and Tele Novella covering "Adventures Close to Home." All three were tracks from the self-titled *The Raincoats*, which was, by 2021, part of the KRS discography.

Covers, as Alex Murray-Leslie suggests, are political—they confirm there's something significant about the song to consider in the present. On the KRS compilation album, the three covers underscored that songs from *The Raincoats* retain their relevance across time and place.

"If you look at a lot of the Kill Rock Stars bands I signed during my time there, there's a real through-line that goes back to The Raincoats, to what they started," Portia says. "It's a cliché to say that a band is timeless," Slim remarks, "but one of the ways you can actually *be timeless* is to have such a particular alchemy of how you play that no one before you or after you will ever play that way again. You can see their influences and then you can see the long trail of influences coming from them. A lot of smart, artistic musicians aspire to that, but it's very, very hard—impossible, usually—to do." Portia agrees, "The Raincoats are endlessly inspirational."

AT LAST: THE RAINCOATS PLAY THE PACIFIC NORTHWEST ON OCTOBER 13, 2009

Despite becoming the godmothers of the Olympia fairytale, The Raincoats had never played in the Pacific Northwest. They finally made it to the region during their third life for shows in Seattle and Portland that Portia planned as part of the KRS campaign for *The Raincoats* on its thirtieth anniversary.

For both Gina and Ana, the dates are a bit of a blur. Gina had spent time in the area previously with The Hangovers, and Ana recalls relatively little from the shows. Gina does recall that Heather Dunn came to see them in Portland at the Holocene, and Gina was so glad to see her. She felt an immense release of her anxiety from that spell in the nineties. Heather remembers it, too. She sat with Gina backstage "just talking" for a while before reconnecting with Ana, too. "Ever since then, we've been besties on Instagram," Heather laughs.

Portia was in the audience, which she describes as "*super packed*" with "a lot of cool kids." Carrie of Sleater-Kinney was also present, seeing The Raincoats live for the first time after years of idolatry.

"It was one of those shows where your mouth is just hanging open and you can't even really comprehend that you're there. It's so rare to see a band that is just 100 percent not giving a fuck, saying this is what we do, and doing it really well. This is our art, like it, love it, or leave it," Portia says of the Portland gig. "Seeing The Raincoats live was so empowering. It's what we hope for women, and I hope there were some little girls who went to that show and were like, 'Holy shit, I could totally do that. I don't have to do the thing boys are doing, and I don't have to do things exactly the way everybody else says!' It's so transformative to see people color outside the lines and express themselves. And the Raincoats show was transformative in that way."

Transdisciplinary artist Nadia Buyse was on the bill that night, opening for Grass Widow and The Raincoats. She'd actually grown up in Olympia, where it was impossible *not* to be a Raincoats fan. "Gina and Ana said, 'If you're ever in London, come hang out,'" Nadia remembers. She eventually moved to the UK and did just that.

Portia didn't remain in close touch with the band but still says, "I don't get to meet a lot of real rock stars in my line of work, and The Raincoats definitely felt to me like *real* rock stars. I was intimidated to finally meet them. They're heroes, you know?"

The Raincoats stopped for brunch with Tobi in Olympia. "And I've only just found out Tobi hates brunch," Ana laughs.

To date, The Raincoats have yet to play a show in Olympia.

VIV ALBERTINE AND SOFT POWER AT NEW YORK'S KNITTING FACTORY

After playing Portland, The Raincoats traveled to the East Coast for a New York City gig at Brooklyn's Knitting Factory. They invited Viv Albertine of The Slits along to celebrate songs from her first solo album. Gina and Ana both joke that it turned into a kind of punk pajama party, with Viv sharing a hotel room with The Raincoats. Palmolive even remembers coming to the show and crashing in the room, too. "I was there, too!" Molly Neuman of Bikini Kill adds. Tobi Vail and Kathi Wilcox of Bikini Kill were also in the crowd. "It was like a mini reunion," Tobi laughs.

Viv was on the bill with The Raincoats, along with Soft Power—a band you might not know by name, but surely you know their fierce guitarist, Mary Timony. She got started on Dischord Records in Washington, D.C. with her first band Autoclave (cofounded with Christina Billotte of future Riot Grrrl band Slant 6). By 2009, she'd already had a luminous musical life as a solo artist and in the much-loved Matador indie band Helium. If not for The

Raincoats, some of her subsequent music might never have come to be. "I had this cassette of *Odyshape*," Mary remembers. "I'd go on these walks and listen to it, and it was pretty magical. The thing that has always resonated with me is how singular they are, how they're so much *more* than punk because they've created something so different, their own world, with their music." The chance to open for them in 2009 gave her the strength, and the kick, she really needed.

"I had been really struggling about whether I should just give up music," Mary says. "I was at the end of my thirties, and I really thought, I should just stop. I was playing in this band with a couple of friends from D.C. at the time, Soft Power, and we got a chance to open for The Raincoats at the Knitting Factory. I was still planning to quit at this point. But then seeing Viv Albertine of The Slits playing solo, seeing The Raincoats creating this world with their music, and reflecting about being on the same bill as these women who I get so much spiritual energy from ... it was such a fucking awesome experience!" Mary smiles and flashes a knowing look. "They showed me that I have to keep going. It was a really, *really* profound turning point in my life. It meant so much to me." Since that show, Mary has recorded more critically acclaimed solo music, formed supergroup bands the Spells (with Carrie Brownstein of Sleater-Kinney), Ex Hex, and Wild Flag (with Carrie and Janet Weiss of Sleater-Kinney). And she's making a lot of music plans for the future.

October 16, 2009 was also a pivotal night for Viv. The Slits broke up back in 1981, and she essentially gave up music. She'd gone to art school and had a child. But she still had an itch to make music. In the early 2000s, Viv started writing music again, this time solo. As friends and supporters of hers, The Raincoats invited her to play those new songs in New York that autumn night at the Knitting Factory. A few months later, Viv did an interview about her forthcoming solo record, with music drawn from the songs she'd played in Brooklyn. She said she'd never imagined herself as "a solo performer," yet "being a bit older, there comes a point when I looked around and thought, *Look at all the people you do know who do that and the people you know who don't do that and what have* they got that's any different—except the bottle to do it." She was nervous about getting on stage again, but reminded herself that the crowd wasn't there to judge her skill as a musician. They were there for something much more important. "They don't mind if it's not technically brilliant," she reflected. "That's such a great legacy of punk—that technical ability comes pretty low down the list about what's necessary live."[18]

The Knitting Factory would be the last date on a brief reunion tour to support the reissue of *The Raincoats*. A couple days after the show, the print edition of *The Village Voice* remarked, "Why their brief reunion tour isn't an overwhelmingly big deal, I'm not sure ... the band sold out the Knitting Factory's new venue in Williamsburg, though the show still felt like a kind of secret."[19]

For those in the know who were at the Knitting Factory that night, the show became a point of intergenerational inspiration.

ATP GIGS—LOOKING FORWARD, LOOKING BACK

In case The Raincoats weren't quite certain that they'd inspired an entire generation of musicians, the "All Tomorrow's Parties" (ATP) festivals confirmed it. The concept involved a temporal collapse in which artists would "curate" experiences, bringing a lineup of handpicked artists from past, present, and future. Barry Hogan conceived the idea for ATP in 2001 as an anti-corporate festival that would reinvent the form. Curators ranged from original punk pioneers such as Patti Smith and Iggy Pop, to Mogwai and Pavement, and the events ran for a total of fifteen years until a spectacular collapse in 2016.

Backstage pass for All Tomorrow's Parties

In late 2009, the lineup for the Pavement ATP was announced. The show would be the first for Pavement after the band broke up many years prior. The curated lineup was described in *Consequence* as, simply, "bands that Pavement likes." Alongside the re-formed Pavement, The Raincoats joined The Fall, Mission of Burma, The Clean, Blitzen Trapper, The Walkmen, Broken Social Scene, and others.

At some festivals, curators who selected The Raincoats weren't just musicians, but artists of other forms such as *The Simpsons* creator Matt Groening or British comedian Stewart Lee. When Matt Groening announced his curated lineup, he emphasized that he'd put together a bill of "outsiderness seeking world domination."[20]

BIG IN JAPAN

The Raincoats finally made it to Japan in 2010 after an original invitation to play back in 1984. Koki Yahata, the A&R person for Tokyo's P-Vine Records (who'd licensed The Raincoats' first three albums), was key in bringing the band over. For decades, they'd been big in Japan, but fans had to wait until the twenty-first century to see The Raincoats live.

Electronic, atmospheric artist Phew was supporting The Raincoats in Tokyo. She was already a fan herself, and recalls how, "in 1979 or early 1980, when I had just broken up my own band [Aunt Sally], a familiar clerk at a record store I visited every few days let me listen to the first album that had just arrived." Initially, says Phew, "I was attracted by the colorful jacket, which was unusual for those days, and then I was fascinated by the sound. I was especially fascinated by the drums, which sounded unlike anything I had ever heard before." When she got the chance to open for The Raincoats in Tokyo, she wouldn't have been anywhere else. As Phew remembers it, "The Raincoats' first show in Tokyo was packed, so at first I was backstage listening to them play. But eventually I couldn't stay, so I went to the audience and sang 'Lola,' swaying my body almost in the front row." Phew continues, "I generally watch the other performers backstage or in the last row, but this was the first and probably the last time I waded through the audience to almost the front row."

Collection of Raincoats badges,
including designs by the band and by fans

Ana also remembers a girl from one of the audiences approaching her and Anne after a Raincoats set, saying, "I want to be like The Raincoats!" Anne quickly interjected, "But you become like The Raincoats by being yourself! That's what The Raincoats is, it's to just be yourself and not copy someone else!"

Japan also became a crucial place for Ana's own experimentation and collaborative impulse, because it's where she met Phew. It was the first time Ana had heard of her, but she was immediately intrigued by the sounds Phew created. "I can't remember exactly what instruments she was using, but they were all on a table, there was no guitar, and it was ... mysterious," Ana remembers. A collaboration would develop within the decade.

The Raincoats have also become an enduring element of Tokyo's underground fashion scene. Minami Yamaguchi, founder of fashion label and boutique VIVA Strange, has long been a Raincoats fan and saw them live in Japan's capital. (She's also a musician herself, with a solo project titled "She Talks Silence.") Her goal isn't to make products described as fashion, or even clothing, necessarily, but *music*. And for the artists she loves, her aim is "to give back," she repeatedly says. "The most important thing is to create things in a manner that suits them."

Nothing is bootleg; everything Yamaguchi designs is a collaboration with the artist or band. She's made a Raincoats raincoat with the cutout figures from *Moving* on the back. An *Odyshape* long-sleeve. A "No One's Little Girl" embroidered pink T-shirt reflecting the design on the 7-inch single. A bag with Ana's and Gina's portraits on either side, their images from the back of *The Raincoats* sleeve.

Yamaguchi's wearable music bucks the gender binary and any age considerations—"Something that could be appreciated by a wide range of backgrounds, regardless of gender or age," she says.[21] Unsurprisingly, she's also done a collab with Phew.

Mostly, when they look back on their time in Japan together now, Ana and Gina remember the karaoke. The entire band went to a karaoke bar together and Ana sang the Nirvana song "Lithium." In so many ways, that's absolutely perfect.

INSIDE THE MOMA, INFINITY

You know what Dylan says happens inside museums: Infinity goes up on trial.

The Museum of Modern Art (MoMA) has been courting radicalism, feminism, protest, and controversy since it opened in 1929 at the height of Modernism. In the present, its library and archives hold the largest concentration of materials related to modern art anywhere on the globe, with more than 320,000 individual objects and primary source materials from more than 90,000 artists of all forms, canonical and experimental.

But it wasn't always seen as a space where sonic performance and visual art converged.

"The modern museum has always been attacked as a symptom of cultural ossification by all those speaking in the name

LIFE NUMBER 3

of life and cultural renewal against the dead weight of the past," cultural historian Andreas Huyssen wrote in the late 1990s, just as the new millennium approached.[22] At that point, he argued, there was a need to reconceive the nature of the museum as one where "counter-hegemonic memory" was possible—where something could happen "to claim some anchoring space in a world of puzzling and often threatening heterogeneity, non-synchronicity, and information overload."[23] Inside the museum, The Raincoats helped to usher in that new paradigm in the twenty-first century.

Setlist for The Raincoats' 2010 show at MoMA in New York City

As the end of the 2000s approached, the then editor of *Artforum*, Tim Griffin, who'd soon become director of The Kitchen, commissioned an issue of the magazine titled "The Museum Revisited."[24] He was interested in exploring what he perceived as a "growth of dialogues across disciplines," making it possible to reimagine the contours of museum space. In that first decade of the new millennium, Tim observed "art audiences exploding" and museums experiencing a sharp rise in the number of visitors. It was an "experience economy" taking shape, and that meant the vocabulary surrounding museum visits had become accessible to a broader public. As Tim argues, for many museums it was still about numbers; the word "democratic" came to be synonymous with capacity rather than establishing a heterogeneous public. But as artists like The Raincoats began entering those spaces, a meaningful shift became possible—one in which diverse audiences, in large numbers, could begin to learn a shared vernacular. Art need not fit within an understood range of forms, displayed traditionally in a museum space, or discussed in terms of its permanence. In spaces like MoMA, genres and forms could finally collapse into one another.

On November 20, 2010, The Raincoats played at MoMA to inaugurate the museum's Modern Women initiative, a project and publication designed to illuminate "the modern and contemporary women artists whose diversity of practices and contributions to the avant-garde movements of the twentieth century have been enormous, if often underrecognized."[25] The initiative and accompanying exhibition featured works by more than 300 female artists working across moments and media, including Marina Abramović, Chantal Akerman, Laurie Anderson, Diane Arbus, Anna Banana, Gretchen Bender, Lynda Benglis, Louise Bourgeois, Margaret Bourke-White, Leonora Carrington, Judy Chicago, Imogen Cunningham, Maya Deren, Ray Eames, Barbara Ess, Helen Frankenthaler, Su Friedrich, Katharina Fritsch, Nan Goldin, the Guerrilla Girls, Eva Hesse, Nancy Holt, Jenny Holzer, Mary Kelly, Lee Krasner, Yayoi Kusama, Dorothea Lange, Ida Lupino, Marisol, Ana Mendieta, Georgia O'Keefe, Yoko Ono, Faith Ringgold, Cindy Sherman, Kiki Smith, Trinh T. Minh-Ha, Cosey Fanni Tutti, Agnès Varda, Kara Walker, and Carrie Mae Weems.

The Raincoats became part of that collective as they performed in those "hallowed" halls. "At college," Ana says, "I always felt The Raincoats was as much art as anything that was shown in that place, a kind of performance art. And I felt that what we did should be part of how they saw our artistic practice, by the college, but they didn't. But when we were playing at MoMA, I thought, *Well done Raincoats, here we are performing at one of the most famous art museums in the world.*"

Kathleen Hanna DJ'd, and she sang "Fairytale in the Supermarket" with The Raincoats on stage. The event took place shortly after Ari Up had died, so The Raincoats also played a Slits song for her in her memory that she'd written, titled "Vindictive," with the chorus, "let's do the split / I wanna shit on it!"

Both Gina and Ana were asked to share reflections with MoMA after the performance. Gina said, "Here in 2010, to be invited to perform at MoMA is significant for us—thirty-three years after we first played together. Women curators, women's photography, women's art, The Kitchen show and us, at MoMA ... Thank you to Kathleen for being an inspiration and playing records and performing on Saturday night. Thank you to all those who turned up and yelled and danced and listened on Saturday night ... Let's all continue to try to make a difference, because it really does matter ..." Ana said, "The most important thing about art is its power to communicate. The audience at MoMA showed such a warm response that we felt we did to some degree what many of the artworks there do every day." She concluded by saying, "Having Kathleen Hanna collaborating in the event was a real treat. It was Kathleen and her generation that helped our work become better known and validated ... shouting out loud."[26]

That night, just five avenues over from the Ramones' 53rd and 3rd, The Raincoats showed that punk is indeed art, just like Gina and Ana always intended.

A RETURN TO THE KITCHEN

The Kitchen laid the groundwork for new conceptions of art that gave artists permission to smash disciplinary boundaries. In recognition of that pioneering work and those artists it helped to shape, The Kitchen began hosting galas in the 2010s. As director of the organization, Tim Griffin wanted to celebrate linchpin artists who'd performed at the venue early on, as well as those who'd been overlooked. The events were about bringing the history of The Kitchen decidedly into the present, illuminating its contemporary significance and "activating intergenerational bonds," Tim says.

Kim Gordon and Dan Graham were chosen as honorees for the 2015 spring gala, for which they'd curate a schedule for the night. Graham had been a mentor for Kim, and both had illuminated in their own distinct ways how the worlds of fine art and music could be bridged. Naturally, they invited The Raincoats. "Kim really propelled it," Tim explains. Stephen Malkmus of Pavement and the Feelies were also on the bill.

Nearly thirty-five years after they'd appeared in Lower Manhattan to play the gig that would be released as *The Kitchen Tapes*, The Raincoats brought together a new kind of heterogeneous crowd to celebrate Kim Gordon and Dan Graham. When it comes to bringing together an audience with diverse perspectives and identities, across generations, "you couldn't ask for a better band to do that than The Raincoats," Tim declares.

He acknowledges that The Kitchen galas, including this one, weren't accessible to all given the price tag. But by the end of the gala night, before The Raincoats took the stage—they were scheduled to close out the evening—Tim and his team opened the doors and allowed all the fans hovering outside to imbibe the beautiful cacophony.

PLAYING FOR THE NEO NATURISTS

For British fans, one of the more recent and memorable Raincoats performances was a 2016 gig with the Neo Naturists. "Everybody was naked!" Jon Slade of Huggy Bear exclaims. Naz echoes the memory, adding, "And it was great!"

Joe Scotland of Studio Voltaire "loves the Neo Naturists, and he loves The Raincoats," Shirley explains, and he wanted The Raincoats to play a Neo Naturists event at the ICA. "They perform on sets with odd objects," Shirley says, describing seemingly disparate materials such as "hay bales and lobsters." And, she emphasizes, "They're completely naked and their bodies are painted." The Raincoats went to the ICA to discuss how this could work; the Neo Naturists asked The Raincoats to play a couple of songs. "They insisted The Raincoats play this absolutely hideous song 'Chirpy Chirpy, Cheep Cheep.' And, well, they did it," Shirley laughs. ("Chirpy Chirpy, Cheep Cheep" is a 1971 song by the "bubblegum" Scottish pop band Middle of the Road. In 2006, the *Observer* named it one of the most "unintentionally creepy" songs of all time.)

The Neo Naturists are a live art collective originally formed in 1981 by Jennifer Binnie, Christine Binnie, Wilma Johnson, and Grayson Perry. Like other artists emerging during the early years of UK punk, they came out of squatting communities in West London, contributing to the burgeoning subculture. The Neo Naturists had each been experimenting with body painting, the role of the physical body in art, and radical acts centering women. They sought to rebel against the cultural commodification and sexualization of women's bodies, and to celebrate the female form in ways that undercut visual misogyny inherent in London, and even across subcultural punk realms of the time.

When Studio Voltaire presented the retrospective of their work in 2016, it declared that, "The group achieved a unique artistic voice, which contrasted with the highly polished esthetic of 1980s London." The gallery went on to explain that, "In a cultural landscape that was decidedly slick, urban, and modern, the Neo Naturists' work celebrated a particular kind of anarchic innocence, making frequent references to the English pastoral and homely pursuits such as camping, girlguiding, and harvest festivals."[27]

For the Neo Naturists' performance, The Raincoats were just three on stage: Ana, Gina, and Anne (no drummer). Gina painted dresses for them to wear so that they appeared nude but weren't. "With the naked dresses, I bleached black and/or navy cotton dresses and they turned a pinky flesh color; then I applied paint to them to represent the naked female body," Gina explains. So Gina and Anne wore the painted dresses while Ana wore a T-shirt with her own drawings of two cups of tea and, lower down, a spinning record. "My signature black T-shirt," Ana says and laughs, explaining, "I just wouldn't want to be naked in public. I guess maybe I'm old-fashioned."

Jon remembers running into Liz Naylor in the crowd, a Huggy Bear reunion of sorts. "*Everybody* was naked, and there were bales of hay everywhere . . . Liz [Naylor] will back me up! This did happen!" Jon laughs. "But The Raincoats were *NOT* naked, a very important part of that story," he adds. "Gina made nude body dresses, and she and Anne were in them on either side of Ana, who clearly was not having any of it."

This wouldn't be the last time The Raincoats could be heard playing in connection with the Neo Naturists. In 2023, when Tate Britain put on *Women in Revolt!*, Gina's Super 8 film *3 Minute Scream* served as the de facto soundtrack to photographic images of the Neo Naturists and dozens of creative works by other female rebels—the sound from the Super 8 film permeated much of that gallery space, turning Gina's rage-filled voice into the exhibition's refrain.

SHOUTING OUT LOUD WITH GABY AGIS

The Neo Naturists certainly weren't the only artists contemplating the role of women's bodies in performance spaces. In early-eighties London, dance choreographer and performance artist Gaby Agis was going to a lot of gigs. Living in a London squat two doors down from Viv Albertine, she'd seen The Slits, of course, but remembers, "There just weren't many women musicians performing at that time." It wasn't until she saw The Raincoats at Brixton Town Hall that her perspective changed.

"It was staggeringly magnificent," Gaby says, and she became obsessed with *Odyshape* and the song "Shouting Out Loud" in particular. "I had the cassette on repeat for at least a month. I was *obsessed*. I was dreaming the music, dreaming The Raincoats." Gaby was most taken with the band's "ability to be with a kind of pure rage and visceral experience, but to flip that and show incredible tenderness and vulnerability, and a kind of playfulness." The idea that all of those emotions can exist in the same bodies—it was language Gaby was seeking in her own exploration of physical movement.

By 1984, right around the time of her self-proclaimed obsession with "Shouting Out Loud," she was invited to contribute to an evening of performance work and remembers, "I immediately knew I wanted to work with 'Shouting Out Loud' and thirteen women. I had it plotted already, and it filled me with excitement." Gaby wrote a letter to Ana who, it turned out, also lived a couple doors down from her on the same London street. She told Ana about her idea for a choreographed dance performance, asked if she could use "Shouting Out Loud," and inquired about the two of them meeting. They met, and an abiding friendship unfolded.

The Raincoats were no more at this point, and Ana was eager to sustain her own creativity. Since the song "Shouting Out Loud" was

Flyer for Gaby Agis's *Shouting Out Loud*

only a little over four minutes and Gaby was imagining a dance performance of thirty-plus minutes, she asked Ana if she'd be interested in doing additional sonic work for the piece. *Absolutely*, Ana told her. Ana attended rehearsals for the dance performance, also to be titled *Shouting Out Loud*, in order to improvise a score that worked in dialogue with the thirteen women on stage. Gaby would then go back to Ana's flat and listen to what she'd come up with. Ultimately, "a long durational work was composed," Gaby says.

This collaborative version of *Shouting Out Loud* was imbued with the politics that surrounded them—Gaby, Ana, and the thirteen women in the performance. "So much of the world we were all inhabiting, as young women—the chaos, the riots, Thatcherism, all amid the rising anti-racist, feminist movements taking shape and resisting the sense of a world closing inward—it felt pretty gruesome," Gaby remembers. But creating *Shouting Out Loud* allowed

Gaby, with Ana's help, to flip the script. They built a different kind of encapsulating world. The cosmos created through Ana's music and the choreographed women's bodies imagined "exteriors at night, the images of fury and all the visions that come through in the song, but it also established a solidarity among the performers, and the possibility of tenderness and support—all those reverberating echoes of the feminist movement," Gaby says. Gaby and Ana revealed it was "possible to create a feminist community within performance"—the dancers, along with Gaby and Ana, already "knew the language."

Part of the language was tethered to resistance. In creating a dance piece with a significant number of performers who were all women, Gaby was eager to "resist the heteronormative idea of a man and woman on stage." The performance was about "a woman and a woman, and a woman and a woman," Gaby explains. She wanted to illuminate the different ways women "organize themselves into different communities," the way they imagine their artistic practices in relation to gender.

Ana approached the sonic extension of the song "Shouting Out Loud" for the performance—the extra twenty-six or so minutes she had to create—in the same experimental and considered way she'd written in The Raincoats. When The Raincoats initially recorded "Shouting Out Loud" for *Odyshape*, Ana'd had the idea to use a shruti box at the end of the song. An instrument derived from a harmonium, the shruti box originates from the Indian subcontinent and makes sounds through a system of bellows. It's handheld and portable, constructed of wood and pipes. In Indian classical music, the shruti box often appears in devotional pieces. Like other instruments that use just-intonation tuning, the shruti box emits sounds that often seem to mimic the sounds of human sighing and weeping, the deep groans and wails the body can emit in lamentation. It was perfect to establish a dialogue with the female bodies on stage, and Ana decided to use it as the base for those twenty-six extra minutes. She also added other sounds of life—of trains, traffic, and running water. "A bit like Gaby's dance piece," Ana says of her soundtrack for the work, "things come in and out and evolve in different ways."

LIFE NUMBER 3

The choreographed piece illuminates various tropes of gendered identity, and the movements we make to resist them. Missed connections, changing degrees of speed, sudden rapidity, urgency, (running away), holding each other both physically and metaphorically, carrying the weight of one another, bodies dead and bodies rising in resurrection, intertwining female bodies in opposition to gender norms. The work as a whole suggests there are many different ways of "shouting out loud" and being heard.

The piece took Gaby in a new direction, and it "opened a back and forth, symbiotic relationship between Ana and I, like working with water and breath ... it was extraordinary."

When Gaby first created the *Shouting Out Loud* performance piece, she knew she was seeking representations of lived experience through dance. It's something she continued to pursue, yet without repeating a performance—that is, until she decided to come back to *Shouting Out Loud* three decades later in 2014. Thirty years on, Gaby had new language to talk about the piece's power and the political stakes in (re)creating it.

The Raincoats song "Shouting Out Loud" started as a way of portraying "an atmosphere of solitude, being in time and space with yourself and what surrounds you," Ana says. There's a significant difference between solitude and loneliness, the former a state of intentional reflection, the latter wounding. In the original 1984 piece, there's a tension between the two, as then-present politics expanded and foreclosed possibilities. That dynamic became more pronounced in the 2014 recreation of *Shouting Out Loud* as dancers across generations, ethnic and cultural backgrounds, and experiences came together to perform what Gaby describes as "improvisational" with "very specific spatial relationships." In deciding to stage *Shouting Out Loud* again, Gaby was less interested in what she calls "the actuality" of the original, and more in exploring "how much of the time we live in inevitably impacts on the work that we make."

In 2014, four of the original dancers came back for the reprise. Gaby also brought dancers ranging in age from teenagers to septuagenarians. To prepare them to come together in the collective intricacy required of *Shouting Out Loud*, Gaby held a *Shouting Out Loud* seminar in which she and Ana met with the performers and moderated discussion around the piece. Gaby told everyone in attendance that the politics of the present "consciously and unconsciously affect our making," and noted how "miners' strikes, squatting, gay pride, feminism, and Thatcherism ... were raging" when she initially conceived *Shouting Out Loud*. Recreating the piece thirty years later, Gaby clarified how she was interested in new ways that women create community and express their relationships to their political environments. *Shouting Out Loud* is ultimately, Gaby suggests, a way of addressing the "turbulent and uncertain times in which we live."

The 2014 recreation was followed by additional performances around the UK from 2015 through 2018, including a 2016 London performance at Greenwich Dance where The Raincoats performed live. *Shouting Out Loud* was advertised that night as a "double bill." Gaby, herself, performed her solo dance piece *In Anticipation of Surrender* with the music of "No One's Little Girl." (Gina worked previously with Gaby on that latter piece, which she remembers "was performed by the amazing dancer Ellen van Schuylenburch.")

The politics of the recreated *Shouting Out Loud* became most evident and urgent in Gaby's final staging of the piece to date: a 2019 performance in Istanbul, Turkey, on International Women's Day, at Mimar Sinan Fine Arts University. Gaby had been working in the city for about a decade and was there during the attempted coup in 2016. She knew she wanted to stage *Shouting Out Loud* in Istanbul on International Women's Day, and she planned to personally extend the performance into the streets in the women's march down the Istiklal. She trained the dancers, who found the piece particularly challenging due to the "layer of threat, and fear of violence that could just spring up when you turn a corner." There was a constant sense of "fight or flight," Gaby says.

"They were brilliant," Gaby adds, describing the Turkish dancers, "and those women needed the piece more than women in other places in some ways." The audience was "just packed." After the crowd began to disperse, Gaby and several others headed uphill toward the top of the Istiklal where the International Women's

Day march was starting. They joined in and were met with riot police and tear gas.

In the years before and since that day in March, Turkish leader Recep Tayyip Erdoğan, a president in name but strongman of the country, enforced a ban on International Women's Day protests and withdrew the country from the Istanbul Convention aimed at preventing violence against women. In response, on each International Women's Day, thousands of women have gathered on the Istiklal and marched toward Taksim Square at the top of Istanbul's famous street, exposing themselves to the threat of state violence in order to combat its inherent misogyny and oppression.

At that moment on the Istiklal on March 8, 2019, Gaby was immediately taken back to the first time she'd been tear-gassed in the midst of a protest. "For a moment," Gaby says, "I thought I was in a performance art piece." It's that very layering of real, political life and performance—lived experience and play—and the easily crushed line between, that Gaby's *Shouting Out Loud* has now illuminated across time and geopolitical space to the sounds of The Raincoats.

THE SECRET LANGUAGE OF THE RAINCOATS: FROM RIOT GRRRL TO BIG JOANIE

It would all be a shame if they got too well known, Jon Slade ruminates of The Raincoats. Shouldn't they stay just a bit underground, he asks, "Because how would you pick your friends, then?"

The secret language of The Raincoats has been connecting people for decades—through shared punk ideologies, queer underground kinship, and much more.

The Raincoats were the language that solidified a deep and lasting friendship between Kurt Cobain and Patty Schemel. "I knew Kurt before Courtney," Patty says. "Kurt loved The Raincoats. I loved The Raincoats. So we knew we had the same interests." Jon Slade agrees. "Whenever someone knew The Raincoats, this was impressive to us," he says, referring to himself and his Huggy

Bear bandmates. "The Raincoats is how I choose my friends. If The Raincoats are a common point of interest, that's how I know I'll get together with anyone."

Knowledge of The Raincoats' singularity is part of that secret language. As soon as you hear someone compare The Raincoats to another band, you realize they just don't get it. "Comparisons are invidious," Lucy Sante says, "because The Raincoats really knocked out a place for themselves. They have their own pedestal, they are engraved, and they are irreducible. They did something that wasn't like what anybody else was doing, and you have to actually listen to their records because you can't describe it in words."

Big Joanie get it, perhaps more than any other band to form in the twenty-first century.

In 2013, Stephanie Phillips was attending Black feminist meetings in London, monthly gatherings for women of color. She was carrying a Raincoats bag at one of the meetings, when Chardine Taylor-Stone, a fellow attendee, noticed the bag. "I was carrying that Raincoats bag," Steph remembers, "and Chardine liked The Raincoats. And not many people there had heard of The Raincoats." So Chardine tracked Steph down on social media, and as soon as Steph posted about wanting to start a Black feminist punk band, Chardine replied. Thus was born Big Joanie.

"The DIY punk scene then," Steph refers to the early 2010s when Big Joanie formed, "was very led and influenced by The Raincoats' approach to punk. When I thought of punk, I never thought of hardcore, and I never thought about the kind of pop punk that has become popular. And I never thought of the Sex Pistols or a masculine idea of punk. For me, punk was always about deconstructing the idea of what a song should be, or even what an idea should be—and going your own way to create a sound rather than being led by the kind of overwhelming idea of what a song structure is supposed to look like, sound like." Steph cites other London bands that came up temporally and ideologically alongside her own band, like Wet Dog, Shopping, Trash Kit, and Woolf. "Everything then felt like it was aiming towards building on what The Raincoats created," she reflects. "It was like The Raincoats laid the foundation, and we were all trying to build up from it."

As Big Joanie bassist Estella Adeyeri explains it, The Raincoats play in a way that's "unconstrained, very intuitive," and they eschew any need for the typical "formalities" of songwriting. For Estella, The Raincoats taught her it's entirely unnecessary to approach music or creative practices in the same way as anyone else; you can always make it your own.

Unlike artists of earlier eras, the members of Big Joanie could Google The Raincoats and track down their music pretty easily. Steph remembers seeking out information about The Raincoats online and falling in love with the song "No Looking" on the self-titled LP. "That was really such an influential song for me," she explains. "It sounds like a spoken-word piece, and it has this poetic element to it, and it really sets a scene between two people sharing this moment that's played out dramatically."

ROUGH TRADE'S FORTIETH ANNIVERSARY: OCTOBER TO NOVEMBER 2016

Rough Trade celebrated its fortieth anniversary in the autumn of 2016 and planned a range of collaborative events to mark the date. It couldn't have been a true celebration of Rough Trade over the years, or its significance to the history of independent music, without The Raincoats front and center.

The Rough Trade *40th Anniversary Journal* published a written piece by Shirley, titled "seventh heaven," and two of Ana's drawings. In addition, for Rough Trade anniversary shows at the Barbican and Islington Town Hall, some of Gina's films were screened, as well as Shirley's photos and a film by Ana.

As Shirley explains, the anniversary was also a celebration of her own creative coming of age, which began with seeing Patti Smith at the Roundhouse in 1976 and The Slits a year later—where Ana and Gina were also in the audience. That was the beginning of The Raincoats and her time working at Rough Trade:

SHOUTING OUT LOUD

seventh heaven

she moves onto the stage.
she punches, pounds the air like a boxer.
she spits on the floor – nothing moves – except my thumping,
    pounding heart.
this is the first woman i have ever seen in my life.
"jesus died for somebody's sins but not mine" . . .

boys everywhere, crashing, thrashing into each other, smashing
    into bodies.
i smell the tension – fear.
suddenly a girl in a raincoat dancing wildly, dreadlocks flying,
    pounding drums,
manic rhythms, off the rails – pure joy.
"oh oh oh sweet love and romance" . . .

the tenderest pain hits my chest, pierces it, my skin falls off.
the building collapses and i fall on the floor.
blistering, soaring violin makes me fly.
her dark brown voice embraces me, takes me on a journey of
    love and despair.
"a scar is open i make mistakes" . . .

in october 1978 i jumped into a van on the corner of portobello road and started working at rough trade records. a drawing of 3 chords in a fanzine had given everyone permission to form a band and that's what everyone i knew was doing – energy. scritti politti brought out their first single on their own label and the cover told you how – diy – empowerment. rough trade was really the only place on earth where i wanted to be.

i was managing the raincoats, taking photographs and setting up the rough trade booking agency with kleenex, the raincoats, essential logic, delta 5, young marble giants, the red crayola and the slits to name just a few. i had the chance to work with carmen knoebel from pure freude in duesseldorf, and with ruth polsky in new york city, sending all the bands over there to play for the first time.

in october 2015 here i am reflecting on all this nearly forty years since patti smith played the roundhouse – the night the slits and the raincoats were conceived and my own life was changed. and looking down at my laptop i begin to contemplate the full potential of the means of production i am holding in my hands.

"Writing that really made me revisit and think about what I had at the time working at Rough Trade," Shirley says, "and what it gave me."

Rehearsal for The Raincoats and Angel Olsen collaboration to celebrate Rough Trade's fortieth anniversary, 2016

The Raincoats met Angel Olsen for the first time in 2015 when she was about to play at an outdoor venue in Lisbon. Angel's friend Sérgio, who'd booked the show, told her, "Shirley and Ana da Silva of The Raincoats are coming to your show. Originally, they weren't going to be able to make it, but Shirley sprained her knee, so they have some extra time in Lisbon." They came and introduced themselves. Angel and bandmate Emily Elhaj have made a point of staying in touch with Gina, Ana, and Shirley to this day.

For Angel, her musical relationship with Emily—a friendship and lengthy collaborative connection—felt akin to Ana's and Gina's. "We felt there was a sort of parallel," Angel says, "being in this long-term thing together, developing and growing, changing, dealing with trouble, disagreeing, all of it that comes up, as it inevitably does ... we felt a *huge* connection to these women, even though we hadn't even met Gina yet!"

When the Rough Trade fortieth anniversary was in the works, Shirley was in the thick of planning. She contacted Angel and asked if her band would be interested in performing with The Raincoats. "I was just like ... honored," Angel says, having trouble finding the right word to convey her swelling heart. "Immediately, I just said *YES!* And I just said yes for everyone else, too." Emily was up for it immediately, too, scheduling conflicts and other difficulties be damned.

"They sent us a list of, like, twenty songs, and we were like, *Oh my God, Jesus Christ*, so scared, terrified," Angel laughs. "It was going to be Emily and Heather from my band, and the guys held back. Almost immediately, Elhaj [Emily] and Heather were so confused, like, *Who is playing what instrument? Are we all playing the same instruments? Will there be two of everything?*" Eventually, like me, they realized that this was all part of the experiment, the whole spirit of The Raincoats—to just decide to *try something*, to pick up and just try it."

VC was excited to play the gig and says it was "just another example of The Raincoats being a magnet that pulls amazing people into these incredible scenarios, right into their orbit, where things just happen. And afterward, I'm like, *wow, that just happened*."

The gig with Angel Olsen was one of those, where we had maybe six hours tops to prepare and rehearse, so it seemed like there was no way it was going to work, and then we played the show and it *just worked.*"

They collaborated on a playlist comprised of Angel's songs, Raincoats songs, and a Patti Smith cover, "Because the Night." Nearly twenty in total. "I learned so much from them, playing that day," Angel reflects. "Because I'm such a control freak. It was really hard for me to let go." Emily agrees: "They really pushed the limits of what we thought we could do."

On the last night of the two-week party, Rough Trade also had a karaoke band. Ana sang Nirvana's "Lithium," bringing a little bit of nineties Rough Trade history into the fortieth anniversary celebration. "It was so brilliant, just fabulous," Shirley says.

THE ETERNAL RETURN TO THE KITCHEN: BIKINI KILL REUNITES FOR THE RAINCOATS

The Raincoats returned to The Kitchen in 2017 to celebrate the release of Jenn Pelly's 33⅓ book about their first LP, *The Raincoats.*

In case there was any lingering doubt about the significance of The Raincoats on the long historical trail of experimental feminist punk, Bikini Kill reformed at the event after a decades-long hiatus—specifically for and *only for* The Raincoats. It could only have happened at The Kitchen.

Back in 2015, Tim Griffin had contacted Shirley about the gala, so by 2017, she felt comfortable getting back in touch. The Raincoats needed to come back to The Kitchen, she told him. "I've always hoped they'd see it as another home," Tim says. Shirley started making handwritten notes about the ideal lineup for the event, sketching out the stage area at the venue. She contacted Tobi to ask if she'd consider doing something for the event, and Ana invited Kathleen. What ultimately happened is now the stuff of legend.

"So, Shirley got in touch and asked if I'd do something for the event," Tobi remembers. "At first I thought, there's no way I can do that. But Shirley was relentless," she laughs. Once Tobi agreed, she told Shirley she had no idea what to play and suggested a friend, Becca Albee (a visual artist who lived in New York and played in the Riot Grrrl band Excuse 17) join her on stage. "Initially, Becca and I were going to do something," Tobi explains, "and then I was talking to Kathi, and I asked if she'd do something, too. But then Kathi came back to me and asked, 'What if we did something with Kathleen?'"

Kathi explains it from her perspective: "I think Tobi didn't want to go up there by herself. At this point, of course, Tobi and Kathleen were not really speaking. But me being the connector, I said, 'Why don't the three of us do something?' I framed it as, 'It's not a big deal, it'll just be the three of us, Bill's not gonna be there, and we'll just do a song from before Bill [Billy Karen, Bikini Kill guitarist] was in the band, one connected to our feelings about The Raincoats.'"

Kathleen admits, "It was pretty much all Kathi. She's the mastermind behind anything good that ever happens." According to Kathi, she broached the topic with Tobi first. "Of course," Kathi remembers, "Tobi said, 'What did Kathleen say?' and I had to tell her I hadn't talked to her about it yet and was just asking if she'd [Tobi] be interested. And Tobi said, 'If Kathleen says yes, then OK, sure.'" Kathi dialed Kathleen.

"She called me and suggested we plan to do something, the three of us, at this event, and I said no," Kathleen remembers. "I didn't really believe that Tobi wanted me to be involved, and I thought Kathi was doing one of her sneaky spin things where she tells me Tobi wants to do it, and then she tells Tobi that I want to do it. I told her I didn't believe Tobi actually wanted to play with me, so no."

Kathleen had wondered what it could be like if the three of them played together again, but lamented that she and Tobi "hadn't been friends in a really, really long time," so she assumed Tobi would never be interested. "And then Kathi said to me, but Tobi really wants to do it, and I was like, *what the fuck?*" For Kathleen, in that immediate moment, it still didn't seem like an actuality. "So I drove to the store, and while I was driving, I thought, *What* the fuck is wrong with you? You're gonna get to see the Raincoats play AT THE KITCHEN?! You'd fly to New York for that anyway! And of course Tobi wants to do it, I mean, we'd do ANYTHING for The Raincoats! Even get back together after twenty years! Definitely, we would! We'd crawl under a barbed wire fence to get to a Raincoats show together, and to play at it, too!" Kathleen realized she was going to blow the chance of being part of a truly historic occasion. "I called Kathi back and said I hoped I hadn't missed the window. Well, what I really said was, I was being stupid! I definitely want to do it! So then I sat around waiting for Kathi to call me back after she talked to Tobi again to say if it was a for-sure thing for Tobi."

Kathi called Tobi again and told her Kathleen said yes. Tobi agreed, too.

Kathleen sat by the phone waiting while Kathi and Tobi talked. "It felt like I was waiting to find out if my crush wanted to go on a date."

The three of them made a plan to meet in New York.

"I saw Tobi that night at The Kitchen before anything started," VC says, "and I'd heard Kathleen was in town. So I was like, *Are you going to do something here with Kathleen?* She was being all mysterious about it, so I just knew: There was gonna be a Bikini Kill reunion! I started running around telling everybody, 'I think there's gonna be a Bikini Kill reunion tonight!' Everyone was saying, *Oh, no way, there's just no way*, and then when I was setting up my drums, Tobi and Kathleen and Kathi all showed up together and I was like, *OH SHIT! IT'S HAPPENING!* Then Tobi asked if she could use my drums for sound check and I was like, *THIS IS FUCKING CRAZY!* So then I went upstairs just telling anyone, *A BIKINI KILL REUNION IS ABOUT TO HAPPEN!*"

"It felt very exciting," Tobi reflects now. "We only played one song ["For Tammy Rae"] and then sat down, but we were like, *whoa, that was crazy!* And then almost immediately, we started to have conversations and realized we really missed each other." For Kathleen, playing with Tobi and Kathi again brought a kind of closure in addition to a resurrected Bikini Kill. "It was about healing the wounds, the chasm," she says, "and mourning the loss of my friendship with Tobi." (Although, Kathleen emphasizes, "I hate that whole language of healing.")

Tobi jokes that she and Kathleen are like Ana and Gina, oil and water, with someone holding the entity together. "I think maybe Kathi is our Shirley," she laughs. "Does Shirley hold all of it together?"

The morning after the event at The Kitchen, Tobi emailed Shirley:

> I forgot to mention it last night, but "For Tammy Rae" is one of the first songs we wrote with Kathleen on guitar as a three-piece in 1990. She may have even brought the song to us, not sure. And I remember Kurt saying it was obviously our best song. Of course, that made me NOT want to record it, and want to write more noisy stuff. But I think he was ultimately right. It is one of our best early songs, and it only has one chord. We didn't record it until 1992. Probably trying not to sound too pop or whatever. It was funny trying to relearn the song from the recording because we never played it live after Billy joined. And so we guessed that we probably just relearned it in the studio to get it on tape. And it seemed like we were just kind of making it up as we went. So in the end, we kind of tried to get the same feel live, instead of cover ourselves note for note ... Thanks again for giving us all a chance to play together.[28]

Shirley replied and asked for a bit more information about the solo song Tobi played, too, which brought Kurt Cobain back into the celebration of The Raincoats along with Bikini Kill. Tobi responded:

> I didn't say most of this, but this is what I remember about that song. In between all of my teenage bands breaking up, Doris and the Go-Team, etc., and starting Bikini Kill with Kathi and Kathleen, there was a period of time where I was kind of isolated and sad in my apartment, listening to records by myself, like The Raincoats, Marine Girls, Young Marble Giants, etc., and some later bands like Shop Assistants from Glasgow and 60s stuff like

the Beatles and Bob Dylan. I spent most of my time alone just playing guitar and making up quiet singer-songwriter type songs and not really being in a band. I would just end up playing them for friends, or before friends' bands, at small shows or parties. Most of them were not very good, but I liked this one enough to bring it to a band I was briefly in with Kurt. He played drums on this song, as I remember it, and that was in the summer/fall of 1990. But then Bikini Kill started, Dave Grohl joined Nirvana, things changed fast, Bikini Kill moved to Washington, D.C., and I think Nirvana moved to LA. Kurt and I still planned to record our songs, and there were some four-track tapes that have mostly been lost. Anyhow, that never happened. The only time I remember playing that song live at a proper show was by myself at Girl Night, or Girl Day, of the International Pop Underground Festival in Olympia at the Capitol Theater. It was a really cool event. Bratmobile played, and Heavens to Betsy, I think it was Corin Tucker's first show ever. Mecca Normal played, and a lot of women were invited to sing a song that had never played a show before. It was the very beginning of Riot Grrrl. Anyhow, my song is just a lot of memories and feelings about trying to connect and being a little kid and wanting to hold onto that feeling of first getting to know someone but losing them as life goes on and things change.

It's set in 1979 in Naselle, Washington, this small Finnish logging town I used to live in when I was a little kid, in the middle of the woods near the mouth of the Columbia River and the Pacific Ocean, not too far from Aberdeen, Montesano, where Kurt grew up. He really liked this song, so I said something before I played it like, 'This song is dedicated to the memory of Kurt Cobain, who's someone who is very special to The Raincoats.'"[29]

Would Bikini Kill have reformed without the jolt from The Raincoats? According to Tobi, "Being asked to come together for The Raincoats, to celebrate a Raincoats book, one hundred percent was the only reason Bikini Kill got back together. Up until that point, *It. Was. Over.* Our friendship was over, and we didn't need to revisit it."

"It felt *impossible* before that," Kathi echoes Tobi. "Kathleen and I had been doing music as the Julie Ruin, and people would ask us if Bikini Kill would ever play again. In my mind it was definite: *That is never going to happen.* It seemed absolutely impossible." Kathleen agrees, "It could only be The Raincoats to bring us back together." Kathi quickly adds, "If we were ever going to do something together again as Bikini Kill, that's the only band that we would have done it for. I can't think of a single other band that would have brought us together like that. And we *only* did it because it was The Raincoats."

Once they realized a Bikini Kill reunion was possible, they looked once again to The Raincoats for inspiration. "There was no way we were going to do revival shows," Kathleen says, but seeing The Raincoats that night at The Kitchen, she realized, "That was *not* a revival show. It was so of the moment and felt like it could have been any decade. It felt new." Tobi emphasizes how, "Seeing The Raincoats do it, it also felt really genuine, and it was so empowering for all of us, in our forties at the time, to see older women performing their work on their own terms."

Back in 1996, following The Raincoats' first reunion, Gina told Richard Boon: "I like the idea we can affect other women, even at our age, who might think of picking up a guitar in their late thirties or early forties. Why not? That's quite inspiring. I like the idea of us being sixty-year-old women playing rock and roll. We're still punks!" Those words took on additional power in the years that followed, giving "permission," as Kathleen would put it, to female artists across generations.

After The Kitchen, Bikini Kill did officially reunite and toured again to new audiences, and their presence impacted artists such as Estella Adeyeri of Big Joanie. "We're constantly being told by society that if you're in your thirties, your forties, you should probably just keel over and die," Estella says, "remove yourself from public viewing. But that messaging just doesn't make sense anymore when you have role models that show you there's another way. I saw Kathleen Hanna recently, and she's in her fifties now, and she said she still feels like she's just getting started and has so much more do."

Kathleen reflects seriously about that night at The Kitchen in 2017. "To see The Raincoats making something new and magical that was so vital, I realized again that their band was giving us permission, and that we could go out again as Bikini Kill and give other women permission, too. The Raincoats gave us permission thirty years before, and they did it again twenty-five years later. I think we all knew after that night that Bikini Kill *had* to play again."

ANA AND PHEW: ISLAND(S)

Koki Yahata, who'd brought The Raincoats to Japan back in 2010 and licensed their music there, knew Ana had been intrigued by Phew's music. He suggested Ana work with Phew. "And he must have said the same to her," Ana says, "because she sent me some of her records. I wrote to her and said, 'We must work together one day, and she wrote and said, 'Yes, we must work together.' Time went on, and it kept bubbling up. There was still a big physical distance between us," Ana explains, which made working together seem difficult despite the electronic highways of the internet. But then Phew came to play in the UK around 2017. Ana went to see her at IKLECTIK, a London venue dedicated to experimental art, sound, and technology. "It's an avant-garde-ish place," Ana describes it. Ana told Phew about the synth modules she'd bought, "and that's when it became a bit more serious." They started sending one another parts of songs, "and the other one would usually finish it, so it was quite quick," Ana reflects.

Although there was a sizeable geographic distance between them, the electronic nature of their work made the collaboration possible. Phew explains, "The album was made without ever going into the studio together or having a goal of making an album, just exchanging files as we felt like it. We had rarely met in person and had only exchanged emails a few times." Yet that physical distance never created a barrier. Phew continues, "As we exchanged sound files, I felt as if we were communicating with each other on a deeper level than if we had actually met and exchanged words. To use an analogy, it is an unobtainable feeling like each of us is traveling on a boat from a different place and looking up at the starry sky."

Ana recalls how it was "very, very easy to work with each other, and mostly we accepted everything that each other did and just added our own elements to it. Only very rarely did we disagree about something." They called the record *Island* "because we both came from islands," Ana explains, referring to her upbringing in Madeira and Phew's in Japan, "and we both live on islands now." She continues, "It was one of the happiest, most creative times, because I was doing this thing that was completely new." Phew adds, referring to the feeling produced by her collaboration with Ana, "During the pandemic, we exchanged mail from time to time and traveled to different islands around the world in our imagination. It is not a feeling that can be described as exciting or rewarding, but for me it is a very beautiful and precious experience."

It all reminded Ana of the very first Raincoats song she and Gina ever finished. "I loved the feeling of songs shaping up to have them finally formed. It's such a great moment, and it's kind of miraculous. When we did our very first song as The Raincoats, 'Life on the Line,' when we composed it, we got to the end of the song and everybody had parts, and it was a formed thing," Ana says. "I felt so exhilarated in that moment, that *oh God, we have a song*. And that feeling returned with *Island*. You find a way of bringing your own language forward."

ROUGH TRADE BOOKS: LOVE, OH LOVE

While reforming for various Raincoats gigs in the 2000s, both Gina's and Ana's visual art practices were also flourishing. Ana's small paintings first became available to audiences as part of a Rough Trade Books series of pamphlets. Hers was titled *Love, oh Love*.

Nina Hervé bought books for Rough Trade shops during her tenure there from 2008 to 2017, and it gave her the idea to start a new Rough Trade business in 2018. As a neighbor of the shop, Ana heard about the forthcoming Rough Trade Books before almost anyone else. "Nina said she was planning a series of pamphlets and that she wanted to do something with me. She knew I made drawings," Ana says, referring to A4 pieces that incorporate Raincoats lyrics.

Ana has long been interested in making art affordable, taking it outside the realm of the elite. Ever since she started drawing windows on newsprint in the late 1970s, she'd had the "idea to make multiples of things, do the same thing several times in a way that they wouldn't be expensive to buy, if I ever sold them," but still individually unique, she explains. "That was my idea behind what I did, and it connected to the music, because I liked the idea that almost anybody could go and buy a record. I'd like that to be the same thing with visual art." That approach led her to make A4 pieces that would ultimately become the images in the A5-sized *Love, oh Love*.

"Nina said, 'I'm going to do four or five of them,'" Ana explains of the pamphlet plans, "and mine was number four. Shirley helped me put it together. We put the drawings here on the table." She motions toward their large kitchen table. "And we moved everything around until we decided on an edit for printing." The launch took place on May 29, 2018 at Tate Modern, with twelve of Nina's pamphlets, spoken word poetry, and a solo performance by Ana.

Nina settled on the nomenclature of "pamphlets"—rather than books or zines—from the start, because she wanted objects that were similar to zines in that they were affordable and lightweight but with more substance. She once described the pamphlets as the analog to a 7-inch single for a publishing house, a kind of teaser before the release of a full LP.

Ana says *Love, oh Love* is "a nice thing to have done, because if I just make the drawings, then they're in a drawer, kind of forgotten, or people buy them, but the pamphlet is much cheaper than buying a drawing, so it's nice that it's out there for people to have." The pages are akin to the "icon" drawings Ana gave out at the National Portrait Gallery back in 2009.

Geoff Travis still describes Ana as the "poet" of the band. That idea is reflected in the pages of *Love, oh Love*, which become flash poems that are at once visual and textual. "The lines come to stand by themselves," Ana says, "and they go with the individual objects

I put them together with. I don't need to put the whole song on it. In a way, the line gains its own meaning by being by itself."

LISSON GALLERY/DAN GRAHAM, OCTOBER 30, 2018

Dan Graham was a long-time Raincoats fan. But he was also a friend and ally. Gina thinks that connection was made through English conceptual art pioneer and fellow Raincoats fan Stephen Willats. Early on, Willats planned to bring The Raincoats over to play Berlin for an exhibition, but some funky pay rate stuff got in the way. "I think in the end, the Germans went, 'Who *are* these people, and what are they doing?!'" Gina says. "But the point is, I think he introduced Dan Graham to The Raincoats."

Gina explains how Graham had lived above Kim Gordon in New York. When Kim first saw Graham giving a lecture, she witnessed him arguing with the artist Mike Kelley about who had invented punk rock, "trying to apply art-world lineage and the formation of the avant-garde to popular culture/subculture," she explains.[30] For Graham, music and performance art were always intertwined, never binaries. Graham was particularly interested in the relationship between performer and audience, distinctions between subjectivity and objectivity, and the role of physical bodies in space. To explore his ideas, Graham put together an all-female band for his performance piece *Performer/Audience/Mirror* (1975). The members included Kim Gordon, Miranda Stanton (of Factory Records band Thick Pigeon), and Christine Hahn (of the Static). Miranda introduced Kim to Thurston Moore, and the future was Sonic Youth. Thurston emphasizes how Graham "really valued what was happening in the nascent work of punk rock ... really considered it radical art music, experimental music." So, naturally, Graham was thinking about The Raincoats.

"He was very interested in women who played music," Gina says, "and the way young women were perceived, and as a result, he became quite interested in The Raincoats."

The interest was circular, as it turned out. Graham's early videography had been a starting point for Gina to build her knowledge about film and performance art. "I didn't know where to start with video," Gina says, referring back to her early days at Hornsey, "but I thought if I do what Dan Graham did, maybe it will take me somewhere. And in the end I did make quite a lot of films that were inspired by his practice." She discusses reading extensively about him without having any sense he'd come into her life more meaningfully later on. "But anyway, he'd done this work where him and another person rolled on the floor filming each other filming, and I thought, well, let's give that a go! So I persuaded another woman to do that. We rolled around on the floor filming each other filming, and I thought, it's a bit of a stolen idea, but it later became a reenactment of a Dan Graham piece. It's great how you can redefine these things in grander terms," Gina says.

When The Raincoats went to play New York in 1994, they all stood together inside one of Graham's sculptures on the roof of the DIA Foundation. By that point, Gina had developed a friendship with the American artist. Graham sent at least a half-dozen mix CDs to Gina in London with collaged booklets he'd designed. Each was titled "Dan Graham Greatest Hits" with a corresponding volume number. Tracks included some original rock and punk favorites from bands like Patti Smith, Sex Pistols, the Mekons, Iggy Pop, Big Star, the Kinks, and Young Marble Giants, as well as much older tracks from artists like Spike Jones and his Orchestra. Graham also mixed in newer releases from the late eighties and early nineties by Bob Dylan, the Feelies, the Vaselines, and Lucinda Williams. Graham taught Gina it was possible to push back against what she felt was a very British adage of "stay in your lane," as far as an artist's medium and discipline were concerned.

When Graham was planning an exhibition at London's Lisson Gallery in 2018, he knew he wanted The Raincoats to play. As Shirley recalls it, they'd created a setlist, but it didn't include "In Love." Graham quickly insisted it was his favorite Raincoats track and hoped it could get added. He'd even written about the song, analyzing how its "polyphonic counterpoint—an indistinguishable babble—nearly cancels out the meaning of the lead vocal ... [which] itself breaks down at the chorus phrase 'this is love' at the end of each stanza, enunciating the line like this: 'This/is/es/ee/lo/la/love/la/ov/oh/ho/ha/ha/hey/this/is/love/ha/ha/ha.'"[31]

They added "In Love" that night, to close out his show. "It was half a circle, his sculpture, and we played inside it, really close to the sculpture, the artwork itself," Ana remembers. "He was there and watched us play inside his art."

RAINCOATS FORTIETH ANNIVERSARY SHOWS

The Raincoats celebrated the fortieth anniversary of their self-titled LP *The Raincoats* with a series of shows in the UK and Europe. As Gina reflected at the time, marking that anniversary shouldn't be seen as a celebration of something past, but honoring an album that, by 2019, had "grown and become something else."

New and long-time fans alike booked tickets to multiple shows. The Raincoats played the same set each night, including *The Raincoats* in its entirety, although anyone who attended more than one gig remarked on the incredible variation at each performance. The Raincoats revealed, again, how their work is ever-evolving, forever taking new shapes in experimental fashion.

Sometimes the rhythm will speed up, sometimes there's a change in duration. The atmosphere of a particular venue space, the emotional connection between the artists, and the specific time and cultural or political moment can all affect the performance. The songs remain living things, responding to their environment, and to the constrictions and opposing latitudes in their midst. "You'll never hear a song sound the same way twice. And that's *really* a compliment," VC says.

At EartH, a venue in north London, Big Joanie played one of these fortieth anniversary gigs on a bill that also included Scritti Politti, and Lora Logic guested on "Black and White," the song on which she'd originally played tenor saxophone. "It was a warm, intimate atmosphere, like somebody's living room," Lora describes the event and her joy of joining up with The Raincoats again. "I didn't have a soprano sax anymore, though," she laments, "so I played tenor, and it was great fun."

Ana's touring suitcase, complete with tour passes and stickers from The Raincoats' many lives

Estella Adeyeri remembers the sense of sheer "freedom and joy" the evening emitted into the atmosphere. It helped that, when Shirley reached out and asked Big Joanie to play, she requested "something different than they usually do"—to experiment with a new way of playing. The "ask" was all part of celebrating The Raincoats' own anniversary and the new approach toward punk they brought into the universe. So Big Joanie went acoustic that night. For Estella, in playing the event with The Raincoats and watching them perform later on, she discovered a new sense of what freedom means on stage.

CENTRE POMPIDOU, PARIS, FEBRUARY 2020

The final live performance of The Raincoats' fortieth anniversary dates was at the Centre Pompidou in Paris, one of the world's great contemporary museums dedicated to art across genres and forms. It took place shortly before the world locked down, as the Covid-19 pandemic changed our collective thinking about mortality, autonomy, and the frailty of the human condition.

The Pompidou opened in 1977—the same year The Raincoats formed and played their first show—as "a venue like no other: a center for art and culture capable of housing both the National Museum of Modern and Contemporary Art, with an international dimension, a large public library, a center for industrial creation, and a center for musical research and creation, all together in one and the same building situated in the heart of the capital."[32] From the start, the Pompidou was intended as a place where art world boundaries could be broken down, a "place where all disciplines could meet" and "artists could converse with the public." A perfect space for The Raincoats to perform the final show celebrating forty years of *The Raincoats*.

The curator, Delphine Le Gatt, had been trying for years to bring The Raincoats to the Pompidou. "I want to push women's bands and women's artists up and in front of the audience, and we tried several times for The Raincoats," she says. "They're iconic, the global Raincoats image and sound."

Shirley drafted a press release that highlighted connections between The Raincoats and the broader art world: "Robert Wyatt's Meltdown at the South Bank in London in 2001; at the British Film Institute and the National Portrait Gallery in 2009; at MoMA in 2010; and more recently, in 2017, also in New York, at The Kitchen." By this point, they'd also performed at other prominent cultural spaces, such as the Museum of Contemporary Art Detroit in 2011, Centre de Cultura Contemporània de Barcelona in 2013, Centre for Contemporary Arts Glasgow in 2016, and London's Feminist Library that same year.

Without doubt, The Raincoats and their music have broken boundaries fabricated by the traditional art world, proving that punk is art and has a home in the lofty museums and galleries in which culture is said to be preserved for all time. And in so doing, their presence allays historian Andreas Huyssen's fears that the museum is merely a "symptom of cultural ossification."[33]

After all, "their message," Delphine adds, "is still so relevant. What is that line?" *No one teaches you how to live.*

LIFE NUMBER 3

WHITE CUBE AND IMI KNOEBEL

"Wherever The Raincoats play, they bring that older sense of a pulsating space with them, like into a gallery—with the music, they say anything goes," Anne Wood says knowingly. "It whips up a storm, wherever we are. Places like White Cube, other galleries, *could* feel so clinical, very clean, but the raw experience that was part of the gigs in the nineties comes into those seemingly sterile spaces and The Raincoats make it something new."

The Raincoats' most recent official performance (at the time of writing this book) occurred at the White Cube Gallery, Bermondsey, London, amid the paintings of Imi Knoebel, Carmen's husband. The gallery drove home the dual and seemingly contradictory notion that punk music is indeed "art" worthy of a gallery space, and that the sterility of such a location can be changed through the sounds brought to it—reshaped into a radical sonic refuge by the artists operating within.

The stark white walls of White Cube, the medicinal atmosphere, played on the very same bright white walls that Carmen Knoebel instituted when she remade the iconic Düsseldorf punk club the Ratinger Hof in 1979. "It was a quiet, quite prestigious gallery," Estella Adeyeri says of White Cube, which made her nervous to walk in for a Raincoats performance. "And then they brought that gallery to life."

"They've been here for so long, and they'll continue to be here inspiring new DIY punk artists," Steph Phillips says. "It's to the point that the mainstream will pretend that they've always been giving them praise, that they've always cared about The Raincoats when in reality they haven't always."

GINA PLAYS HER BASS LOUD

For Gina, much of The Raincoats' third life was spent occasionally collaborating with Ana while expanding her own artistic sensibilities. She returned to early dreams of painting on large-scale canvases at Hornsey and pushed the world of visual art far beyond traditional bounds. "I get obsessed!" Gina explains as she begins describing the creative endeavors she found herself immersed in. She also co-directed a documentary with Helen Reddington (aka Helen McCookerybook of The Chefs) on female musicians titled *Stories from the She-Punks* (2018). Part of Gina's creative burst evolved around motherhood. "In the middle of it all, I raised my two daughters," she says, "and in a lot of ways, I was really a full-time, full-on mum. I just wanted to be with them all the time." (Gina and Mike traveled to China on two separate trips to adopt Honey and Lei Lei, and they raised them in the same thoughtful, creative spirit in which Gina originally formed The Raincoats.)

"We played, sang, and banged on things and danced!" Gina exclaims. She also talks about making films with Honey and Lei Lei, written by them. "Honey was a really good storyteller, and if I had a song or a backing track, I'd get them to dance. And they'd dress up. Very domestic things, maybe." Gina describes how they'd turn their home into performance art of a sort, although she describes it as "just playing around." She recalls happily, "We'd make great big things. I'd have them lie on the floor and draw around them," outlining the shapes of Honey's and Lei Lei's beings as they became temporary features of the flooring, not so different from the video work she'd done in homage to Dan Graham years prior. It was "a creative hub," Gina explains, "where Honey and Lei Lei could find ways to play and make things, and make a mess and have wonderful films and videos to look back on."

Honey, Gina's daughter, reflects on how "having a mum whose ethos is punk, and who's in a punk band" taught them just how important it is to be creative, and that when you're thinking creatively, nothing is impossible. "Anything I've ever wanted to do," Honey says, "there's never been a question of, 'Could I do it?' The mantra is always, 'You're trying to do something you've never done before? Well, why not!'" Honey continues, "Because of my mum and dad, my brain has been wired not to question whether I *could* do something, but to try to figure out *how* to do it. And that's super punk."

As Gina's best friend, Petra is uniquely positioned to speak to it all. "When Gina puts her mind to something, from painting a wall to knitting, she gets a wonderful obsessiveness that's all based on play and not being frightened of throwing yourself in there. And if it's all bollocks in the end, that's fine. But most of us are too scared to ever go there."

In addition to her other "obsessions," Gina continued writing lyrics and creating sounds on her bass. As early as 2014, The Raincoats included some of her new songs on their setlists, including "Feminist Song" and "Pussy Riot." Around the fortieth anniversary of *The Raincoats*, Third Man Records approached the band about potentially doing something new. Ana wasn't interested in coming back to The Raincoats, although she was doing some remixes for Gina. "Back in 2009, 2010, The Raincoats did talk about making a new record," Jean-Marc says, but nothing came to pass.

Without Ana on board, David Buick at Third Man asked Gina if she had anything she'd been working on herself. As it happened, "I'd been doing a lot on my computer at home," Gina told him, referring to the songs that would make up the bulk of her first solo album, *I Play My Bass Loud*, released by Third Man Records in February 2023. "I made almost the entire thing on my Logic software at home. And it made me really wish I'd had Logic in The Raincoats, especially for *Moving* and *Looking in the Shadows*. Had Ana and I had that technology then, they'd have been very different records, and very different experiences.

WOMEN IN REVOLT!

The Raincoats have always been women in revolt, and Gina's artwork became the central face—quite literally—of Tate Britain's exhibition, *Women in Revolt!: Art and Activism in the UK 1970–1990*, which ran from November 8, 2023 until April 7, 2024.

Linsey Young, the Tate Britain curator of *Women in Revolt!*, explains that the exhibition was centered on remedying historical exclusions of women—in the stories being told through the exhibition, and within the walls of Tate Britain. "Joining the Tate, I realized I couldn't tell the stories I was interested in, because we simply didn't have the work and the collections," Linsey explains, so part of the exhibition "was about trying to rectify that, and also about showing parts of British culture and life that are so important and so normal, but are outside the mainstream narrative." To put together what would ultimately become the largest-ever exhibition at the Tate galleries, Linsey and her team traveled throughout the UK to personal archives and homes off the beaten path, seeking objects that would be crucial to telling stories of women in revolt.

For Linsey, The Raincoats have always been central to that narrative. As she reflects, "The Raincoats were a big part of my teenage life, so this show was about fulfilling my fantasies in a way." She wanted to bring some of The Raincoats' art into the space, and as luck would have it, she got connected with Gina, who'd already heard the exhibition was in the works.

"Caroline Coon told me at the opening of her first major show at Stephen Friedman Gallery about an exhibition that was in the pipeline, featuring over a hundred 'women in revolt,'" Gina recalls, "and she was sure I would be invited to be in it." Caroline introduced Gina to Linsey, who'd been told by Studio Voltaire's Joe Scotland about her early Super 8 films. Linsey went to see Gina's painting exhibition *In My Fucking Room* at Gallery 46, and it went from there. Initially, Linsey wanted to feature Gina's Super 8 film *Joanna*, which grapples with women's rights and abortion, but she was concerned with logistical issues, namely the long length of the work. So instead, as Gina tells it, Linsey chose *3 Minute Scream*. The *Scream* was, simply, "much more direct," Linsey confirms.

The film *3 Minute Scream* was originally going to be projected on a smaller scale, but Linsey realized they could use a much larger screen and the sound could reverberate throughout the massive space. So, Gina was asked to supply "as high a resolution version as possible." She started thinking, a bit skeptically, "If it's going to be shown on a monitor in the gallery, the resolution is fine." But Tate Britain kept coming back to her, asking "for better, better" in terms of resolution.

That film soon became larger than life, an image and sound to which women across generations and experiences could relate: a close-up female face shrieking with frustration, rage, despair, and resistance. Within Gina's art, finally, we could all see ourselves and our bottled-up misogynist indignation released.

LIFE NUMBER 3

As Linsey was considering how to position Gina's film in relation to the rest of the exhibition, she was "very conscious of making a show that avoided cutesy feminism, institutional feminism, or capitalist feminism." The *3 Minute Scream* perfectly encapsulated what Linsey wanted. "You can read the scream in loads of different ways," she explains, but at its heart, "The image is very confrontational and relentless, because that's what most women's lives are like, right? Just relentlessly having to go *oh for fuck's sake* about one thing or another." It's also an image that's about "wanting more, and wanting a life that seems so hard to reach," Linsey says.

"When I discovered it was to be projected at two and a half meters by three meters," Gina says, "I was astonished." And "even more so," she adds, when she saw her screaming face "all over London for several weeks, on the underground, on billboards, and in giant format, outside the front and back of Tate Britain." As Linsey confirms, "Gina's scream ended up being the iconic image of the show."

Posters, flypapers, multistory banners ran through the streets of London from October 2023 through to April 2024. That extreme close-up image of Gina's screaming face brought thousands of people into the exhibition. Inside, Raincoats materials helped to paint intertwining narratives of art-based resistance in a misogynist society.

Thanks to a conscious and determined effort to center women in the history of revolution through art, Tate Britain finally recognized The Raincoats and the other women within that space as the rebels they were and have remained. As Ana suggests, The Raincoats have long been viewed as "Other" by the (primarily male) writers and curators who have narrated histories of punk, artistic resistance, and cultural revolution. But at the same time, they also shaped themselves as intentional Others, beacons to artists themselves on the periphery who wanted to find inspiration in something unknown: "We loved the sound of difference, of dissonance and melody, of disruption and joy, speeding up and slowing down, crescendos and dips, bowing, banging and scratching, whispering, singing and shouting. Some people covered their ears, some covered their eyes and some opened their hearts and minds and embraced our songs of love, politics, poetry and humor."[34]

Moving beyond the scream and into a room dedicated to women in punk, Gina's voice continued to aurally punctuate articles, badges, videos, clothing, and album art for bands ranging from The Raincoats to X-Ray Spex (and Poly Styrene) to Ludus (and Linder Sterling). Much of the other Raincoats materials, as well as other key pieces representing female punk artists, came on loan from the archive of Lucy Whitman, cofounder of Rock Against Racism and Rock Against Sexism. It's fitting that The Raincoats would be essential to tearing down the walls of misogynist museum practices that allowed male artists to shape culture for centuries at Tate Britain.

Linsey couldn't be happier with the optics. "I'd always intended to leave the Tate [after the exhibition closed]," she says, "so I thought, *fuck it*, I'm just going to do whatever I want."

But it takes more than one exhibit; the trajectory must continue, and meaningful change must continue to be made.

Has Tate Britain acquired any of the objects from the exhibition, recognizing the need to include women's work in its permanent collections?

"I don't think I can say specifics, legally," Linsey says, but she smiles, "yes."

CIRCULAR TIMING

Across their three lives, The Raincoats reveal that the truest feminist project is circular engagement: inspire, and continue to be inspired by.

It happened in the early nineties when Bikini Kill, inspired by The Raincoats, made music their own way and rocked international stages, and in so doing, inspired The Raincoats to play once again. For Naz, that same circularity became apparent anew at BFI London in 2009: "The very work of The Raincoats at that point in time was to speak with the people who had been inspired by them, but in doing it, they became inspired in reverse *again*, like with Riot Grrrl before. They've done it with multiple generations now, and it's just ... beautiful."

It's a cycle with no temporal end. Klaudia Schifferle of Kleenex/LiLiPUT sums it up in her own version of English, which she says she learned entirely by listening to songs: "The Raincoats' music is in the air, it's all around, it's not a material thing."

The Raincoats have never made music to a traditional time signature. For Joe Dilworth, it's his most salient memory of The Raincoats. "There was never a beat to keep," he explains, "but a physical heartbeat that slows, swells, and skips. It wasn't that timing didn't matter. Timing actually mattered quite a lot. But it was a different kind of timing," he says. As Anne Wood puts it, the music is impossible to count because, "on any given song, sometimes it will be in three, four, five, ten, something else." To learn the time signature of The Raincoats, the language they've created, "you have to try to forget the time," Anne explains.

And "through all of it," Petra adds, "they've maintained a Raincoatsness. They still play with the same profound sense of playfulness—in the profound sense of the word—they started with. They're always experimenting in a way that allows their process to take over, where they go into a new world with no time bounds."

The Kitchen's manifesto says: "Emergence is durational. There is no time-limit on being 'emerging.' To emerge is to grow and growth is an ongoing process, not limited to one generation or stage of life."[35] For The Raincoats, time never repeats on a loop but goes backward and forward at uneven and sporadic intervals. It becomes a process, an experiment, a tool, and sometimes even a weapon. They're forever emerging themselves, and urging others to do the same in response to their music.

In the world created by The Raincoats, metronomes are never set, timepieces refuse to tick uniformly. When you keep your own time, it's yours to define. Beginnings and endings are merely inventions of the ordinary.

As The Raincoats sang out from the start, cups of tea are a clock, a clock, a clock ...

The Raincoats action figure dolls by the fabulous
Jen Lemasters of Chicago's Bric-a-Brac Records

NOTES

All citations from news and magazine clippings are sourced from The Raincoats archive.

Author's Note: On Methodology
1   Huyssen, A. *Twilight Memories: Marking Time in a Culture of Amnesia.* London: Routledge, 1995 (p.7).
2   Blouin, F.X. "History and Memory: The Problem of the Archive," in *PMLA*, 119(2), March 2004, pp.296–8 (p.296).
3   Dever, M. "Archives and New Modes of Feminist Research," in *Australian Feminist Studies*, 32(91–2), August 2017, pp.1–4 (p.3).

Introduction
1   Hesse, E. *Eva Hesse: Diaries* (eds. Barry Rosen and Tamara Bloomberg). New Haven: Yale University Press, 2016.
2   Hildegard of Bingen, from "A Vision of Love," c. 1163–1174

LIFE NUMBER 1
1   Nairn, T. "Hornsey," in *New Left Review*, Issue 50, July/August 1968. Available at: https://newleftreview.org/issues/i50/articles/tom-nairn-hornsey [accessed December 3, 2024].
2   Page, D. "Hornsey College of Art Uprising," in *Tate Etc.*, Issue 18, January 2010. Available at: https://www.tate.org.uk/tate-etc/issue-18-spring-2010/journeys-past [accessed December 3, 2024].
3   Wright, N. "What happened at Hornsey on 28 May 1968," 21 century manifesto blog, May 2012. Available at: https://21centurymanifesto.wordpress.com/2012/05/28/what-happened-at-hornsey-on-28-may-1968/ [accessed December 3, 2024].
4   McIntyre, I. "Squats Across the Empire: A Comparison of Squatting movements in Post-Second World War UK and Australia", in Grashoff, U. (ed.). *Comparative Approaches to Informal Housing Around the Globe.* London: UCL Press, 2020.
5   Layers of London. Available at: https://www.layersoflondon.org/map/overlays/bomb-damage-1945 [accessed December 3, 2024].
6   Barnett, D. "Republic of Frestonia: How squatters in a 1970s London street declared independence from the UK," *Independent*, August 2018. Available at: https://www.independent.co.uk/news/long_reads/frestonia-squatters-london-declare-independence-uk-1970s-free-independent-a8514576.html [accessed December 3, 2024].

NOTES

7. Kamvasinou, K. and Milne, S.A. "Surveying the Creative Use of Vacant Space in London, c.1945–95," in Campbell, C., Giovine, A. and Keating, J. (eds.). *Empty Spaces: Perspectives on Emptiness in Modern History*. London: University of London Press, 2019 (pp.151–78).
8. Ibid (p.159).
9. Anger, A. *ZigZag*, Issue No. 86, August 1978 (pp.36–37).
10. Ibid.
11. Dominic McKenzie Architects. "An Architect's Guide to Notting Hill," blog at www.dominicmckenzie.co.uk. Available at https://www.dominicmckenzie.co.uk/an-architects-guide-to-notting-hill/ [accessed December 3, 2024].
12. Puckey, T. "Performances: Reindeer Werk and Solo, 1973–1981," www.thompuckey.com. Available at: https://www.thompuckey.com/oeuvre/?category=performances [accessed December 3, 2024].
13. "These Punks Have Polish," *Evening Standard*, March 1978.
14. Lupinin, N. "Samizdat," in Encyclopedia of Russian History, ed. Millar, J.R. Farmington Hills: Thomson Gale, 2004.
15. Bromke, A. "Czechoslovakia 1968 to Poland 1978: A Dilemma for Moscow," in *International Journal*, 33(4), Autumn 1978, pp.740–62 (p.750).
16. Bloom, J.M. "The Solidarity Revolution in Poland, 1980–1981," in *The Oral History Review*, 33(1), 2006, pp.33–64.
17. Thane, L. *It Changed My Life: Bikini Kill in the UK*, documentary film. Dir. Thane, L. 1993.
18. See, e.g., The Women's Liberation Music Archive (https://womensliberationmusicarchive.co.uk/j/)
19. Punk 77. "Mike Kemp and Spaceward Studios," *Punk 77*. Available at: https://www.punk77.co.uk/punkhistory/spaceward.htm [accessed December 3, 2024].
20. Marder, M. *KLEENEX / LILIPUT* (ed. Ambrose, G.; trans. Calleja, J.) Kansas City: Thrilling Living, 2023 (p.100).
21. BBC, "Peel Sessions," https://www.bbc.co.uk/radio1/johnpeel/sessions/
22. Palmolive quoted in Goldman, V. "New Raincoats Don't Let You Down," *Melody Maker*, 1979.
23. *NME*, November 24, 1979, p.77; *Melody Maker*, December 1, 1979, p.51.
24. Ferreira, A.P. "Loving in the Lands of Portugal: Sex in Women's Fictions and the Nationalist Order," in Quinlan, S.C. and Arenas, F. (eds.). *Lusosex: Gender and Sexuality in the Portuguese-Speaking World*. Minneapolis: University of Minnesota Press, 2002 (pp.107–29).
25. Roseneil, S. *et al.* (eds.). "The Portuguese Intimate Citizenship Regime,' in *The Tenacity of the Couple-Norm: Intimate Citizenship Regimes in a Changing Europe*. London: UCL Press, 2020 (pp.92–106).
26. Cardina, M. "To Talk or Not to Talk: Silence, Torture, and Politics in the Portuguese Dictatorship of 'Estado Novo',". *The Oral History Review*, 40(2), Summer/Fall 2013, pp.251–70 (p.254).
27. Kyle, J. Personal correspondence with The Raincoats, 1979.
28. ACT Initiative. "About Us," www.act-ni.co.uk. Available at: https://act-ni.co.uk/about [accessed December 3, 2024].

NOTES

29 O'Halloran, S. "Memories of Sinn Féin Britain, 1975-85," in Dawson, G., Dover, J. and Hopkins, S. (eds.). *The Northern Ireland Troubles in Britain: Impacts, engagements, legacies and memories*. Manchester: Manchester University Press, 2016 (pp.127–136); Hepworth, J. "Feminism and Women's Activism," in *'The Age-Old Struggle': Irish republicanism from the Battle of the Bogside to the Belfast Agreement, 1969–1998*. Liverpool: Liverpool University Press, 2021 (pp.129–160).

30 Renwick, A. "Something in the Air, the Rise of the Troops Out Movement," in Dawson, G., Dover, J. and Hopkins, S. (eds.). *The Northern Ireland Troubles in Britain: Impacts, engagements, legacies and memories*. Manchester: Manchester University Press, 2016 (pp.111–126).

31 Cooke, R. "US feminist Susan Brownmiller on why her groundbreaking book on rape is still relevant," *Observer*, February 2018. Available at: https://www.theguardian.com/world/2018/feb/18/susan-brownmiller-against-our-will-interview-metoo [accessed December 3, 2024].

32 McKay, S. "Soldier Dolls in Belfast," *London Review of Books*, 38(8), April 2016. Available at: https://www.lrb.co.uk/the-paper/v38/n08/susan-mckay/diary [accessed December 3, 2024].

33 Interview with *Meikel Clauss* In: *Rüdiger Esch: Electri_City — Elektronik Musik aus Düsseldorf* (Suhrkamp Verlag AG, 2014).

34 Thane, L. (no.17).

35 Thane, L. (no.17).

36 Garcia, J. "Never Mind the Gannex: The Impermeable Jane Garcia Hangs Out With The Raincoats," *New Music News*, 1980.

37 Garcia, J. Personal correspondence with The Raincoats, July 1980.

38 Pohrt, T. "Painting in Miniature: Rosina Cox Boardman's Self-Portrait and the Paint Box," *Yale University Art Gallery Bulletin*, 2015, pp.97–101 (p.97).

39 Stewart, S. *On Longing: Narratives of the Miniature, the Gigantic, the Souvenir, the Collection*. Durham: Duke University Press, 1992 (p.41).

40 Pelly, J. *The Raincoats' The Raincoats (33⅓)*. London: A&C Black Advantage, 2017.

41 McLeod, K. "The Day the Mercer Arts Center Collapsed," in *The Downtown Pop Underground: New York City and the Literary Punks, Renegade Artists, DIY Filmmakers, Mad Playwrights, and Rock 'n' Roll Glitter Queens Who Revolutionized Culture*. New York City: Abrams Press, 2018; Herman, D. "The Collapse of the Broadway Central Hotel and the End of the Mercer Arts Center," Off the Grid: Village Preservation blog, August 2022. Available at: https://www.villagepreservation.org/2022/08/03/the-collapse-of-the-broadway-central-hotel-and-the-end-of-the-mercer-arts-center/ [accessed December 3, 2024].

42 Jaeger, H. Personal correspondence with Shirley O'Loughlin, May 1980.

43 Polsky, R. Personal correspondence with Shirley O'Loughlin, May 1980.

44 Bither, D. "Under a London Fog," *New York Rocker*, September 1980 (p.41).

45 Rough Trade, press release for "Animal Rhapsody," November 1983.

NOTES

LIFE NUMBER 2

1. Fortnightly College Radio Report, Westfield, Massachusetts, United States, July 15, 1981.
2. Cobain, K. Liner notes for *Incesticide* compilation album by Nirvana (DGC Records, 1992).
3. Schemel, P. *Hit So Hard*. New York: Da Capo Press, 2017 (p.88).
4. Cobain, K. (no.2).
5. Boon, R. *Puncture* magazine, "The Raincoats Come Again Another Day," No.35, Spring 1996, pp.59–62.
6. Thane, L. *It Changed My Life: Bikini Kill in the UK*, documentary film. Dir. Thane, L. 1993.
7. Rough Trade. Business correspondence with The Raincoats, 1986.
8. Vail, T. Personal correspondence with Ana da Silva, November 1993.
9. Elliot, N. Personal correspondence with Shirley O'Loughlin, August 1993.
10. Bhatia, A. Liner notes for *Moving* album reissue by The Raincoats (Rough Trade, 1994).
11. Sparrow, D. Liner notes for *Moving* album reissue by The Raincoats (Rough Trade, 1994).
12. Shelley, S. Personal correspondence with The Raincoats, 1994.
13. Da Silva, A. Tribute to Kurt Cobain, *Melody Maker*, 1994.
14. Paul Stolper exhibition press release. "Factual Nonsense: The Art and Death of Joshua Compston 21 June–31 August 2013," paulstoper.com. Available at: https://www.paulstolper.com/exhibitions/73-factual-nonsense-the-art-and-death-of-joshua-compston/press_release_text/ [accessed 3 December 2024].
15. Worrall, S. "ORGAN THING: Joshua Compston, East London, closed doors, a visionary, A Fete Worst Than Death, an anniversary exhibition and ... ," The Organ, 2014. Available at: https://organthing.com/2014/03/27/organ-thing-joshua-compston-east-london-closed-doors-a-visionary-a-fete-worst-than-death-an-anniversary-exhibition-and/ [accessed December 3, 2024].
16. Lindsay, T. Personal correspondence with Shirley O'Loughlin, 1995.
17. Petrusich, A. "In Retrospect/John Cale's Inventive Retrospection," *New Yorker*, January 2017. Available at: https://www.newyorker.com/magazine/2017/01/30/john-cales-inventive-retrospection [accessed December 3, 2024].
18. Marder, M. Personal correspondence with Shirley O'Loughlin, April 1995.
19. Mochnacz, M. Personal correspondence with The Raincoats, January 1996.
20. Dutton, J. 'Memory Dress', available at: http://www.jennidutton.com/memorydress.html [accessed January 7, 2025].
21. Ottawa Start, 'René Trim's Arts & Crafts: The Memory Dress Project', July 18, 2015. Available at: https://ottawastart.com/rene-trims-arts-crafts-the-memory-dress-project/ [accessed January 7, 2025].
22. Elizabeth A. Sackler Center for Feminist Art, "Women's Work". Brooklyn Museum. Available at: https://www.brooklynmuseum.org/eascfa/dinner_party/womens_work [accessed December 3, 2024].
23. Thorp, C. "Lady Gaga meat dress: The outfit that shocked the world," BBC

NOTES

Culture. Available at: https://www.bbc.com/culture/article/20230921-lady-gaga-meat-dress-the-outfit-that-shocked-the-world [accessed December 3, 2024].
24 Ibid.
25 Milroy, S. "The Flesh Dress: A Defence," in Robinson, H. (ed.) *Feminism –Art– Theory: An Anthology, 1968–2000*. Oxford: Blackwell, 2001.
26 Wilcox, K. Personal correspondence with Ana da Silva, January 1995.
27 Topper, S. Personal correspondence with The Raincoats, 1994.
28 Flanagin, C. Personal correspondence with Ana da Silva, 1997.
29 Chaudhuri, A. Fan letter to The Raincoats, 1980.
30 Chaudhuri, A. "Women Macs to the Future; From Feminist Punk Combo to, er, Feminist Punk Combo: Anita Chaudhuri on the Reforming of The Raincoats," *Guardian*, April 15, 1996.
31 Palmolive and other family members left the church in around 2013, as in Desroches, S. "The Music and Activism of Tianna Esperanza," *Provincetown Magazine*, June 2018. Available at: https://provincetownmagazine.com/2018/06/27/the-now-sound/ [accessed March 5, 2025].

LIFE NUMBER 3
1 Mitchell, K. Personal correspondence with The Raincoats, September 1994.
2 O'Hagan, S. "The Great Wyatt Hope," *Observer*, May 2001. Available at: https://www.theguardian.com/theobserver/2001/may/27/featuresreview.review5 [accessed December 3, 2024].
3 Ladyfest. "Ladyfest 2000 Info Center," August 2000. Available at: http://ladyfest.org/index3.html [accessed January 8, 2025].
4 Ladyfest Leeds. 'Music Line Up for Ladyfest Leeds April Festival,' Indymedia UK. Available at: https://www.indymedia.org.uk/en/2007/03/363993.html [accessed January 8, 2025].
5 Beaven, K. "Performance Art: The Happening," The Tate. Available at: https://www.tate.org.uk/art/art-terms/h/happening/happening [accessed December 3, 2024].
6 Spencer, C. *Beyond the Happening*. Manchester: Manchester University Press, 2020.
7 *Performance Art* magazine, Vol. 1, January 1979, pp. 22–23, https://doi.org/10.1162/pam.1979.0.1.1
8 Linsley, J. "Invasive Action: Girl Monster @ The Donau Festival," More Milk Yvette: A Journal of the Broken Screen, 2009. Available at: https://moremilkyvette.blogspot.com/2009/07/johanna-linsley-on-invasive-action-girl.html [accessed December 17, 2024].
9 Glasgow Women's Library Archive. 'Archive Catalogue'. Available at: https://archive.womenslibrary.org.uk/
10 Dyer, R. and Toksvig, S. *Gay Icons* book description. The National Portrait Gallery Company Limited, 2009. Available at: https://www.npg.org.uk/business/publications/gay-icons1.php [accessed January 8, 2025].

NOTES

11 The National Portrait Gallery. 'Gay Icons, Past Exhibition Archive'. Available at: https://www.npg.org.uk/whatson/exhibitions/20091/gay-icons/ [accessed January 8, 2025].

12 Toksvig, S. quoted in "Gay Icons", Past Exhibition Archive, The National Portrait Gallery. Available at: https://www.npg.org.uk/whatson/exhibitions/20091/gay-icons/ [accessed December 17, 2024].

13 Kay, D. "We're here, we're queer, we're not going shopping! Clause 28 and the birth of the LGBTIQ+ community," Brighton and Hove Museums. Available at: https://brightonmuseums.org.uk/discovery/history-stories/were-here-were-queer-were-not-going-shopping-clause-28-and-the-birth-of-the-lgbtiq-community/ [accessed December 3, 2024].

14 Walthamstow Rock'n'Roll Book Club conversation. Walthamstow Trades Hall, London, May 7, 2024.

15 Moon, S. and Hanna, K. Insert in "Mean" b/w "Rock Star" By Slim Moon and Kathleen Hanna, KRS, 1991.

16 Courtesy Glasgow Women's Library (GWL) Archive. Available at: https://womenslibrary.org.uk/explore-our-collections/the-archive-collection/ [accessed January 8, 2025].

17 Brownstein, C. 'The Raincoats', *Monitor Mix* blog, NPR, October 14, 2009. Available at: https://www.npr.org/sections/monitormix/2009/10/the_raincoats.html [accessed January 8, 2024].

18 McKay, S. "Viv Albertine (Slits)," *Electric Sleeve Notes*, November 2009. Available at: https://www.eccentricsleevenotes.com/viv-albertine-slits [accessed December 3, 2024].

19 Powell, M. 'Live: The Raincoats Keep It Like a Secret at the Knitting Factory'. Village Voice, October 19, 2009. Available at: https://www.villagevoice.com/live-the-raincoats-keep-it-like-a-secret-at-the-knitting-factory/ [accessed January 8, 2025].

20 Gehr, R. "The 9 Best Moments of All Tomorrow's Parties," *SPIN*, May 2010. Available at: https://www.spin.com/2010/05/9-best-moments-all-tomorrows-parties/ [accessed December 3, 2024).

21 Osumi, Y. "Communicating intent; the founder of VIVA Strange Boutique, Minami Yamaguchi," *Tokion*, April 2021. Available at: https://tokion.jp/en/2021/04/14/viva-strange-boutique-minami-yamaguchi/ [accessed December 3, 2024].

22 Huyssen, A. *Twilight Memories: Marking Time in a Culture of Amnesia*. London: Routledge, 1995 (p.13).

23 Ibid, p.7, 15.

24 Griffin, T. 'The Museum Revisted', *Artforum International*, 48(10), 2010.

25 Museum of Modern Art. "Modern Women: The Book", 2010. Available at: https://www.moma.org/interactives/modern_women/book/ [accessed December 17, 2024].

26 Patton, E. and Raimondi, M. "The Raincoats: Shouting Out Loud at MoMA," Inside/Out blog at moma.org, December 2010. Available at: https://www.

NOTES

moma.org/explore/inside_out/2010/12/16/the-raincoats-shouting-out-loud-at-moma/ [accessed December 3, 2024].

27 Studio Voltaire. "The Neo Naturists," studiovoltaire.org, 2016. Available at: https://studiovoltaire.org/whats-on/the-neo-naturists-2016/ [accessed December 3, 2024].
28 Vail, T. Personal correspondence with Shirley O'Loughlin, November 2017.
29 Ibid.
30 Gordon, K. "Dan Graham (1942–2022)," *Texte Zur Kunst*, Issue 126, June 2022. Available at: https://www.textezurkunst.de/en/126/kim-gordon-dan-graham-obituary/ [accessed December 3, 2024].
31 Graham, D. *Rock My Religion: Writings and Art Projects, 1965–1990*. Cambridge: MIT Press, 1993 (p. 123).
32 Centre Pompidou. 'Who are we?', 2021. Available at: https://www.centrepompidou.fr/en/the-centre-pompidou/who-are-we [accessed January 8, 2024].
33 Huyssen, A. (no.20).
34 From a treatment that Ana, Gina, and Shirley collaborated on for a 2012 BBC pitch. Ana reused the language in a 2024 talk she gave in Madeira.
35 The Kitchen. 'About'. Available at: https://thekitchen.org/about/ [accessed January 8, 2025].

Quoted Lyrics

p.39: "You're a Million" by The Raincoats (Rough Trade). Lyrics by Ana Paula da Silva © 1979 (We ThRee).

p.59: "Fairytale in the Supermarket" by the Raincoats (Rough Trade) © 1979 (We ThRee).

p.234: "The Void" by The Raincoats (Rough Trade) © 1979 (We ThRee).

p.326: "Visions of Johanna" by Bob Dylan (Columbia). Lyrics by Bob Dylan © 1966 (Sony/ATV Music Publishing LLC).

P.328: "Vindictive" by The Slits (Island Records). Lyrics by Ari Up © 1977 (Universal Music Publishing Group).

p.356 "Fairytale in the Supermarket" by the Raincoats (Rough Trade) © 1979 (We ThRee).

p.363 Ibid.

LIST OF IMAGES

p.8   courtesy of Ana da Silva / photograph by Maria Helena da Silva
p.15 courtesy of Shirley O'Loughlin / photograph by Shirley O'Loughlin
p.26 courtesy of Shirley O'Loughlin / photographs by Shirley O'Loughlin
p.28 courtesy of Ana da Silva / poster design by Neal Brown
p.33 courtesy of Ana da Silva
p.35 courtesy of The Raincoats archive / photograph by Jerzy Kośnik
p.43 courtesy of Shirley O'Loughlin / photograph by Shirley O'Loughlin
p.43 courtesy of Ana da Silva / design by Ana da Silva
p.48 courtesy of Shirley O'Loughlin / photograph by Shirley O'Loughlin
p.55 courtesy of Shirley O'Loughlin / photograph by Shirley O'Loughlin
p.60 courtesy of The Raincoats archive
p.62 courtesy of The Raincoats archive
p.63 courtesy of Shirley O'Loughlin
p.66 courtesy of Ana da Silva
p.69 courtesy of The Raincoats archive / design by Simon Bramley
p.75 courtesy of Shirley O'Loughlin / photograph by Ana da Silva
p.81 courtesy of Ana da Silva / photograph by Maria Helena da Silva
p.86 courtesy of William Mitchell, ACT Initiative
p.89 courtesy of Francesca Scott / lyrics by Caroline Scott
p.94 courtesy of The Raincoats archive / photographs by Carmen Knoebel
p.99 courtesy of Shirley O'Loughlin / photograph by Shirley O'Loughlin
p.101 courtesy of The Raincoats archive / flyer design by Neal Brown
p.105 courtesy of Shirley O'Loughlin / photograph by Shirley O'Loughlin
p.110 courtesy of Ana da Silva / design and text by Ana da Silva / photograph by Audrey Golden
p.113 courtesy of Hilary Jaeger
p.122 courtesy of Hilary Jaeger
p.125 courtesy of Shirley O'Loughlin / photographs by Shirley O'Loughlin
p.127 courtesy of The Raincoats archive / design by Simon Bramley
p.129 courtesy of Shirley O'Loughlin / photograph by Shirley O'Loughlin
p.133 courtesy of Hilary Jaeger
p.139 courtesy of Ana da Silva / drawing by Ana da Silva
p.144 courtesy of Jill Furmanovsky / photographs by Jill Furmanovsky
p.158 courtesy of Ana da Silva / lyrics by Ana da Silva
p.161 courtesy of Ana da Silva / design by Ana da Silva and Shirley O'Loughlin
p.163 courtesy of Gina Birch / photograph by Gina Birch
p.168 courtesy of Philip Grey / photograph by Philip Grey

LIST OF IMAGES

p.175 courtesy of The Raincoats archive / photographer unknown
p.178 courtesy of Ana da Silva / photograph by Ana da Silva
p.185 courtesy of Kathi Wilcox
p.199 courtesy of The Raincoats archive / text © Kurt Cobain
p.204 courtesy of The Raincoats archive / text © Kim Gordon
p.220 courtesy of Ana da Silva / design by Ana da Silva
p.223 courtesy of Gina Birch
p.229 courtesy of Ana da Silva
p.252 courtesy of The Raincoats archive / photograph by Joe Dilworth
p.253 courtesy of The Raincoats archive / photograph by Joe Dilworth
p.256 courtesy of Maria Mochnacz / photograph by Maria Mochnacz
p.257 courtesy of Maria Mochnacz / photograph by Maria Mochnacz
p.259 courtesy of Ana da Silva / design by Ana da Silva
p.278 courtesy of Ana da Silva
p.286 courtesy of The Raincoats archive / photograph by Mike Hipple
p.291 courtesy of The Raincoats archive / photograph by Florian Schulte
p.299 courtesy of The Raincoats archive / photograph by Florian Schulte
p.313 courtesy of Shirley O'Loughlin / photograph by Shirley O'Loughlin
p.323 courtesy of Shirley O'Loughlin
p.325 courtesy of Ana da Silva
p.327 courtesy of Ana da Silva
p.333 courtesy of Gaby Agis
p.341 courtesy of Vice Cooler / photograph by Vice Cooler
p.355 courtesy of Shirley O'Loughlin / photograph by Shirley O'Loughlin
p.364 courtesy of Jen Lemasters and Audrey Golden / photograph by Jenna Obrizok

LIST OF INTERVIEWEES

All of the following people sat for interviews with me (in person or via video call or phone), responded to questions by email and text, or otherwise corresponded with me for this book:

Ana da Silva
Gina Birch
Shirley O'Loughlin

Adam Kidron	Emily Elhaj
Alex Murray-Leslie	Eric Erlandson
Amy Rigby	Frankie Scott
Angel Olsen	Gaby Agis
Angela Jaeger	G.B. Jones
Anita Chaudhuri	Geoff Travis
Anjali Bhatia	Heather Dunn
Annabel Wright	Hilary Jaeger
Anne Wood	Honey Birch
Beth Ditto	Ingrid Weiss
Bruce Pavitt	Jane McKeown
Carmen Knoebel	Jean Smith
Carrie Brownstein	Jean-Marc Butty
Charles Hayward	Jeremie Frank
Corin Tucker	Joe Dilworth
Cynthia Sley	John Foster
Dana Squires	Jon Slade
David Thomas	Jude Crighton
Delia Sparrow	Julie Panebianco
Delphine Le Gatt	Kathi Wilcox
Derek Goddard	Kathleen Hanna
Dick O'Dell	Kim Gordon
Ed Buller	Klaudia Schifferle

LIST OF INTERVIEWEES

Linsey Young
Liz Naylor
Liz Phair
Lois Maffeo
Lora Logic
Lucy Sante
Lucy Thane
Lucy Whitman
Maciej Magura
Maggie Vail
Manda MacKinnon
Mary Timony
Mayo Thompson
Mike Holdsworth
Molly Neuman
Nadia Buyse
Nazmia Jamal
Neal Brown
Nick Turner
Paloma McLardy
Pat Place
Patrick Keiller
Patty Schemel
Paul Smith
Peaches
Petra Pattinson

Phew
Phil Grey
Phil Staines
Philippa Jarman
Portia Sabin
Ray Farrell
Richard Dudanski
Rob Sheffield
Sean McLusky
Sheri Hood
Simon Bramley
Slim Moon
Steph Hillier
Stephanie Phillips
Stephen McRobbie
Steve Shelley
Sue Donne
Thurston Moore
Tim Griffin
Tobi Vail
Tomek Lipinski
Vice Cooler
Vicky Aspinall
Viv Albertine
Vivien Goldman
William Mitchell

ACKNOWLEDGMENTS

This book would not have been possible without The Raincoats, both present and past, who sat with me for hours and hours of interviews and conversations. I cannot thank Ana, Gina, and Shirley enough for their incredible generosity with their time—in their London homes, over dozens of Zooms, and over dozens more phone calls. When all was said and done, the three of them spoke with me for over 100 hours collectively. A special thank you, too, to Vicky Aspinall, Anne Wood, Ingrid Weiss, Paloma McLardy, Richard Dudanski, Charles Hayward, Jeremie Frank, Nick Turner, Jean-Marc Butty, and Vice Cooler—Raincoats at various points who all gave generously with their time for this book.

I am so grateful to everyone else who agreed to be interviewed and corresponded with me for this book. Thank you to all who provided images, and an especially big thank you to Shirley for photographing so many objects from The Raincoats archive for inclusion.

Greil Marcus, I'm so thrilled this book has your words as its foreword. Thank you so very much.

Thanks for being such a wonderful editor, Lee Brackstone. This book became the best version of itself with your editorial eye. Thanks, too, Ben Schafer, for making this book a reality in America. And thank you so much to everyone at White Rabbit, such a wonderful team to work with.

So many people offered eyes or ears while I was working on this project. You know who you are, and I'm so grateful. A special thank you to Sarah Witt for giving me a London home base from which to do so much in-person work on this book. And a special thank you to Jenna Obrizok, a photography wizard.

And very little would ever be possible without all the love from Evan McCormick, Matin, and Marguerite.

CREDITS

White Rabbit would like to thank everyone at Orion who worked on the publication of *Shouting Out Loud: Lives of the Raincoats*.

Agent
Matthew Hamilton, The Hamilton Agency

Editor
Lee Brackstone

Copy-editor
Sue Lascelles

Proofreader
Piers Martin

Editorial Management
Susie Bertinshaw
Sophie Nevrkla
Jane Hughes
Charlie Panayiotou
Lucy Bilton
Patrice Nelson

Audio
Paul Stark
Louise Richardson
Georgina Cutler-Ross

Contracts
Rachel Monte
Ellie Bowker
Tabitha Gresty

Design
Steve Marking
Nick Shah
Deborah Francois
Helen Ewing

Photo Shoots & Image Research
Natalie Dawkins

Finance
Nick Gibson
Jasdip Nandra
Sue Baker
Tom Costello

Inventory
Jo Jacobs
Dan Stevens

CREDITS

Production
Sarah Cook
Katie Horrocks
Amy Knight

Marketing
Tom Noble

Publicity
Aoife Datta

Sales
Dave Murphy
Victoria Laws
Esther Waters
Group Sales teams across
Digital, Field, International
and Non-Trade

Operations
Group Sales Operations team

Rights
Rebecca Folland
Tara Hiatt
Ben Fowler
Maddie Stephens
Ruth Blakemore
Marie Henckel